Thanks for picking up volume 24! It turns out this volume is wall-to-wall villain stories. I have to say sorry to those of you who were hoping for more Deku... But I think this should be interesting, so please enjoy it!

KOHEI HORIKOSHI

24

SHONEN JUMP Manga Edition

STORY & ART **KOHEI HORIKOSHI**

TRANSLATION & ENGLISH ADAPTATION **Caleb Cook**
TOUCH-UP ART & LETTERING **John Hunt**
DESIGNER **Julian [JR] Robinson**
SHONEN JUMP SERIES EDITOR **John Bae**
GRAPHIC NOVEL EDITOR **Mike Montesa**

BOKU NO HERO ACADEMIA © 2014 by Kohei Horikoshi
All rights reserved.
First published in Japan in 2014 by SHUEISHA Inc., Tokyo.
English translation rights arranged by SHUEISHA Inc.

Printed in the U.S.A.

Published by VIZ Media, LLC
P.O. Box 77010
San Francisco, CA 94107

10 9 8 7 6 5 4 3 2
First printing, June 2020
Second printing, October 2020

 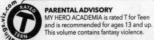

PARENTAL ADVISORY
MY HERO ACADEMIA is rated T for Teen
and is recommended for ages 13 and up.
This volume contains fantasy violence.

MY HERO ACADEMIA Vol. 24

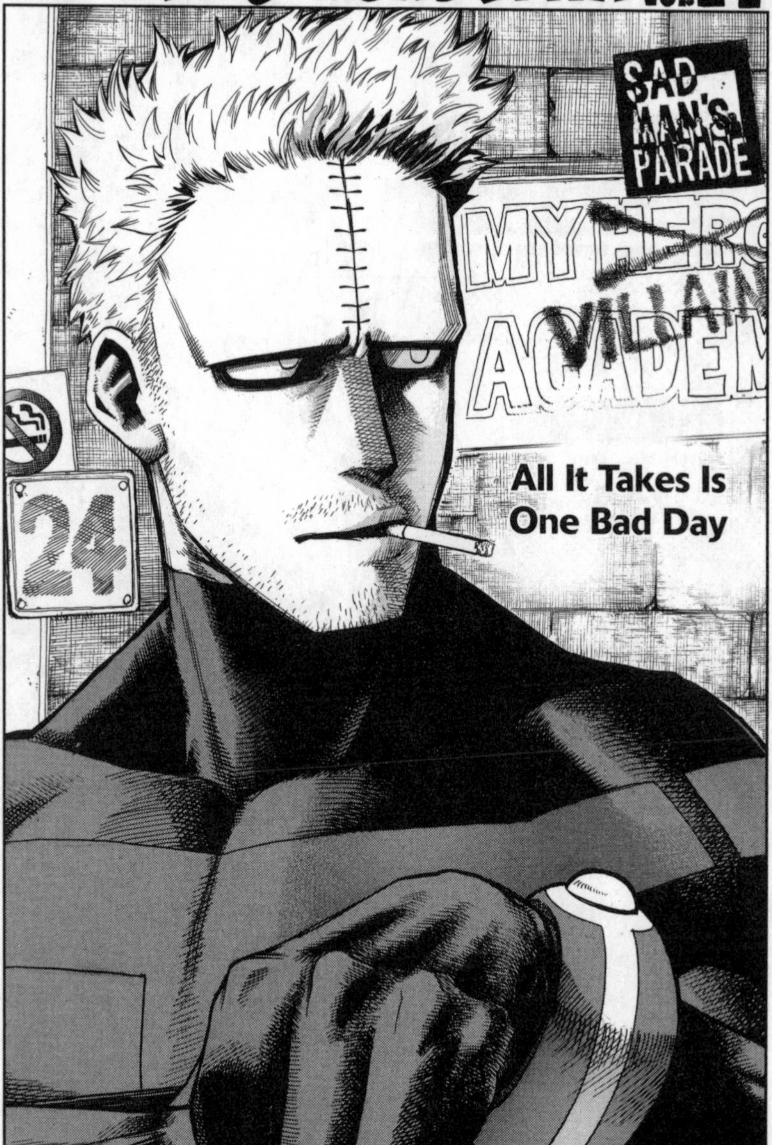
SAD MAN'S PARADE
MY HERO VILLAIN ACADEM
24

All It Takes Is One Bad Day

KOHEI HORIKOSHI

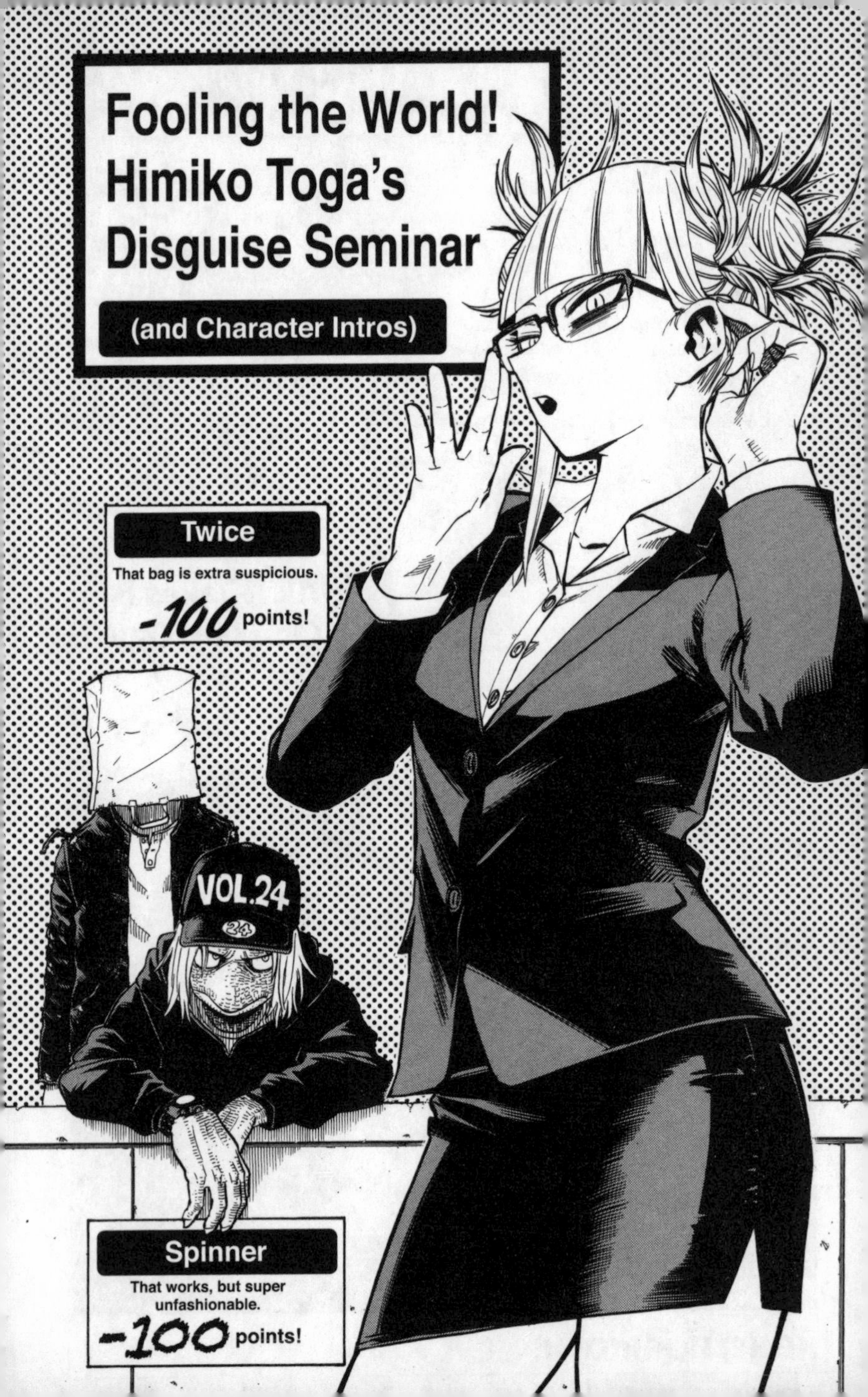
Fooling the World! Himiko Toga's Disguise Seminar
(and Character Intros)
Twice
That bag is extra suspicious.
-100 points!
VOL.24
24
Spinner
That works, but super unfashionable.
-100 points!

One day, people began manifesting special abilities that came to be known as "Quirks," and before long, the world was full of superpowered humans. But with the advent of these exceptional individuals came an increase in crime, and governments alone were unable to deal with the situation. At the same time, others emerged to oppose the spread of evil! As if straight from the comic books, these heroes keep the peace and are even officially authorized to fight crime. Our story begins when a certain Quirkless boy and lifelong hero fan meets the world's number one hero, starting him on his path to becoming the greatest hero ever!

STORY

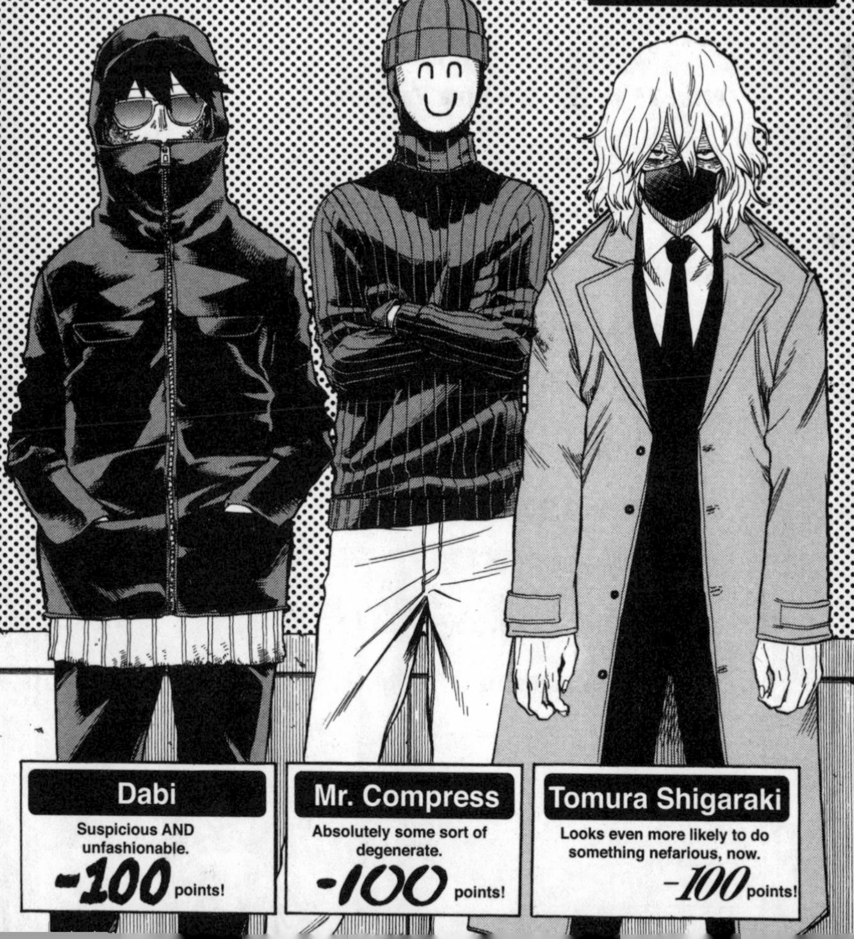
Dabi
Suspicious AND unfashionable.
-100 points!
Mr. Compress
Absolutely some sort of degenerate.
-100 points!
Tomura Shigaraki
Looks even more likely to do something nefarious, now.
-100 points!

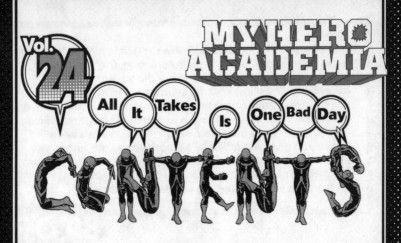

MY HERO ACADEMIA

Vol. 24

All It Takes Is One Bad Day

CONTENTS

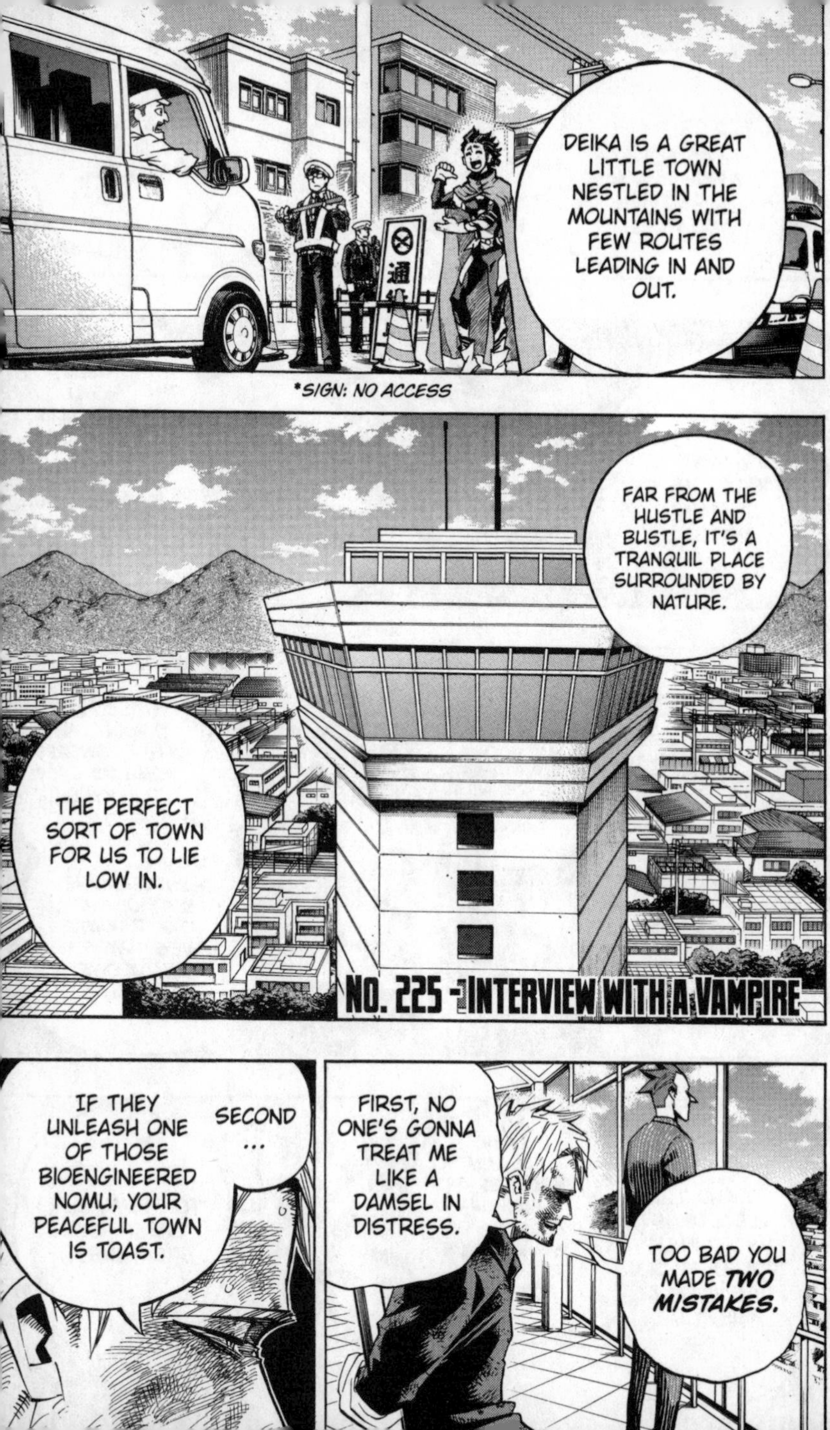
DEIKA IS A GREAT LITTLE TOWN NESTLED IN THE MOUNTAINS WITH FEW ROUTES LEADING IN AND OUT.
*SIGN: NO ACCESS
FAR FROM THE HUSTLE AND BUSTLE, IT'S A TRANQUIL PLACE SURROUNDED BY NATURE.
THE PERFECT SORT OF TOWN FOR US TO LIE LOW IN.
NO. 225 - INTERVIEW WITH A VAMPIRE
TOO BAD YOU MADE TWO MISTAKES.
FIRST, NO ONE'S GONNA TREAT ME LIKE A DAMSEL IN DISTRESS.
SECOND ...
IF THEY UNLEASH ONE OF THOSE BIOENGINEERED NOMU, YOUR PEACEFUL TOWN IS TOAST.

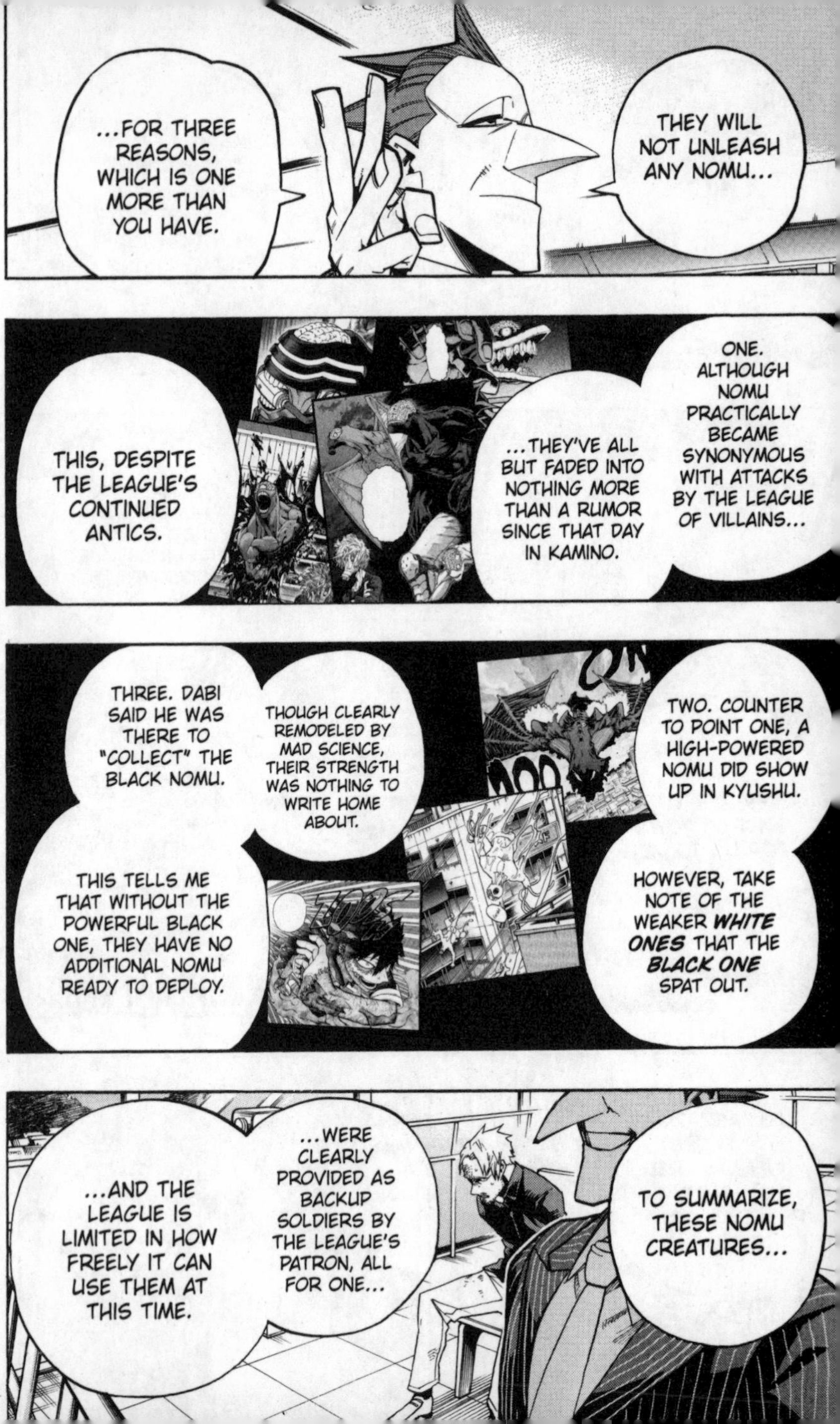
THEY WILL NOT UNLEASH ANY NOMU...
...FOR THREE REASONS, WHICH IS ONE MORE THAN YOU HAVE.
ONE. ALTHOUGH NOMU PRACTICALLY BECAME SYNONYMOUS WITH ATTACKS BY THE LEAGUE OF VILLAINS...
...THEY'VE ALL BUT FADED INTO NOTHING MORE THAN A RUMOR SINCE THAT DAY IN KAMINO.
THIS, DESPITE THE LEAGUE'S CONTINUED ANTICS.
TWO. COUNTER TO POINT ONE, A HIGH-POWERED NOMU DID SHOW UP IN KYUSHU.
HOWEVER, TAKE NOTE OF THE WEAKER ***WHITE ONES*** THAT THE ***BLACK ONE*** SPAT OUT.
THOUGH CLEARLY REMODELED BY MAD SCIENCE, THEIR STRENGTH WAS NOTHING TO WRITE HOME ABOUT.
THREE. DABI SAID HE WAS THERE TO "COLLECT" THE BLACK NOMU.
THIS TELLS ME THAT WITHOUT THE POWERFUL BLACK ONE, THEY HAVE NO ADDITIONAL NOMU READY TO DEPLOY.
TO SUMMARIZE, THESE NOMU CREATURES...
...WERE CLEARLY PROVIDED AS BACKUP SOLDIERS BY THE LEAGUE'S PATRON, ALL FOR ONE...
...AND THE LEAGUE IS LIMITED IN HOW FREELY IT CAN USE THEM AT THIS TIME.

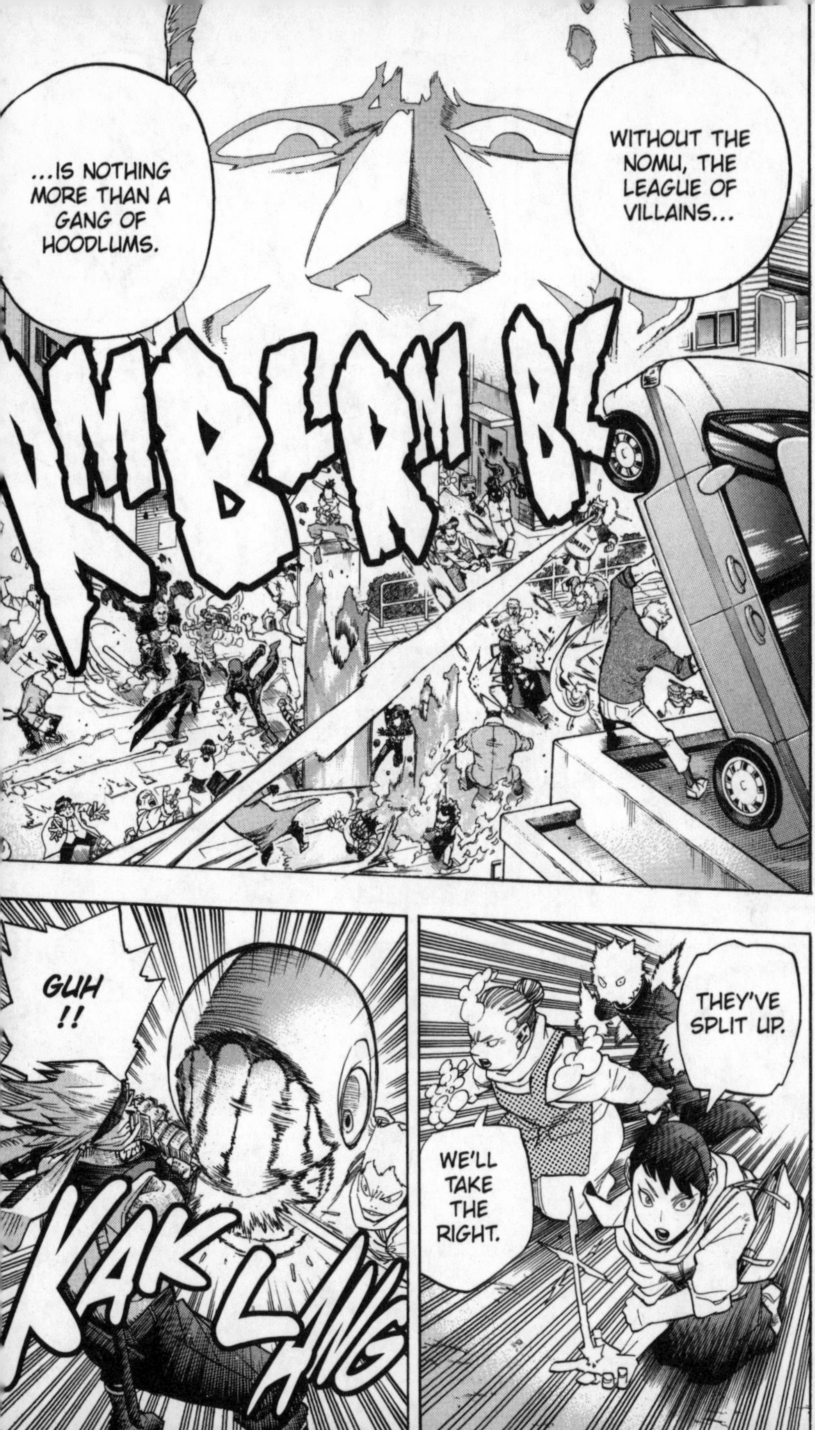
WITHOUT THE NOMU, THE LEAGUE OF VILLAINS...
...IS NOTHING MORE THAN A GANG OF HOODLUMS.
MBLAM BL
THEY'VE SPLIT UP.
WE'LL TAKE THE RIGHT.
GUH !!
KAK LANG

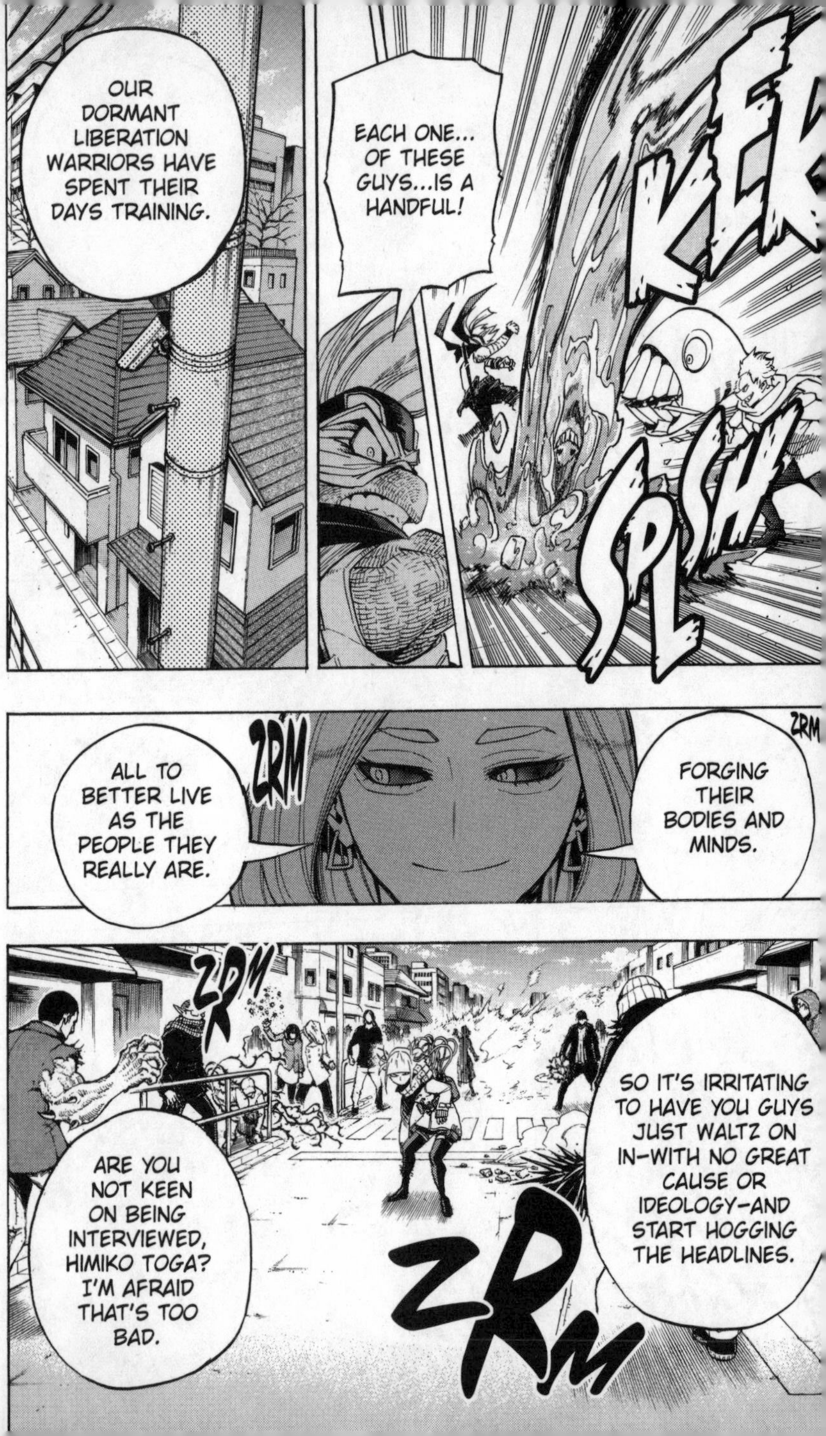
KLK
SPLSH
EACH ONE... OF THESE GUYS...IS A HANDFUL!
OUR DORMANT LIBERATION WARRIORS HAVE SPENT THEIR DAYS TRAINING.
ZRM
FORGING THEIR BODIES AND MINDS.
ZRM
ALL TO BETTER LIVE AS THE PEOPLE THEY REALLY ARE.
SO IT'S IRRITATING TO HAVE YOU GUYS JUST WALTZ ON IN—WITH NO GREAT CAUSE OR IDEOLOGY—AND START HOGGING THE HEADLINES.
ZRM
ZRM
ARE YOU NOT KEEN ON BEING INTERVIEWED, HIMIKO TOGA? I'M AFRAID THAT'S TOO BAD.

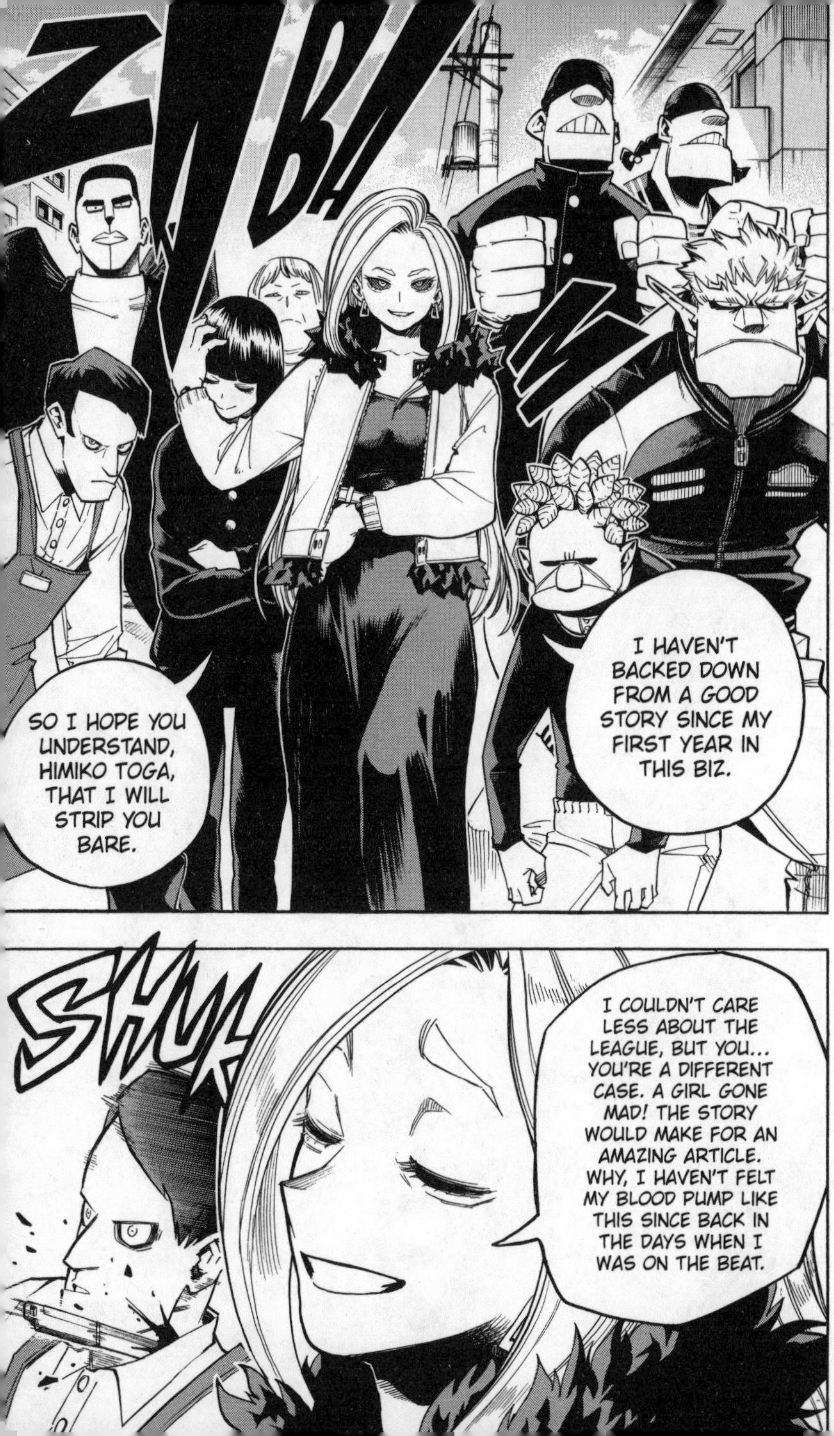
ZABA!
I HAVEN'T BACKED DOWN FROM A GOOD STORY SINCE MY FIRST YEAR IN THIS BIZ.
SO I HOPE YOU UNDERSTAND, HIMIKO TOGA, THAT I WILL STRIP YOU BARE.
I COULDN'T CARE LESS ABOUT THE LEAGUE, BUT YOU... YOU'RE A DIFFERENT CASE. A GIRL GONE MAD! THE STORY WOULD MAKE FOR AN AMAZING ARTICLE. WHY, I HAVEN'T FELT MY BLOOD PUMP LIKE THIS SINCE BACK IN THE DAYS WHEN I WAS ON THE BEAT.
SHUK

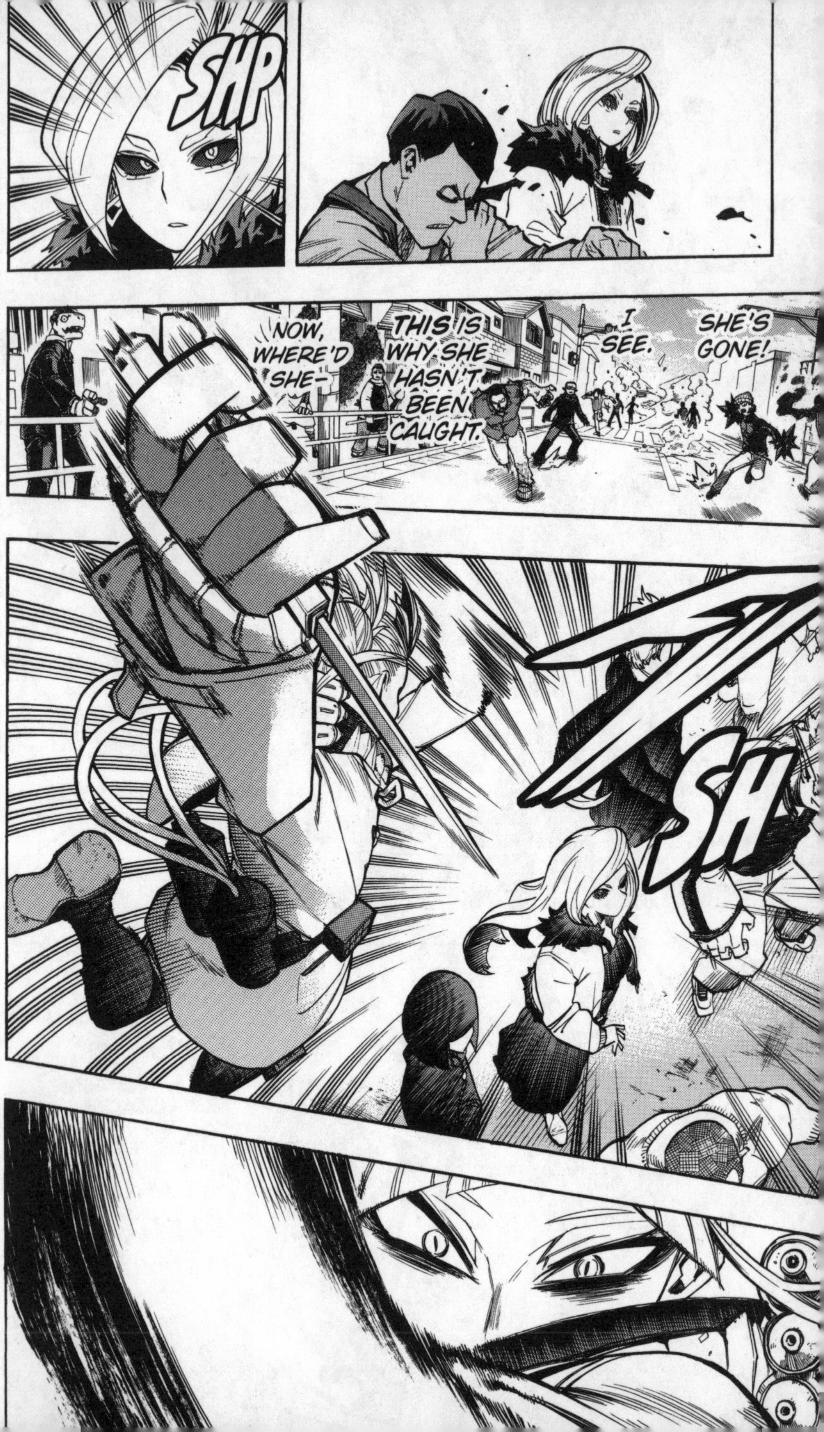
SHP
SHE'S GONE!
I SEE.
THIS IS WHY SHE HASN'T BEEN CAUGHT.
NOW, WHERE'D SHE-
SH

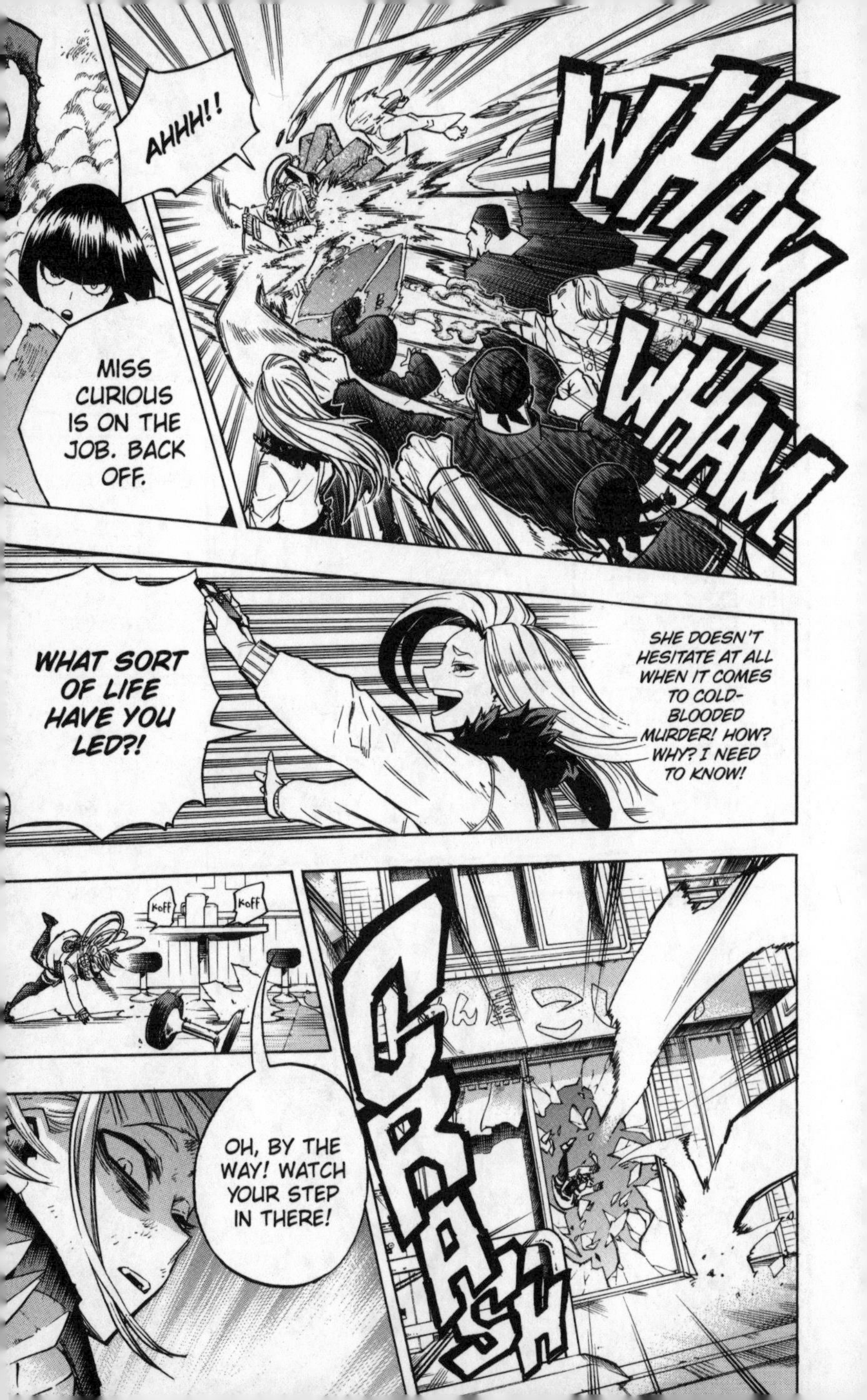
WHAM
WHAM
AHHH!!
MISS CURIOUS IS ON THE JOB. BACK OFF.
SHE DOESN'T HESITATE AT ALL WHEN IT COMES TO COLD-BLOODED MURDER! HOW? WHY? I NEED TO KNOW!
WHAT SORT OF LIFE HAVE YOU LED?!
CRASH
KOFF
KOFF
OH, BY THE WAY! WATCH YOUR STEP IN THERE!

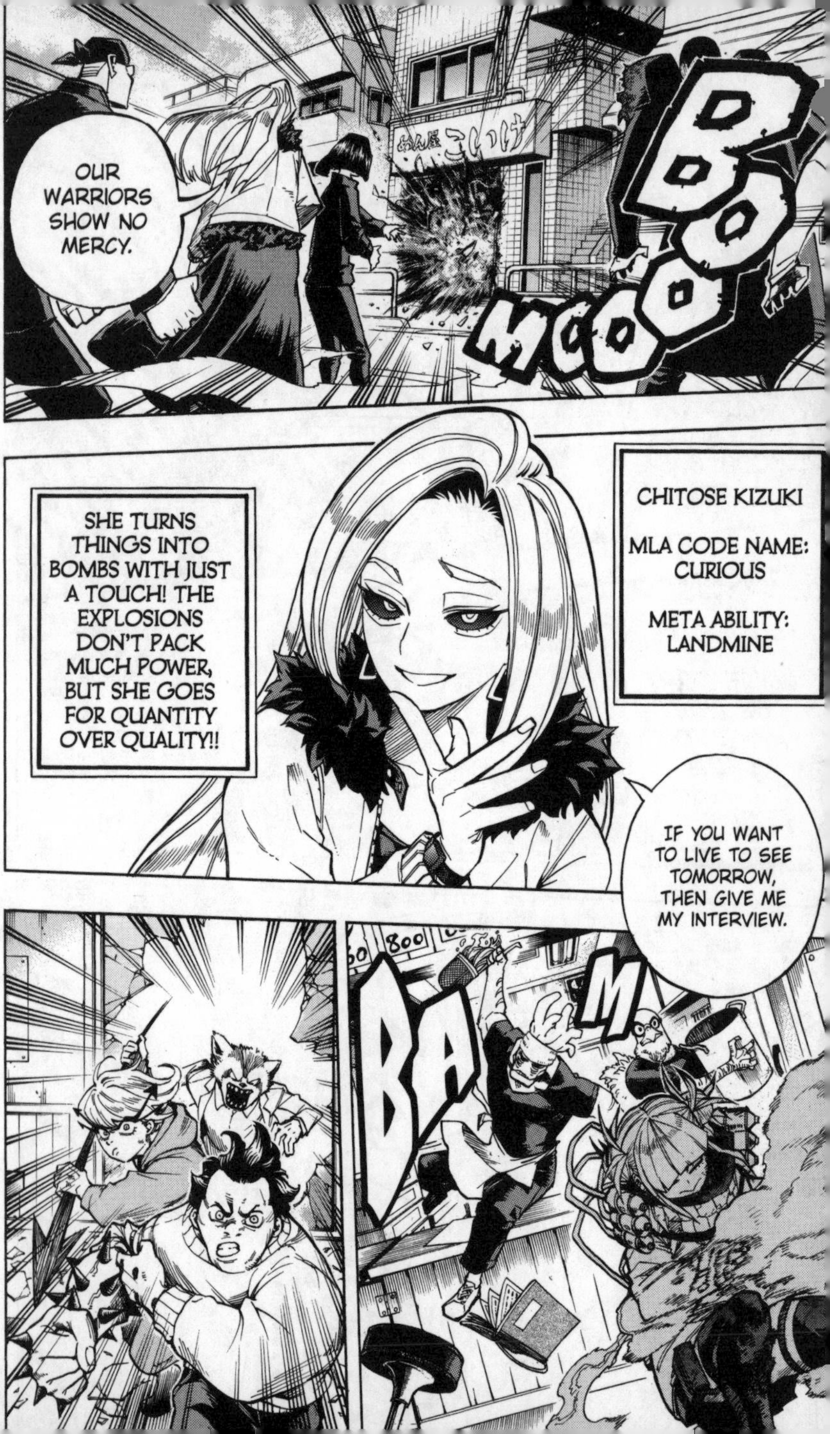
BOOOOOM
OUR WARRIORS SHOW NO MERCY.
CHITOSE KIZUKI
MLA CODE NAME: CURIOUS
META ABILITY: LANDMINE
SHE TURNS THINGS INTO BOMBS WITH JUST A TOUCH! THE EXPLOSIONS DON'T PACK MUCH POWER, BUT SHE GOES FOR QUANTITY OVER QUALITY!!
IF YOU WANT TO LIVE TO SEE TOMORROW, THEN GIVE ME MY INTERVIEW.
BAM

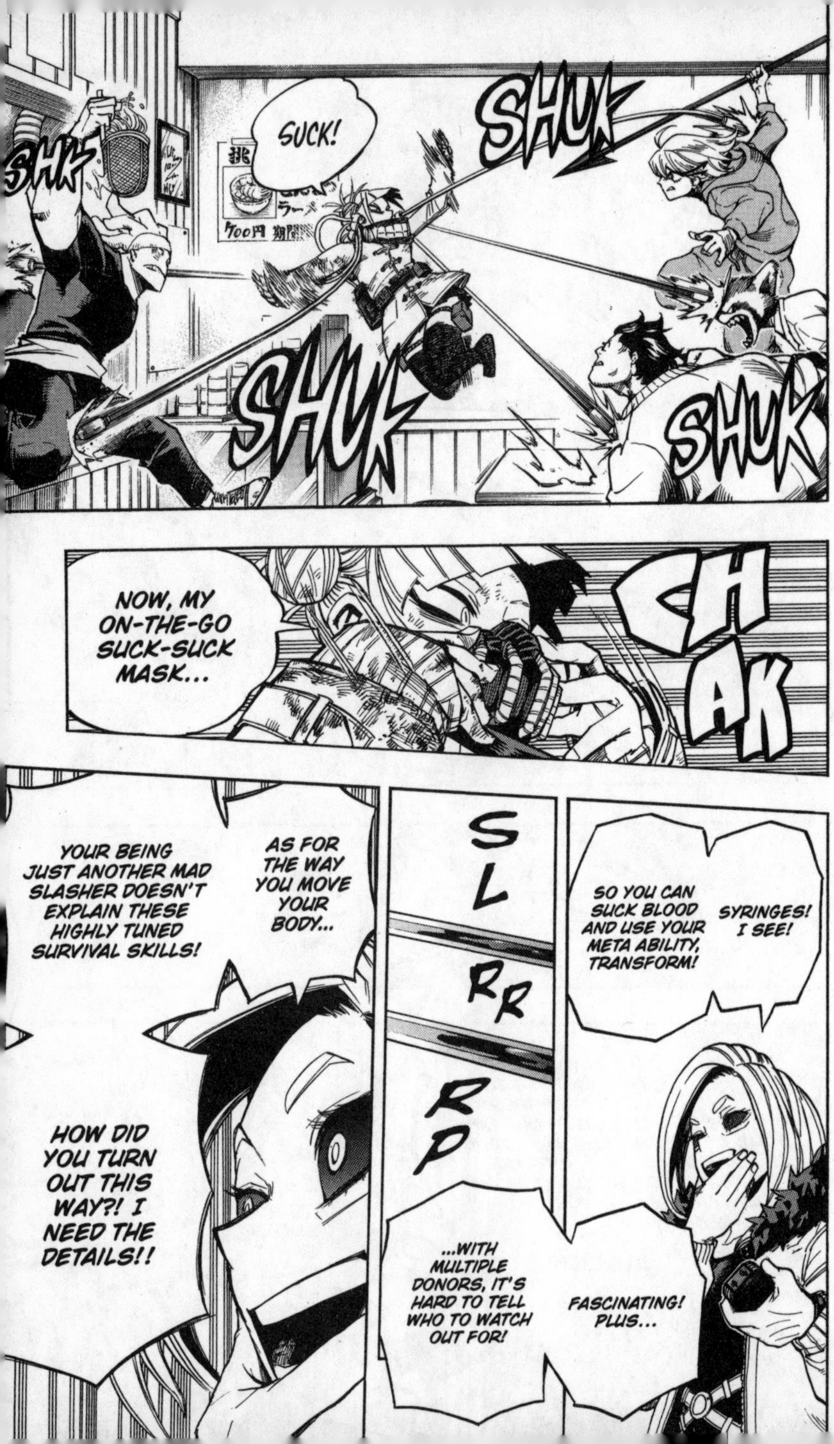
SHUK
SHUK
SUCK!
SHK
SHUK
CHAK
NOW, MY ON-THE-GO SUCK-SUCK MASK...
SYRINGES! I SEE!
SO YOU CAN SUCK BLOOD AND USE YOUR META ABILITY, TRANSFORM!
FASCINATING! PLUS...
SLRRRRP
...WITH MULTIPLE DONORS, IT'S HARD TO TELL WHO TO WATCH OUT FOR!
AS FOR THE WAY YOU MOVE YOUR BODY...
YOUR BEING JUST ANOTHER MAD SLASHER DOESN'T EXPLAIN THESE HIGHLY TUNED SURVIVAL SKILLS!
HOW DID YOU TURN OUT THIS WAY?! I NEED THE DETAILS!!

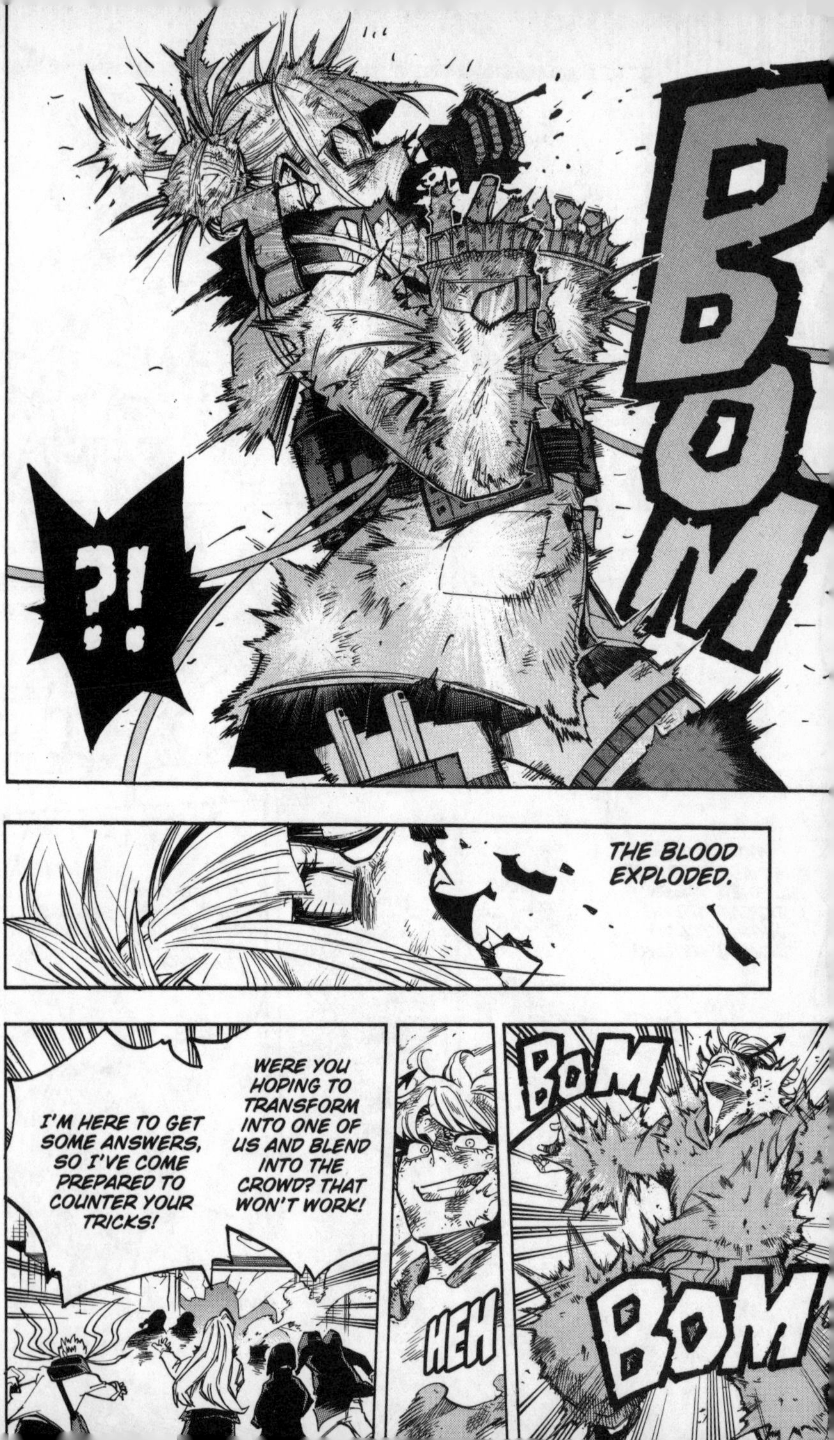
BOM
?!
THE BLOOD EXPLODED.
BOM
BOM
HEH
WERE YOU HOPING TO TRANSFORM INTO ONE OF US AND BLEND INTO THE CROWD? THAT WON'T WORK!
I'M HERE TO GET SOME ANSWERS, SO I'VE COME PREPARED TO COUNTER YOUR TRICKS!

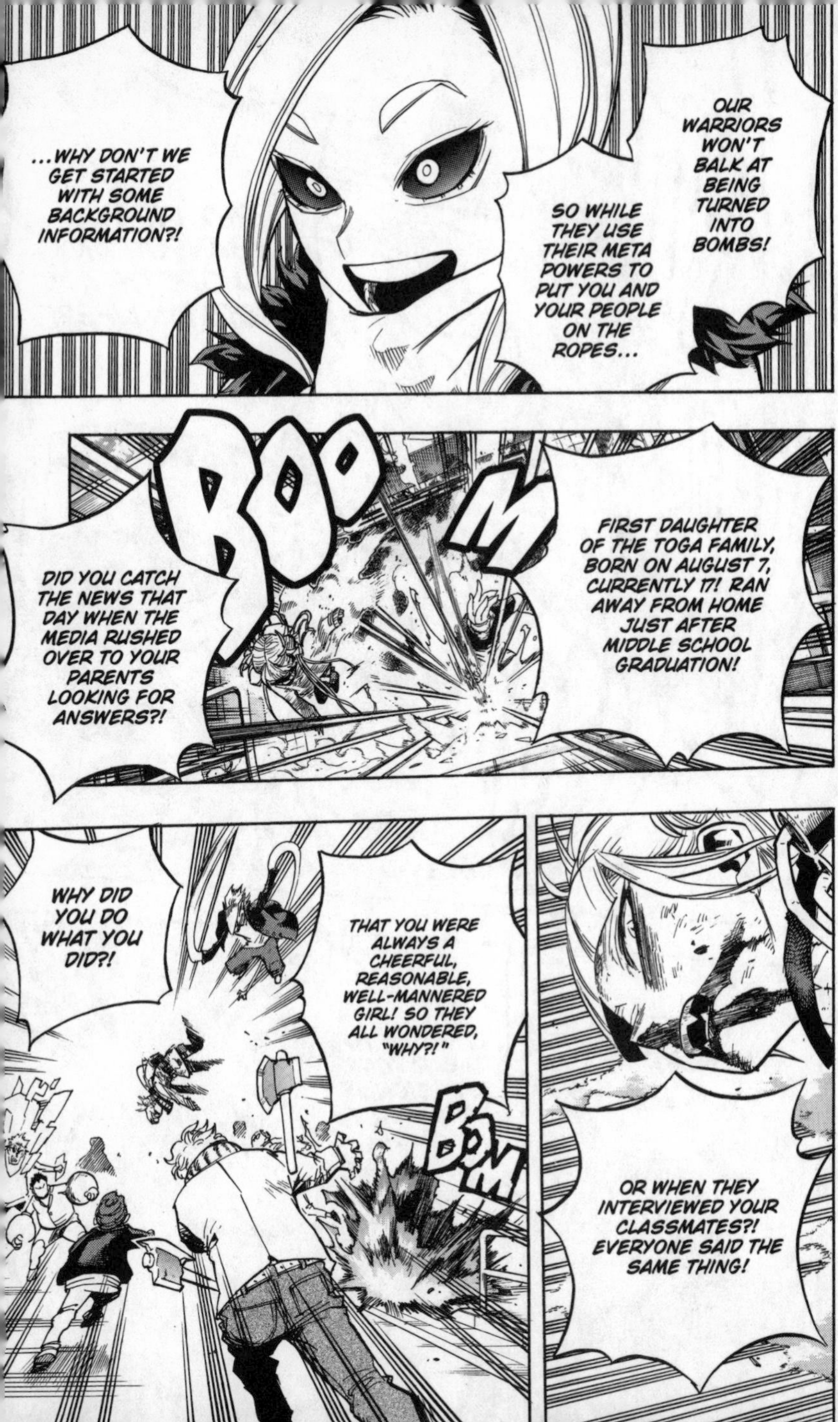
OUR WARRIORS WON'T BALK AT BEING TURNED INTO BOMBS!
SO WHILE THEY USE THEIR META POWERS TO PUT YOU AND YOUR PEOPLE ON THE ROPES...
...WHY DON'T WE GET STARTED WITH SOME BACKGROUND INFORMATION?!
FIRST DAUGHTER OF THE TOGA FAMILY, BORN ON AUGUST 7, CURRENTLY 17! RAN AWAY FROM HOME JUST AFTER MIDDLE SCHOOL GRADUATION!
DID YOU CATCH THE NEWS THAT DAY WHEN THE MEDIA RUSHED OVER TO YOUR PARENTS LOOKING FOR ANSWERS?!
OR WHEN THEY INTERVIEWED YOUR CLASSMATES?! EVERYONE SAID THE SAME THING!
THAT YOU WERE ALWAYS A CHEERFUL, REASONABLE, WELL-MANNERED GIRL! SO THEY ALL WONDERED, "WHY?!"
WHY DID YOU DO WHAT YOU DID?!
BOOM

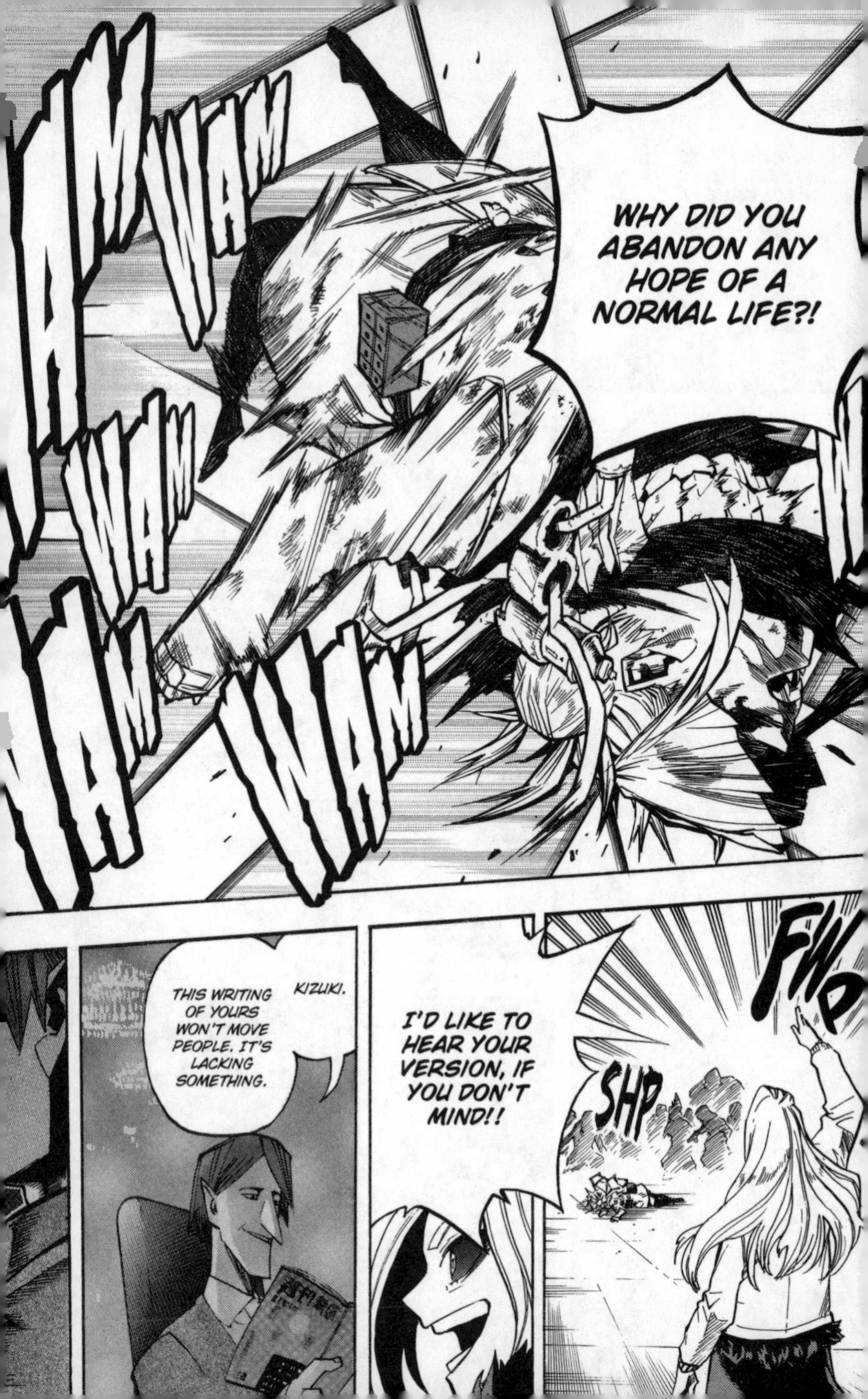
WAM
WAM
WAM
WAM
WAM
WHY DID YOU ABANDON ANY HOPE OF A NORMAL LIFE?!
FWP
I'D LIKE TO HEAR YOUR VERSION, IF YOU DON'T MIND!!
SHP
KIZUKI.
THIS WRITING OF YOURS WON'T MOVE PEOPLE. IT'S LACKING SOMETHING.

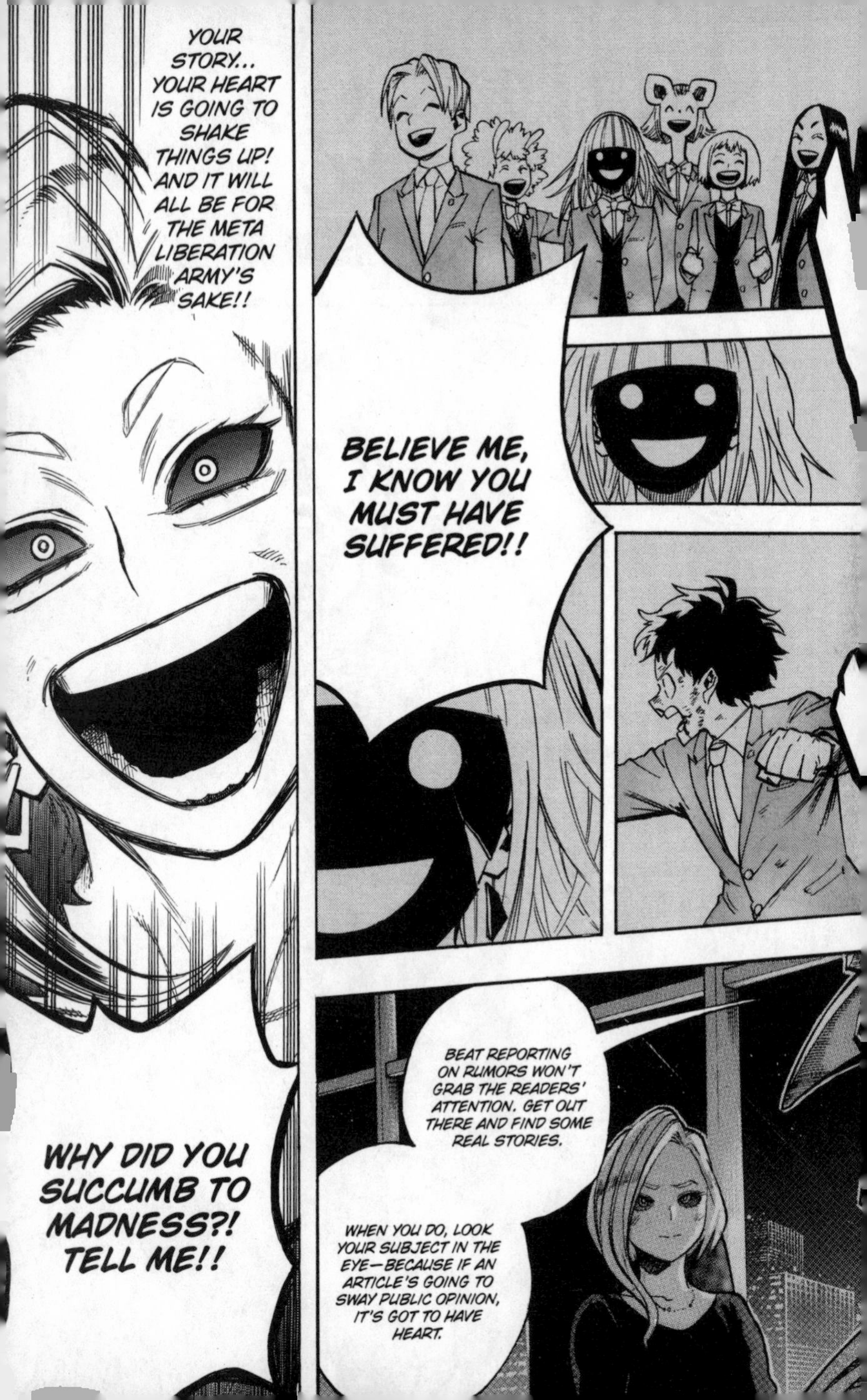
BELIEVE ME, I KNOW YOU MUST HAVE SUFFERED!!
BEAT REPORTING ON RUMORS WON'T GRAB THE READERS' ATTENTION. GET OUT THERE AND FIND SOME REAL STORIES.
WHEN YOU DO, LOOK YOUR SUBJECT IN THE EYE—BECAUSE IF AN ARTICLE'S GOING TO SWAY PUBLIC OPINION, IT'S GOT TO HAVE HEART.
YOUR STORY... YOUR HEART IS GOING TO SHAKE THINGS UP! AND IT WILL ALL BE FOR THE META LIBERATION ARMY'S SAKE!!
WHY DID YOU SUCCUMB TO MADNESS?! TELL ME!!

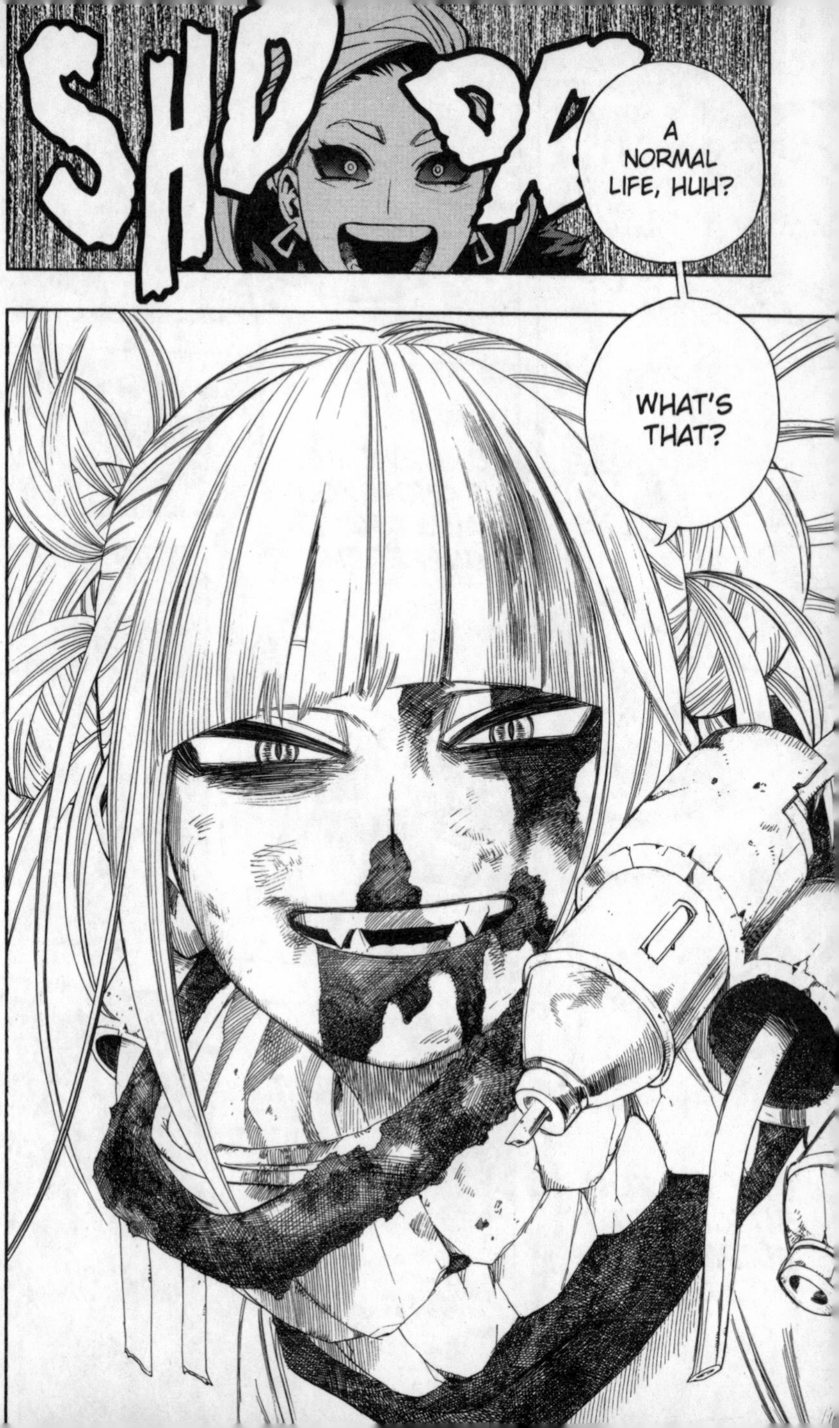
A NORMAL LIFE, HUH?
WHAT'S THAT?

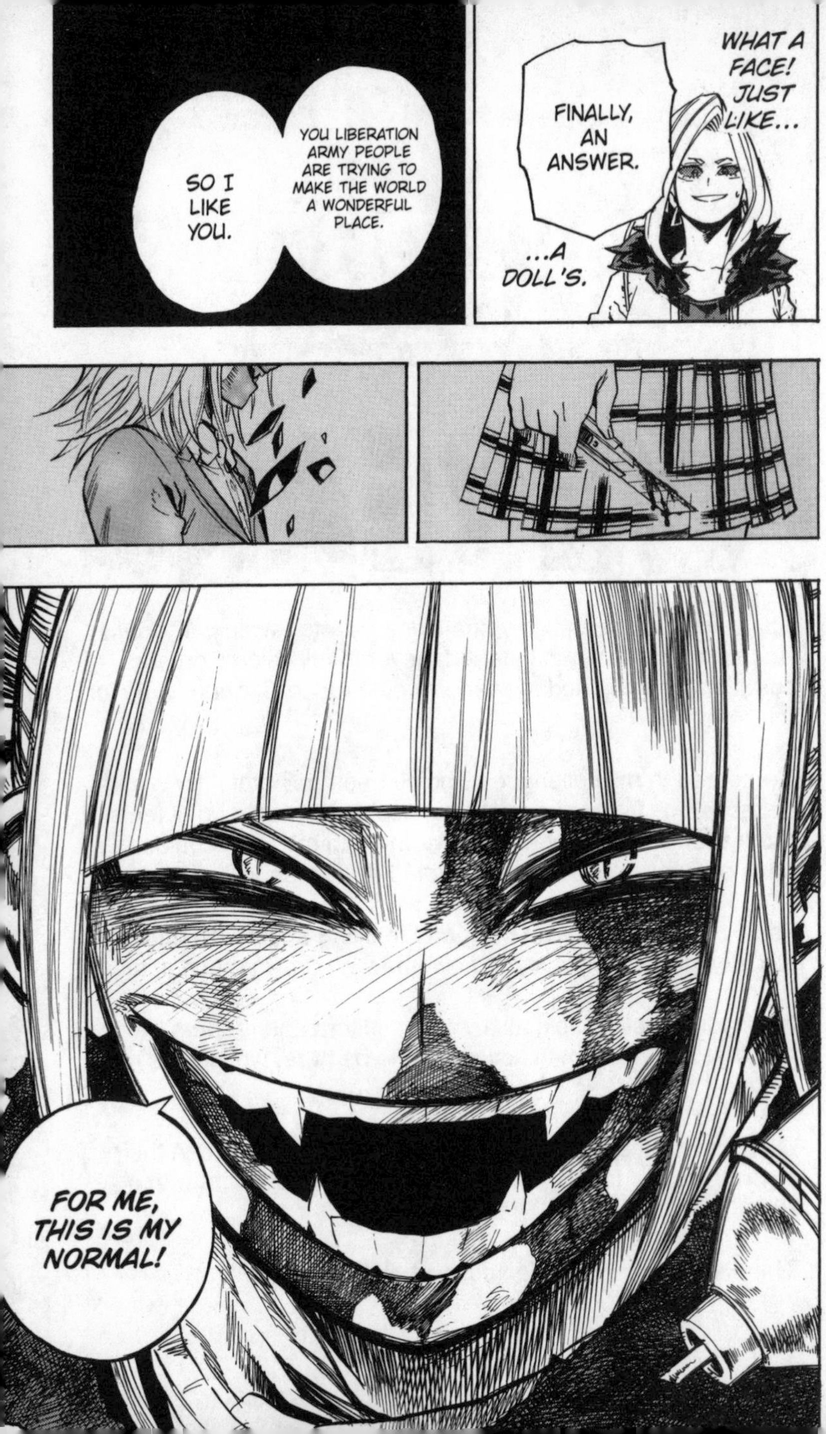
WHAT A FACE! JUST LIKE...
FINALLY, AN ANSWER.
...A DOLL'S.
YOU LIBERATION ARMY PEOPLE ARE TRYING TO MAKE THE WORLD A WONDERFUL PLACE.
SO I LIKE YOU.
FOR ME, THIS IS MY NORMAL!

MY HERO ACADEMIA

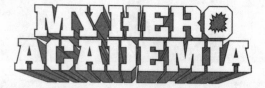

FIVE YEARS

Apparently, it's been five years since I started writing *My Hero Academia*. Back when I started, never in my wildest dreams could I have imagined my series would run in *Shonen Jump* for this long. Wow!

Compared to my colleagues who've been going at it for decades, my five years might not seem like much, but it feels like a pretty significant accomplishment to me, who couldn't have pictured a future where I got to draw manga.

I spend my days looking back and thinking about how much I still have to accomplish and how I haven't grown much at all.

It's thanks to pure luck, all my great editors and readers like you that a dud like me is even able to be here, writing this mini essay.

Jump is a battlefield where masters of the craft sharpen their swords and go to war, so all I can do is keep drawing with a PLUS ULTRA attitude. Draw, draw, draw!

Thanks for your continued support of *MHA*!

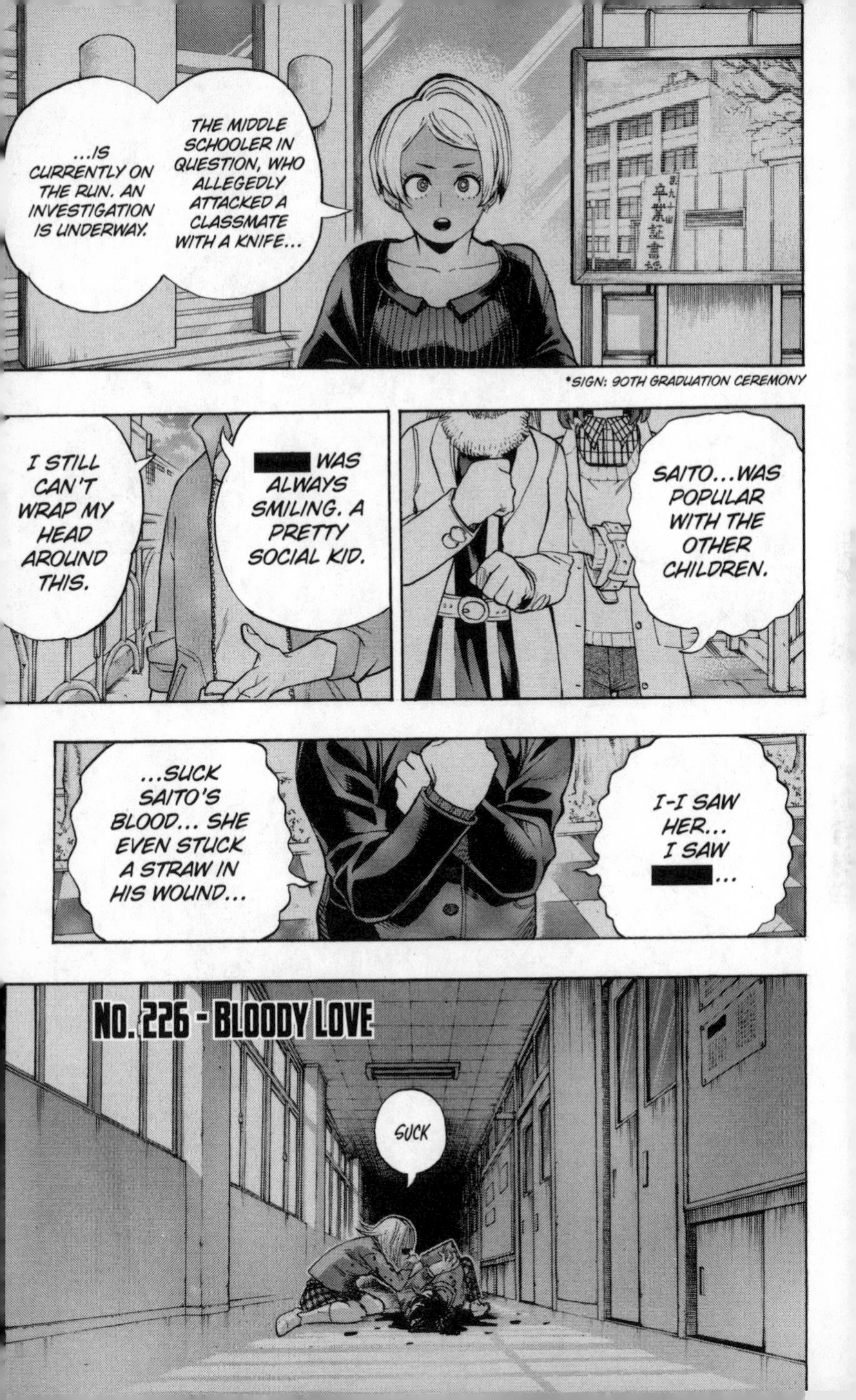
THE MIDDLE SCHOOLER IN QUESTION, WHO ALLEGEDLY ATTACKED A CLASSMATE WITH A KNIFE...
...IS CURRENTLY ON THE RUN. AN INVESTIGATION IS UNDERWAY.
*SIGN: 90TH GRADUATION CEREMONY
SAITO...WAS POPULAR WITH THE OTHER CHILDREN.
[redacted] WAS ALWAYS SMILING. A PRETTY SOCIAL KID.
I STILL CAN'T WRAP MY HEAD AROUND THIS.
I-I SAW HER... I SAW [redacted]...
...SUCK SAITO'S BLOOD... SHE EVEN STUCK A STRAW IN HIS WOUND...
NO. 226 - BLOODY LOVE
SUCK

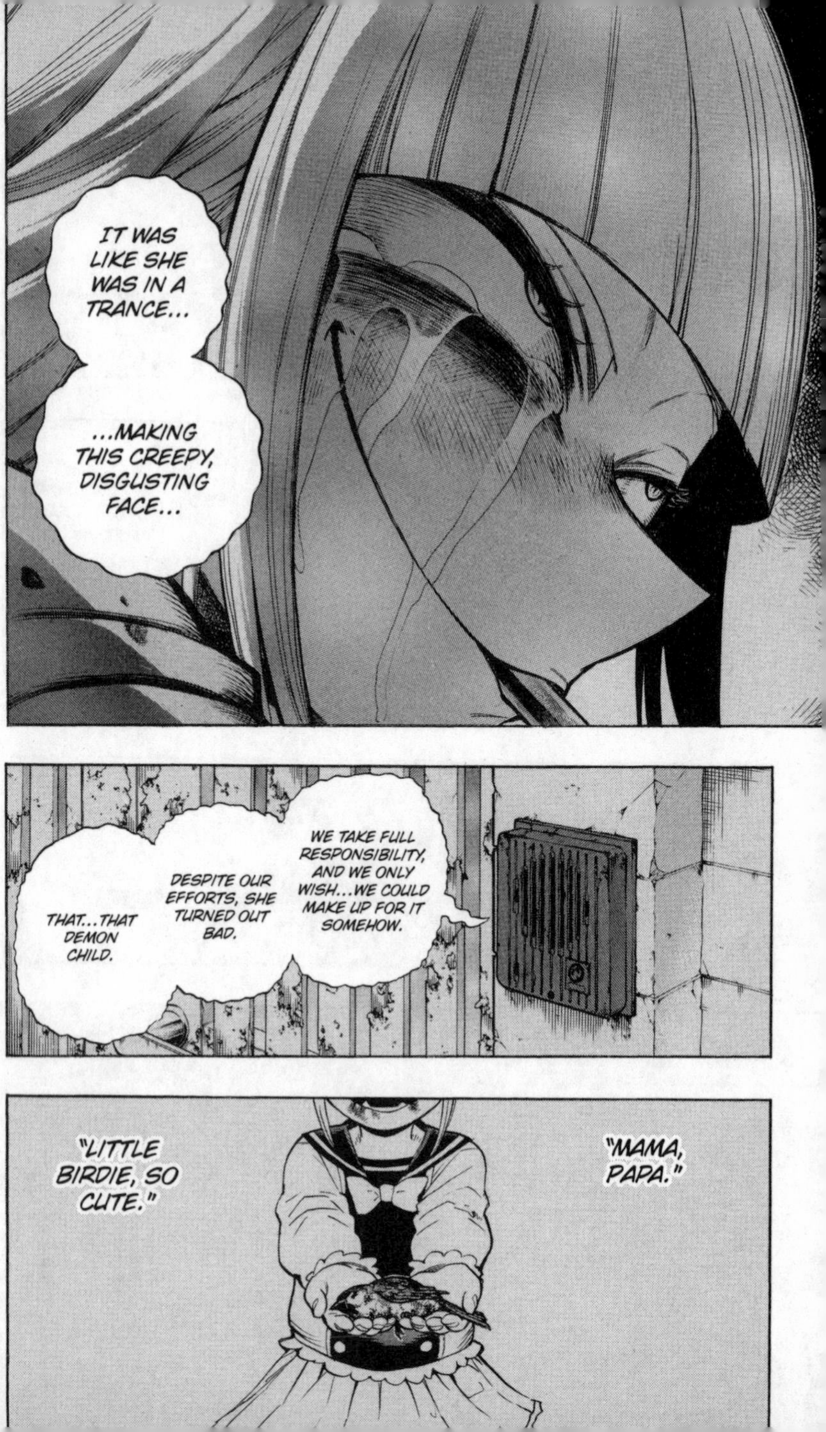
IT WAS LIKE SHE WAS IN A TRANCE...
...MAKING THIS CREEPY, DISGUSTING FACE...
WE TAKE FULL RESPONSIBILITY, AND WE ONLY WISH...WE COULD MAKE UP FOR IT SOMEHOW.
DESPITE OUR EFFORTS, SHE TURNED OUT BAD.
THAT...THAT DEMON CHILD.
"MAMA, PAPA."
"LITTLE BIRDIE, SO CUTE."

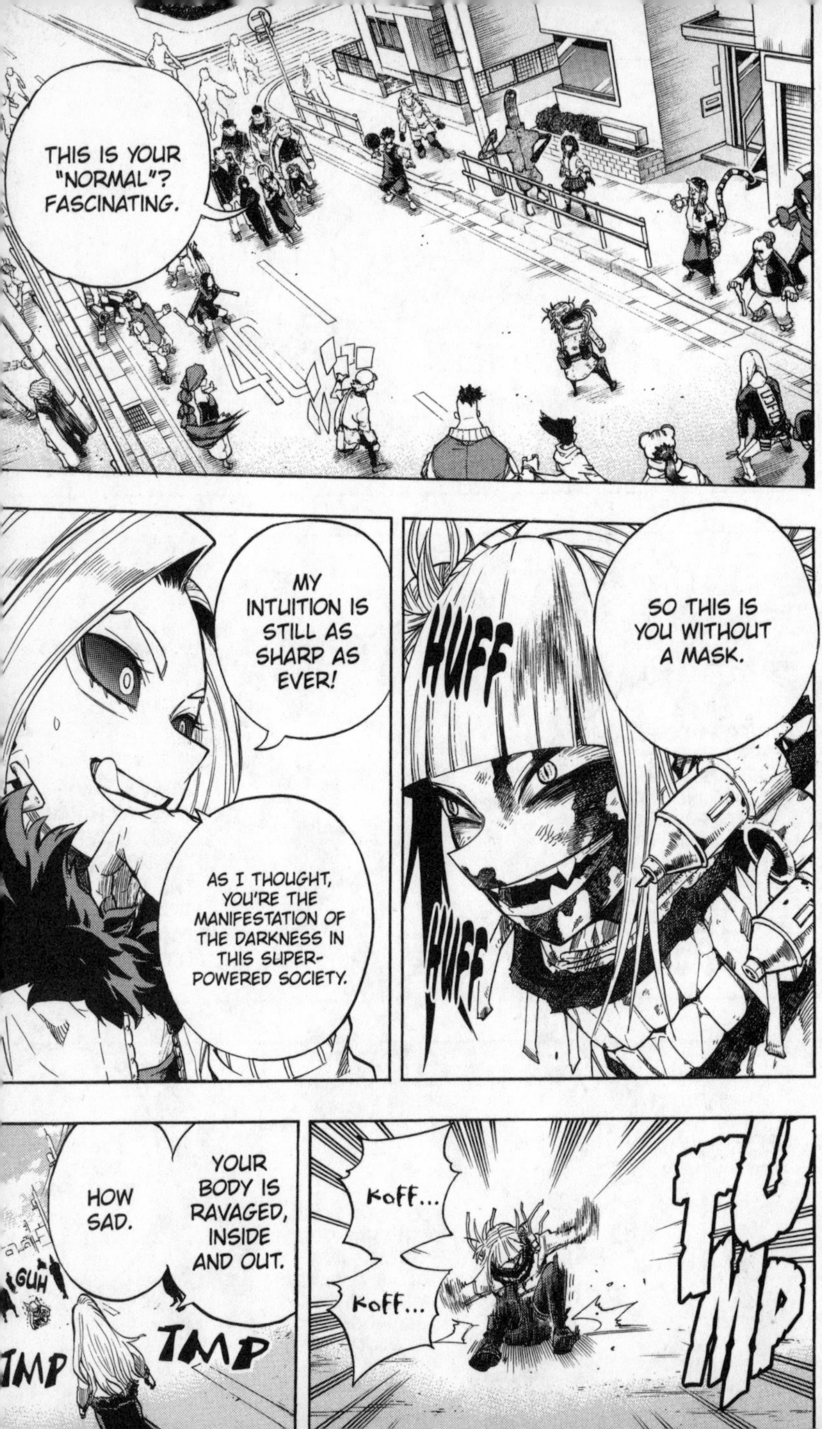
THIS IS YOUR "NORMAL"? FASCINATING.
SO THIS IS YOU WITHOUT A MASK.
HUFF
HUFF
MY INTUITION IS STILL AS SHARP AS EVER!
AS I THOUGHT, YOU'RE THE MANIFESTATION OF THE DARKNESS IN THIS SUPER-POWERED SOCIETY.
TUMP
KOFF...
KOFF...
YOUR BODY IS RAVAGED, INSIDE AND OUT.
HOW SAD.
GUH
TMP
TMP

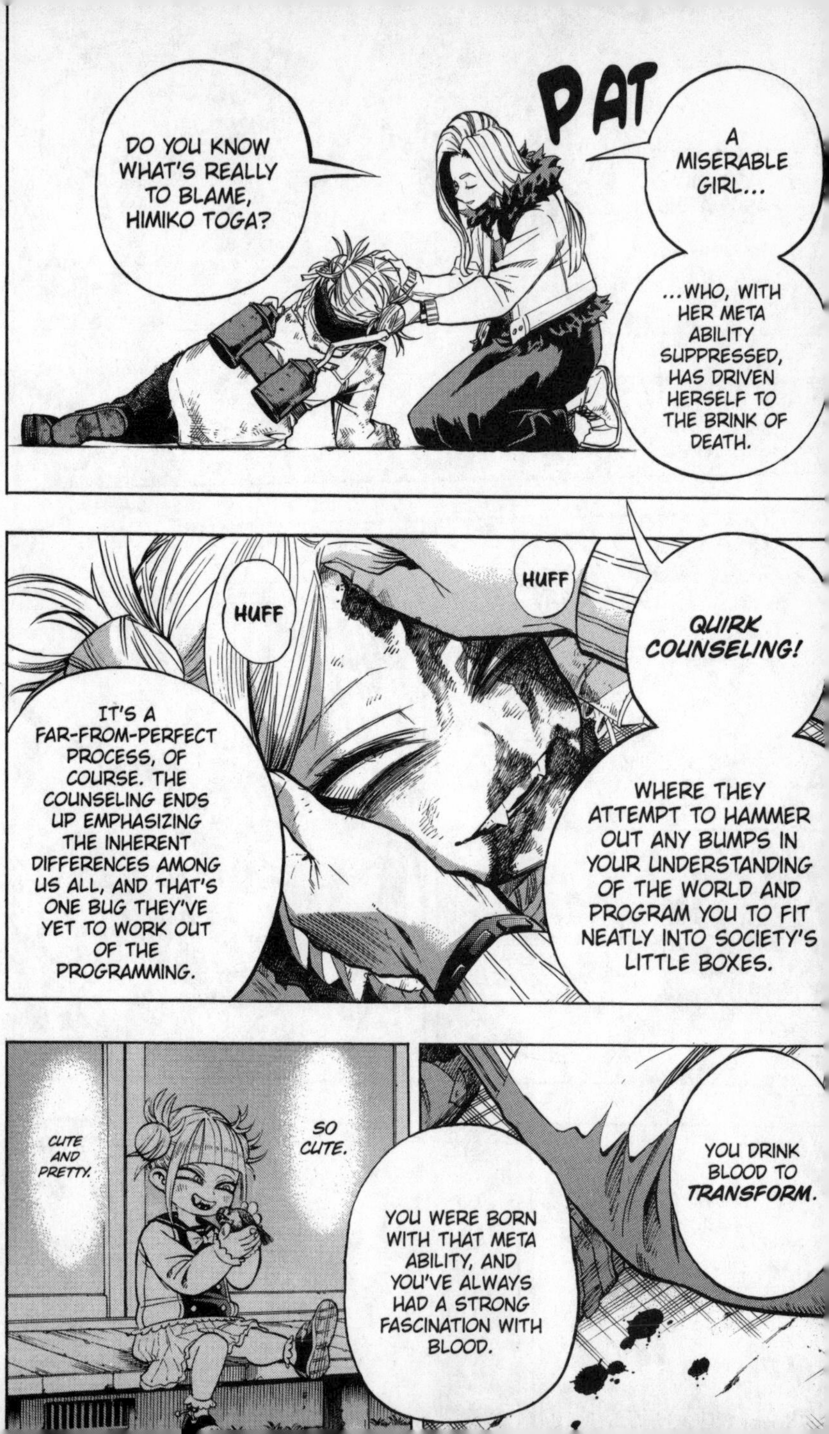
PAT
A MISERABLE GIRL...
...WHO, WITH HER META ABILITY SUPPRESSED, HAS DRIVEN HERSELF TO THE BRINK OF DEATH.
DO YOU KNOW WHAT'S REALLY TO BLAME, HIMIKO TOGA?
HUFF
QUIRK COUNSELING!
WHERE THEY ATTEMPT TO HAMMER OUT ANY BUMPS IN YOUR UNDERSTANDING OF THE WORLD AND PROGRAM YOU TO FIT NEATLY INTO SOCIETY'S LITTLE BOXES.
HUFF
IT'S A FAR-FROM-PERFECT PROCESS, OF COURSE. THE COUNSELING ENDS UP EMPHASIZING THE INHERENT DIFFERENCES AMONG US ALL, AND THAT'S ONE BUG THEY'VE YET TO WORK OUT OF THE PROGRAMMING.
YOU DRINK BLOOD TO *TRANSFORM*.
YOU WERE BORN WITH THAT META ABILITY, AND YOU'VE ALWAYS HAD A STRONG FASCINATION WITH BLOOD.
SO CUTE.
CUTE AND PRETTY.

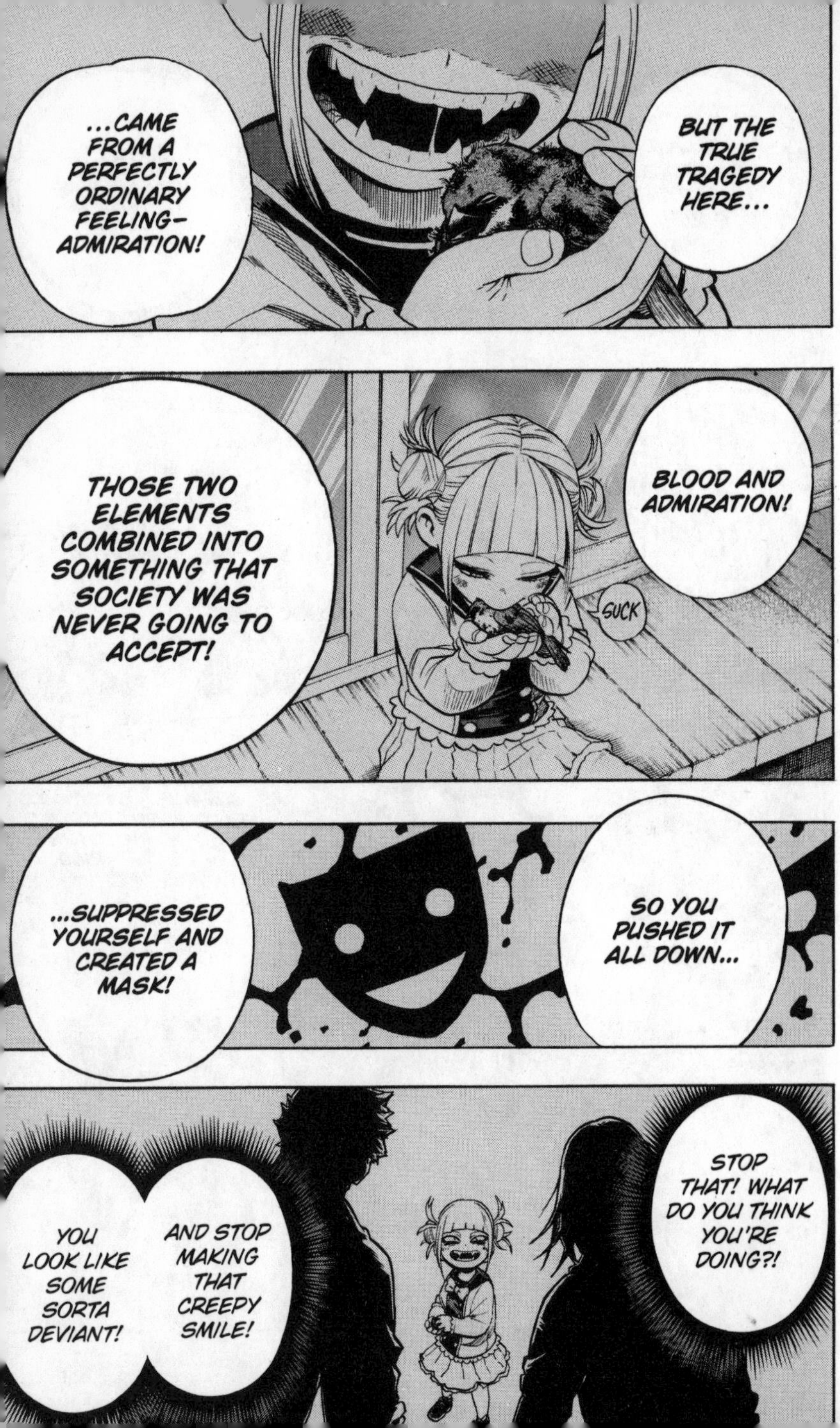
BUT THE TRUE TRAGEDY HERE...
...CAME FROM A PERFECTLY ORDINARY FEELING—ADMIRATION!
BLOOD AND ADMIRATION!
SUCK
THOSE TWO ELEMENTS COMBINED INTO SOMETHING THAT SOCIETY WAS NEVER GOING TO ACCEPT!
SO YOU PUSHED IT ALL DOWN...
...SUPPRESSED YOURSELF AND CREATED A MASK!
STOP THAT! WHAT DO YOU THINK YOU'RE DOING?!
AND STOP MAKING THAT CREEPY SMILE!
YOU LOOK LIKE SOME SORTA DEVIANT!

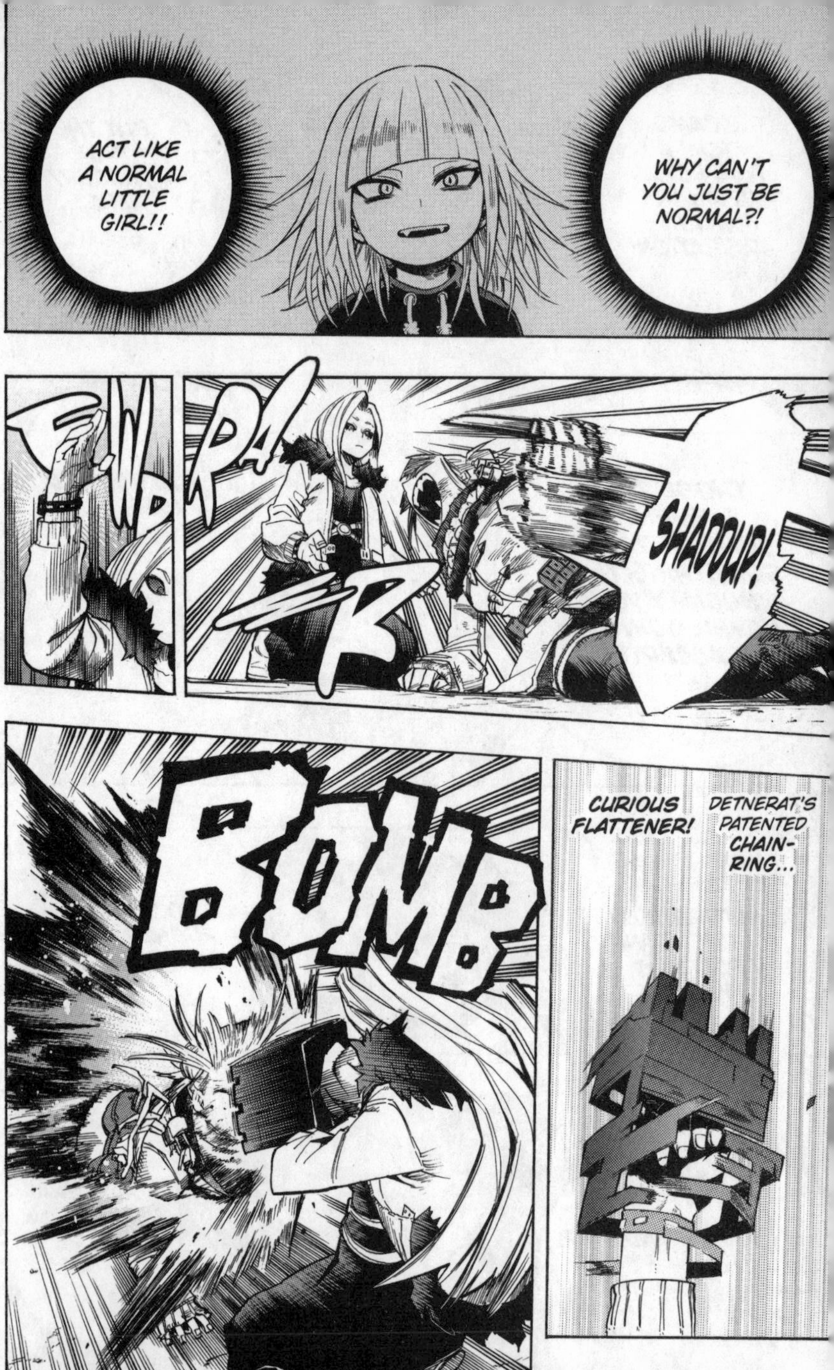
WHY CAN'T YOU JUST BE NORMAL?!
ACT LIKE A NORMAL LITTLE GIRL!!
SHADDUP!
DETNERAT'S PATENTED CHAIN-RING...
CURIOUS FLATTENER!
BOMB

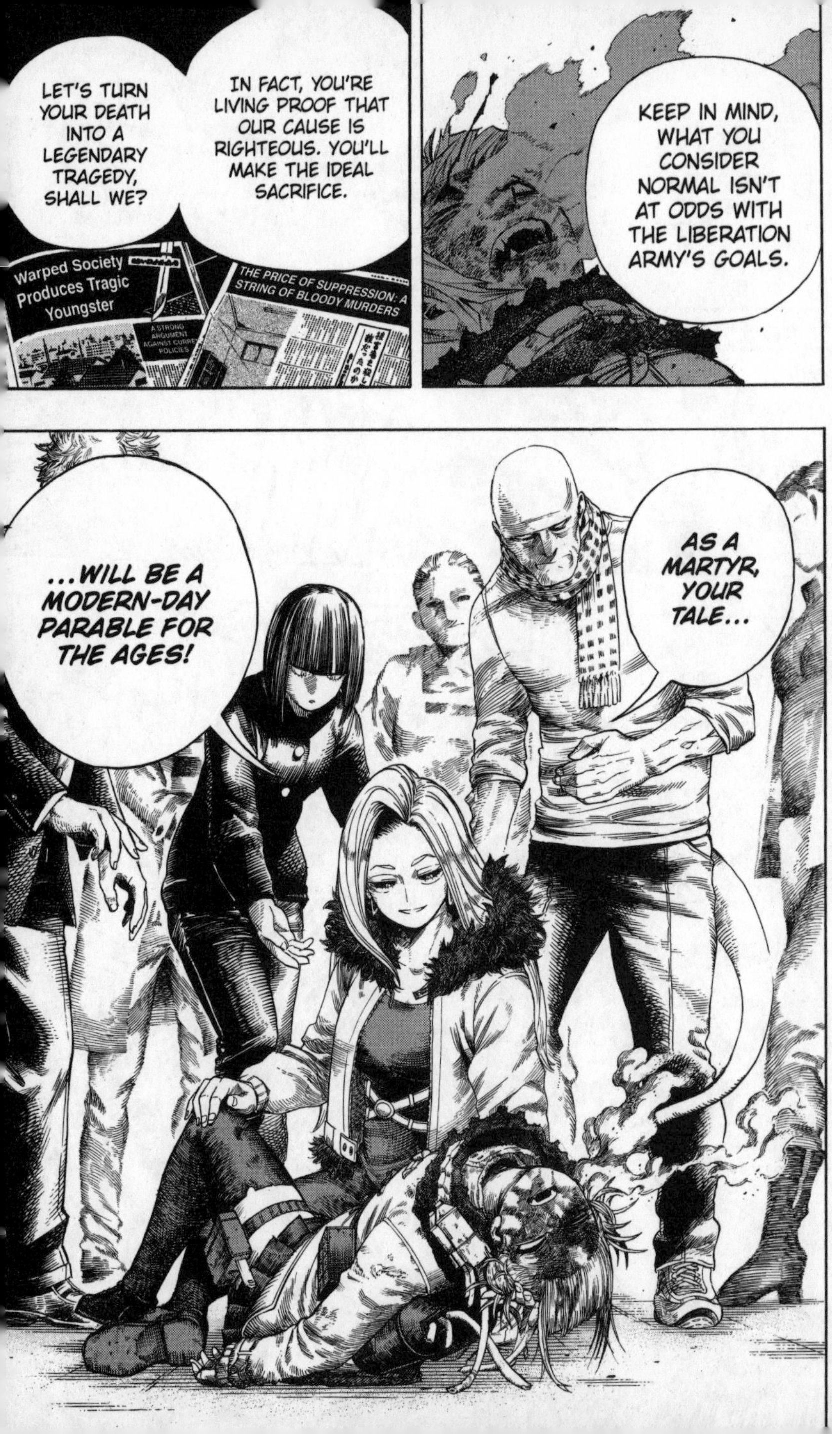
KEEP IN MIND, WHAT YOU CONSIDER NORMAL ISN'T AT ODDS WITH THE LIBERATION ARMY'S GOALS.
IN FACT, YOU'RE LIVING PROOF THAT OUR CAUSE IS RIGHTEOUS. YOU'LL MAKE THE IDEAL SACRIFICE.
LET'S TURN YOUR DEATH INTO A LEGENDARY TRAGEDY, SHALL WE?
THE PRICE OF SUPPRESSION: A STRING OF BLOODY MURDERS
Warped Society Produces Tragic Youngster
AS A MARTYR, YOUR TALE...
...WILL BE A MODERN-DAY PARABLE FOR THE AGES!

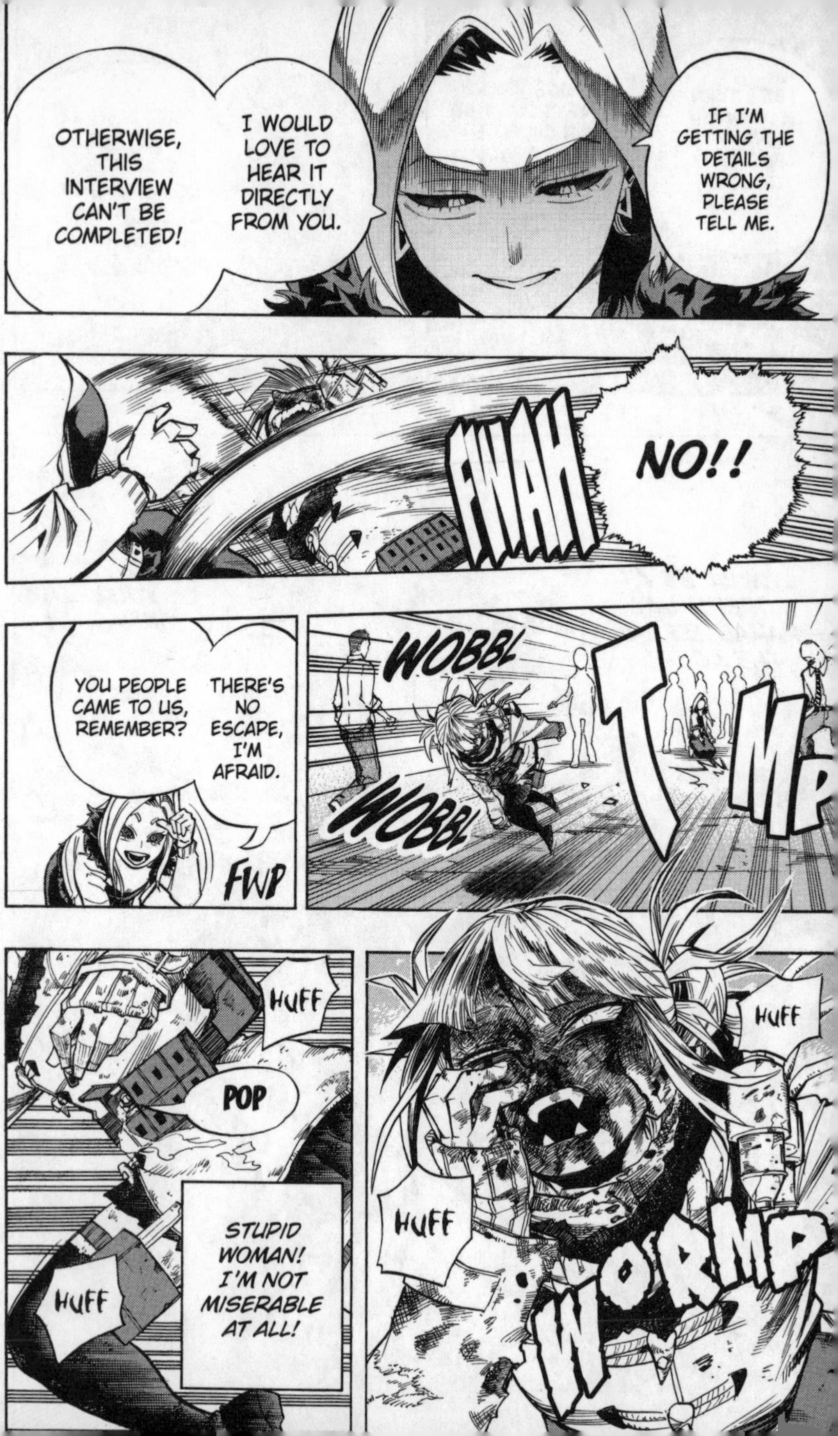
IF I'M GETTING THE DETAILS WRONG, PLEASE TELL ME.
I WOULD LOVE TO HEAR IT DIRECTLY FROM YOU.
OTHERWISE, THIS INTERVIEW CAN'T BE COMPLETED!
NO!!
FWAH
TMP
WOBBL
WOBBL
THERE'S NO ESCAPE, I'M AFRAID.
YOU PEOPLE CAME TO US, REMEMBER?
FWP
HUFF
HUFF
WORMP
HUFF
POP
STUPID WOMAN! I'M NOT MISERABLE AT ALL!
HUFF

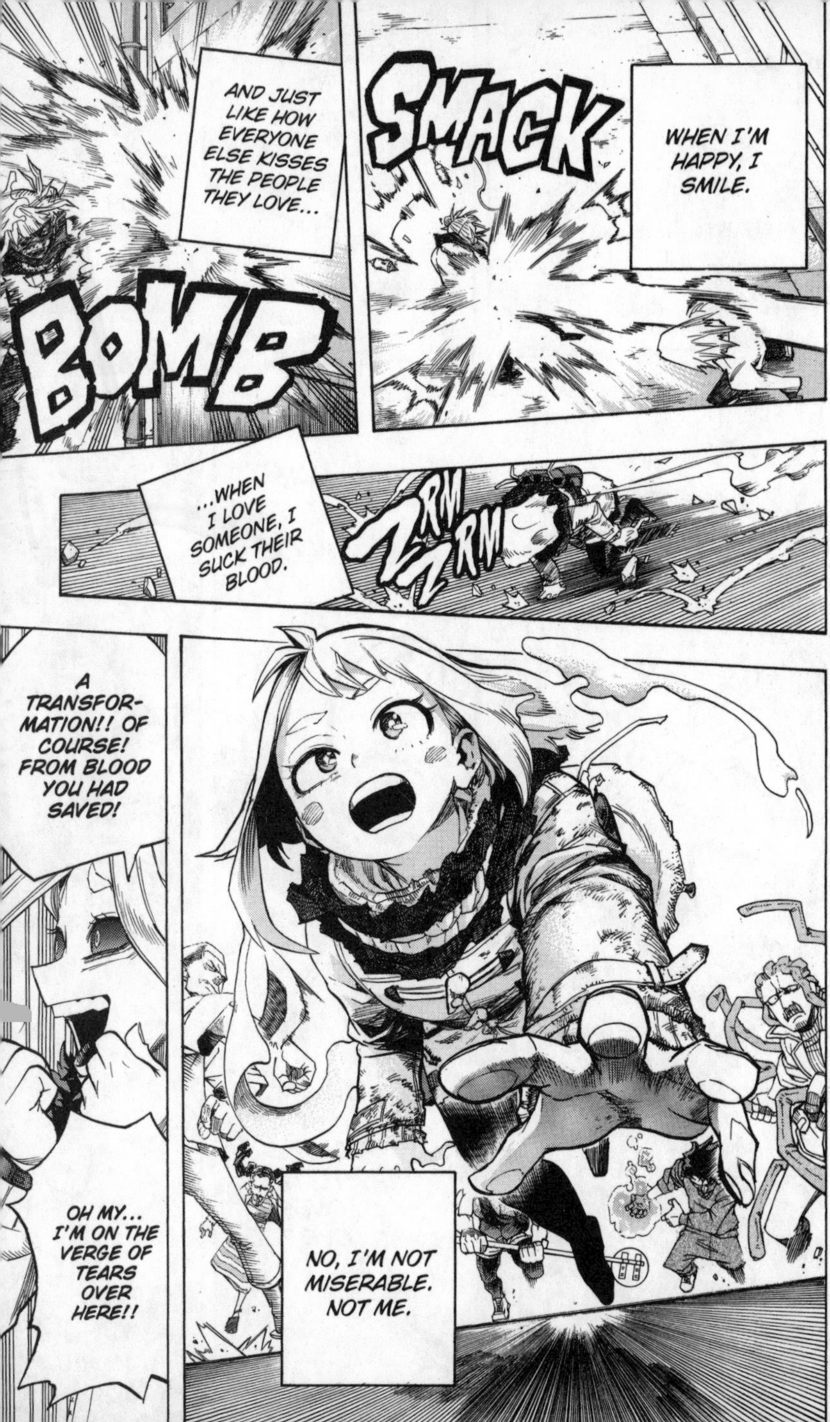
WHEN I'M HAPPY, I SMILE.
SMACK
AND JUST LIKE HOW EVERYONE ELSE KISSES THE PEOPLE THEY LOVE...
BOMB
ZRM ZRM
...WHEN I LOVE SOMEONE, I SUCK THEIR BLOOD.
NO, I'M NOT MISERABLE. NOT ME.
A TRANSFORMATION!! OF COURSE! FROM BLOOD YOU HAD SAVED!
OH MY... I'M ON THE VERGE OF TEARS OVER HERE!!

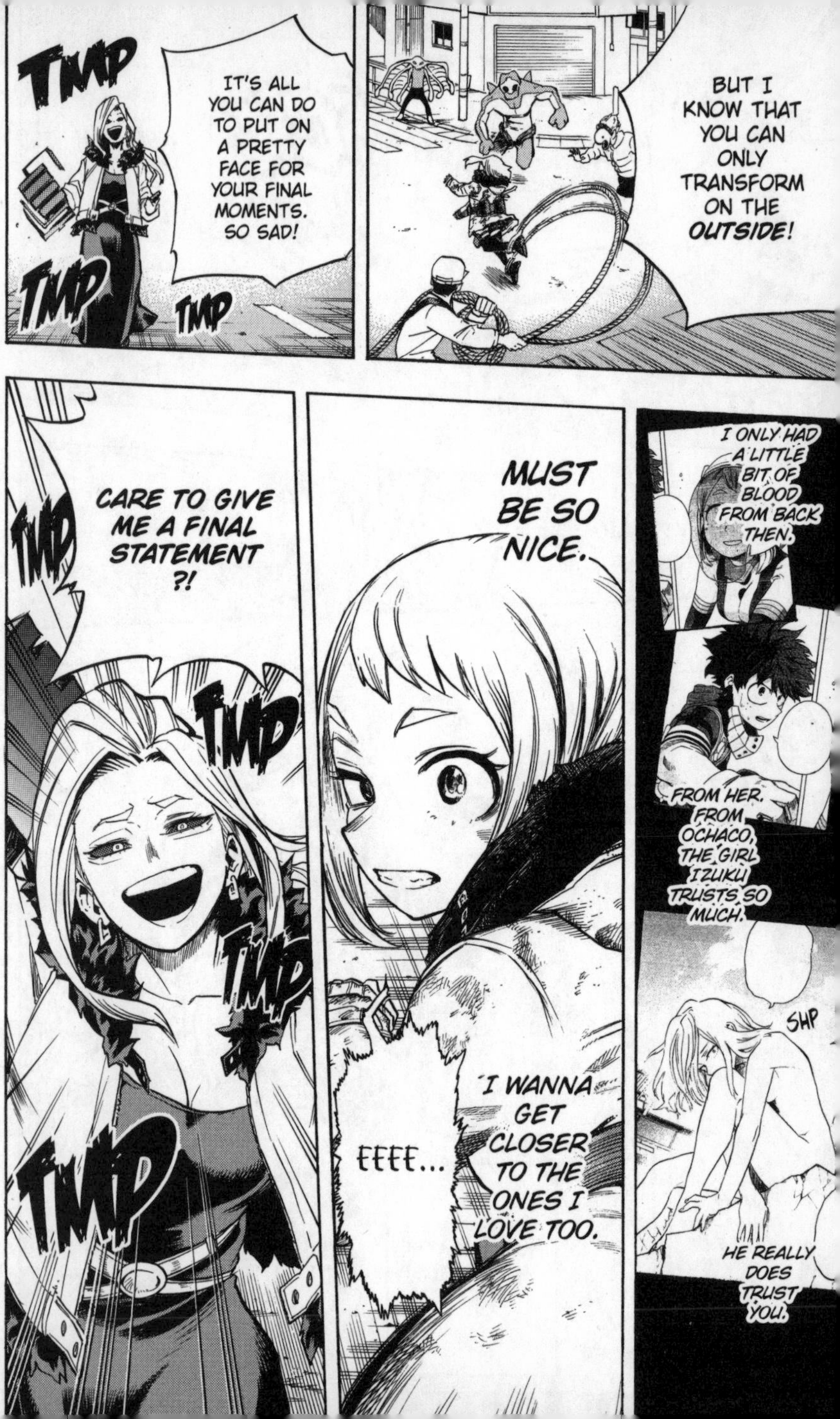
BUT I KNOW THAT YOU CAN ONLY TRANSFORM ON THE OUTSIDE!
TMP
IT'S ALL YOU CAN DO TO PUT ON A PRETTY FACE FOR YOUR FINAL MOMENTS. SO SAD!
TMP
TMP
I ONLY HAD A LITTLE BIT OF BLOOD FROM BACK THEN.
FROM HER. FROM OCHACO, THE GIRL IZUKU TRUSTS SO MUCH.
SHP
HE REALLY DOES TRUST YOU.
MUST BE SO NICE.
"I WANNA GET CLOSER TO THE ONES I LOVE TOO.
EEEE...
TMP
CARE TO GIVE ME A FINAL STATEMENT ?!
TMP
TMP
TMP

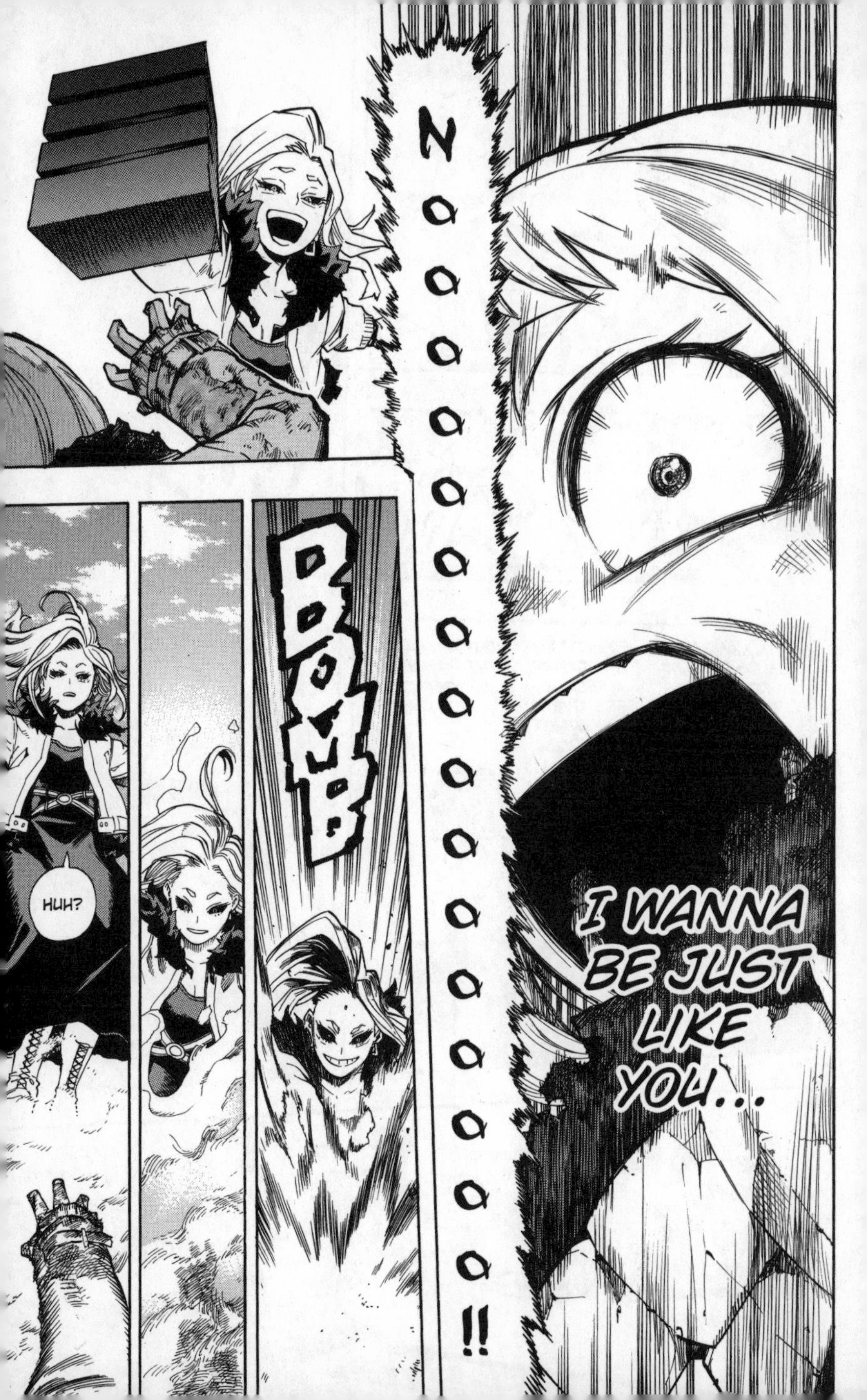
NOOOOOOOOOOOOOOOOOOOOO!!
I WANNA BE JUST LIKE YOU...
DOOMB
HUH?

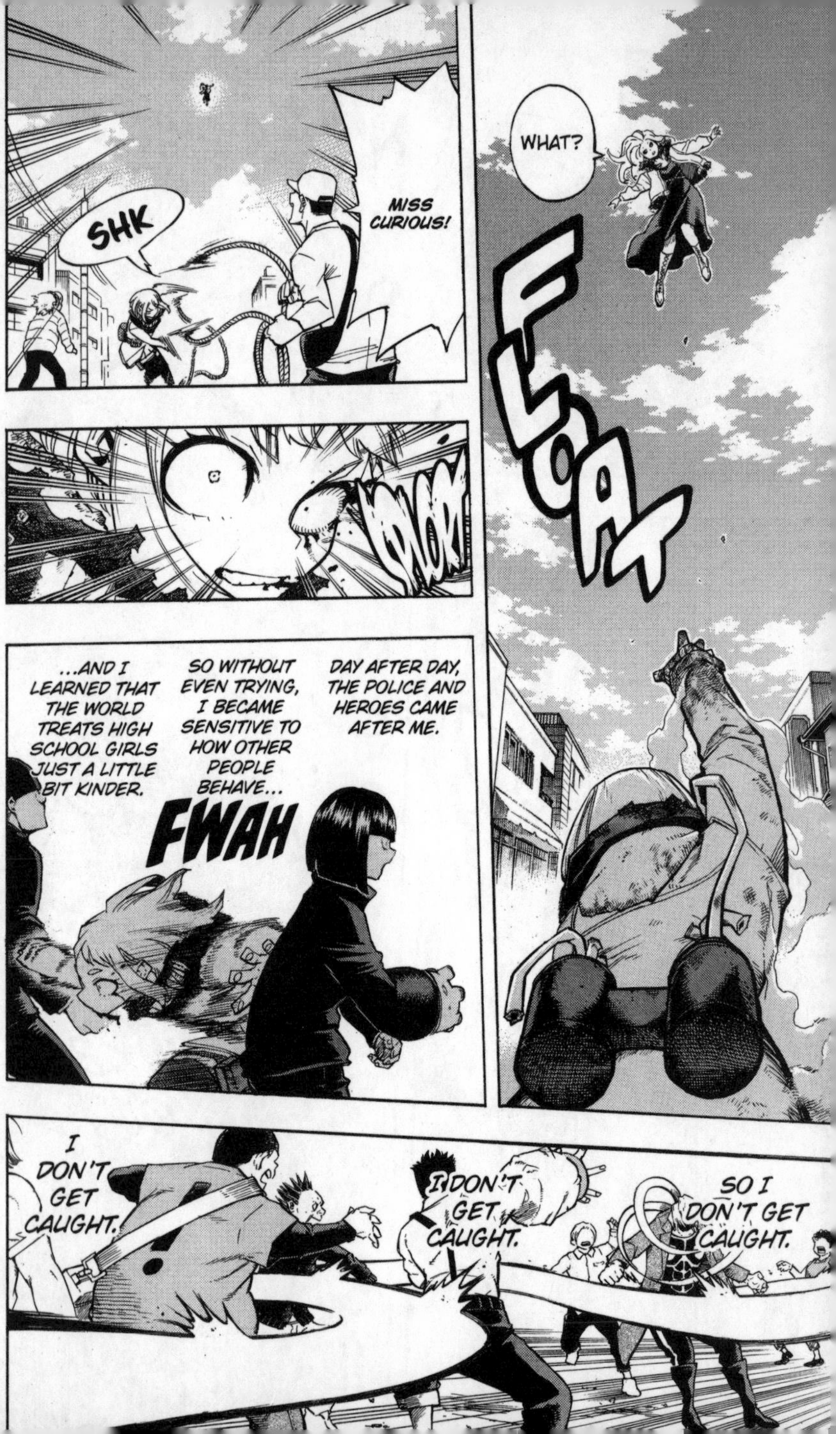
WHAT?
FLOAT
MISS CURIOUS!
SHK
DAY AFTER DAY, THE POLICE AND HEROES CAME AFTER ME.
SO WITHOUT EVEN TRYING, I BECAME SENSITIVE TO HOW OTHER PEOPLE BEHAVE...
...AND I LEARNED THAT THE WORLD TREATS HIGH SCHOOL GIRLS JUST A LITTLE BIT KINDER.
FWAH
SO I DON'T GET CAUGHT.
I DON'T GET CAUGHT.
I DON'T GET CAUGHT.

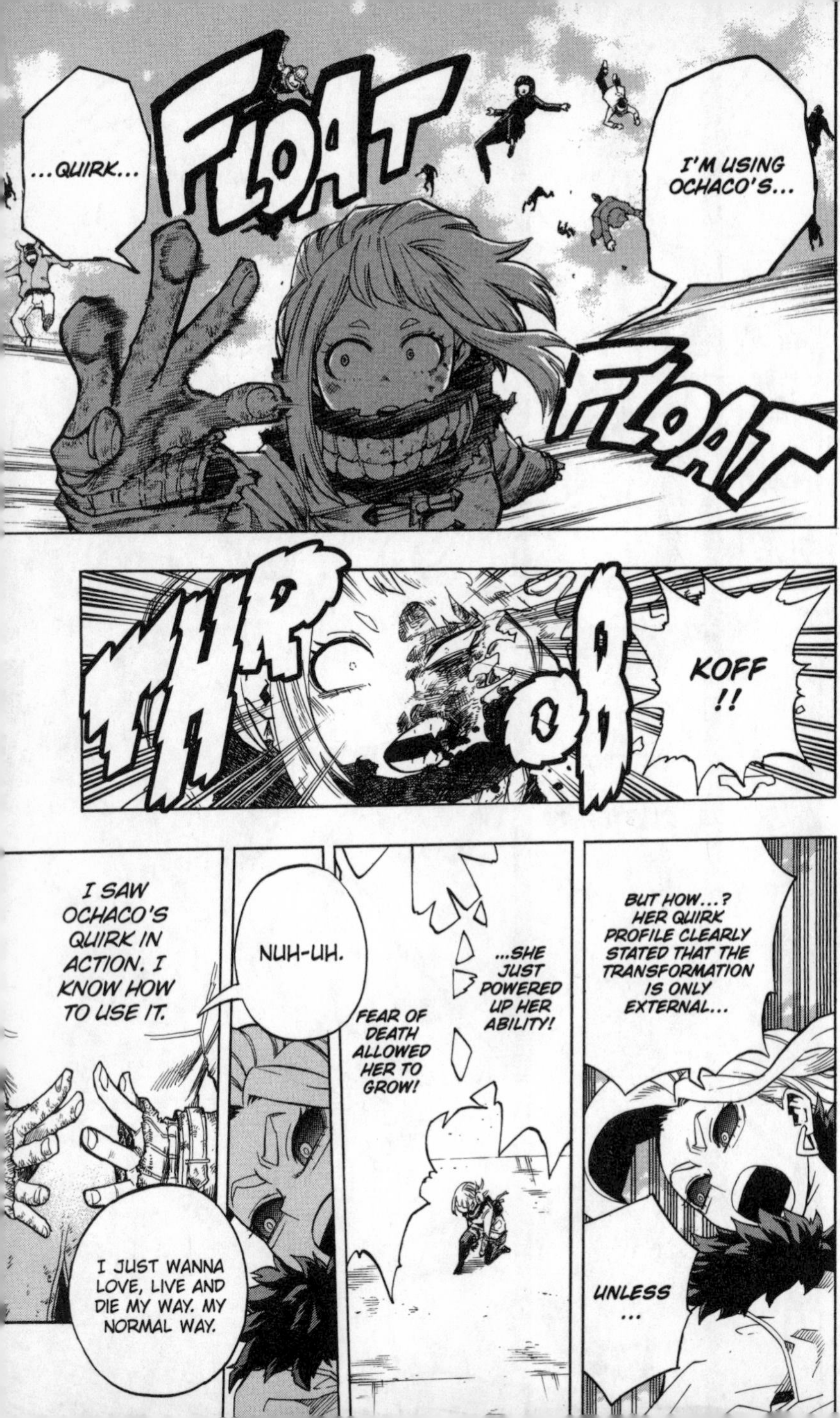
I'M USING OCHACO'S...
FLOAT
...QUIRK...
FLOAT
KOFF !!
THROB
BUT HOW...? HER QUIRK PROFILE CLEARLY STATED THAT THE TRANSFORMATION IS ONLY EXTERNAL...
UNLESS ...
...SHE JUST POWERED UP HER ABILITY!
FEAR OF DEATH ALLOWED HER TO GROW!
NUH-UH.
I JUST WANNA LOVE, LIVE AND DIE MY WAY. MY NORMAL WAY.
I SAW OCHACO'S QUIRK IN ACTION. I KNOW HOW TO USE IT.

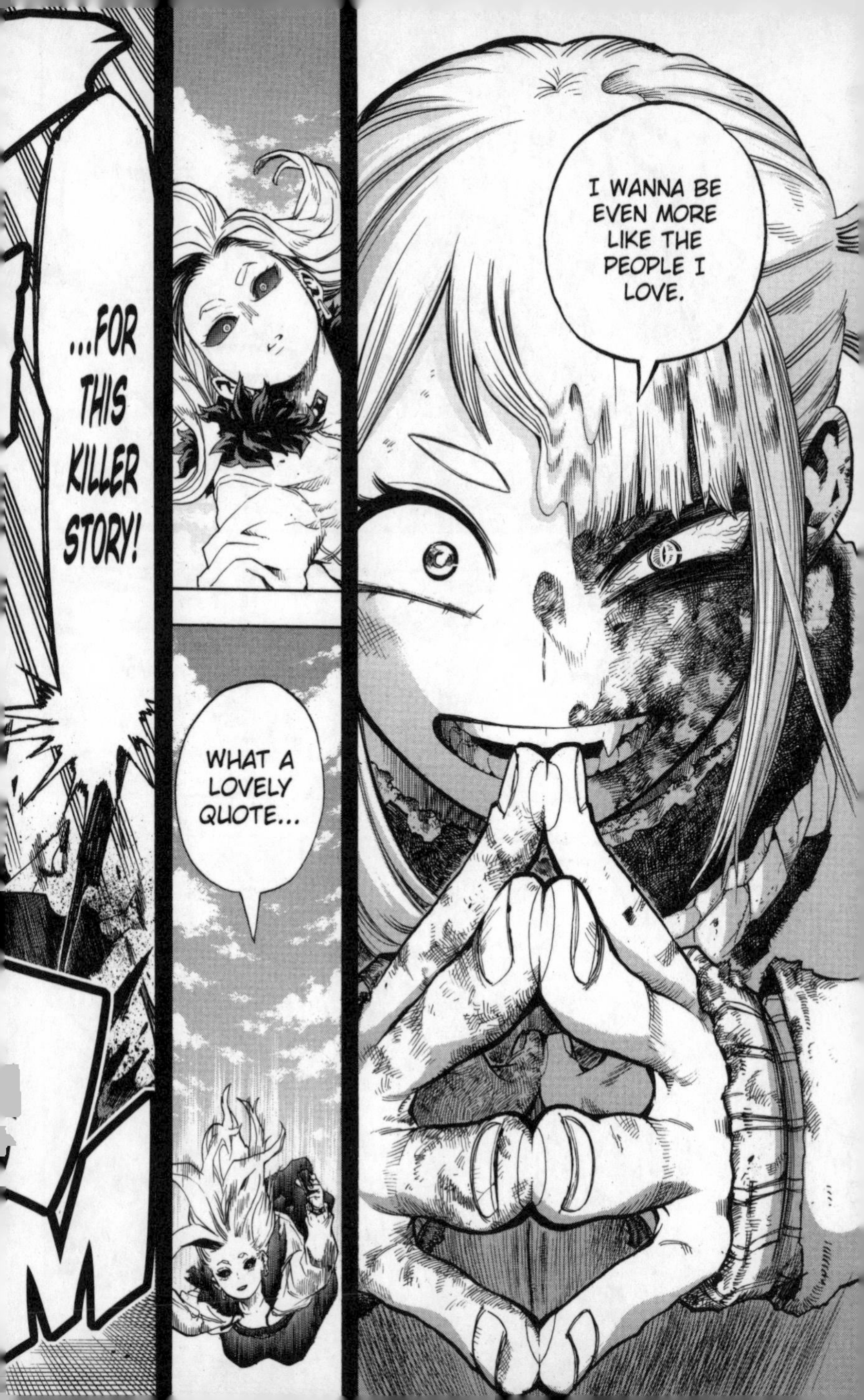
I WANNA BE EVEN MORE LIKE THE PEOPLE I LOVE.
WHAT A LOVELY QUOTE...
...FOR THIS KILLER STORY!

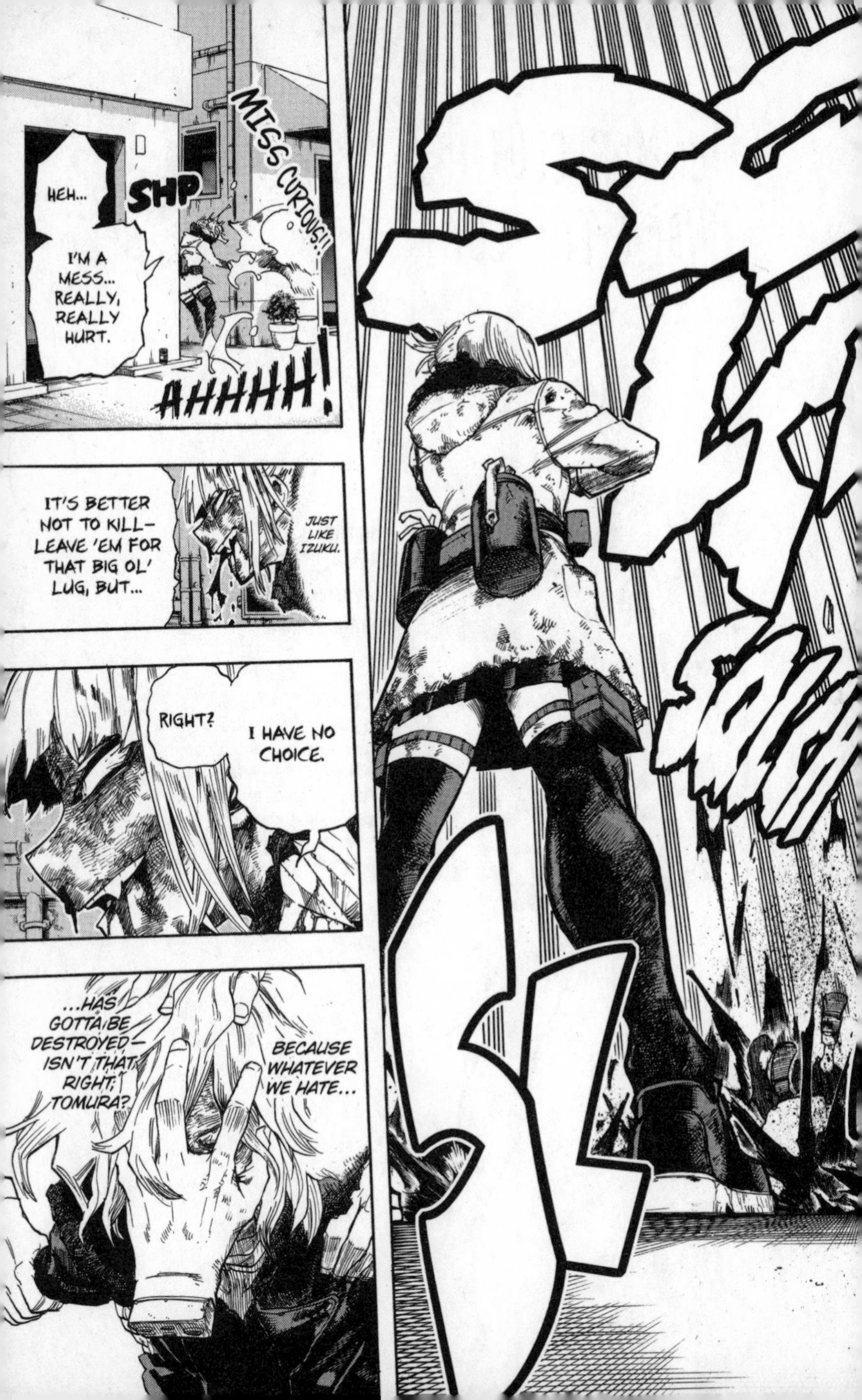
MISS CURIOUS!!
SHP
HEH...
I'M A MESS... REALLY, REALLY HURT.
AHHHHH!
JUST LIKE IZUKU.
IT'S BETTER NOT TO KILL— LEAVE 'EM FOR THAT BIG OL' LUG, BUT...
I HAVE NO CHOICE.
RIGHT?
BECAUSE WHATEVER WE HATE...
...HAS GOTTA BE DESTROYED— ISN'T THAT RIGHT, TOMURA?

SUMMER CLOTHES UNDER THE COAT

Birthday: 8/7
Height: 157 cm
Favorite Things: Blood, pomegranates

BEHIND THE SCENES
In volume 8, I mentioned how hard she is to draw. Sixteen books later, nothing has changed, and she still routinely stumps me. How on earth is that hair held together? Nobody knows…

No. 227 - Sleepy

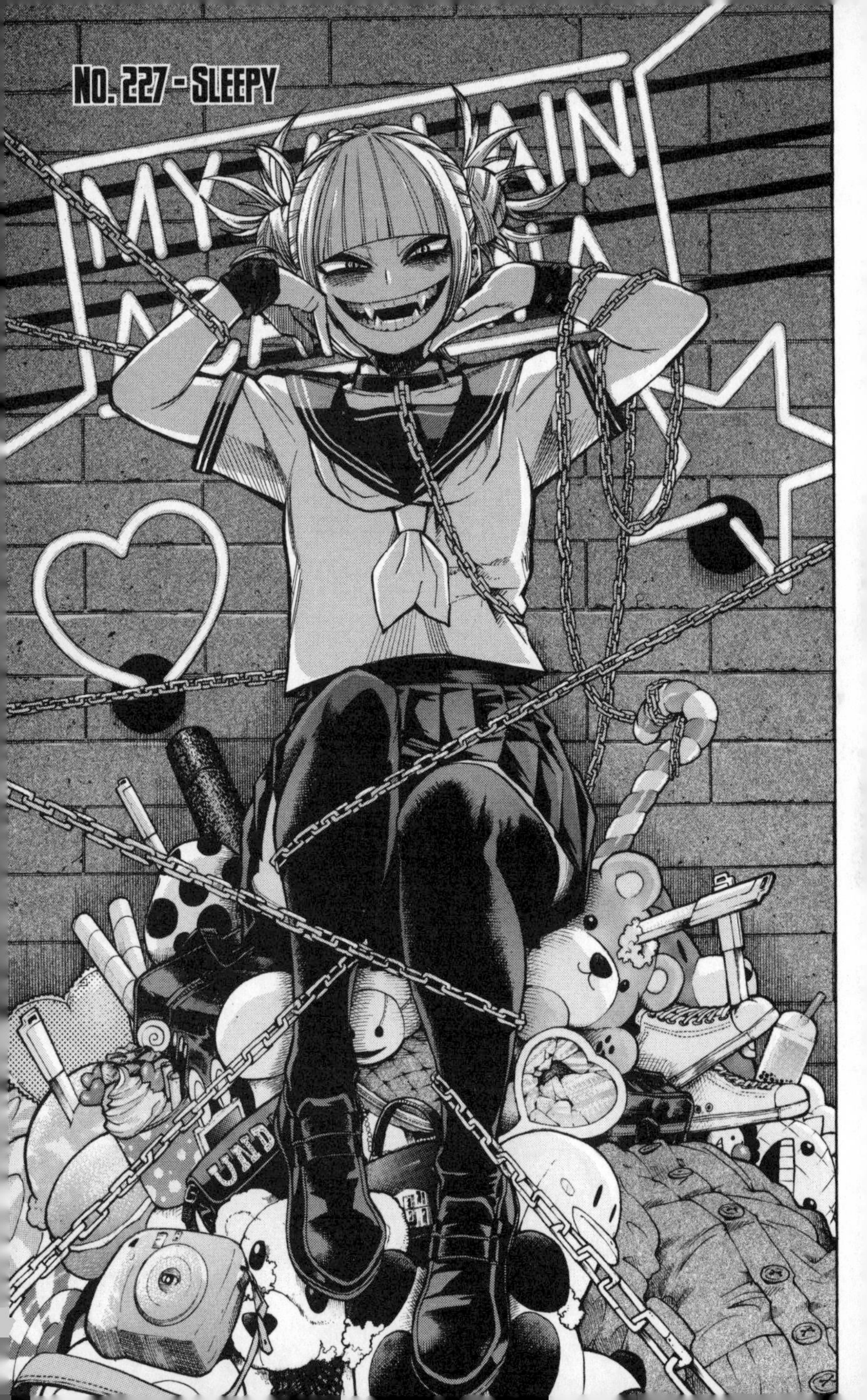
UND

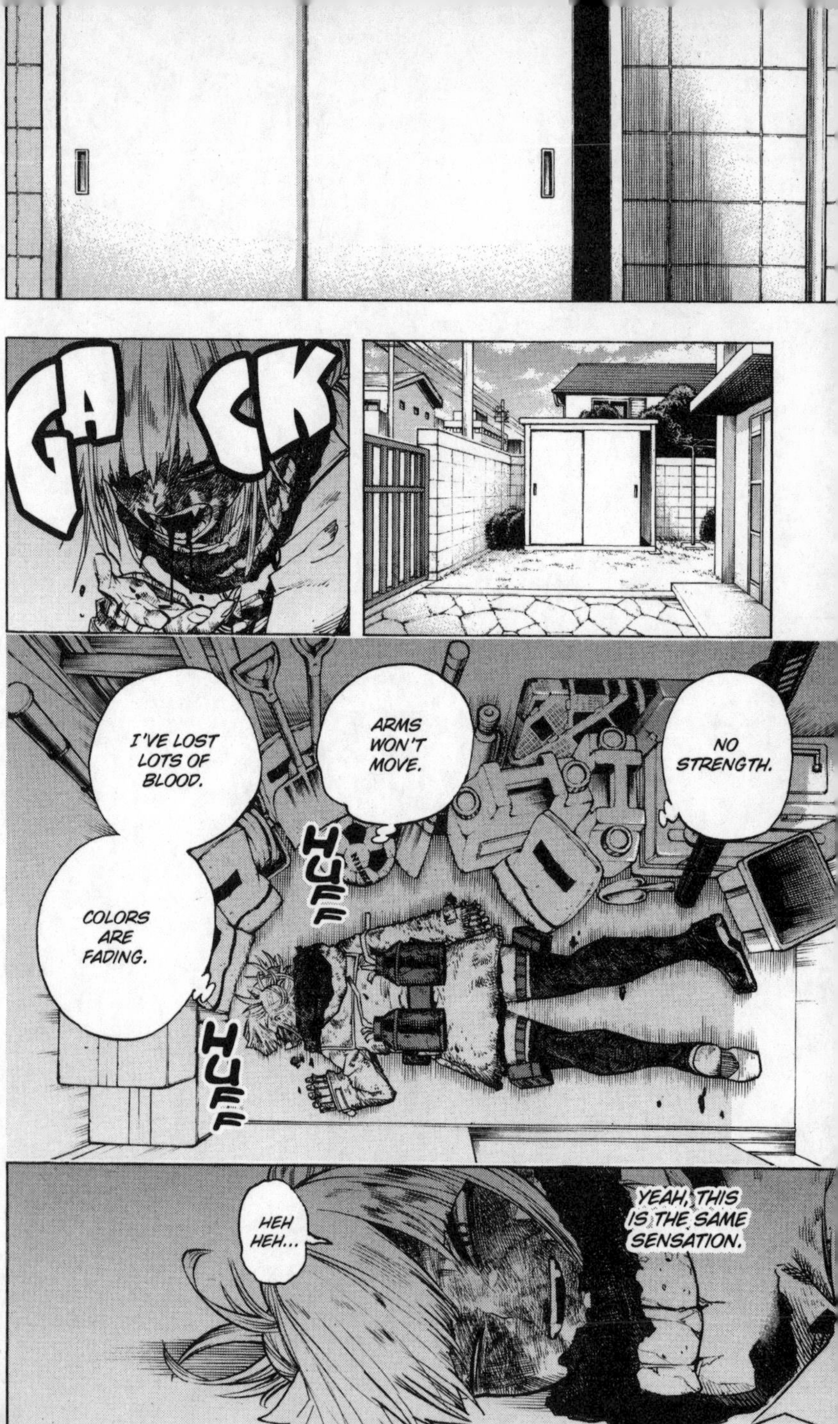
GACK
NO STRENGTH.
ARMS WON'T MOVE.
I'VE LOST LOTS OF BLOOD.
HUFF
COLORS ARE FADING.
HUFF
YEAH, THIS IS THE SAME SENSATION.
HEH HEH...

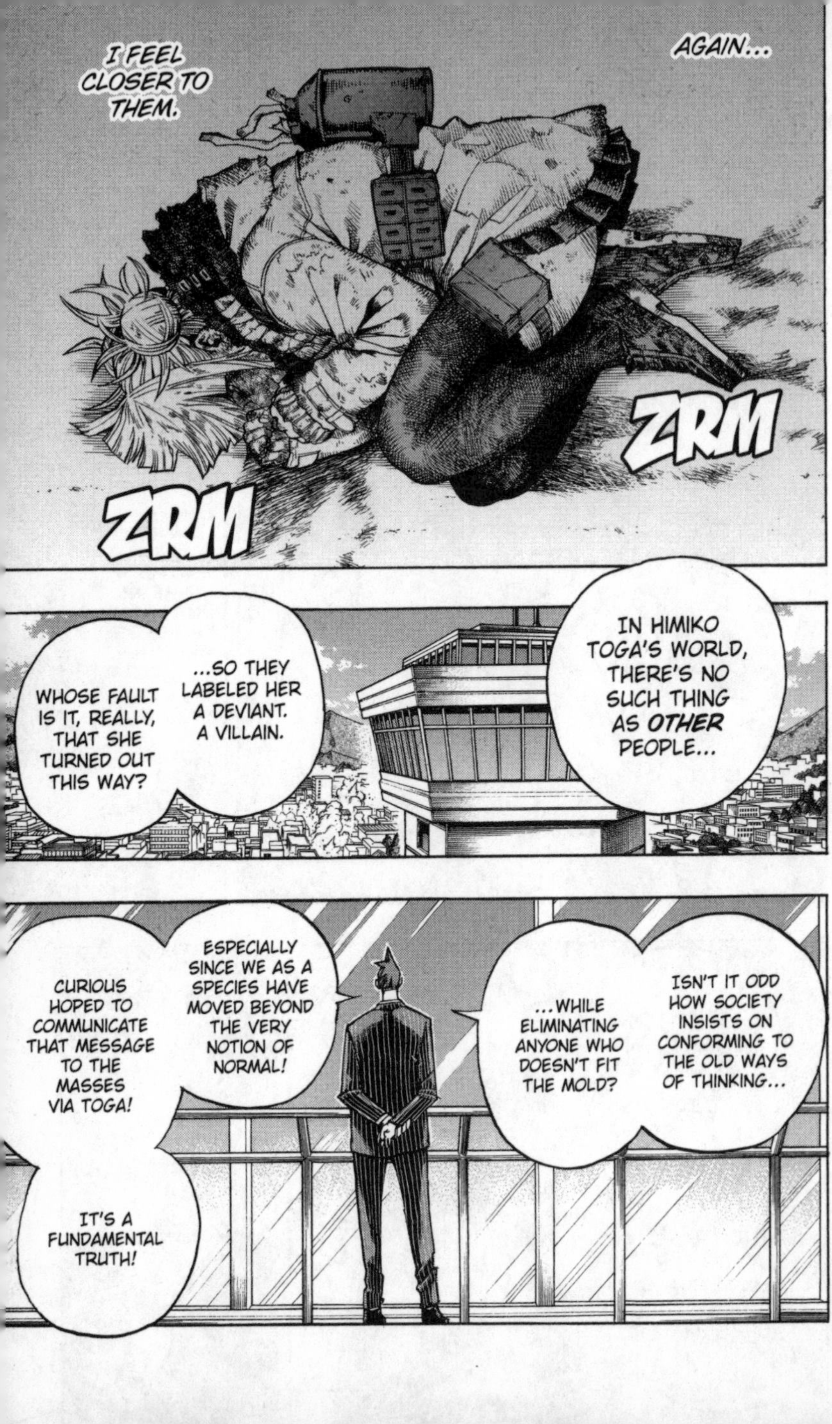
AGAIN...
I FEEL CLOSER TO THEM.
ZRM
ZRM
IN HIMIKO TOGA'S WORLD, THERE'S NO SUCH THING AS *OTHER* PEOPLE...
...SO THEY LABELED HER A DEVIANT. A VILLAIN.
WHOSE FAULT IS IT, REALLY, THAT SHE TURNED OUT THIS WAY?
ISN'T IT ODD HOW SOCIETY INSISTS ON CONFORMING TO THE OLD WAYS OF THINKING...
...WHILE ELIMINATING ANYONE WHO DOESN'T FIT THE MOLD?
ESPECIALLY SINCE WE AS A SPECIES HAVE MOVED BEYOND THE VERY NOTION OF NORMAL!
CURIOUS HOPED TO COMMUNICATE THAT MESSAGE TO THE MASSES VIA TOGA!
IT'S A FUNDAMENTAL TRUTH!

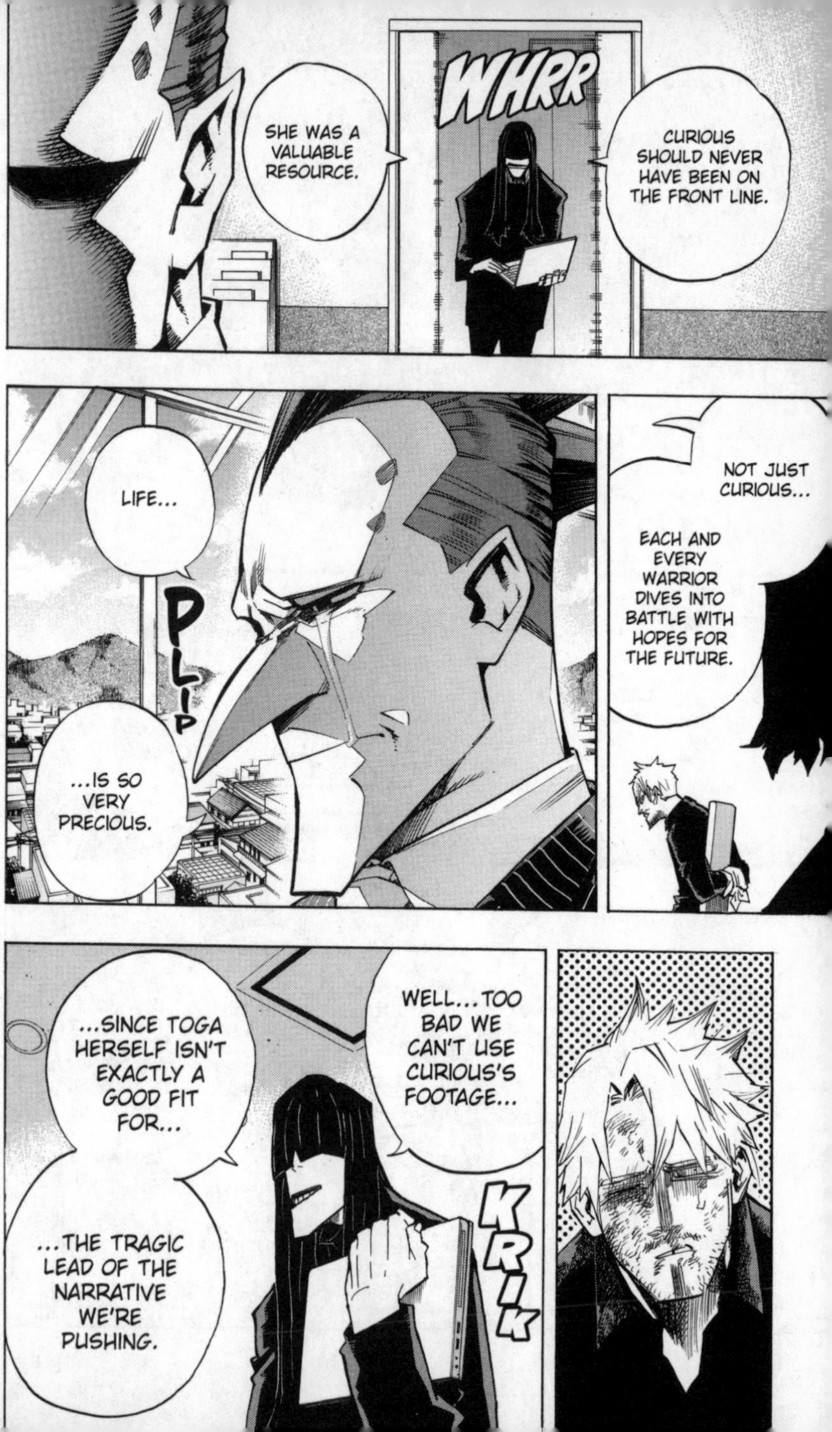
WHRR
CURIOUS SHOULD NEVER HAVE BEEN ON THE FRONT LINE.
SHE WAS A VALUABLE RESOURCE.
NOT JUST CURIOUS...
EACH AND EVERY WARRIOR DIVES INTO BATTLE WITH HOPES FOR THE FUTURE.
LIFE...
PLIP
...IS SO VERY PRECIOUS.
WELL...TOO BAD WE CAN'T USE CURIOUS'S FOOTAGE...
KRIK
...SINCE TOGA HERSELF ISN'T EXACTLY A GOOD FIT FOR...
...THE TRAGIC LEAD OF THE NARRATIVE WE'RE PUSHING.

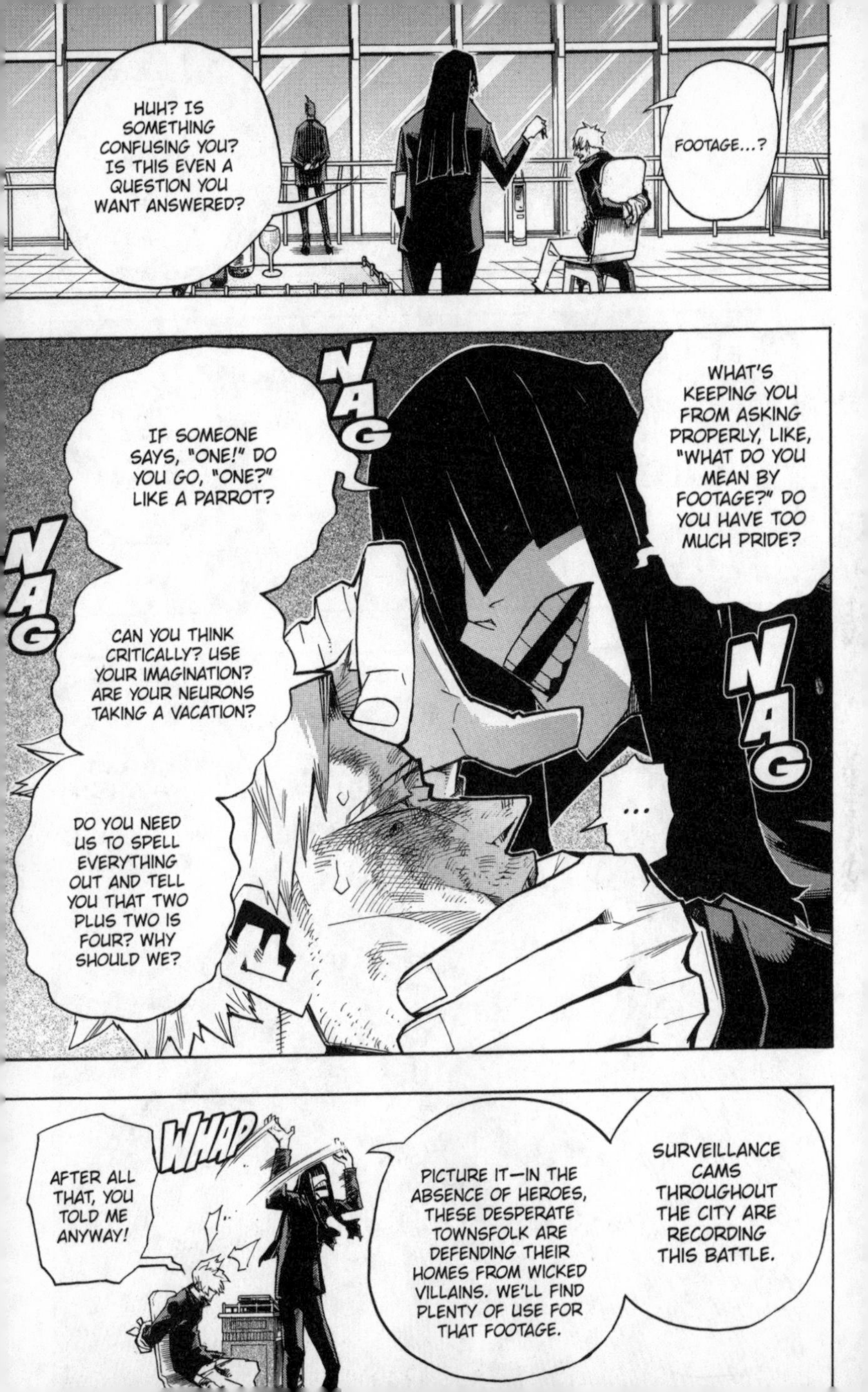
FOOTAGE...?
HUH? IS SOMETHING CONFUSING YOU? IS THIS EVEN A QUESTION YOU WANT ANSWERED?
WHAT'S KEEPING YOU FROM ASKING PROPERLY, LIKE, "WHAT DO YOU MEAN BY FOOTAGE?" DO YOU HAVE TOO MUCH PRIDE?
NAG
IF SOMEONE SAYS, "ONE!" DO YOU GO, "ONE?" LIKE A PARROT?
NAG
NAG
CAN YOU THINK CRITICALLY? USE YOUR IMAGINATION? ARE YOUR NEURONS TAKING A VACATION?
...
DO YOU NEED US TO SPELL EVERYTHING OUT AND TELL YOU THAT TWO PLUS TWO IS FOUR? WHY SHOULD WE?
SURVEILLANCE CAMS THROUGHOUT THE CITY ARE RECORDING THIS BATTLE.
PICTURE IT—IN THE ABSENCE OF HEROES, THESE DESPERATE TOWNSFOLK ARE DEFENDING THEIR HOMES FROM WICKED VILLAINS. WE'LL FIND PLENTY OF USE FOR THAT FOOTAGE.
WHAP
AFTER ALL THAT, YOU TOLD ME ANYWAY!

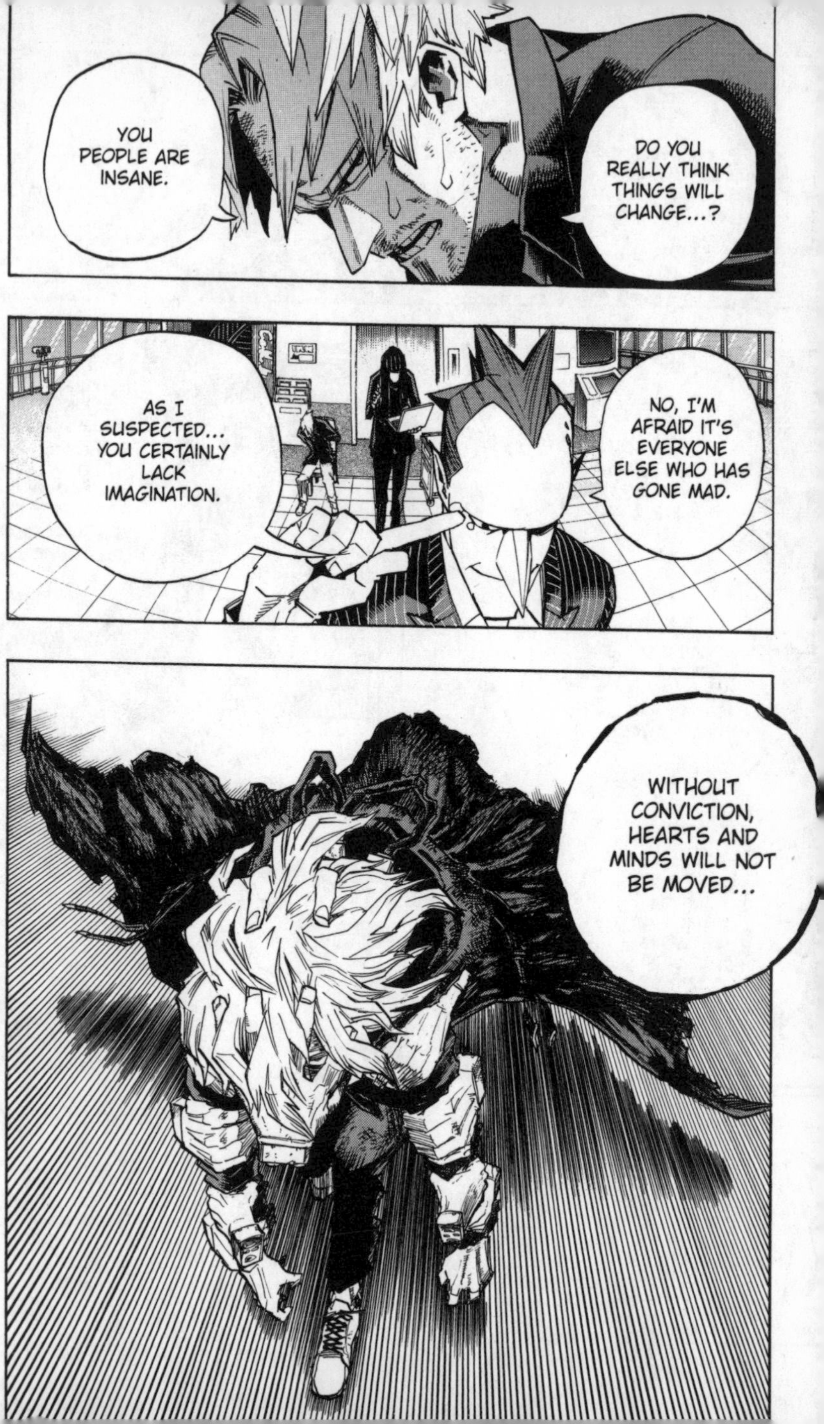
DO YOU REALLY THINK THINGS WILL CHANGE...?
YOU PEOPLE ARE INSANE.
NO, I'M AFRAID IT'S EVERYONE ELSE WHO HAS GONE MAD.
AS I SUSPECTED... YOU CERTAINLY LACK IMAGINATION.
WITHOUT CONVICTION, HEARTS AND MINDS WILL NOT BE MOVED...

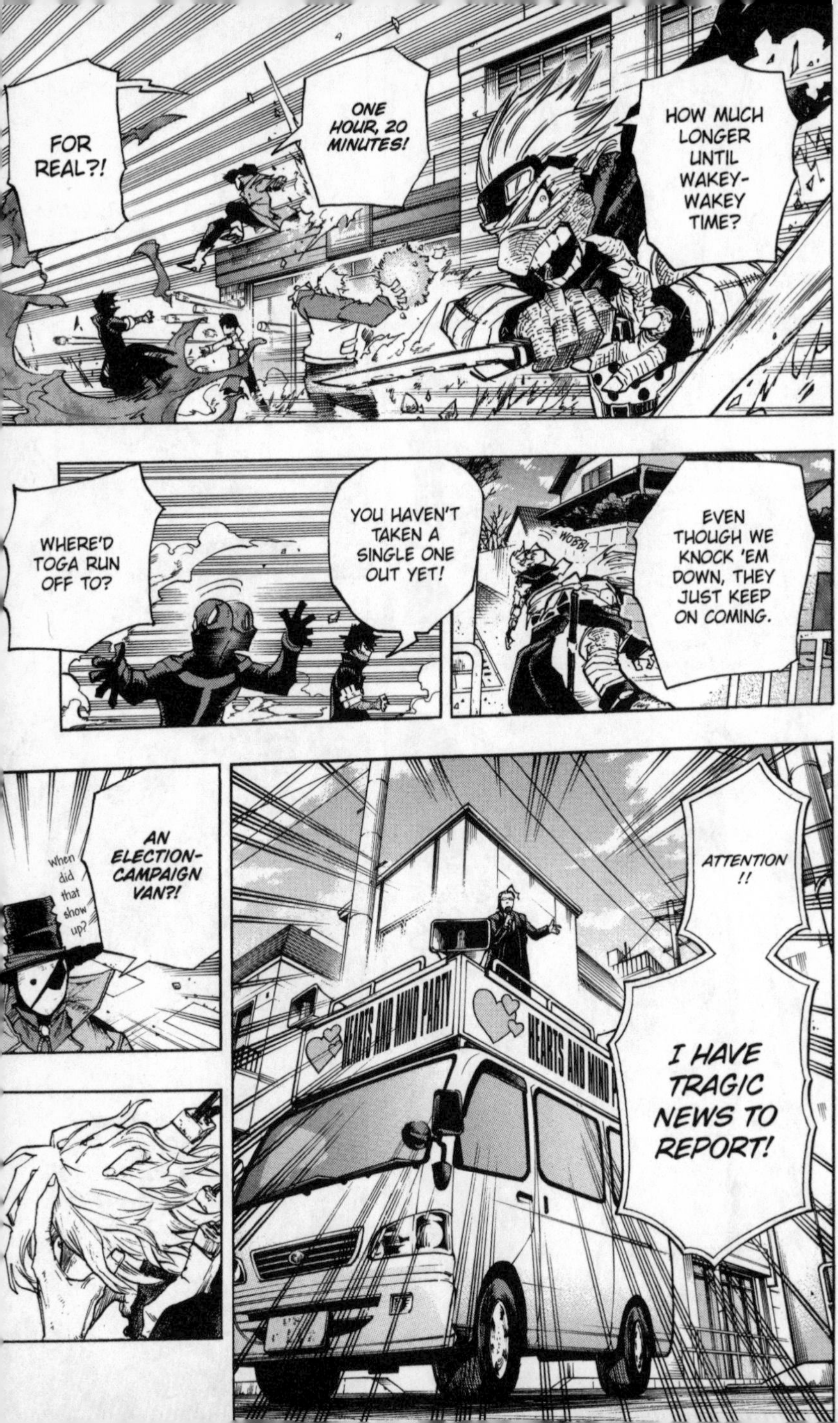
HOW MUCH LONGER UNTIL WAKEY-WAKEY TIME?
ONE HOUR, 20 MINUTES!
FOR REAL?!
WOBBL
EVEN THOUGH WE KNOCK 'EM DOWN, THEY JUST KEEP ON COMING.
YOU HAVEN'T TAKEN A SINGLE ONE OUT YET!
WHERE'D TOGA RUN OFF TO?
ATTENTION!!
HEARTS AND MIND PARTY
I HAVE TRAGIC NEWS TO REPORT!
AN ELECTION-CAMPAIGN VAN?!
when did that show up?

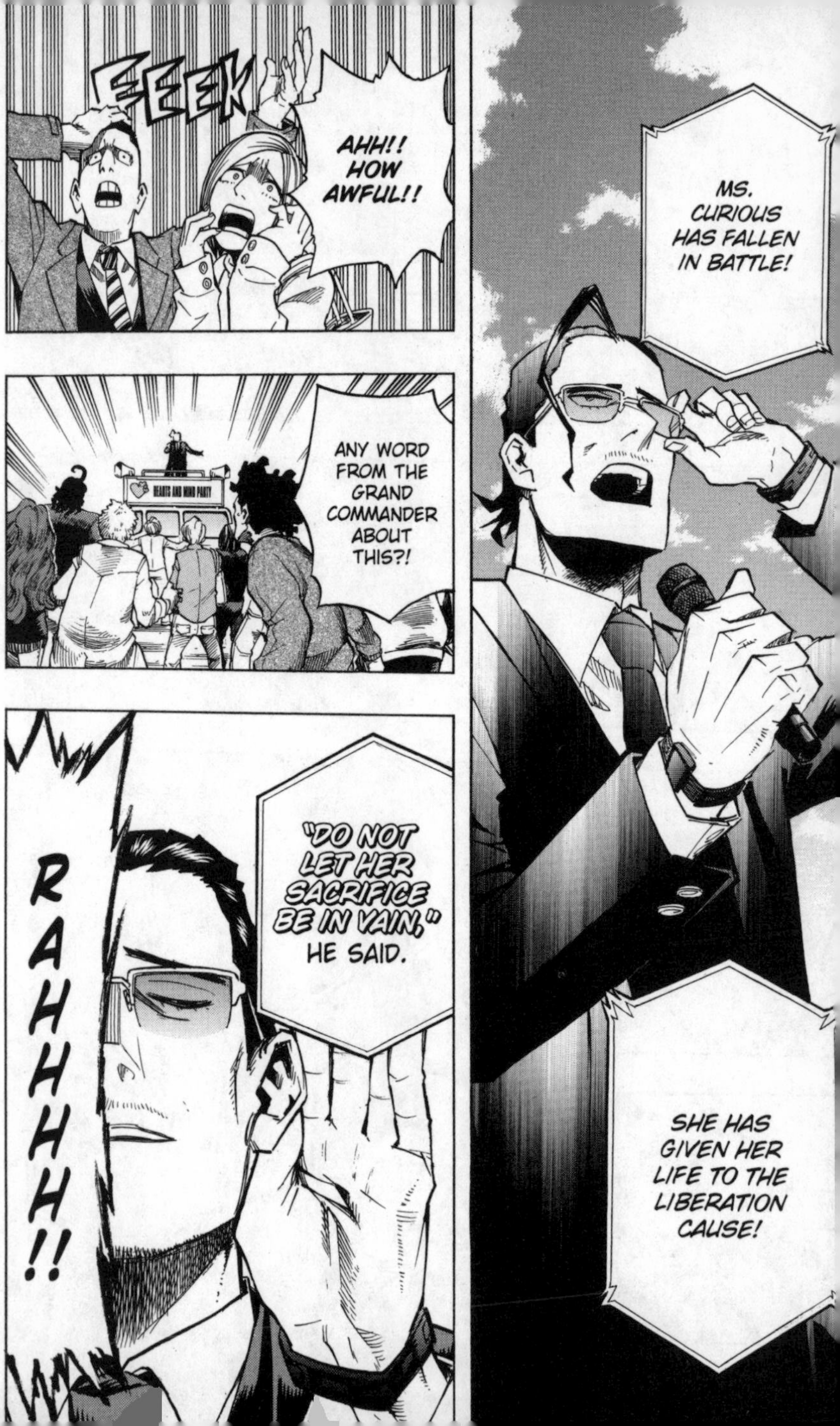
MS. CURIOUS HAS FALLEN IN BATTLE!
SHE HAS GIVEN HER LIFE TO THE LIBERATION CAUSE!
AHH!! HOW AWFUL!!
EEEK
ANY WORD FROM THE GRAND COMMANDER ABOUT THIS?!
"DO NOT LET HER SACRIFICE BE IN VAIN," HE SAID.
RAHHHH!!

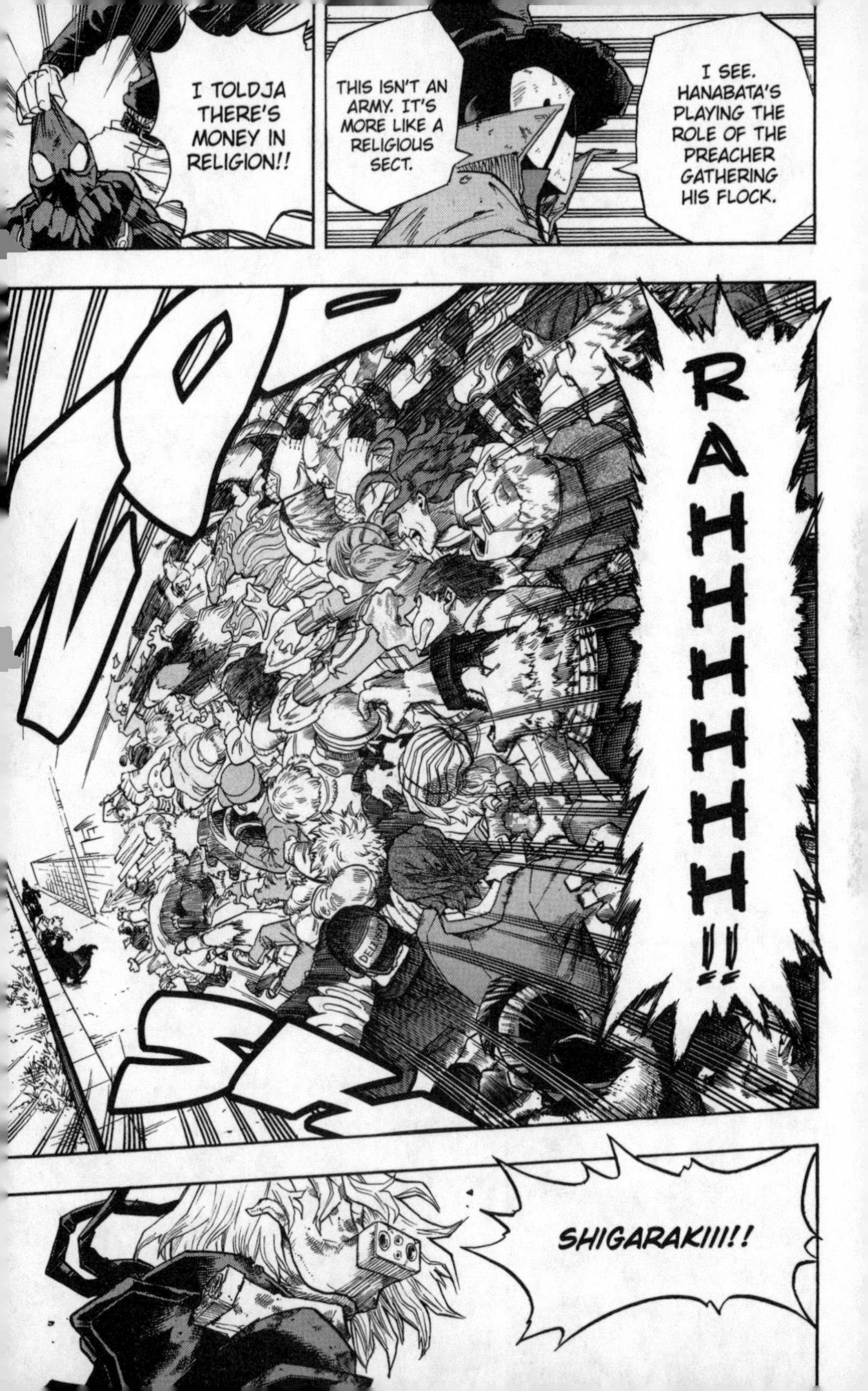
I SEE. HANABATA'S PLAYING THE ROLE OF THE PREACHER GATHERING HIS FLOCK.
THIS ISN'T AN ARMY. IT'S MORE LIKE A RELIGIOUS SECT.
I TOLDJA THERE'S MONEY IN RELIGION!!
RAHHHHHH!!
SHIGARAKIII!!

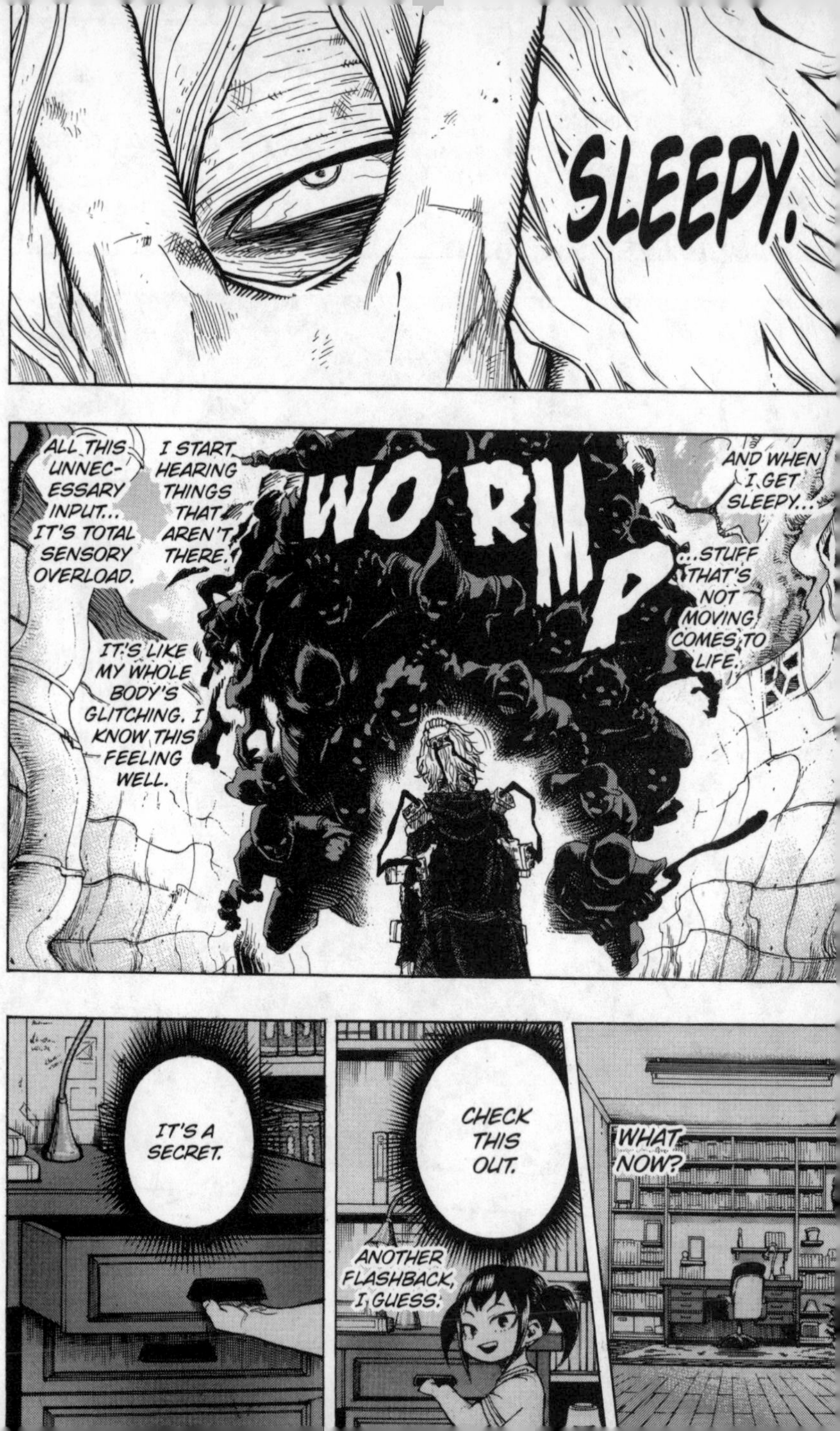
SLEEPY.
AND WHEN I GET SLEEPY...
...STUFF THAT'S NOT MOVING COMES TO LIFE.
WORMP
I START HEARING THINGS THAT AREN'T THERE.
ALL THIS UNNEC-ESSARY INPUT... IT'S TOTAL SENSORY OVERLOAD.
IT'S LIKE MY WHOLE BODY'S GLITCHING. I KNOW THIS FEELING WELL.
WHAT NOW?
CHECK THIS OUT.
ANOTHER FLASHBACK, I GUESS.
IT'S A SECRET.

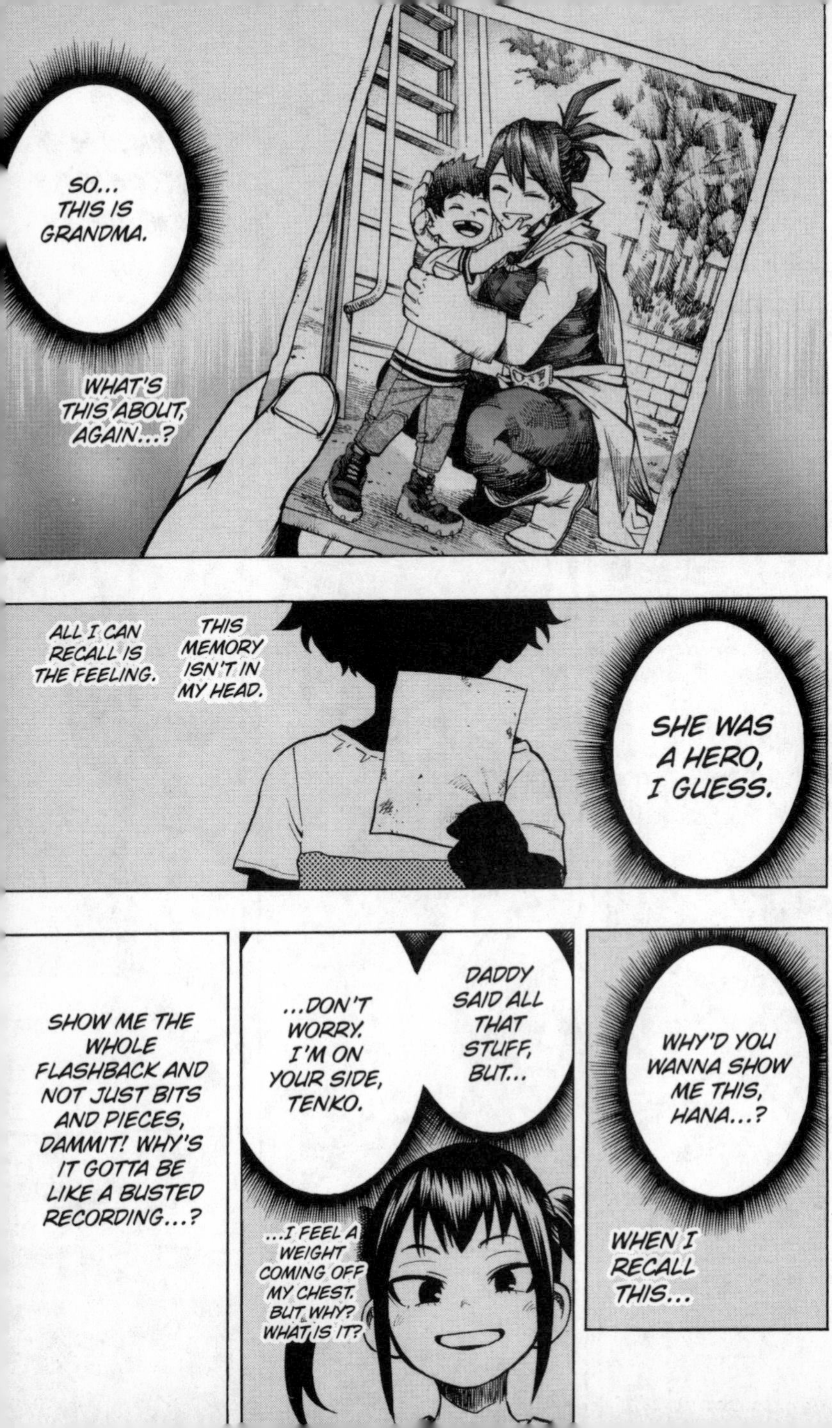
SO... THIS IS GRANDMA.
WHAT'S THIS ABOUT, AGAIN...?
SHE WAS A HERO, I GUESS.
THIS MEMORY ISN'T IN MY HEAD.
ALL I CAN RECALL IS THE FEELING.
WHY'D YOU WANNA SHOW ME THIS, HANA...?
WHEN I RECALL THIS...
DADDY SAID ALL THAT STUFF, BUT...
...DON'T WORRY. I'M ON YOUR SIDE, TENKO.
...I FEEL A WEIGHT COMING OFF MY CHEST. BUT WHY? WHAT IS IT?
SHOW ME THE WHOLE FLASHBACK AND NOT JUST BITS AND PIECES, DAMMIT! WHY'S IT GOTTA BE LIKE A BUSTED RECORDING...?

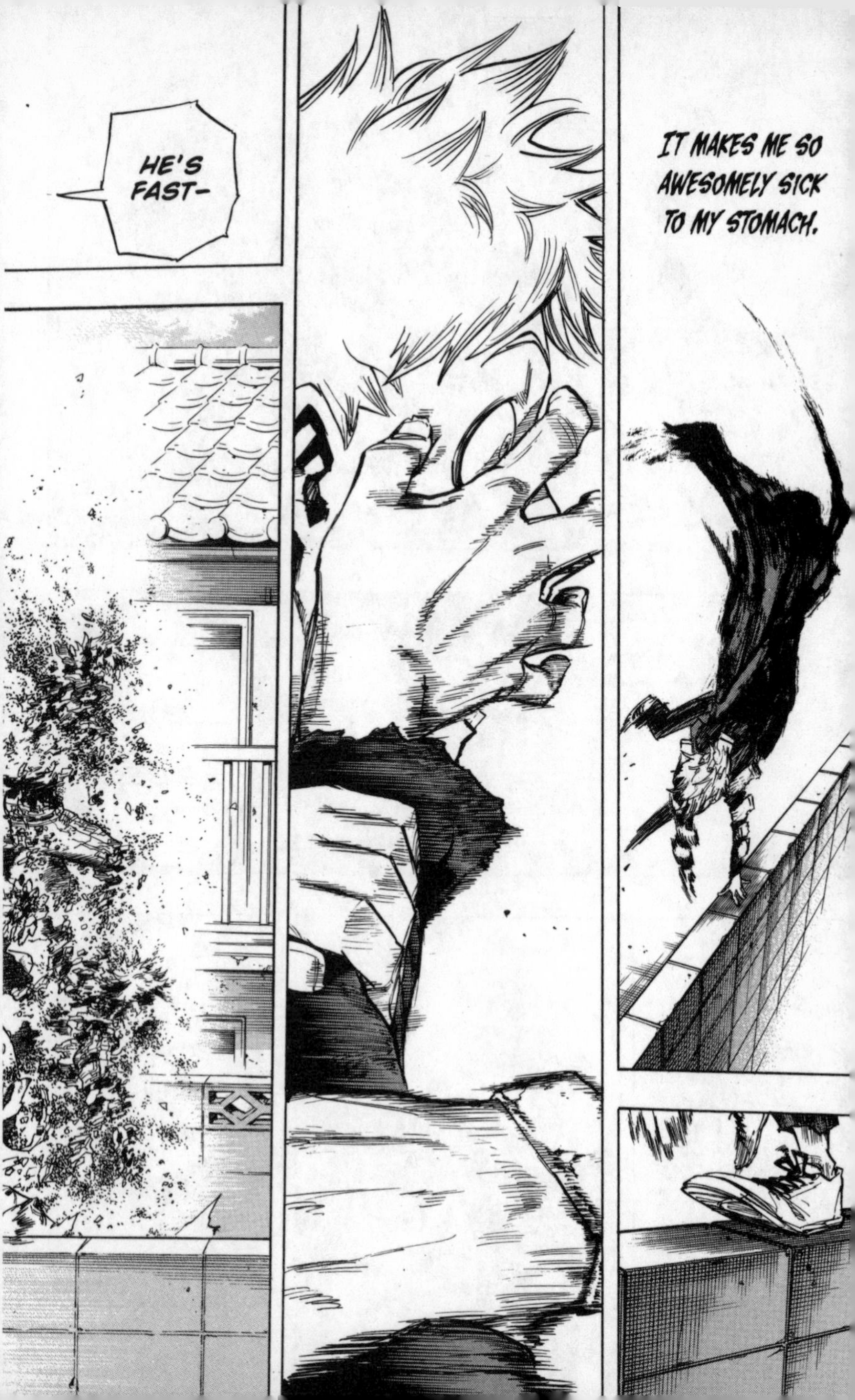
IT MAKES ME SO AWESOMELY SICK TO MY STOMACH.
HE'S FAST-

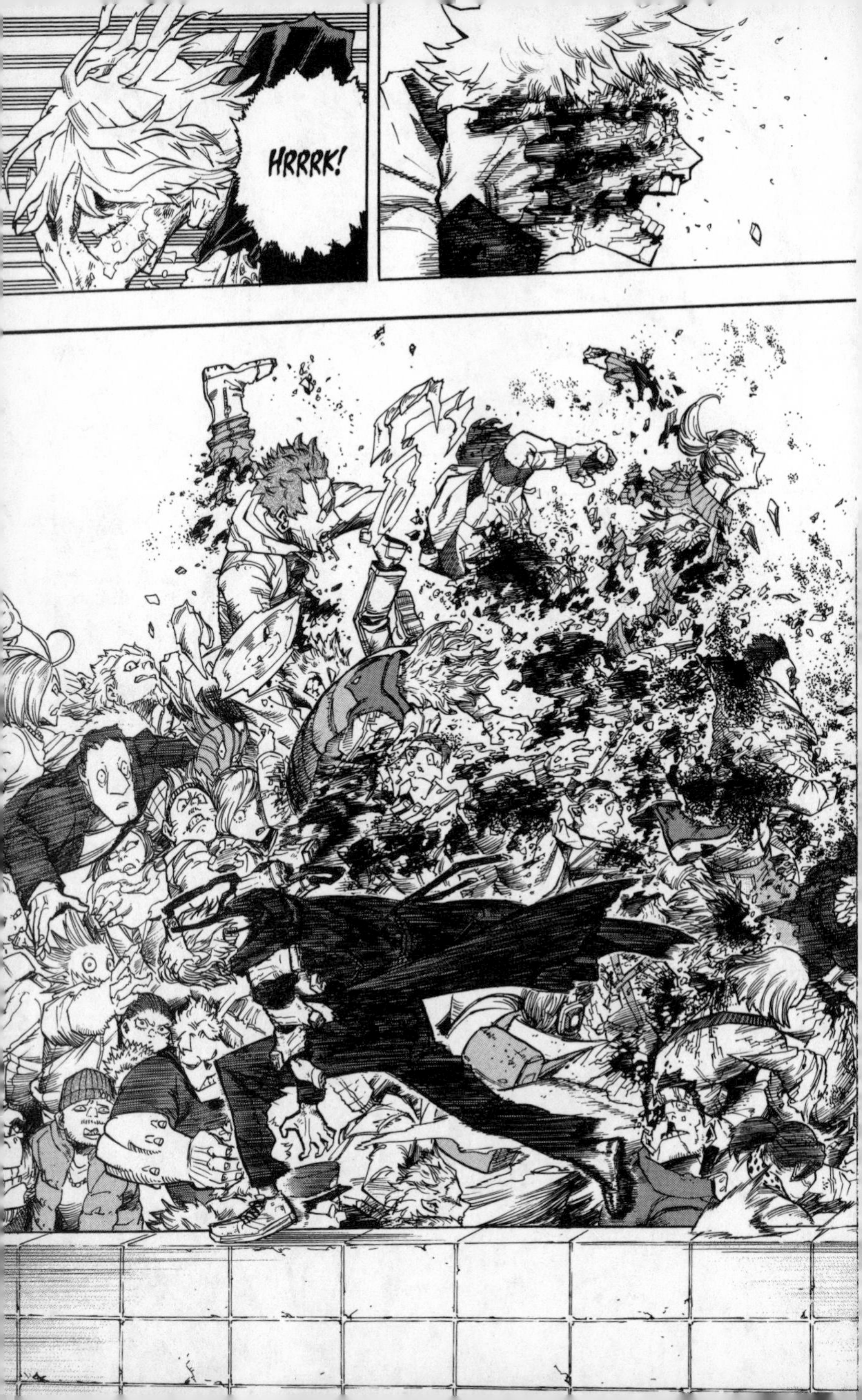
HRRRK!

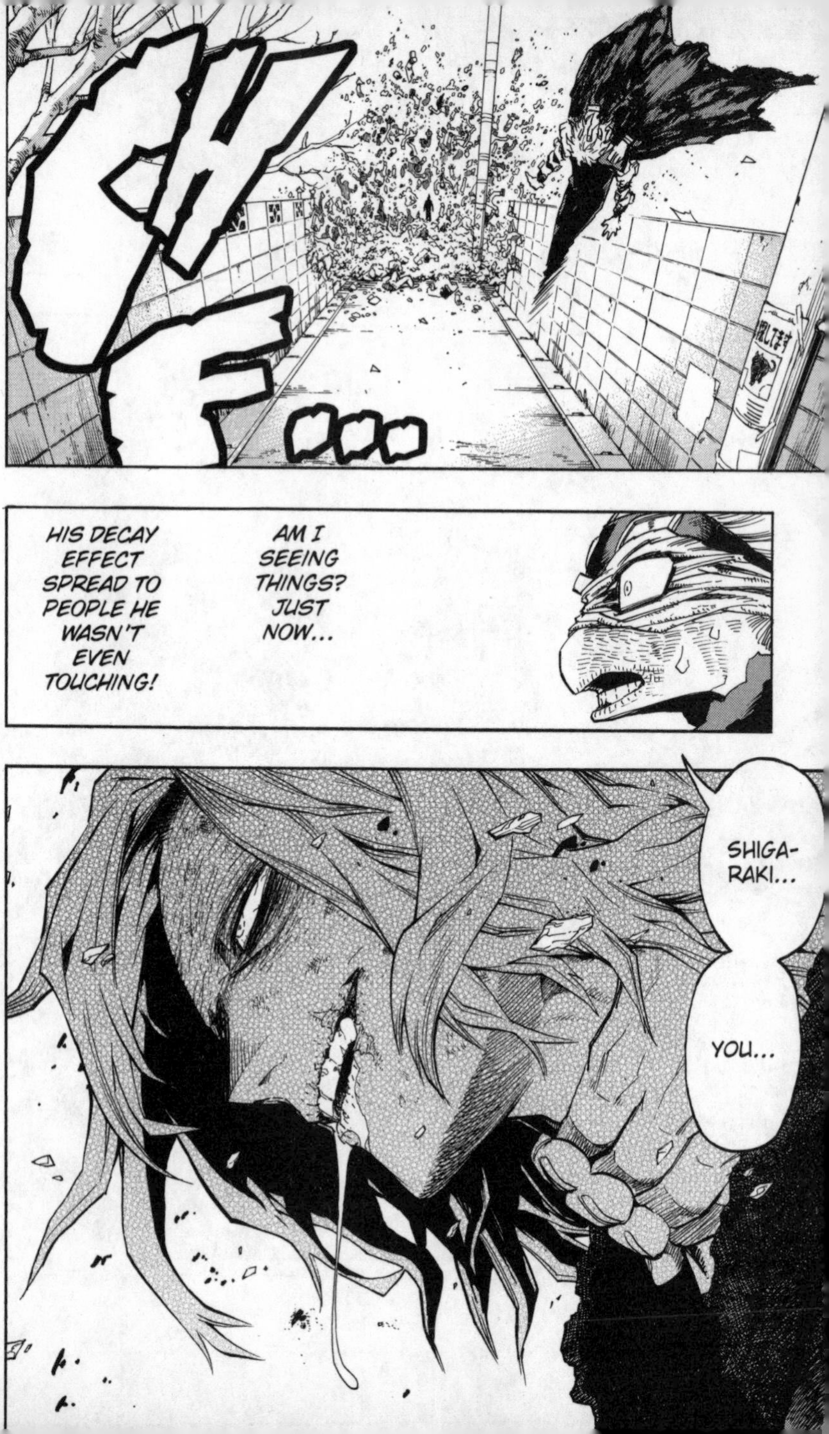
AM I SEEING THINGS? JUST NOW...
HIS DECAY EFFECT SPREAD TO PEOPLE HE WASN'T EVEN TOUCHING!
SHIGA-RAKI...
YOU...

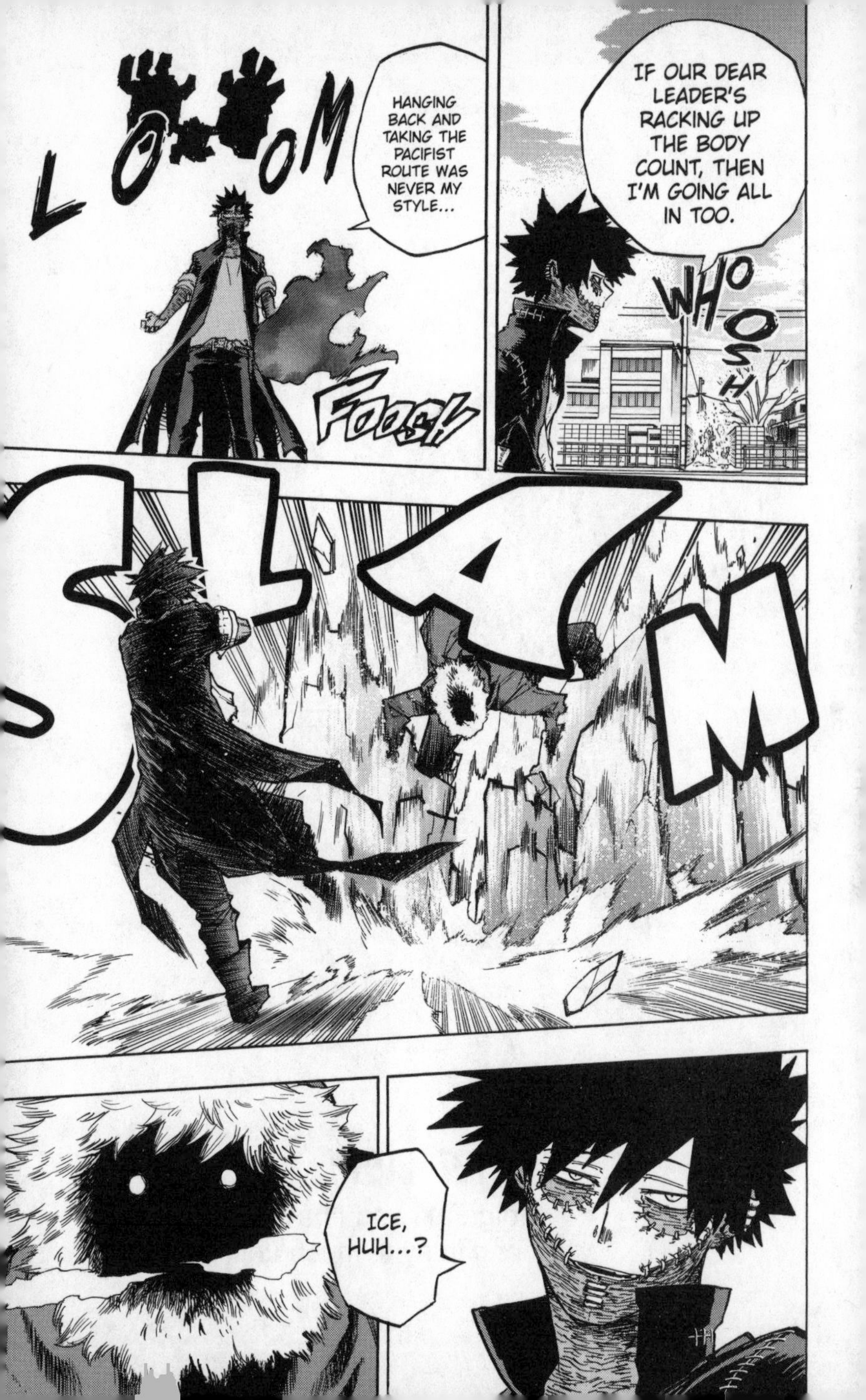
IF OUR DEAR LEADER'S RACKING UP THE BODY COUNT, THEN I'M GOING ALL IN TOO.
WHOOSH
LOOM
HANGING BACK AND TAKING THE PACIFIST ROUTE WAS NEVER MY STYLE...
SLAM
ICE, HUH...?

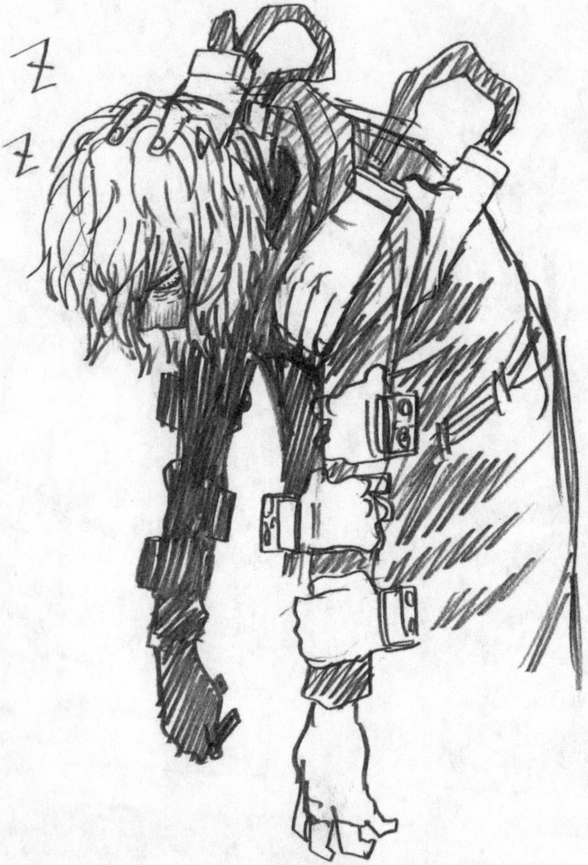
Z
Z
Z

NO. 227 - SLEEPY

Shigaraki and I have never been in sync much until now.

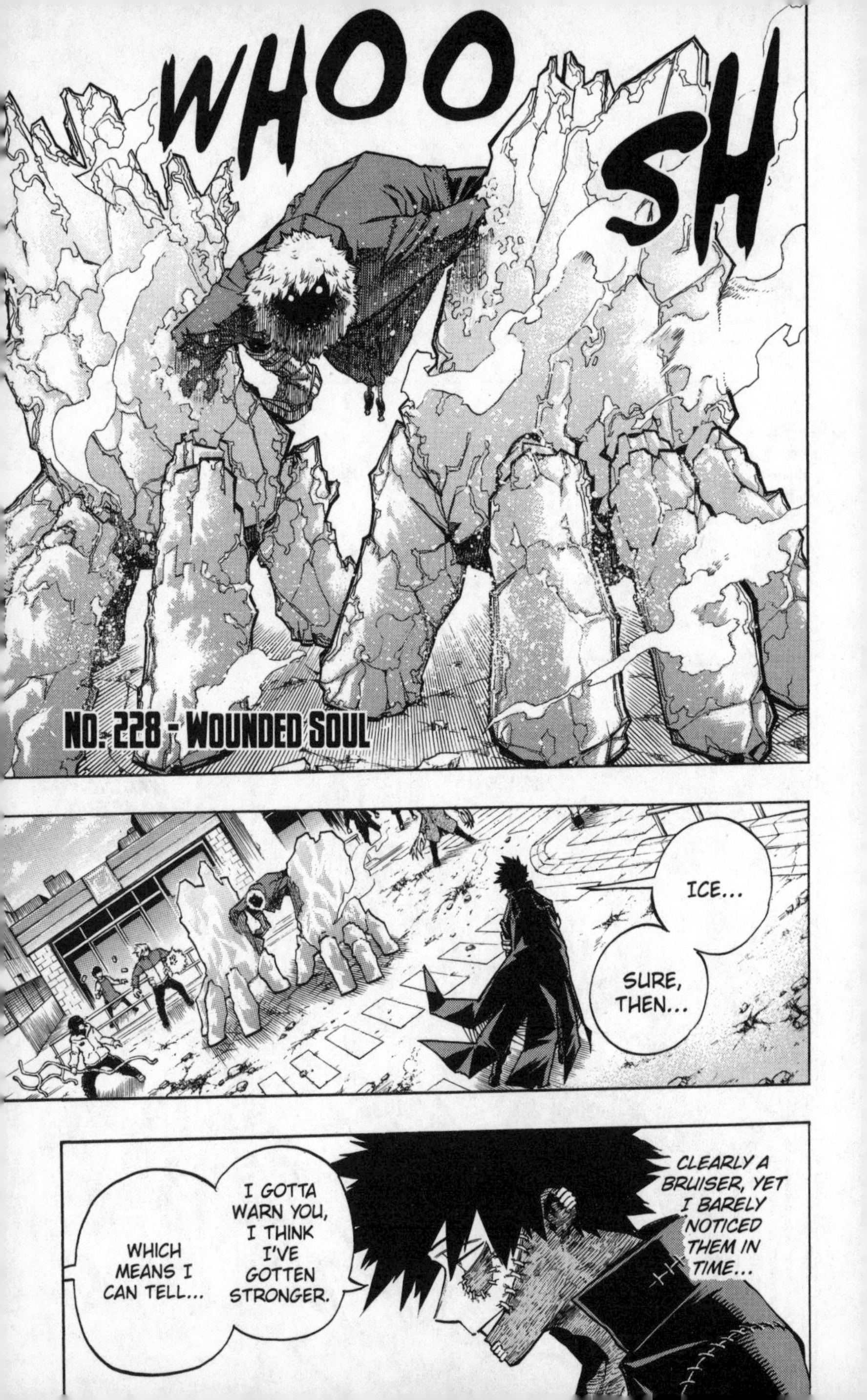
WHOOSH
No. 228 - Wounded Soul
ICE...
SURE, THEN...
CLEARLY A BRUISER, YET I BARELY NOTICED THEM IN TIME...
I GOTTA WARN YOU, I THINK I'VE GOTTEN STRONGER.
WHICH MEANS I CAN TELL...

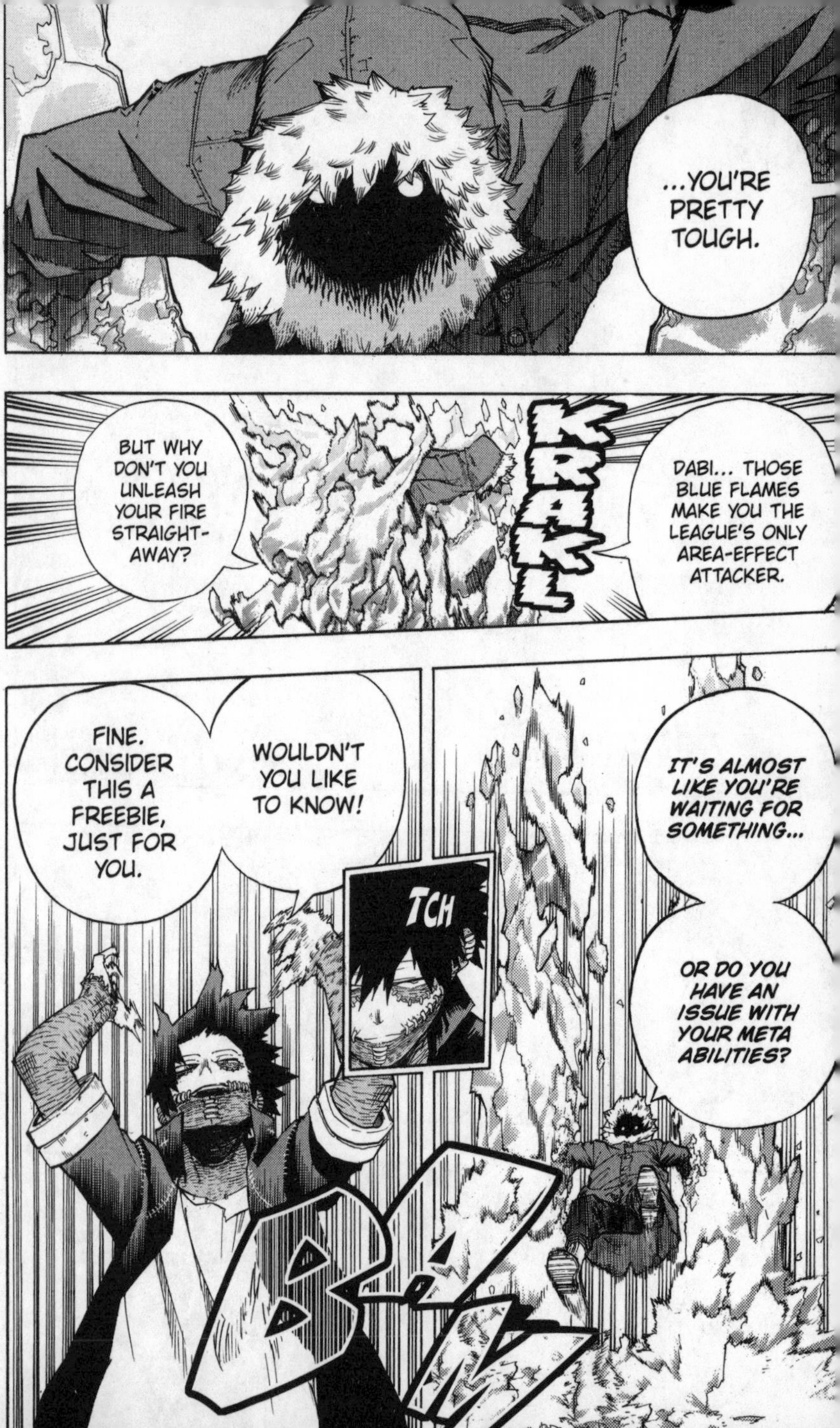
...YOU'RE PRETTY TOUGH.
DABI... THOSE BLUE FLAMES MAKE YOU THE LEAGUE'S ONLY AREA-EFFECT ATTACKER.
KRAKL
BUT WHY DON'T YOU UNLEASH YOUR FIRE STRAIGHT-AWAY?
IT'S ALMOST LIKE YOU'RE WAITING FOR SOMETHING...
OR DO YOU HAVE AN ISSUE WITH YOUR META ABILITIES?
TCH
WOULDN'T YOU LIKE TO KNOW!
FINE. CONSIDER THIS A FREEBIE, JUST FOR YOU.

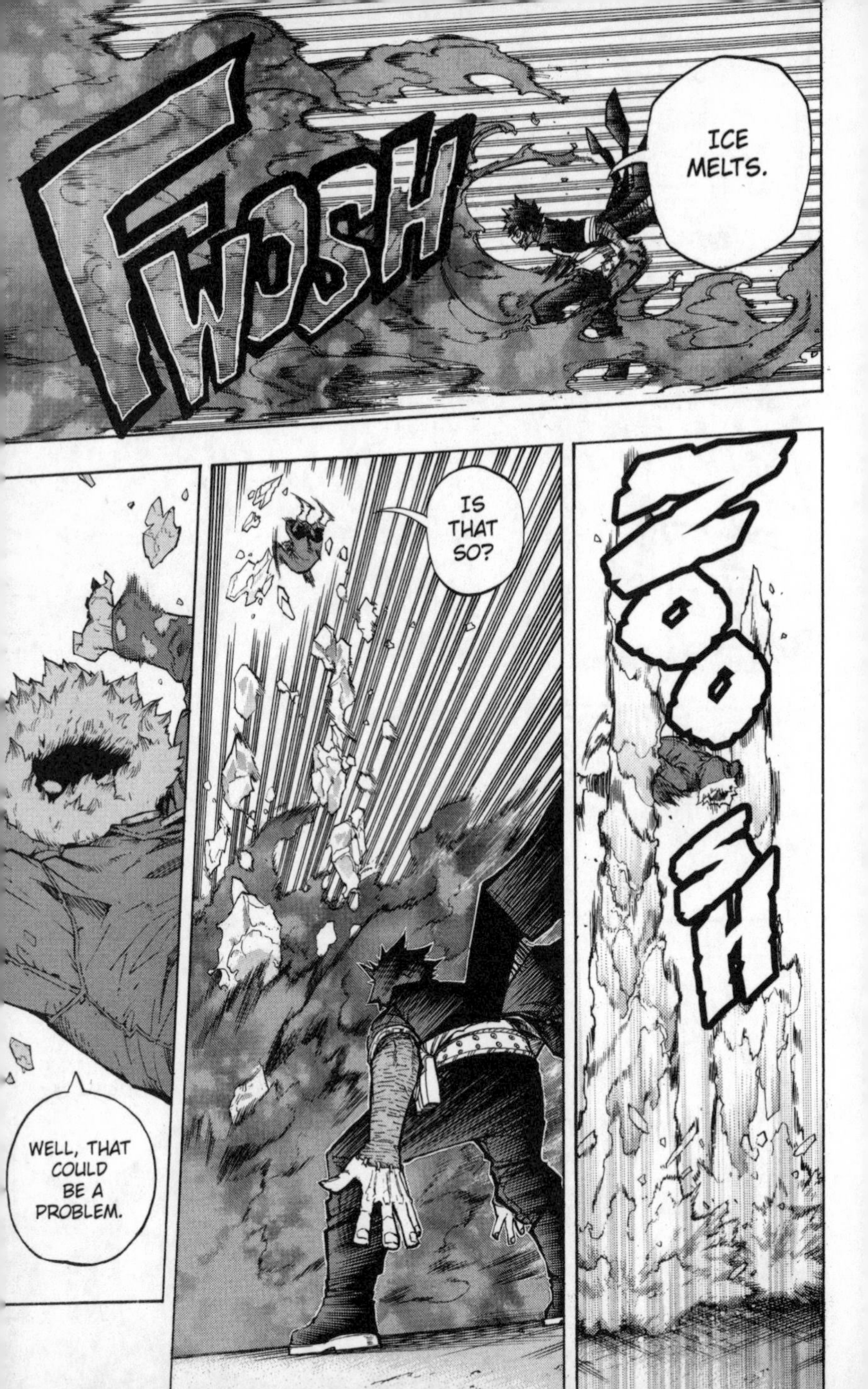
ICE MELTS.
FWOOSH
WOOSH
IS THAT SO?
WELL, THAT COULD BE A PROBLEM.

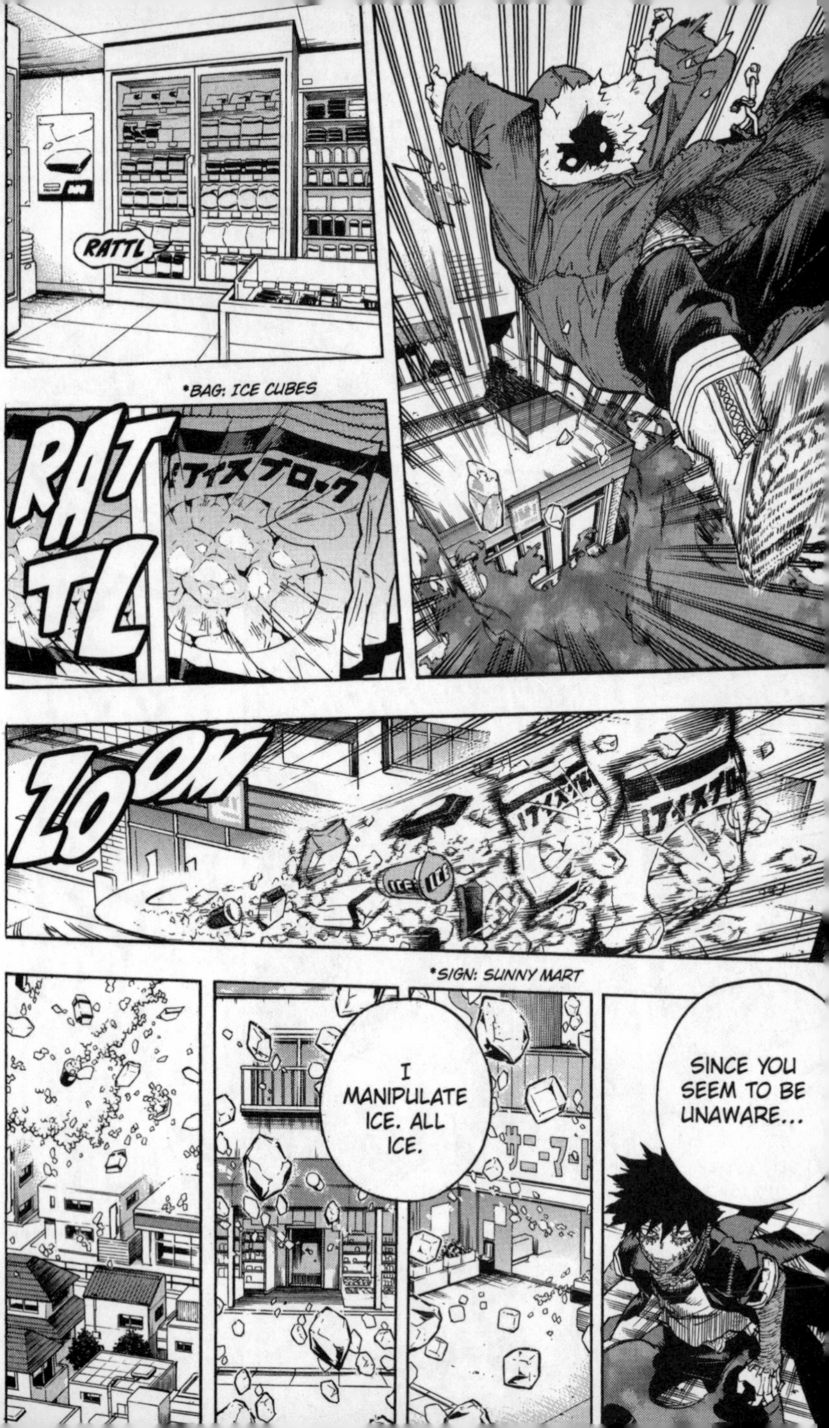
RATTL
*BAG: ICE CUBES
アイスブロック
RAT TL
ZOOM
*SIGN: SUNNY MART
SINCE YOU SEEM TO BE UNAWARE...
I MANIPULATE ICE. ALL ICE.
サニーマート

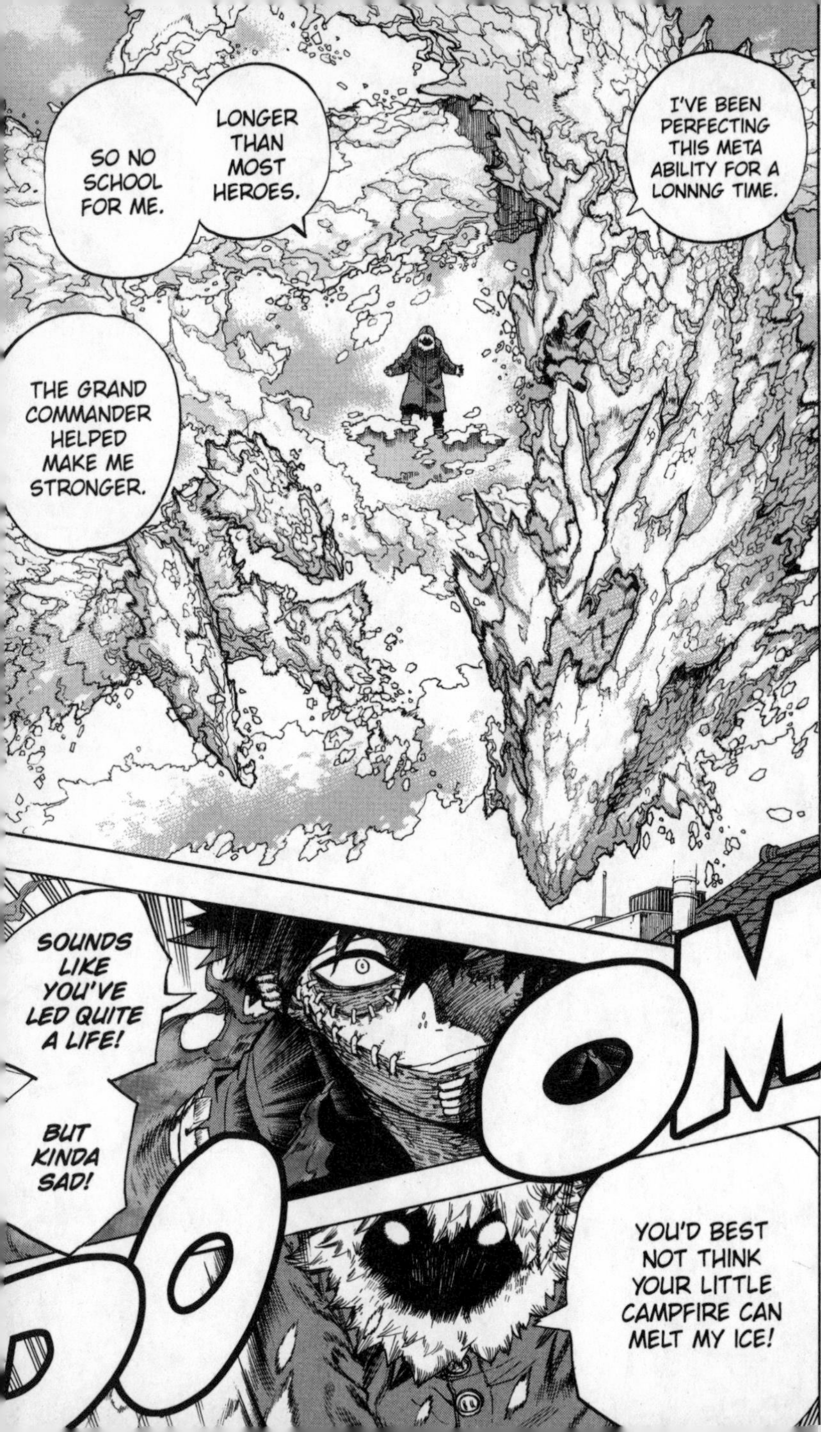

I'VE BEEN PERFECTING THIS META ABILITY FOR A LONNNG TIME.
LONGER THAN MOST HEROES.
SO NO SCHOOL FOR ME.
THE GRAND COMMANDER HELPED MAKE ME STRONGER.
SOUNDS LIKE YOU'VE LED QUITE A LIFE!
BUT KINDA SAD!
DOOOM
YOU'D BEST NOT THINK YOUR LITTLE CAMPFIRE CAN MELT MY ICE!

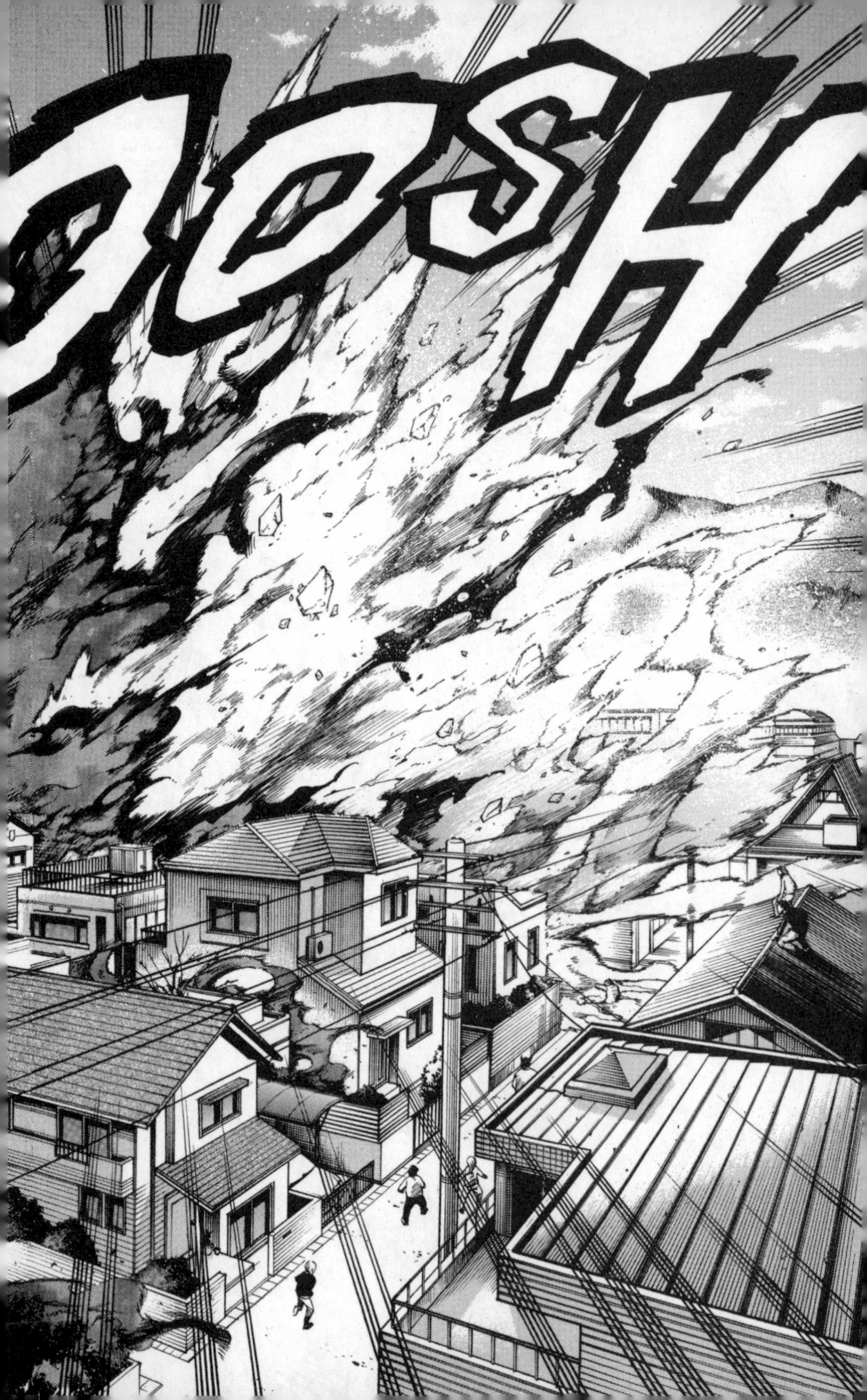

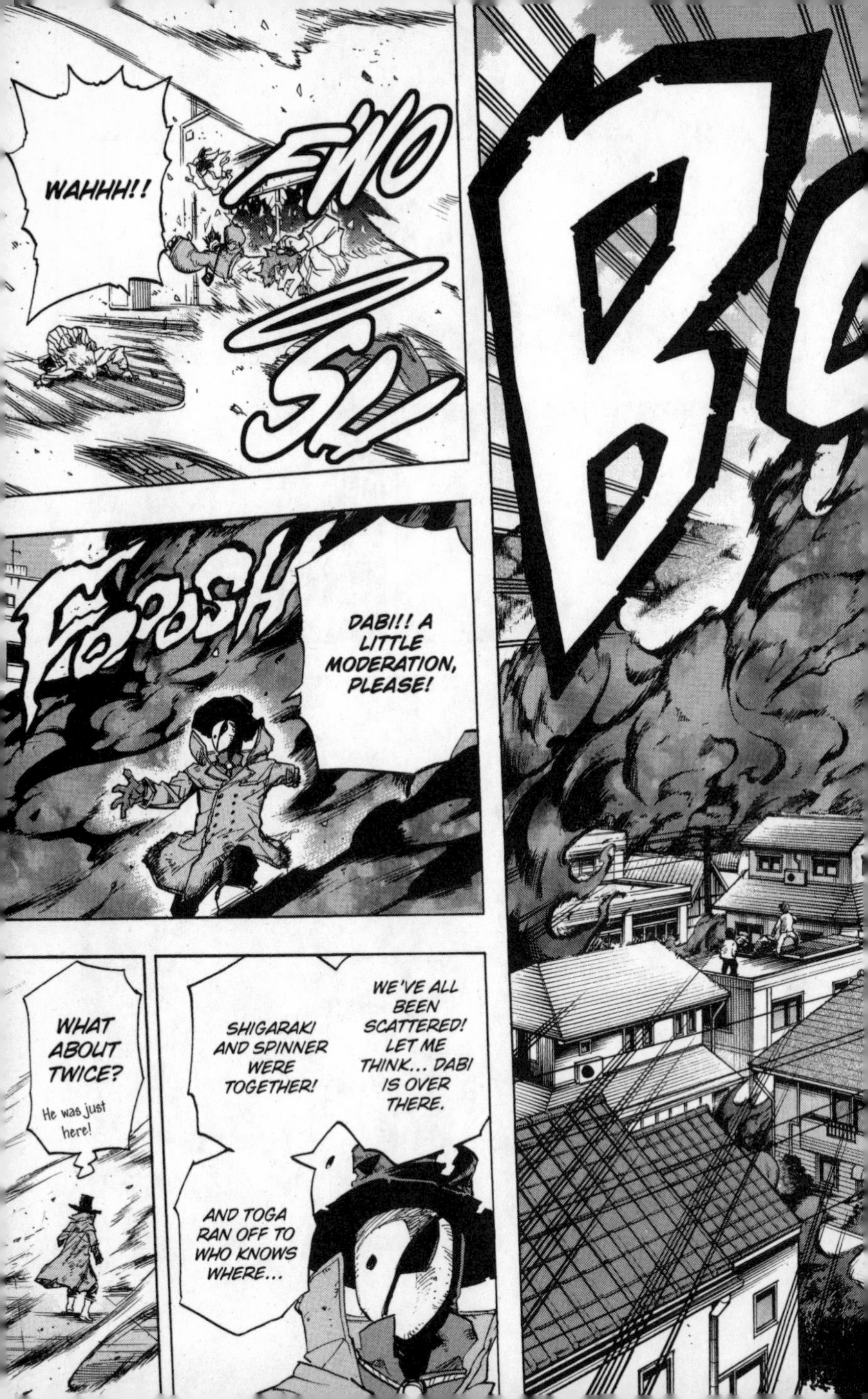
FWO
SH!
WAHHH!!
FOOOSH
DABI!! A LITTLE MODERATION, PLEASE!
WE'VE ALL BEEN SCATTERED! LET ME THINK... DABI IS OVER THERE.
SHIGARAKI AND SPINNER WERE TOGETHER!
AND TOGA RAN OFF TO WHO KNOWS WHERE...
WHAT ABOUT TWICE?
He was just here!

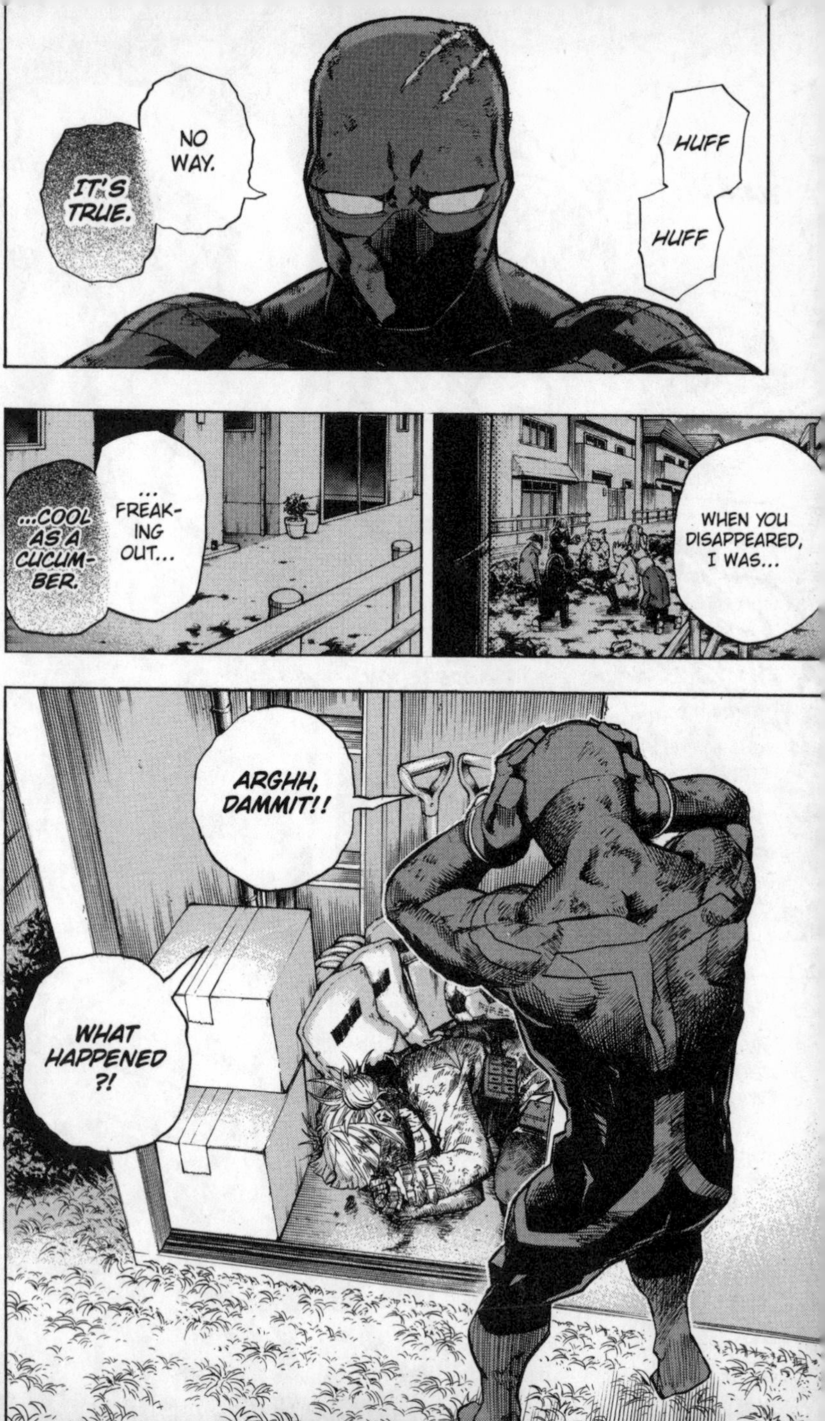
HUFF
HUFF
NO WAY.
IT'S TRUE.
WHEN YOU DISAPPEARED, I WAS...
... FREAKING OUT...
...COOL AS A CUCUMBER.
ARGHH, DAMMIT!!
WHAT HAPPENED?!

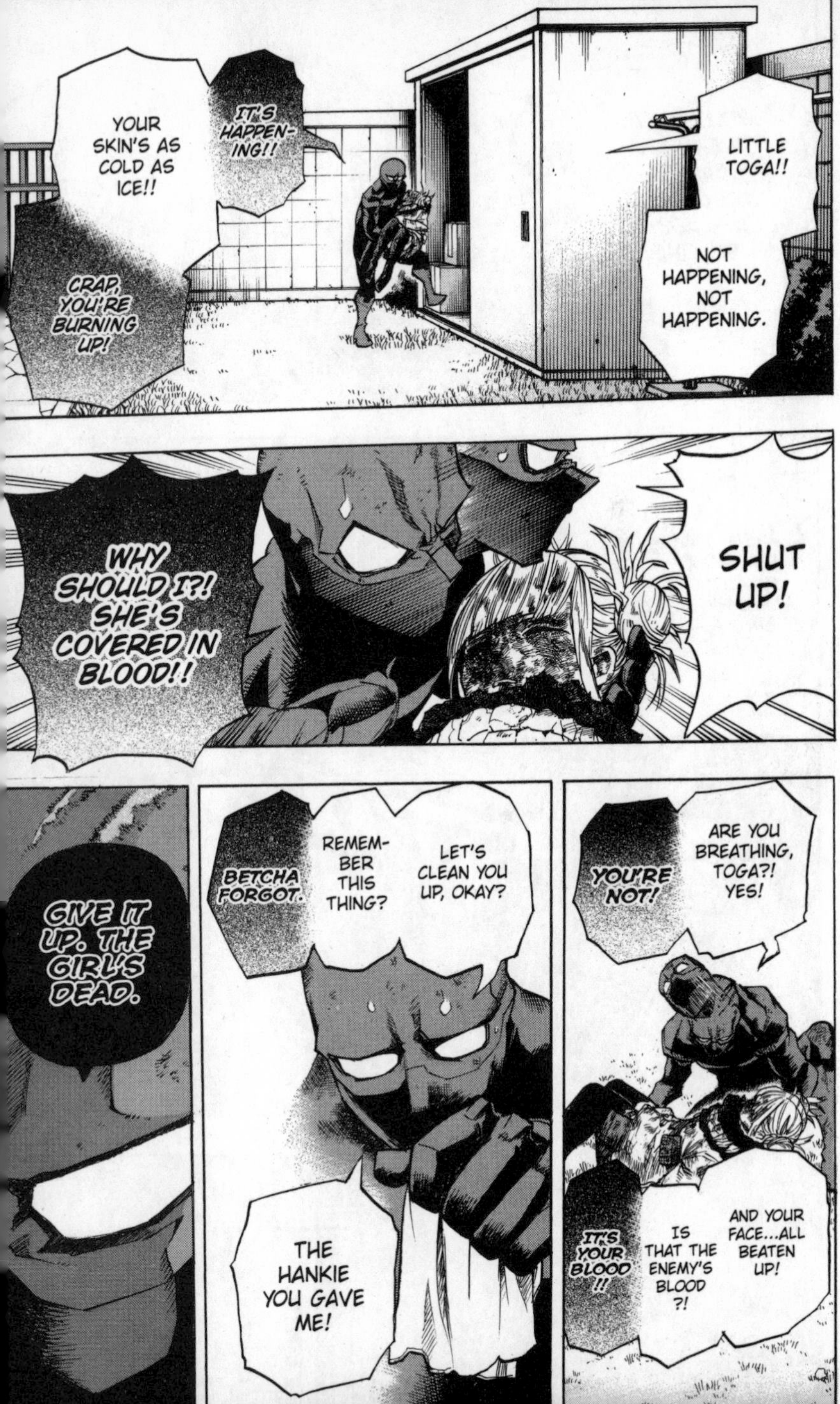
LITTLE TOGA!!
NOT HAPPENING, NOT HAPPENING.
IT'S HAPPENING!!
YOUR SKIN'S AS COLD AS ICE!!
CRAP, YOU'RE BURNING UP!
SHUT UP!
WHY SHOULD I?! SHE'S COVERED IN BLOOD!!
ARE YOU BREATHING, TOGA?! YES!
YOU'RE NOT!
AND YOUR FACE...ALL BEATEN UP!
IS THAT THE ENEMY'S BLOOD ?!
IT'S YOUR BLOOD !!
LET'S CLEAN YOU UP, OKAY?
REMEMBER THIS THING?
BETCHA FORGOT.
THE HANKIE YOU GAVE ME!
GIVE IT UP. THE GIRL'S DEAD.

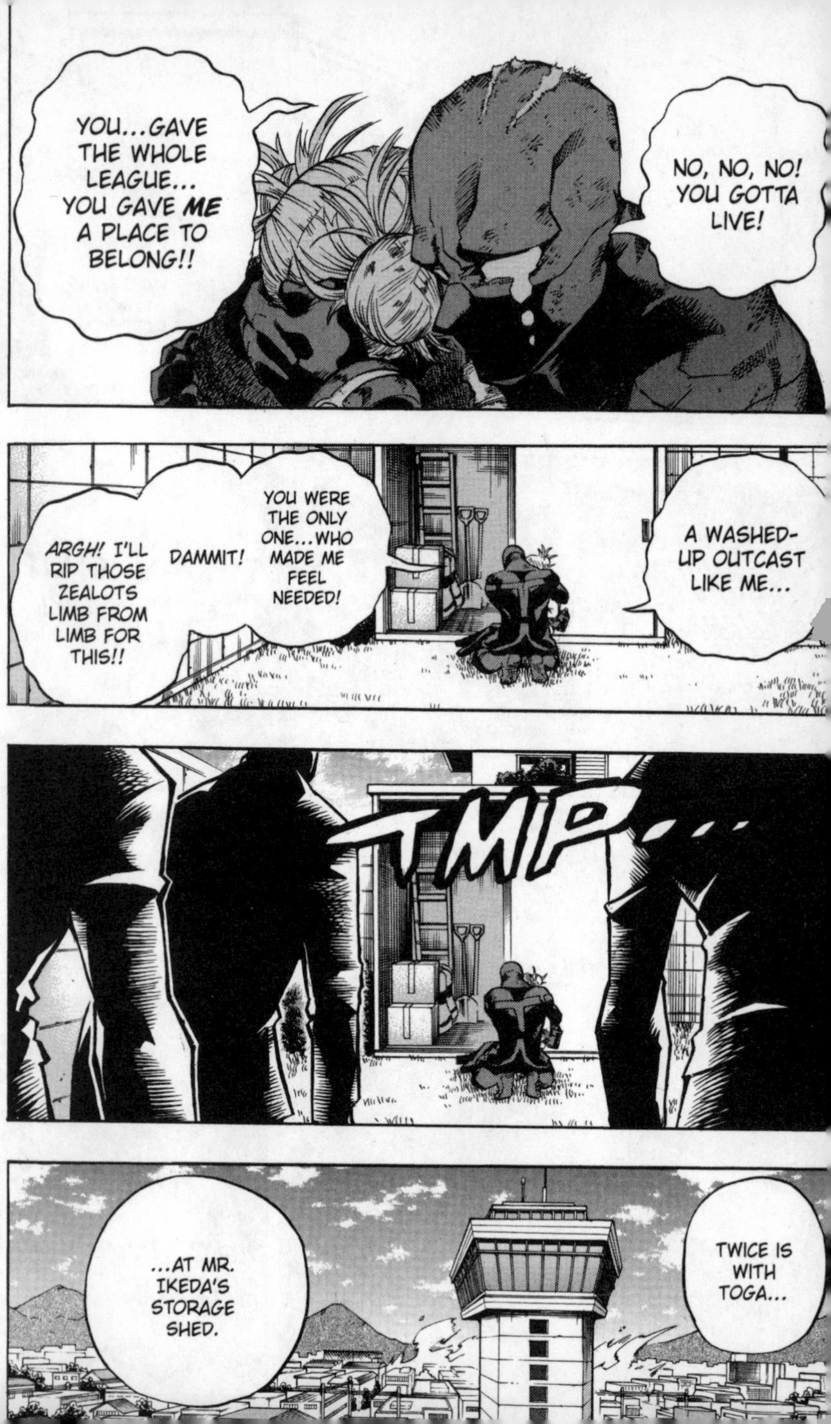
NO, NO, NO! YOU GOTTA LIVE!
YOU...GAVE THE WHOLE LEAGUE... YOU GAVE *ME* A PLACE TO BELONG!!
A WASHED-UP OUTCAST LIKE ME...
YOU WERE THE ONLY ONE...WHO MADE ME FEEL NEEDED!
DAMMIT!
ARGH! I'LL RIP THOSE ZEALOTS LIMB FROM LIMB FOR THIS!!
TMP...
TWICE IS WITH TOGA...
...AT MR. IKEDA'S STORAGE SHED.

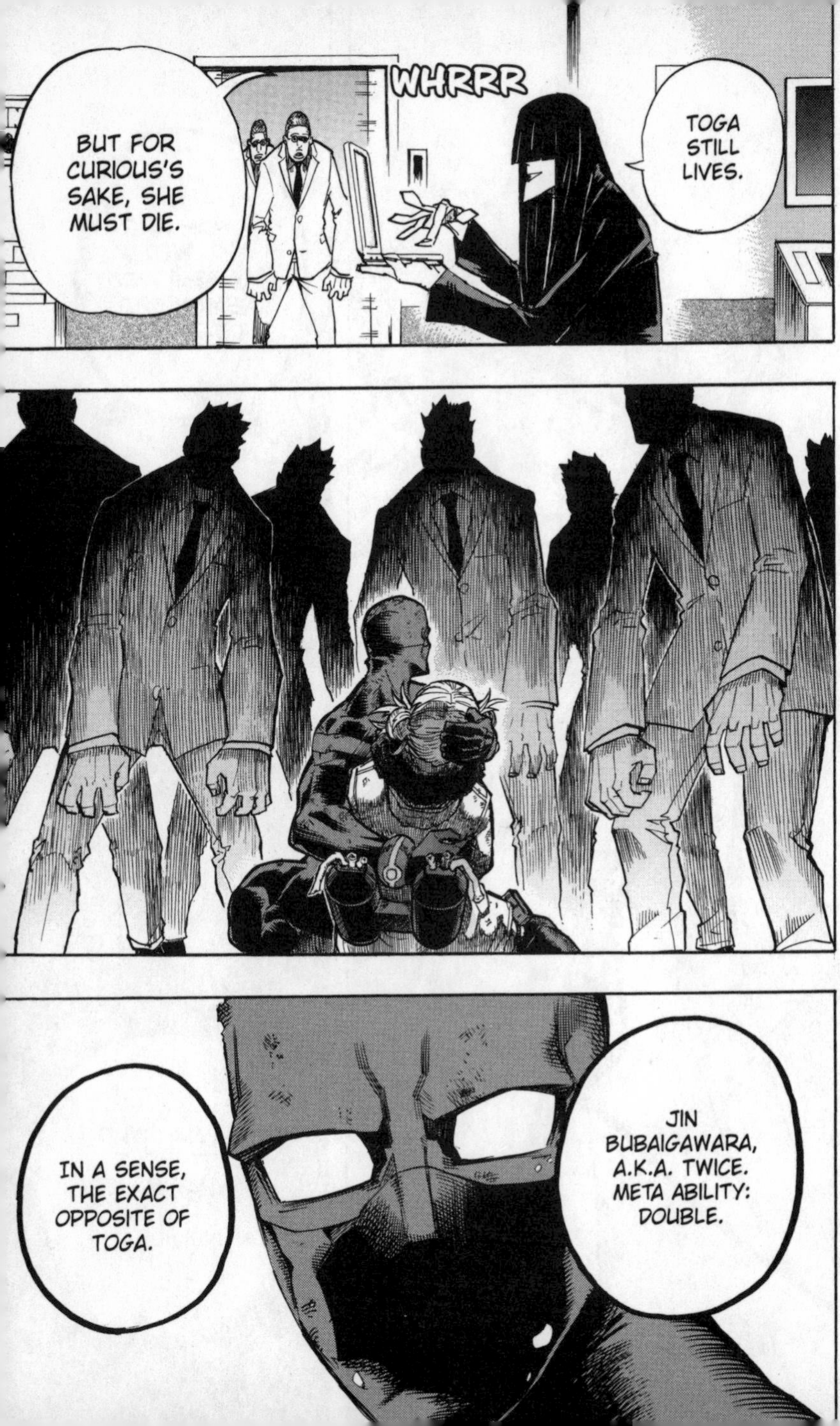
TOGA STILL LIVES.
WHRRR
BUT FOR CURIOUS'S SAKE, SHE MUST DIE.
JIN BUBAIGAWARA, A.K.A. TWICE. META ABILITY: DOUBLE.
IN A SENSE, THE EXACT OPPOSITE OF TOGA.

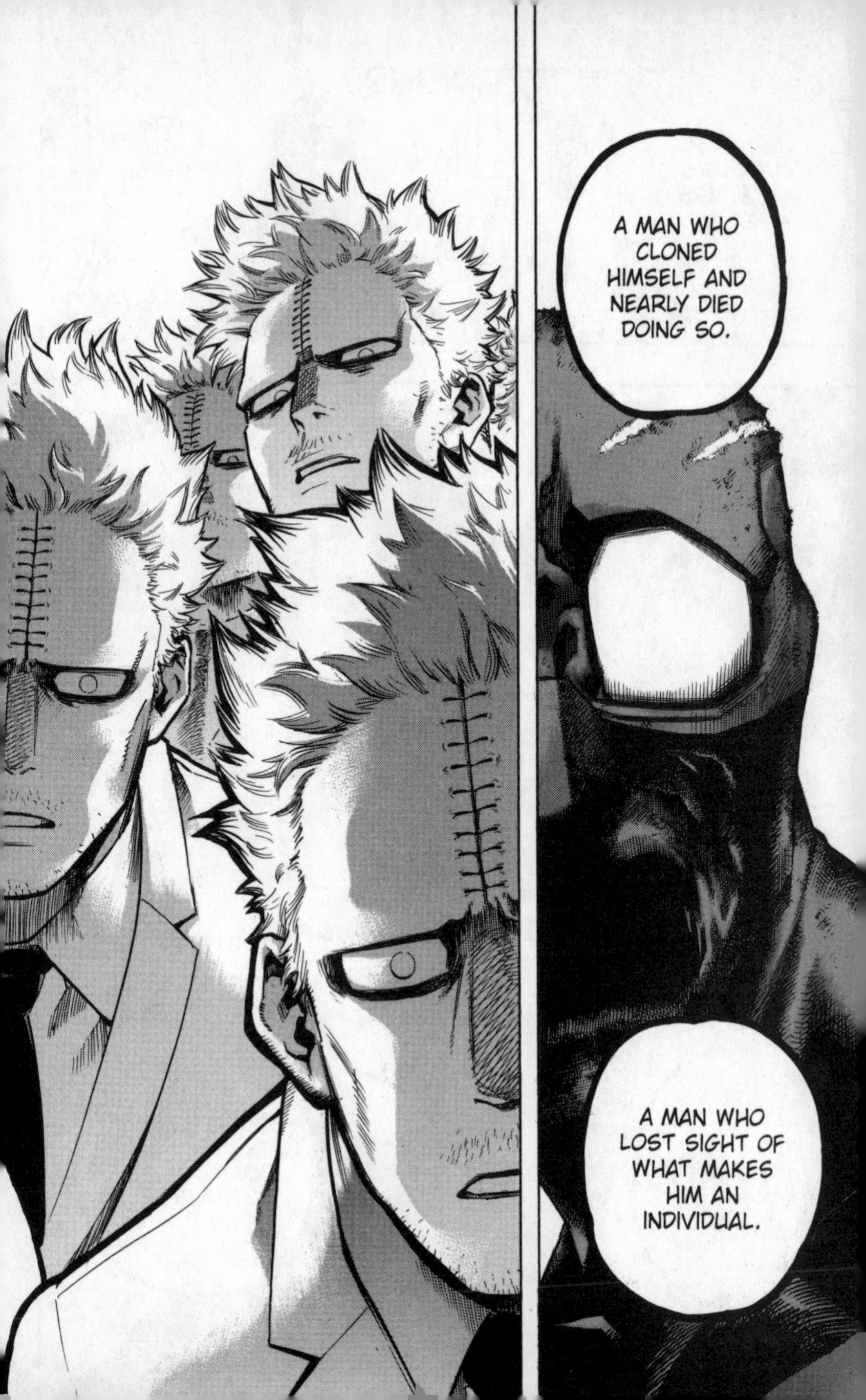
A MAN WHO CLONED HIMSELF AND NEARLY DIED DOING SO.
A MAN WHO LOST SIGHT OF WHAT MAKES HIM AN INDIVIDUAL.

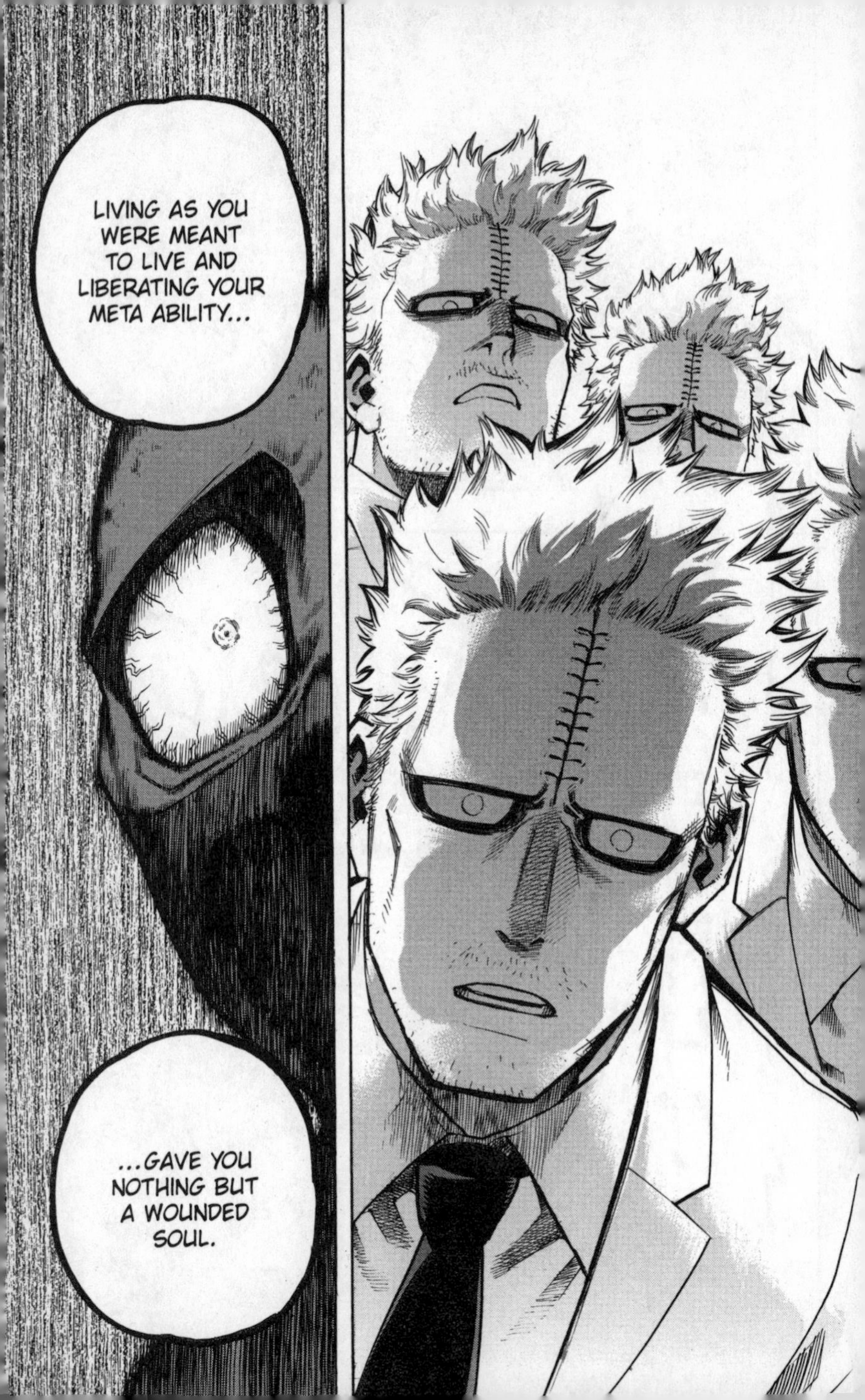
LIVING AS YOU WERE MEANT TO LIVE AND LIBERATING YOUR META ABILITY...
...GAVE YOU NOTHING BUT A WOUNDED SOUL.

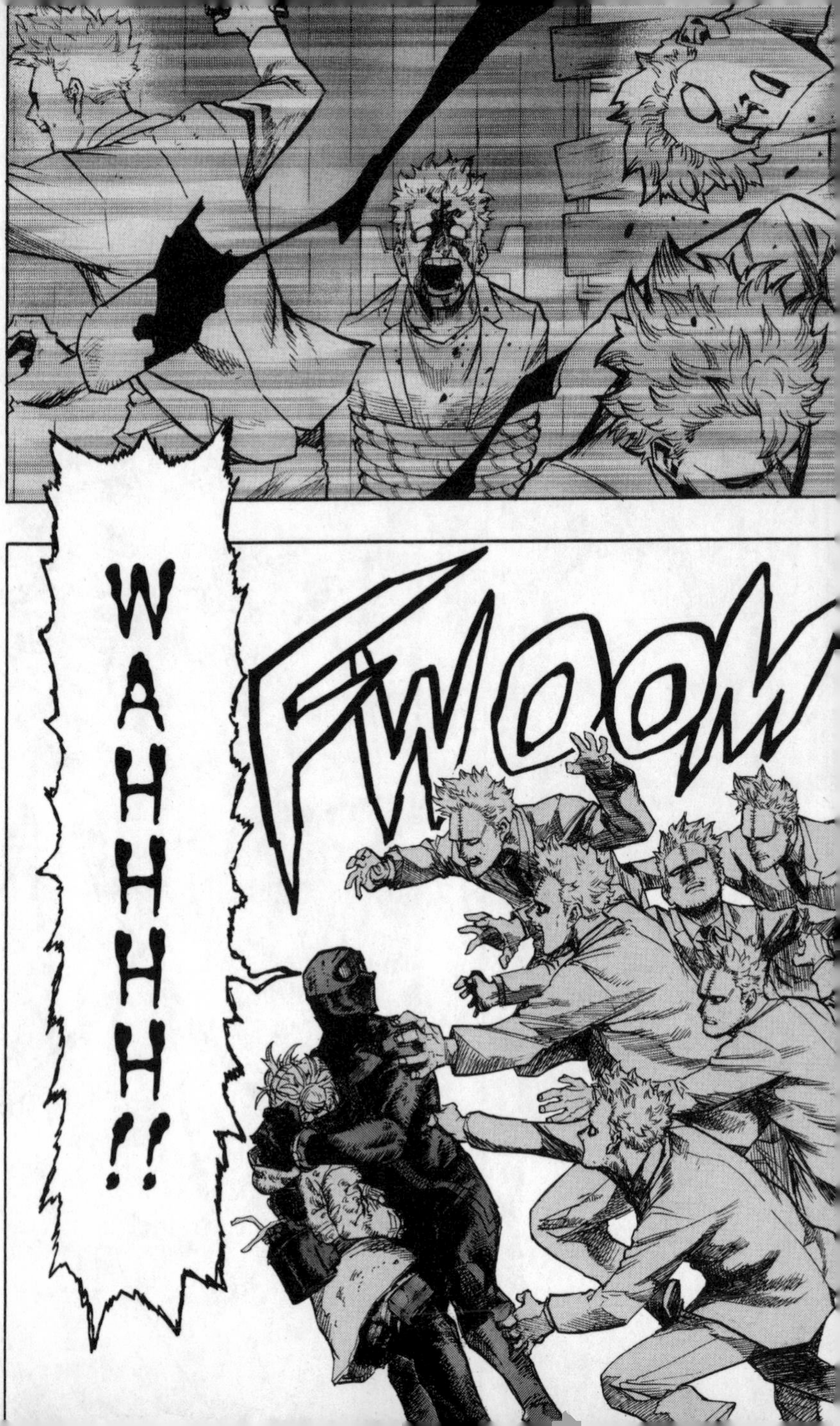
WAHHHH!!
FWOOM

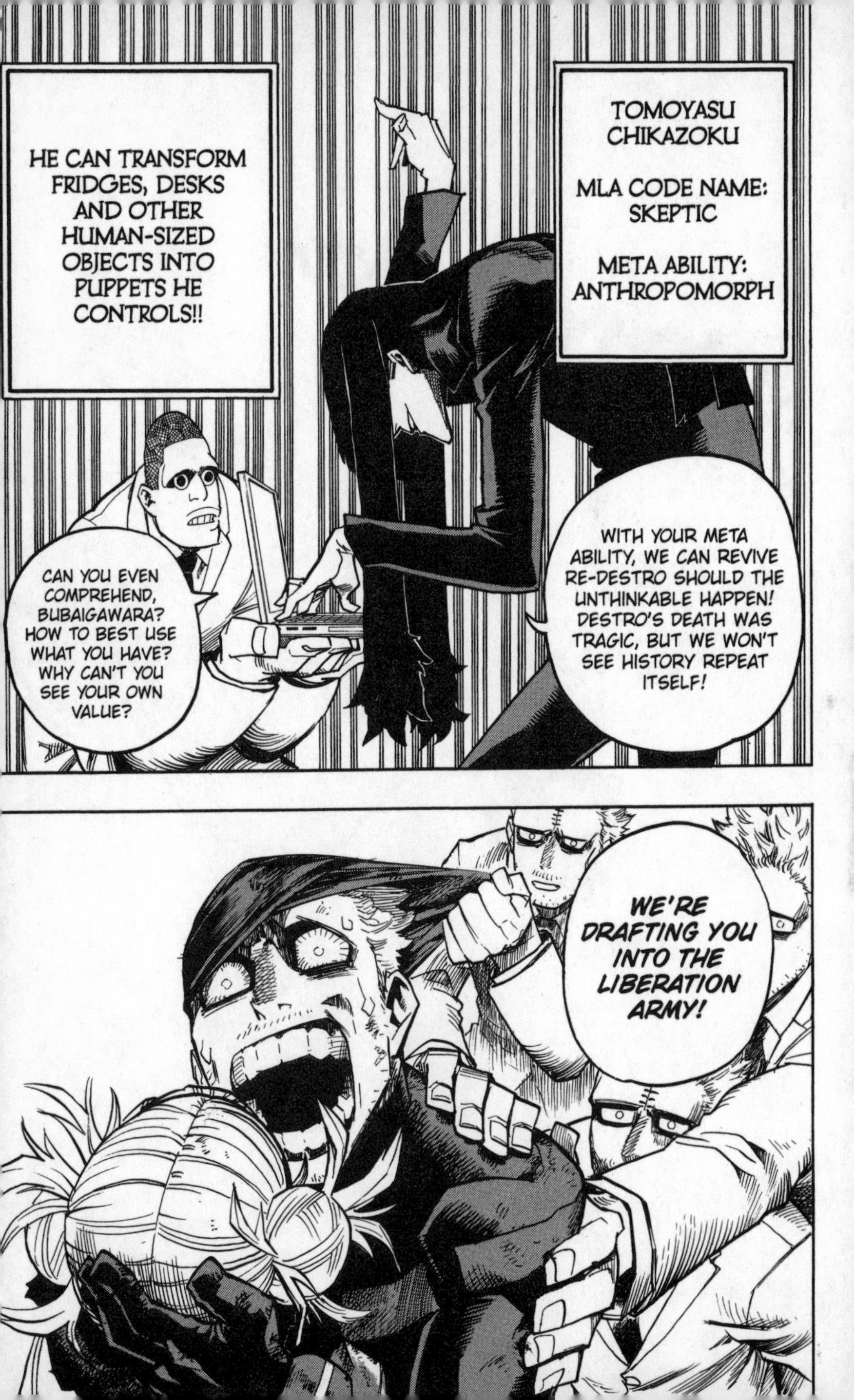
TOMOYASU CHIKAZOKU

MLA CODE NAME: SKEPTIC

META ABILITY: ANTHROPOMORPH
HE CAN TRANSFORM FRIDGES, DESKS AND OTHER HUMAN-SIZED OBJECTS INTO PUPPETS HE CONTROLS!!
WITH YOUR META ABILITY, WE CAN REVIVE RE-DESTRO SHOULD THE UNTHINKABLE HAPPEN! DESTRO'S DEATH WAS TRAGIC, BUT WE WON'T SEE HISTORY REPEAT ITSELF!
CAN YOU EVEN COMPREHEND, BUBAIGAWARA? HOW TO BEST USE WHAT YOU HAVE? WHY CAN'T YOU SEE YOUR OWN VALUE?
WE'RE DRAFTING YOU INTO THE LIBERATION ARMY!

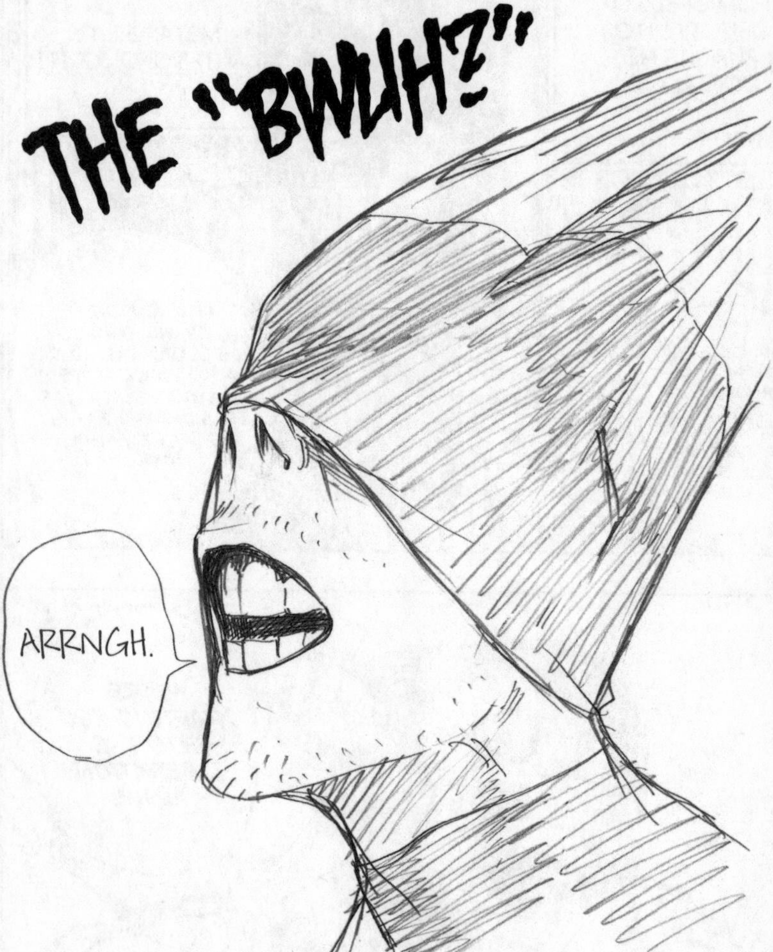
THE "BWUH?!"
ARRNGH.

I had a panel like this in the rough draft of the chapter, but I ended up deleting it.

Good job, me.

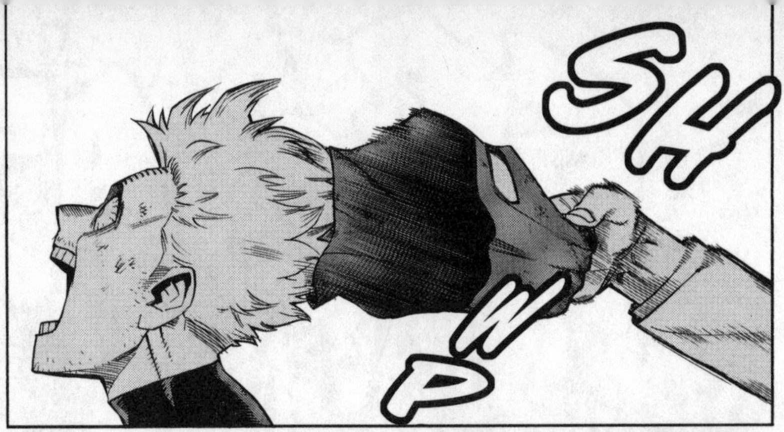
SHWP

No. 229 - All It Takes Is One Bad Day

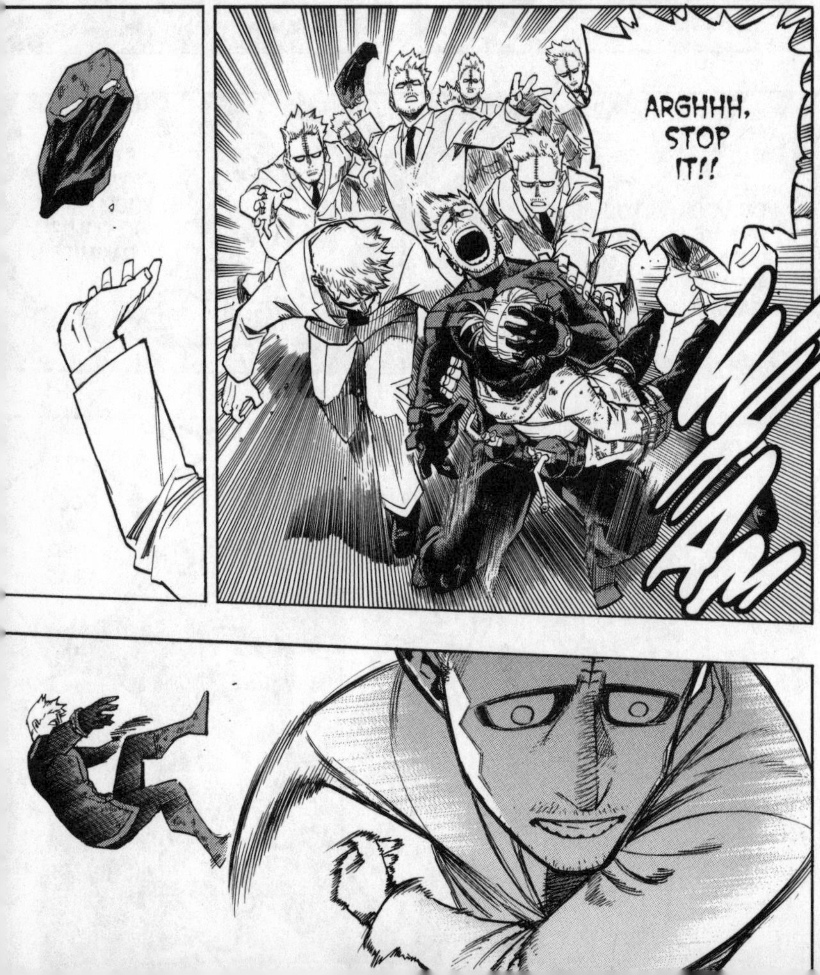
ARGHHH, STOP IT!!
WHAM

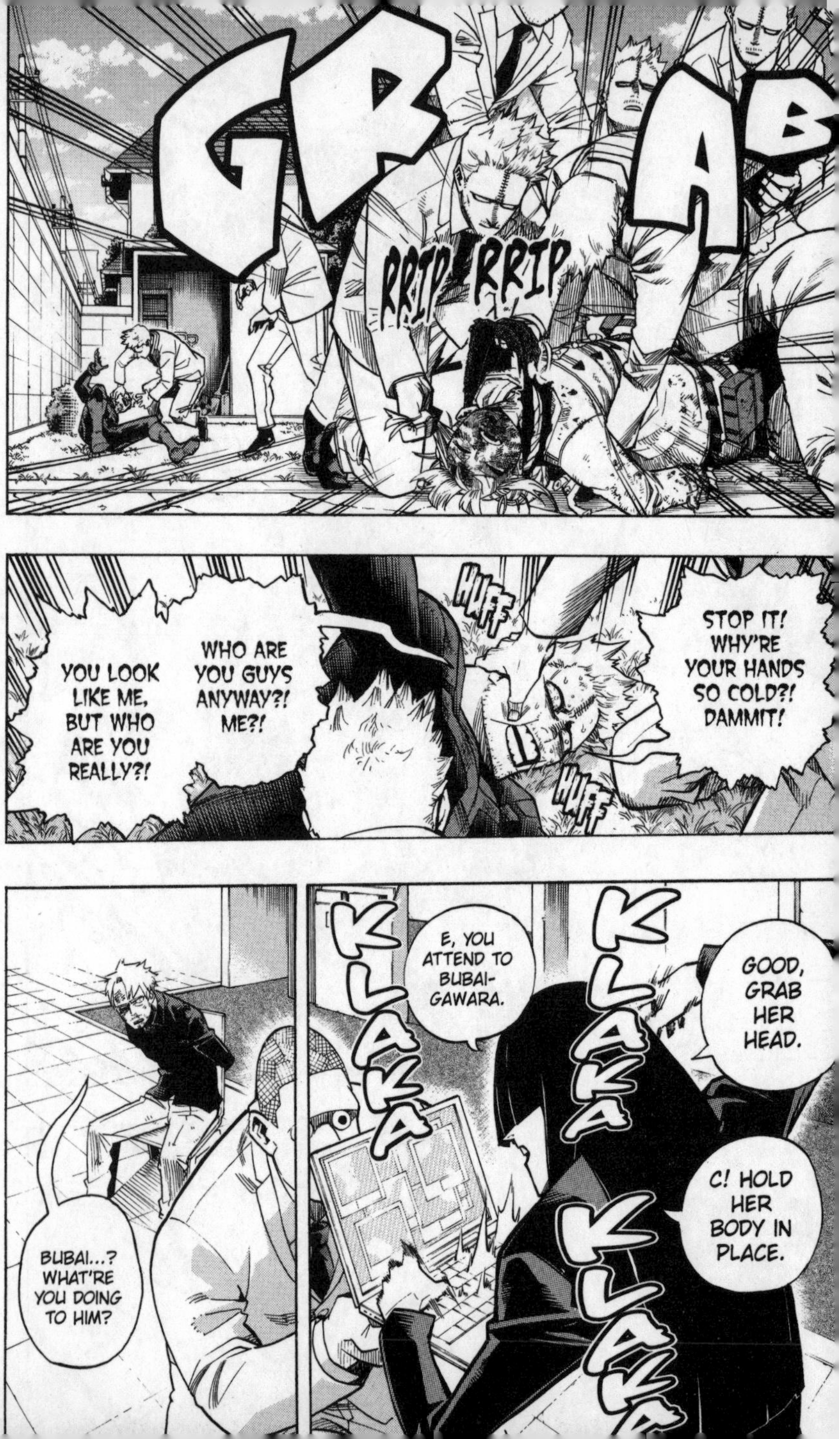
GRAB
RRIP RRIP
STOP IT! WHY'RE YOUR HANDS SO COLD?! DAMMIT!
HUFF
HUFF
WHO ARE YOU GUYS ANYWAY?! ME?!
YOU LOOK LIKE ME, BUT WHO ARE YOU REALLY?!
GOOD, GRAB HER HEAD.
KLAKA
E, YOU ATTEND TO BUBAI-GAWARA.
KLAKA
C! HOLD HER BODY IN PLACE.
KLAKA
BUBAI...? WHAT'RE YOU DOING TO HIM?

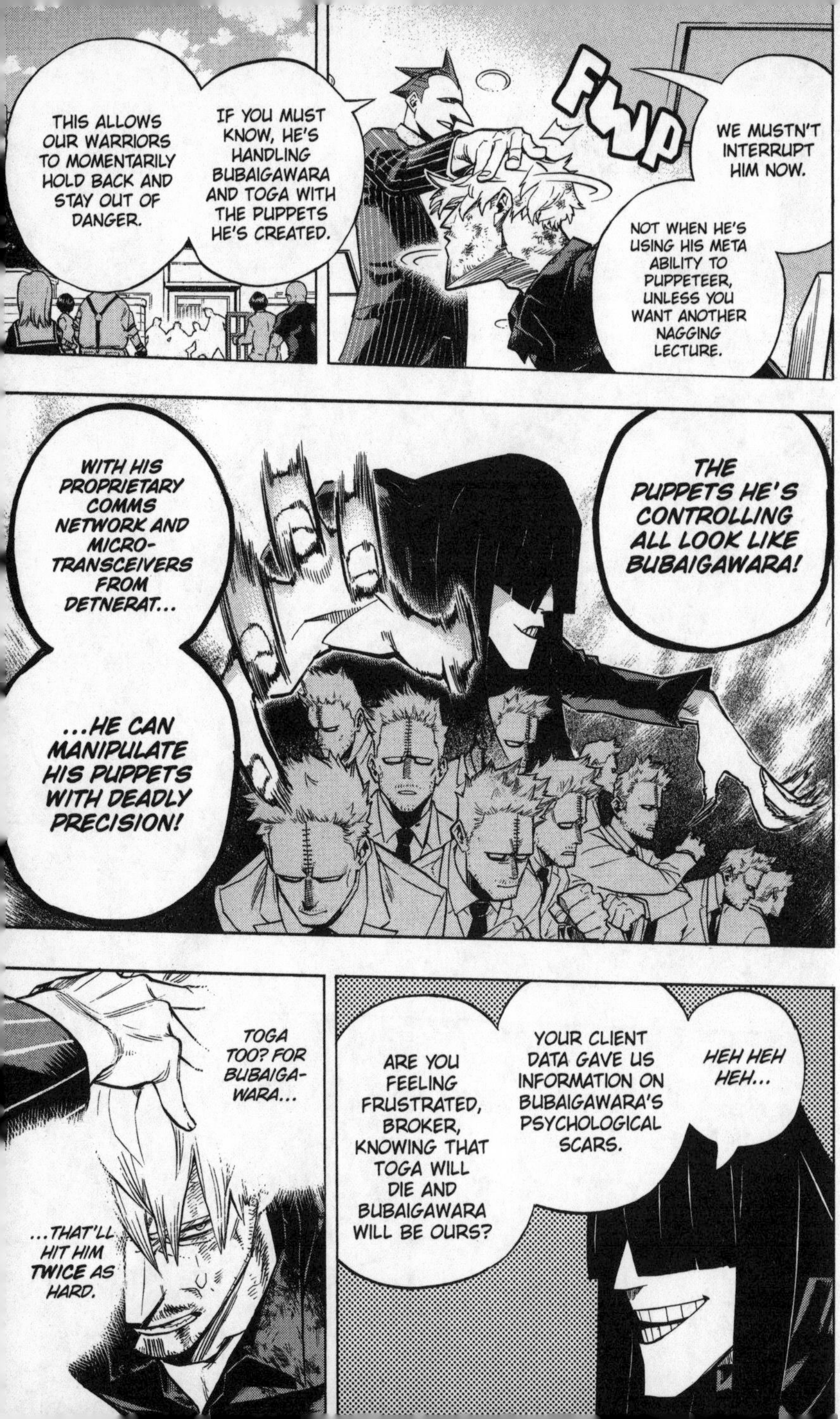
FWP
WE MUSTN'T INTERRUPT HIM NOW.
NOT WHEN HE'S USING HIS META ABILITY TO PUPPETEER, UNLESS YOU WANT ANOTHER NAGGING LECTURE.
IF YOU MUST KNOW, HE'S HANDLING BUBAIGAWARA AND TOGA WITH THE PUPPETS HE'S CREATED.
THIS ALLOWS OUR WARRIORS TO MOMENTARILY HOLD BACK AND STAY OUT OF DANGER.
THE PUPPETS HE'S CONTROLLING ALL LOOK LIKE BUBAIGAWARA!
WITH HIS PROPRIETARY COMMS NETWORK AND MICRO-TRANSCEIVERS FROM DETNERAT...
...HE CAN MANIPULATE HIS PUPPETS WITH DEADLY PRECISION!
HEH HEH HEH...
YOUR CLIENT DATA GAVE US INFORMATION ON BUBAIGAWARA'S PSYCHOLOGICAL SCARS.
ARE YOU FEELING FRUSTRATED, BROKER, KNOWING THAT TOGA WILL DIE AND BUBAIGAWARA WILL BE OURS?
TOGA TOO? FOR BUBAIGA-WARA...
...THAT'LL HIT HIM TWICE AS HARD.

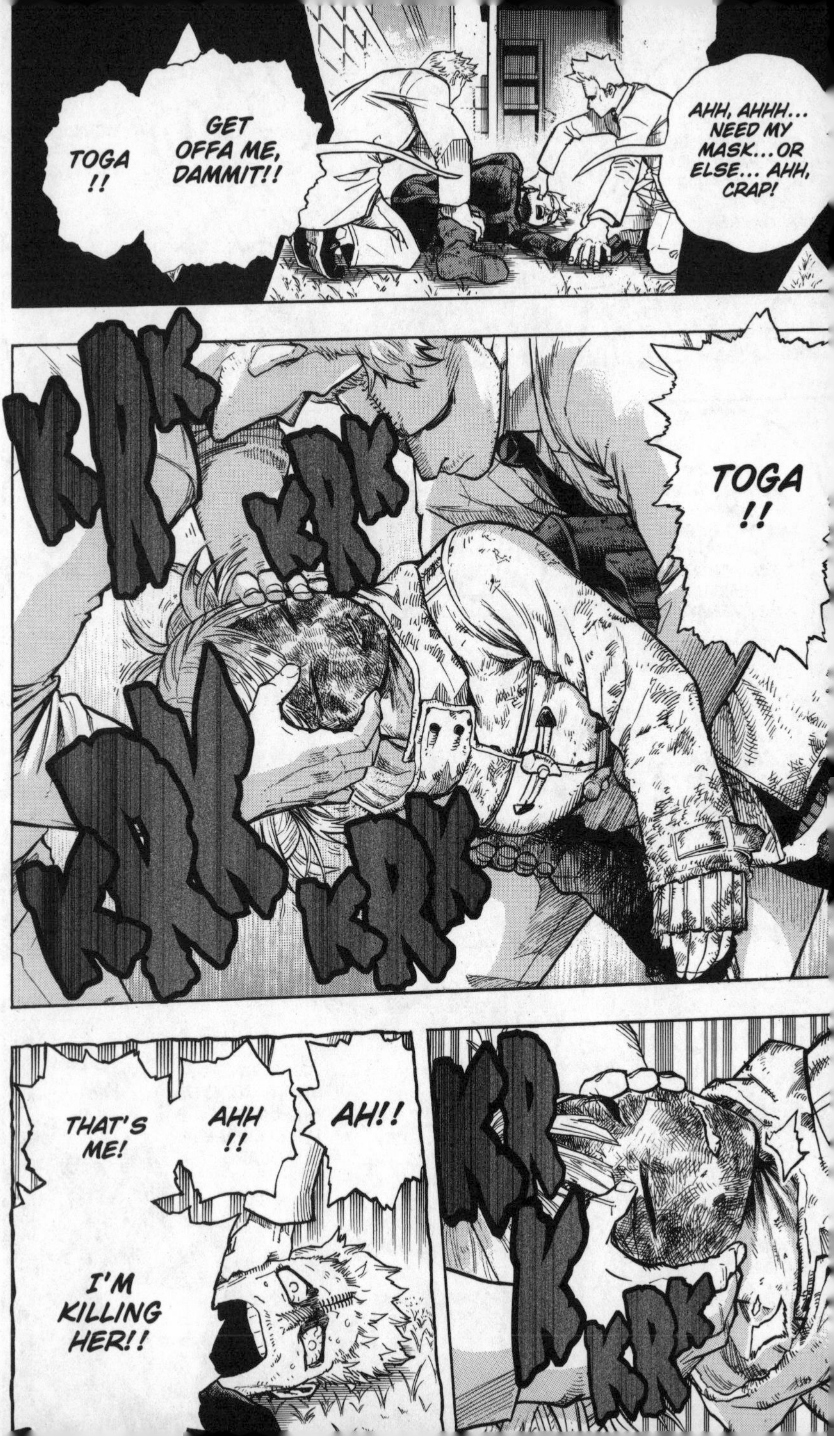
AHH, AHHH... NEED MY MASK...OR ELSE... AHH, CRAP!
GET OFFA ME, DAMMIT!!
TOGA!!
TOGA!!
KRK
KRK
KRK
KRK
KRK
KRK
AH!!
AHH!!
THAT'S ME!
I'M KILLING HER!!

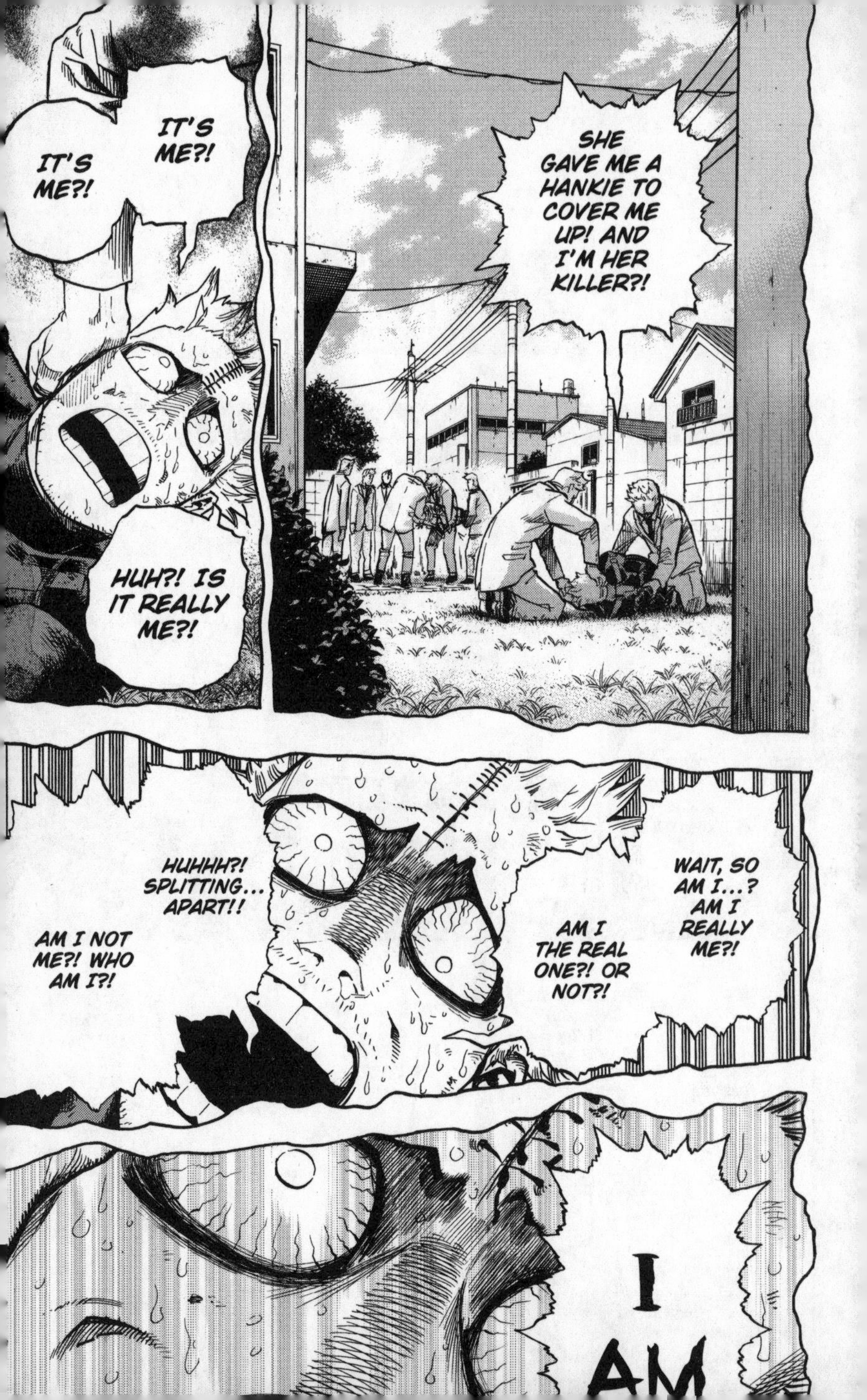
SHE GAVE ME A HANKIE TO COVER ME UP! AND I'M HER KILLER?!
IT'S ME?!
IT'S ME?!
HUH?! IS IT REALLY ME?!
WAIT, SO AM I...? AM I REALLY ME?!
AM I THE REAL ONE?! OR NOT?!
HUHHH?! SPLITTING... APART!!
AM I NOT ME?! WHO AM I?!
I AM

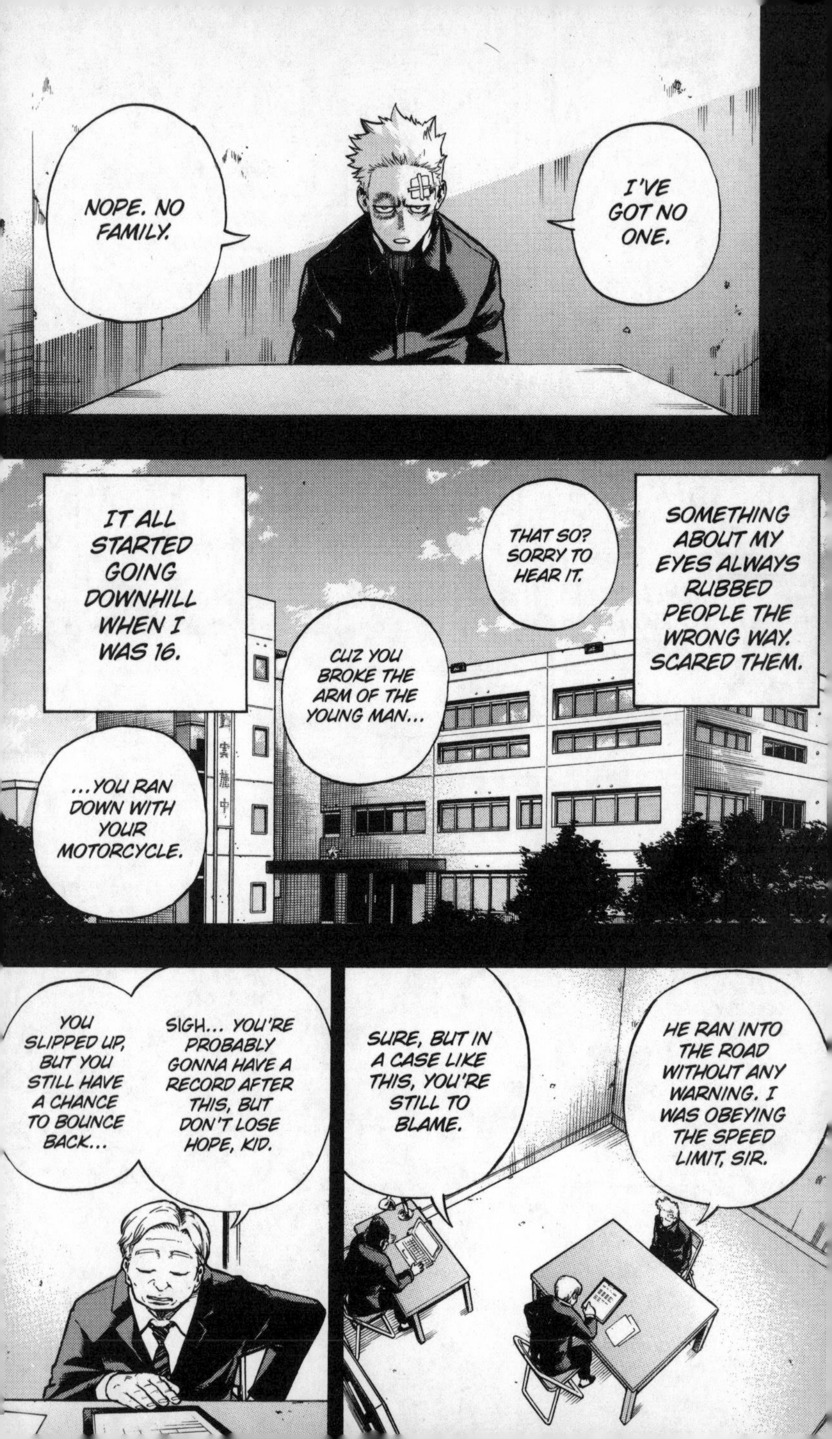
I'VE GOT NO ONE.
NOPE. NO FAMILY.
THAT SO? SORRY TO HEAR IT.
SOMETHING ABOUT MY EYES ALWAYS RUBBED PEOPLE THE WRONG WAY. SCARED THEM.
IT ALL STARTED GOING DOWNHILL WHEN I WAS 16.
CUZ YOU BROKE THE ARM OF THE YOUNG MAN...
...YOU RAN DOWN WITH YOUR MOTORCYCLE.
HE RAN INTO THE ROAD WITHOUT ANY WARNING. I WAS OBEYING THE SPEED LIMIT, SIR.
SURE, BUT IN A CASE LIKE THIS, YOU'RE STILL TO BLAME.
SIGH... YOU'RE PROBABLY GONNA HAVE A RECORD AFTER THIS, BUT DON'T LOSE HOPE, KID.
YOU SLIPPED UP, BUT YOU STILL HAVE A CHANCE TO BOUNCE BACK...

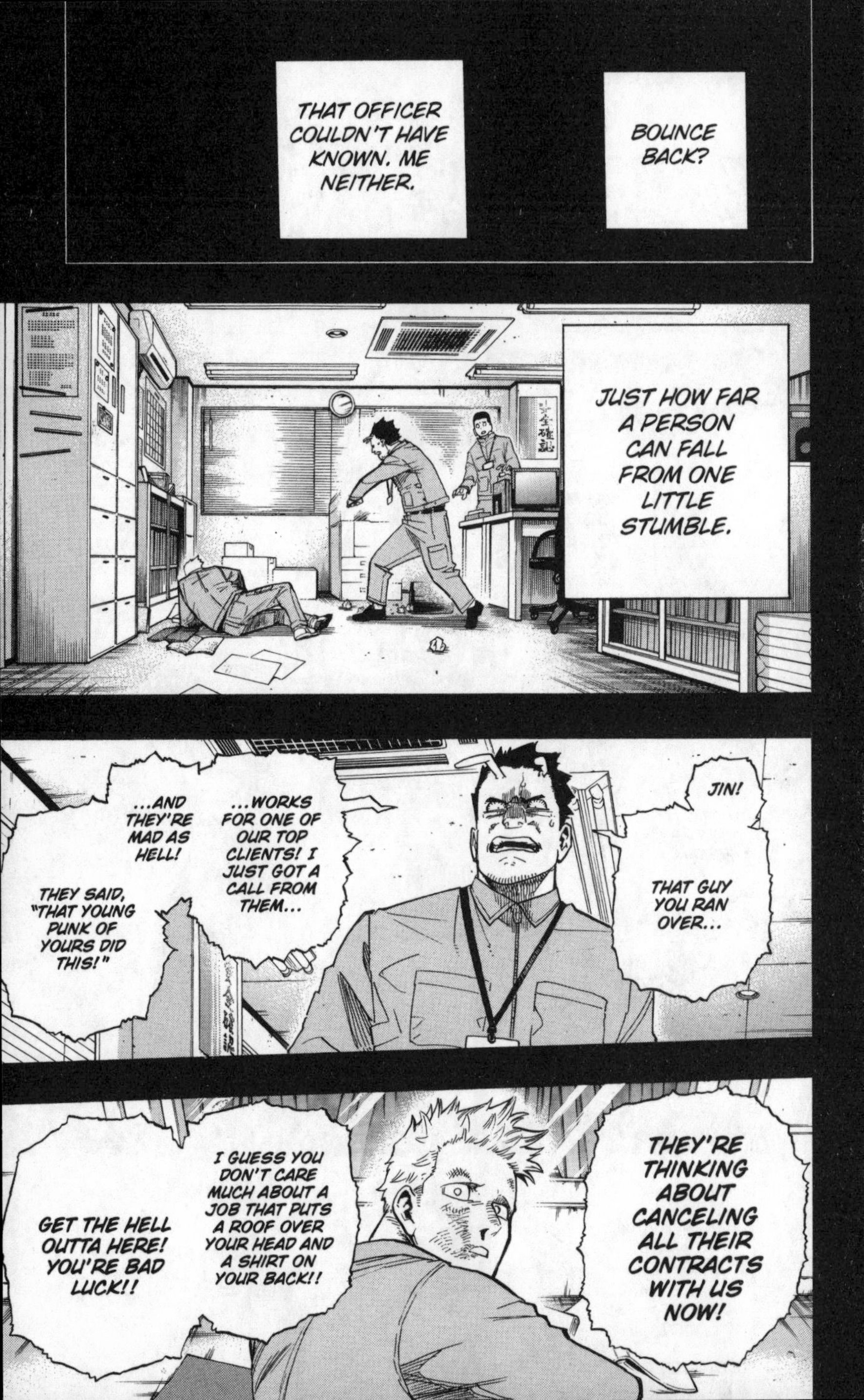
BOUNCE BACK?
THAT OFFICER COULDN'T HAVE KNOWN. ME NEITHER.
JUST HOW FAR A PERSON CAN FALL FROM ONE LITTLE STUMBLE.
JIN!
THAT GUY YOU RAN OVER...
...WORKS FOR ONE OF OUR TOP CLIENTS! I JUST GOT A CALL FROM THEM...
...AND THEY'RE MAD AS HELL!
THEY SAID, "THAT YOUNG PUNK OF YOURS DID THIS!"
THEY'RE THINKING ABOUT CANCELING ALL THEIR CONTRACTS WITH US NOW!
I GUESS YOU DON'T CARE MUCH ABOUT A JOB THAT PUTS A ROOF OVER YOUR HEAD AND A SHIRT ON YOUR BACK!!
GET THE HELL OUTTA HERE! YOU'RE BAD LUCK!!

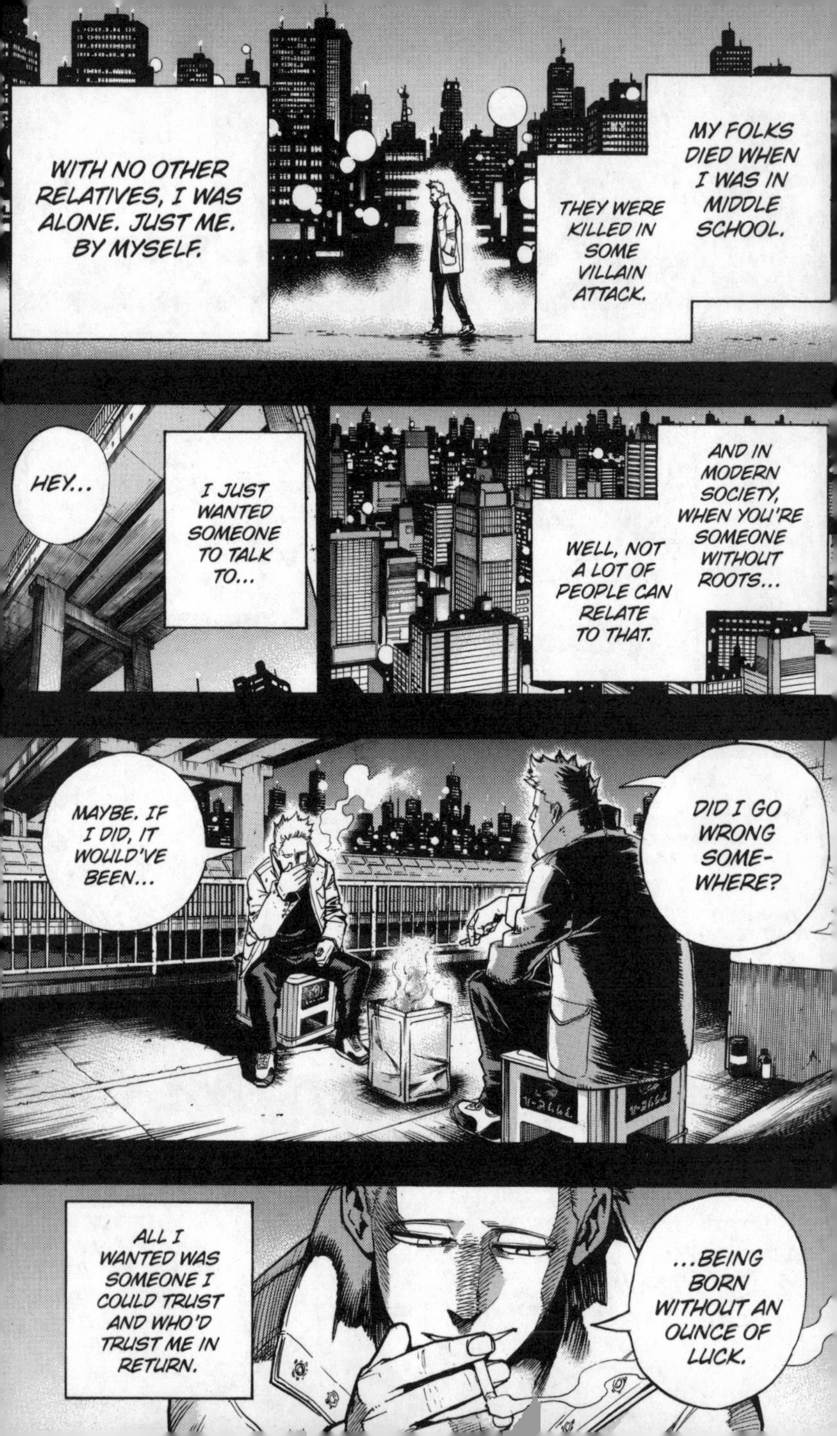
MY FOLKS DIED WHEN I WAS IN MIDDLE SCHOOL.
THEY WERE KILLED IN SOME VILLAIN ATTACK.
WITH NO OTHER RELATIVES, I WAS ALONE. JUST ME. BY MYSELF.
AND IN MODERN SOCIETY, WHEN YOU'RE SOMEONE WITHOUT ROOTS...
WELL, NOT A LOT OF PEOPLE CAN RELATE TO THAT.
I JUST WANTED SOMEONE TO TALK TO...
HEY...
DID I GO WRONG SOME-WHERE?
MAYBE. IF I DID, IT WOULD'VE BEEN...
...BEING BORN WITHOUT AN OUNCE OF LUCK.
ALL I WANTED WAS SOMEONE I COULD TRUST AND WHO'D TRUST ME IN RETURN.

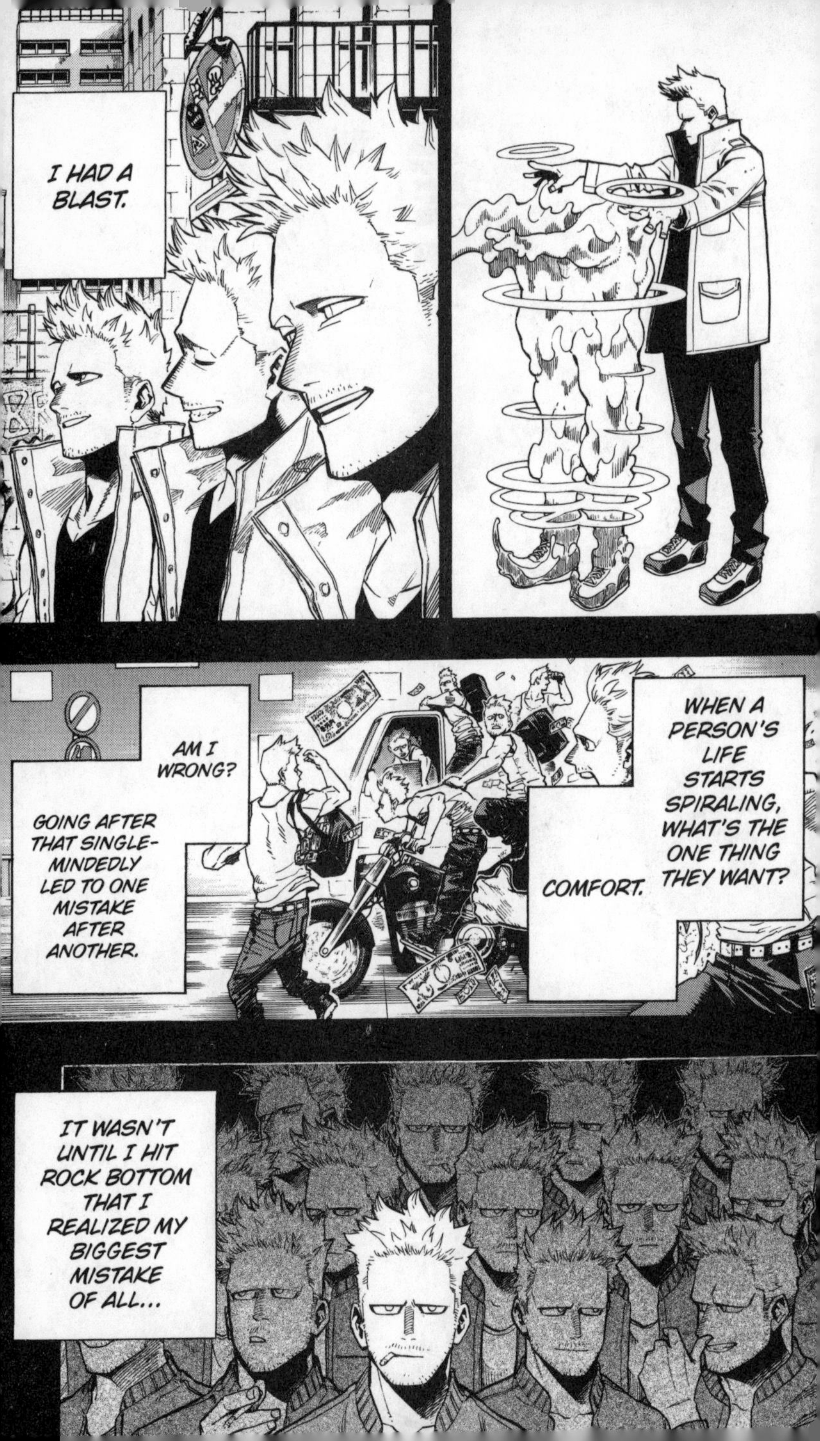
I HAD A BLAST.
WHEN A PERSON'S LIFE STARTS SPIRALING, WHAT'S THE ONE THING THEY WANT?
COMFORT.
AM I WRONG?
GOING AFTER THAT SINGLE-MINDEDLY LED TO ONE MISTAKE AFTER ANOTHER.
IT WASN'T UNTIL I HIT ROCK BOTTOM THAT I REALIZED MY BIGGEST MISTAKE OF ALL...

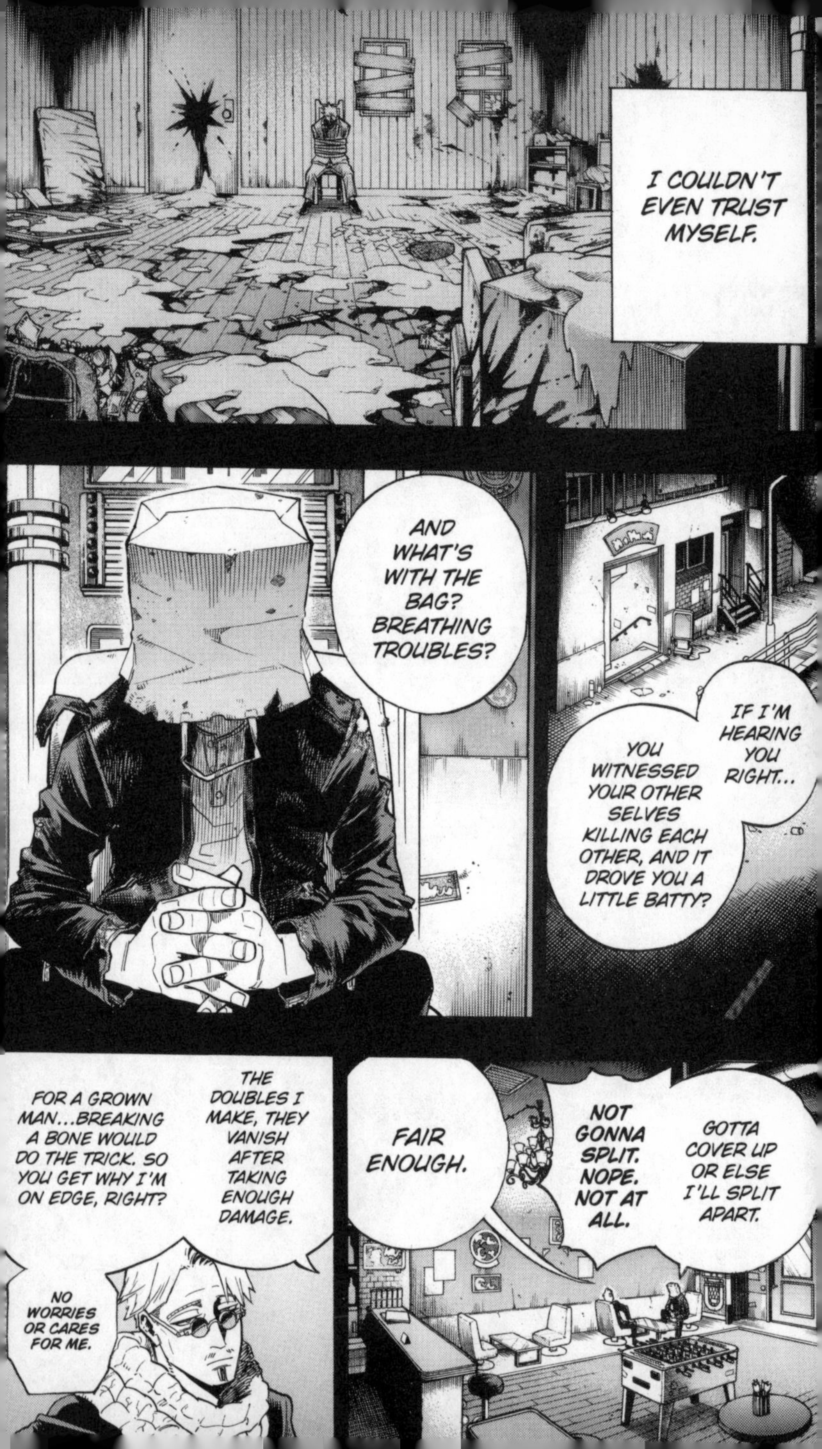
I COULDN'T EVEN TRUST MYSELF.
IF I'M HEARING YOU RIGHT...
YOU WITNESSED YOUR OTHER SELVES KILLING EACH OTHER, AND IT DROVE YOU A LITTLE BATTY?
AND WHAT'S WITH THE BAG? BREATHING TROUBLES?
GOTTA COVER UP OR ELSE I'LL SPLIT APART.
NOT GONNA SPLIT. NOPE. NOT AT ALL.
FAIR ENOUGH.
THE DOUBLES I MAKE, THEY VANISH AFTER TAKING ENOUGH DAMAGE.
FOR A GROWN MAN...BREAKING A BONE WOULD DO THE TRICK. SO YOU GET WHY I'M ON EDGE, RIGHT?
NO WORRIES OR CARES FOR ME.

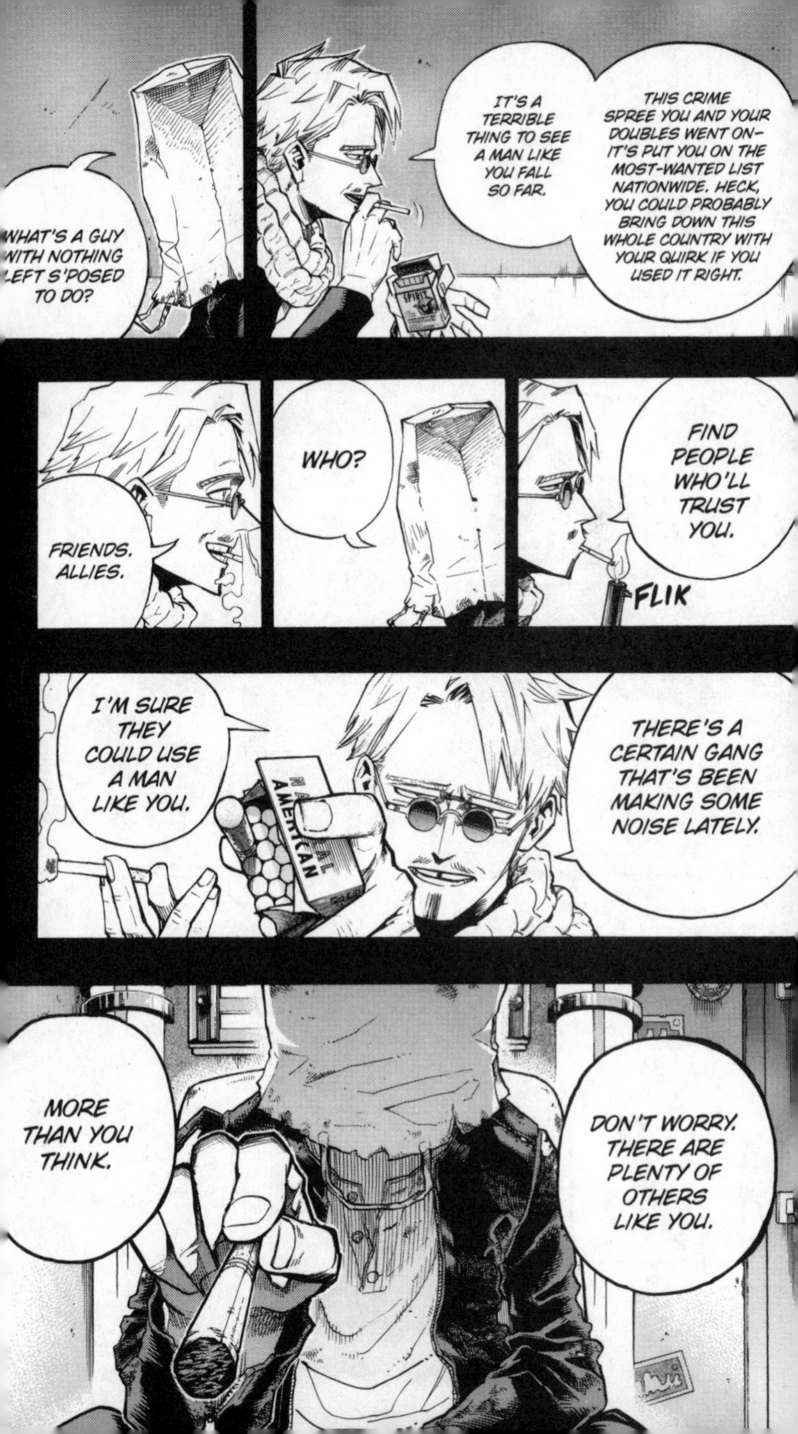
THIS CRIME SPREE YOU AND YOUR DOUBLES WENT ON— IT'S PUT YOU ON THE MOST-WANTED LIST NATIONWIDE. HECK, YOU COULD PROBABLY BRING DOWN THIS WHOLE COUNTRY WITH YOUR QUIRK IF YOU USED IT RIGHT.
IT'S A TERRIBLE THING TO SEE A MAN LIKE YOU FALL SO FAR.
WHAT'S A GUY WITH NOTHING LEFT S'POSED TO DO?
FIND PEOPLE WHO'LL TRUST YOU.
FLIK
WHO?
FRIENDS. ALLIES.
THERE'S A CERTAIN GANG THAT'S BEEN MAKING SOME NOISE LATELY.
I'M SURE THEY COULD USE A MAN LIKE YOU.
DON'T WORRY. THERE ARE PLENTY OF OTHERS LIKE YOU.
MORE THAN YOU THINK.

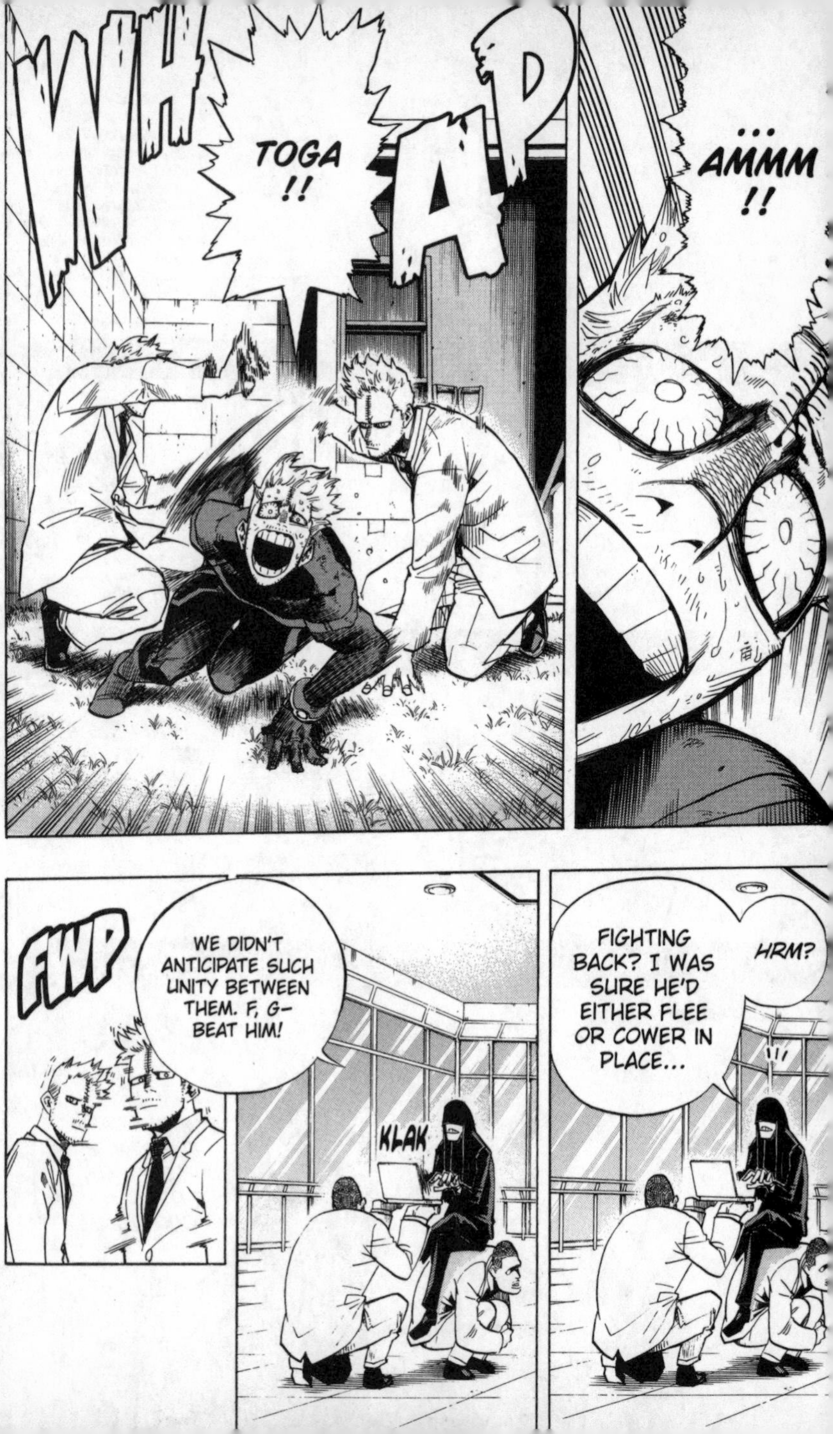
...AMMM!!
WHAP
TOGA!!
HRM?
FIGHTING BACK? I WAS SURE HE'D EITHER FLEE OR COWER IN PLACE...
WE DIDN'T ANTICIPATE SUCH UNITY BETWEEN THEM. F, G- BEAT HIM!
KLAK
FWP

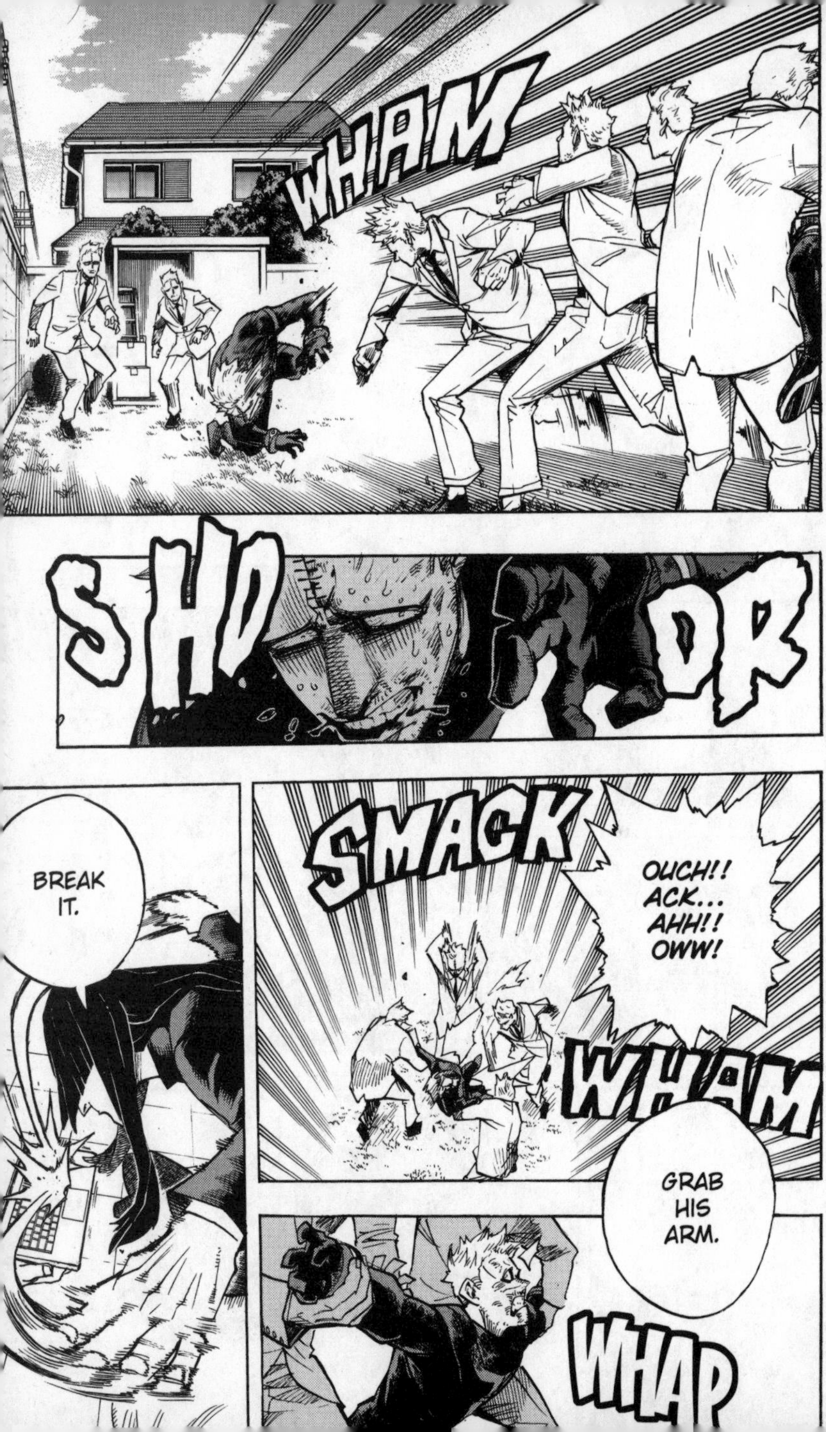
WHAM
SHD DR
SMACK
OUCH!! ACK... AHH!! OWW!
WHAM
GRAB HIS ARM.
WHAP
BREAK IT.

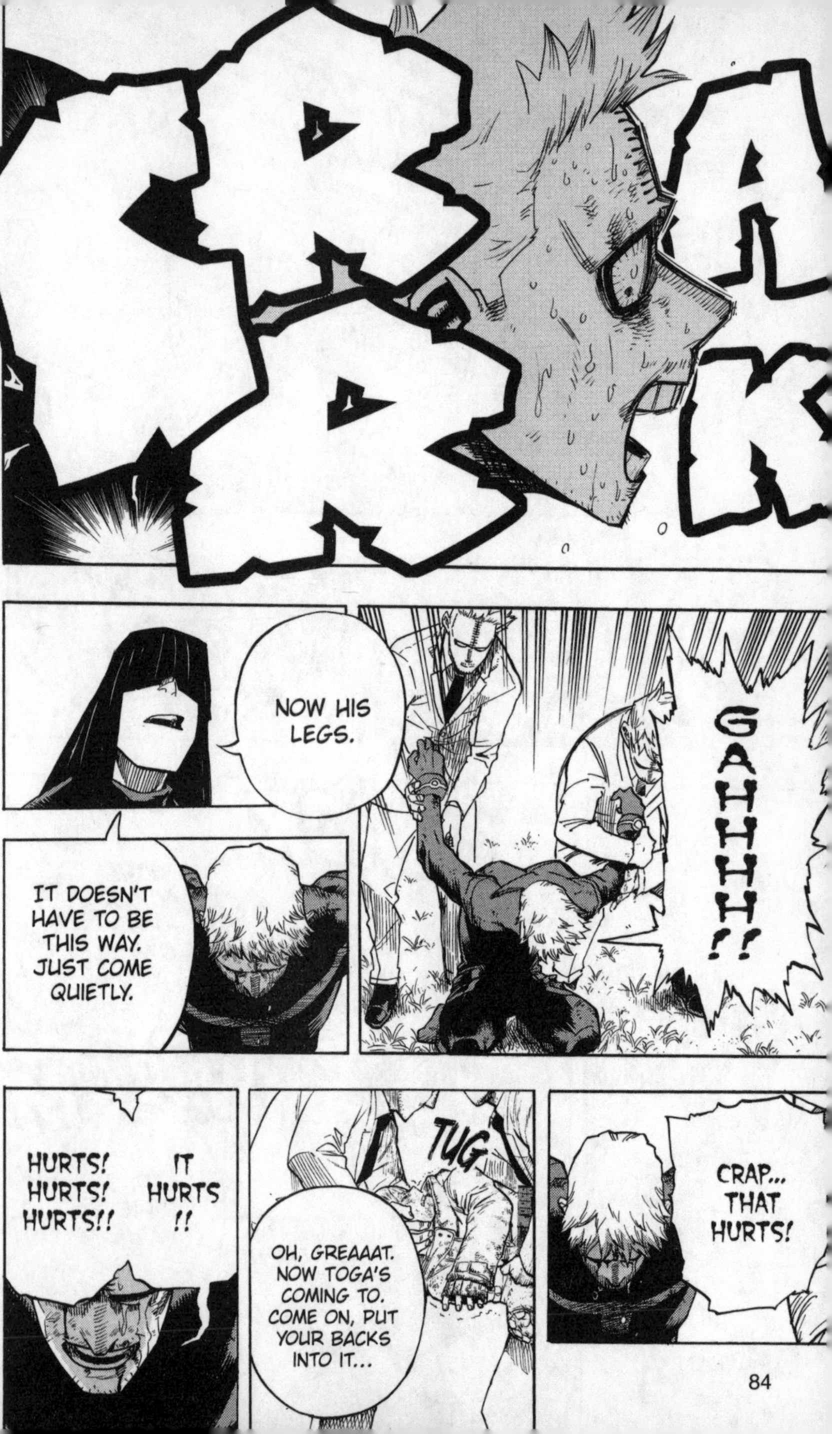
GAHHHH!!
NOW HIS LEGS.
IT DOESN'T HAVE TO BE THIS WAY. JUST COME QUIETLY.
CRAP... THAT HURTS!
TUG
OH, GREAAAT. NOW TOGA'S COMING TO. COME ON, PUT YOUR BACKS INTO IT...
IT HURTS!!
HURTS! HURTS! HURTS!!

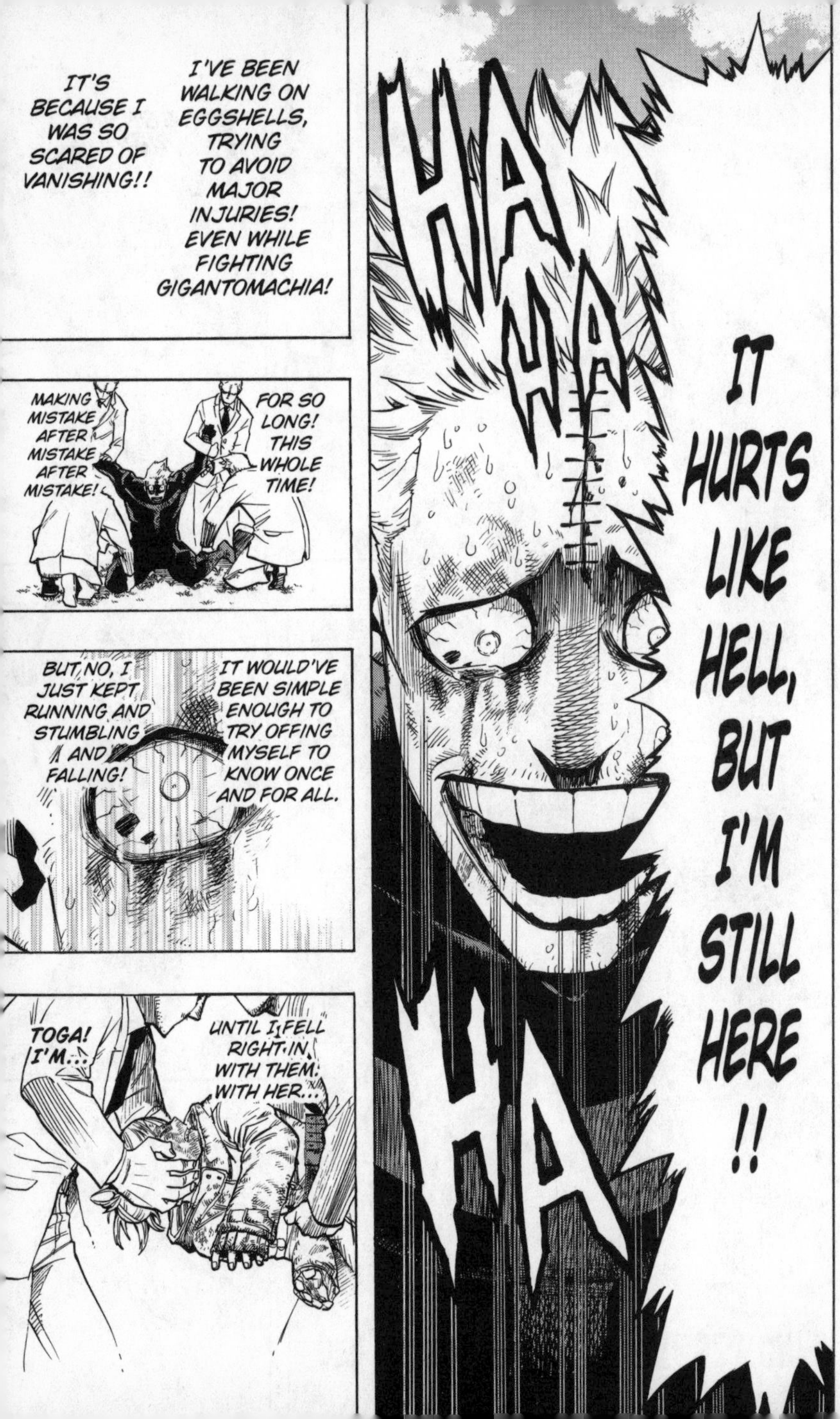
HA HA HA
IT HURTS LIKE HELL, BUT I'M STILL HERE!!
I'VE BEEN WALKING ON EGGSHELLS, TRYING TO AVOID MAJOR INJURIES! EVEN WHILE FIGHTING GIGANTOMACHIA!
IT'S BECAUSE I WAS SO SCARED OF VANISHING!!
FOR SO LONG! THIS WHOLE TIME!
MAKING MISTAKE AFTER MISTAKE AFTER MISTAKE!
IT WOULD'VE BEEN SIMPLE ENOUGH TO TRY OFFING MYSELF TO KNOW ONCE AND FOR ALL.
BUT, NO, I JUST KEPT RUNNING AND STUMBLING AND FALLING!
UNTIL I FELL RIGHT IN WITH THEM. WITH HER...
TOGA! I'M...

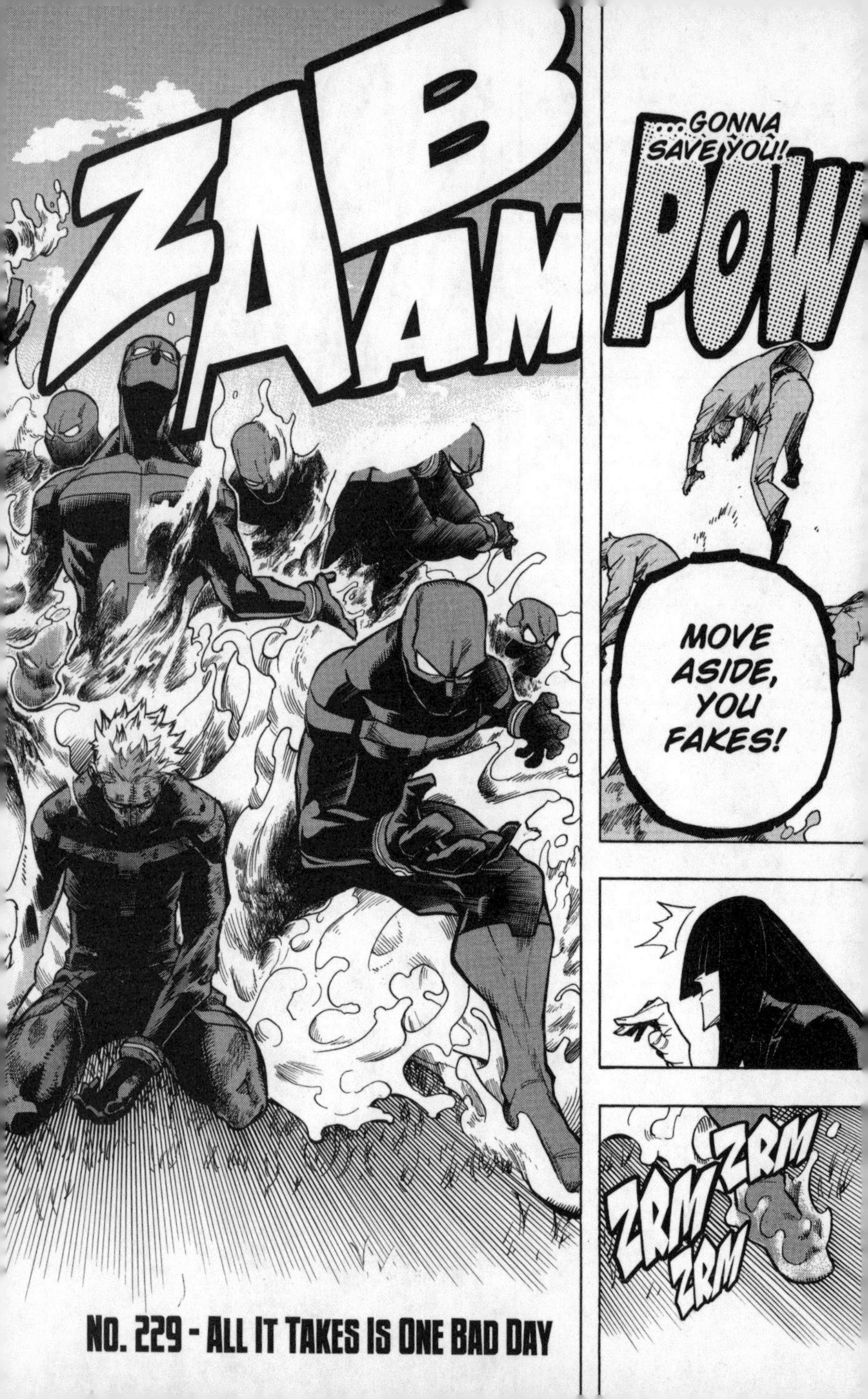
...GONNA SAVE YOU!
POW
MOVE ASIDE, YOU FAKES!
ZRM ZRM ZRM ZRM
ZABAM

No. 229 - All It Takes Is One Bad Day

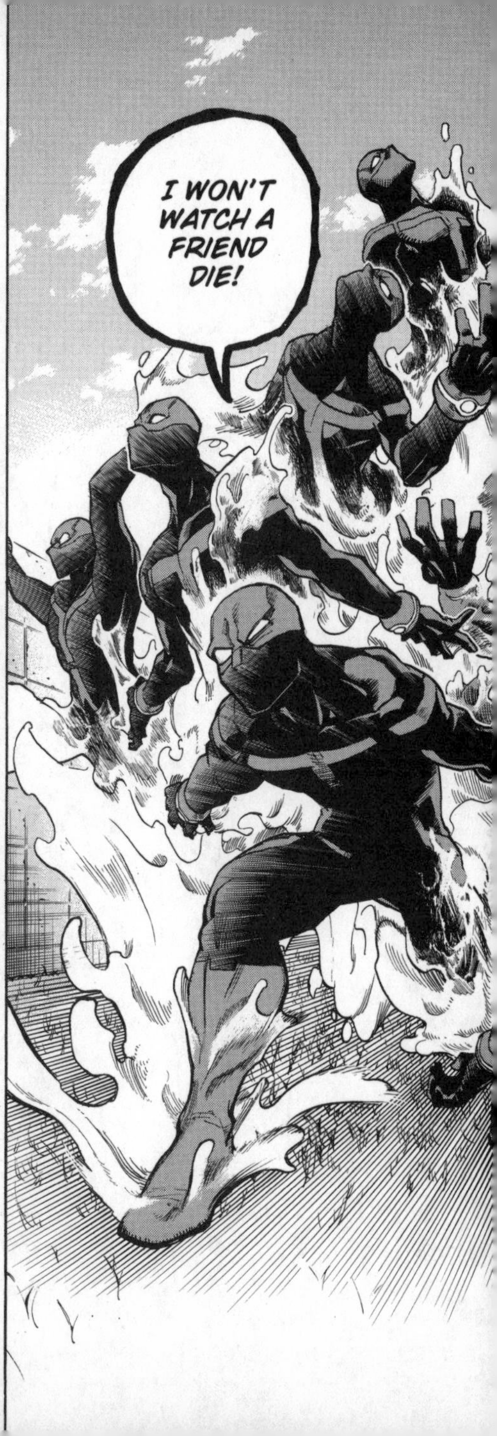
I WON'T WATCH A FRIEND DIE!

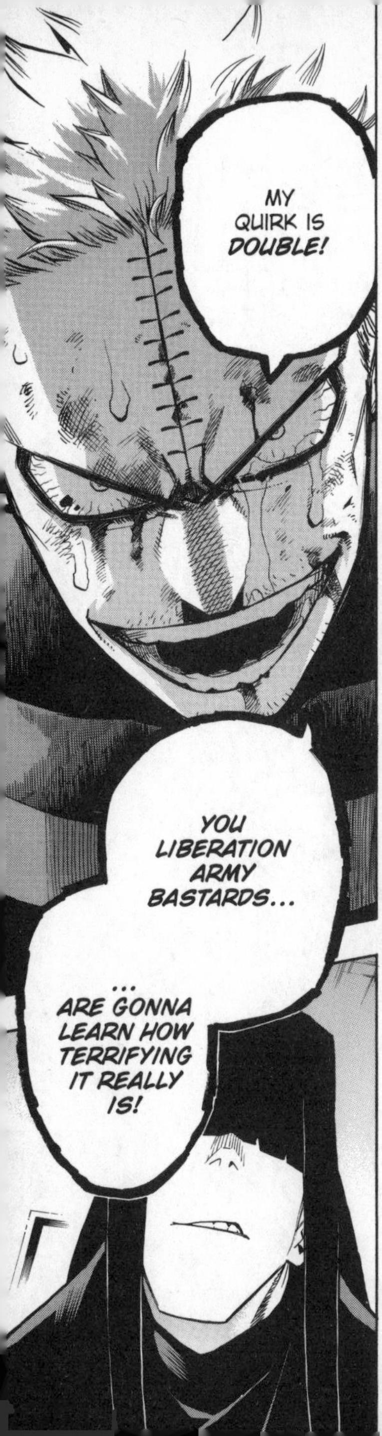
MY QUIRK IS DOUBLE!
YOU LIBERATION ARMY BASTARDS...
...ARE GONNA LEARN HOW TERRIFYING IT REALLY IS!

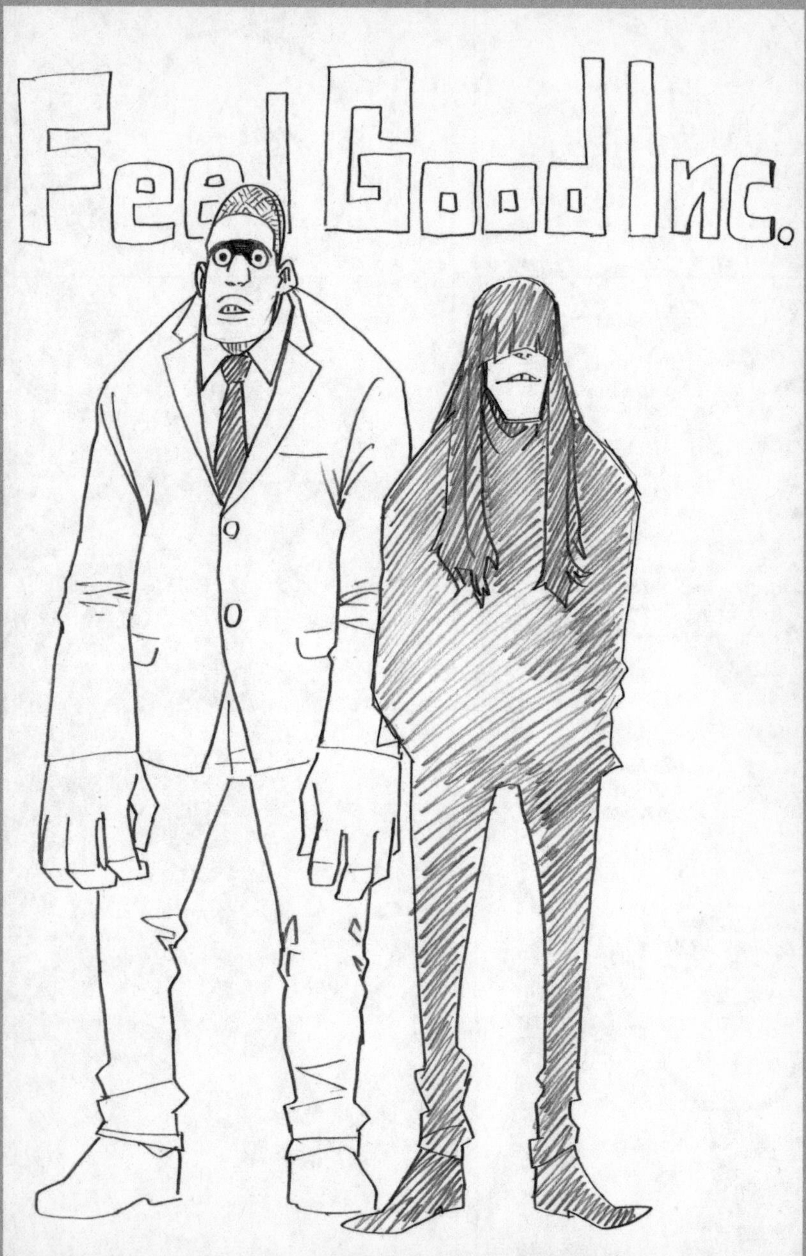
Feel Good Inc.

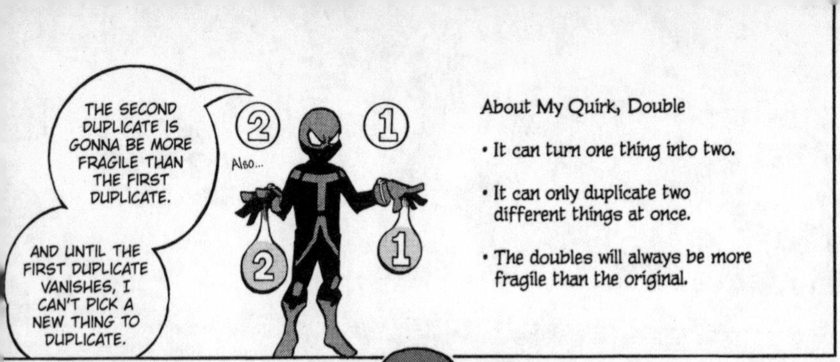
About My Quirk, Double
• It can turn one thing into two.
• It can only duplicate two different things at once.
• The doubles will always be more fragile than the original.
Also...
THE SECOND DUPLICATE IS GONNA BE MORE FRAGILE THAN THE FIRST DUPLICATE.
AND UNTIL THE FIRST DUPLICATE VANISHES, I CAN'T PICK A NEW THING TO DUPLICATE.

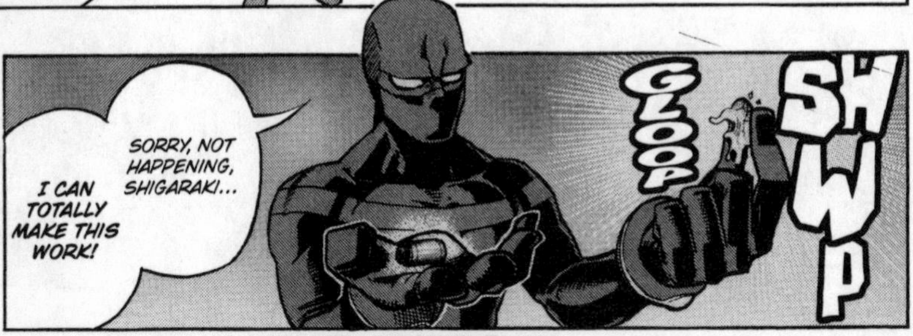
SHWP
GLOOP
SORRY, NOT HAPPENING, SHIGARAKI...
I CAN TOTALLY MAKE THIS WORK!

No. 230 - Sad Man's Parade

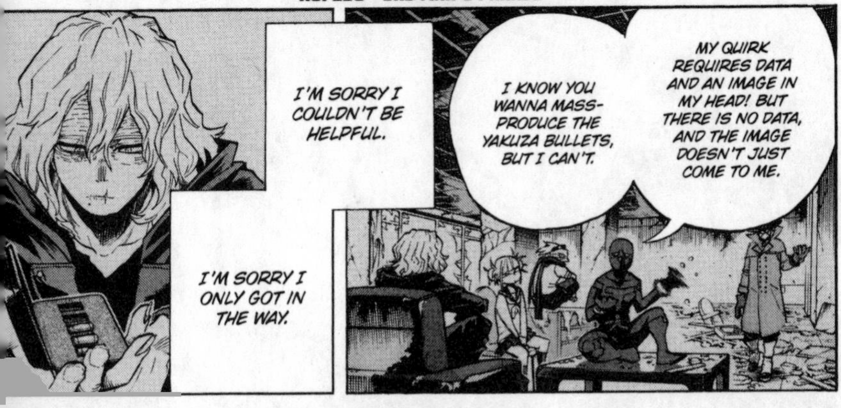
I KNOW YOU WANNA MASS-PRODUCE THE YAKUZA BULLETS, BUT I CAN'T.
MY QUIRK REQUIRES DATA AND AN IMAGE IN MY HEAD! BUT THERE IS NO DATA, AND THE IMAGE DOESN'T JUST COME TO ME.
I'M SORRY I COULDN'T BE HELPFUL.
I'M SORRY I ONLY GOT IN THE WAY.

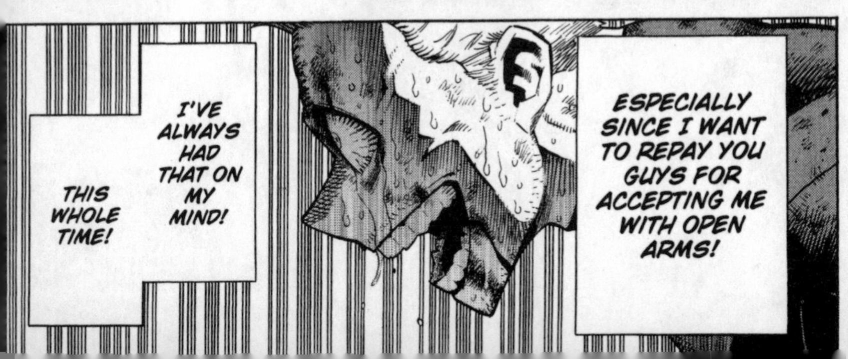
ESPECIALLY SINCE I WANT TO REPAY YOU GUYS FOR ACCEPTING ME WITH OPEN ARMS!
I'VE ALWAYS HAD THAT ON MY MIND!
THIS WHOLE TIME!

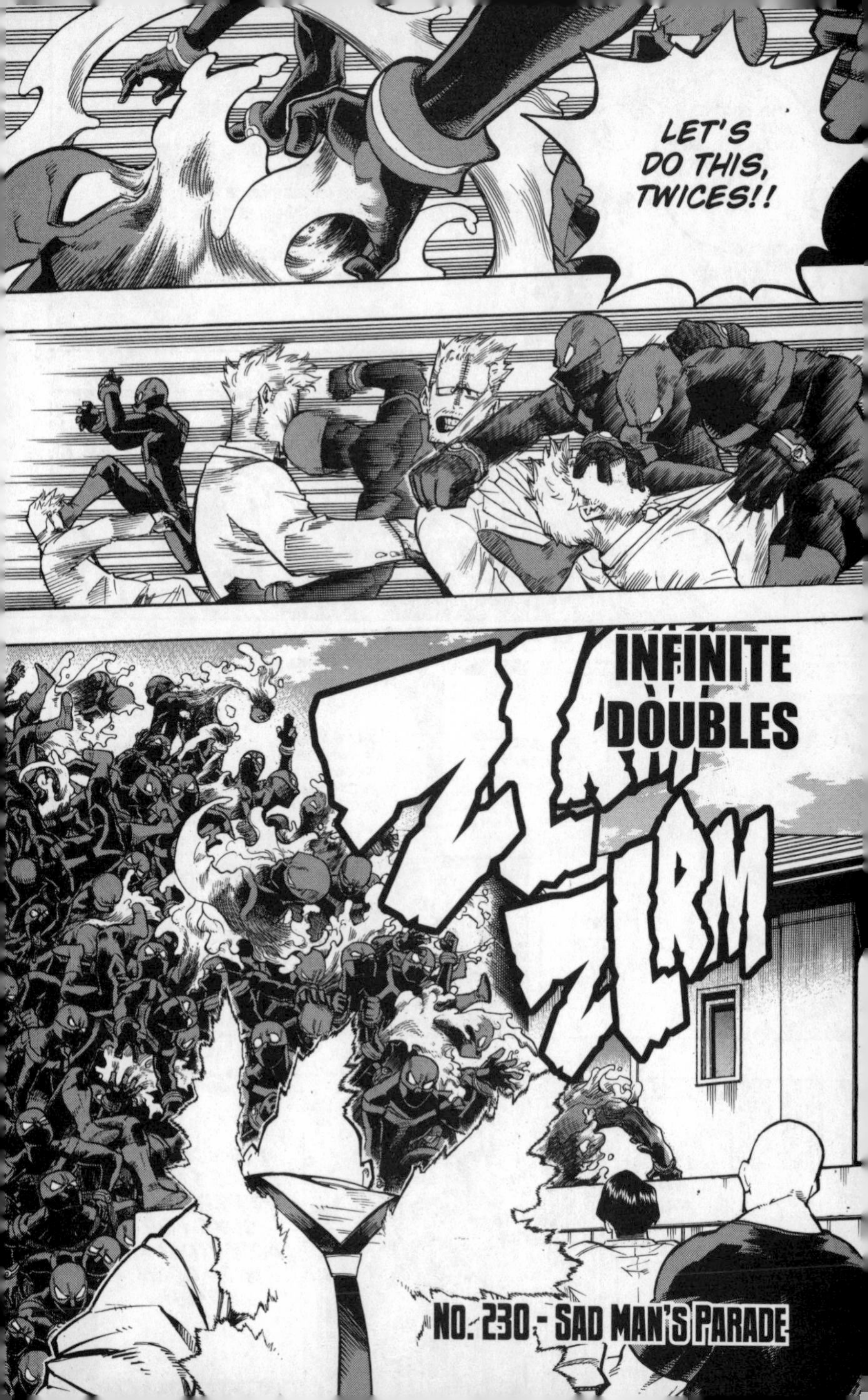
LET'S DO THIS, TWICES!!
INFINITE DOUBLES
ZRRM
NO. 230 - SAD MAN'S PARADE

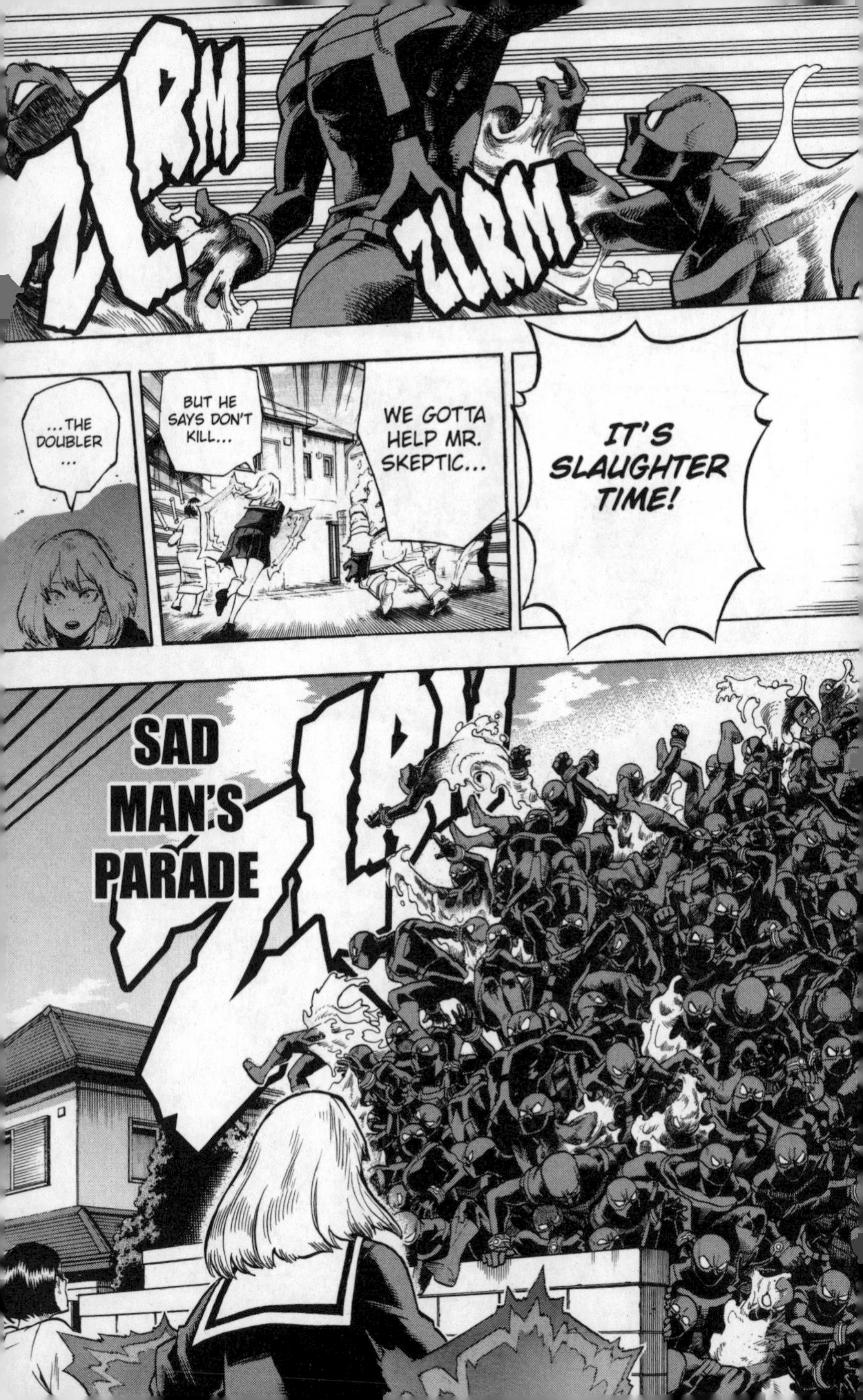
ZLRM
ZLRM
IT'S SLAUGHTER TIME!
WE GOTTA HELP MR. SKEPTIC...
BUT HE SAYS DON'T KILL...
...THE DOUBLER ...
SAD MAN'S PARADE

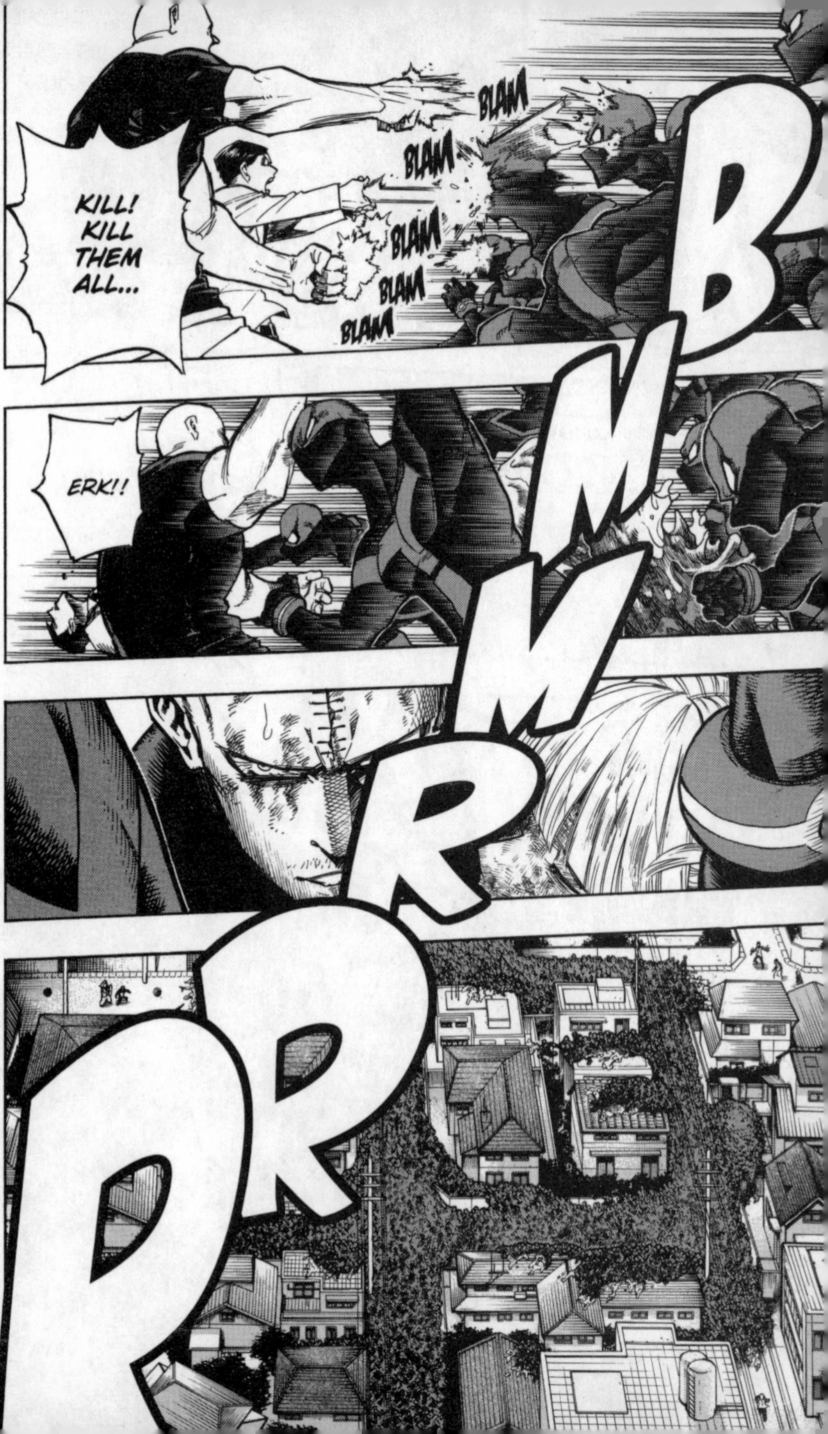
BLAM
BLAM
BLAM
BLAM
BLAM
KILL! KILL THEM ALL...
ERK!!
BMMMRR

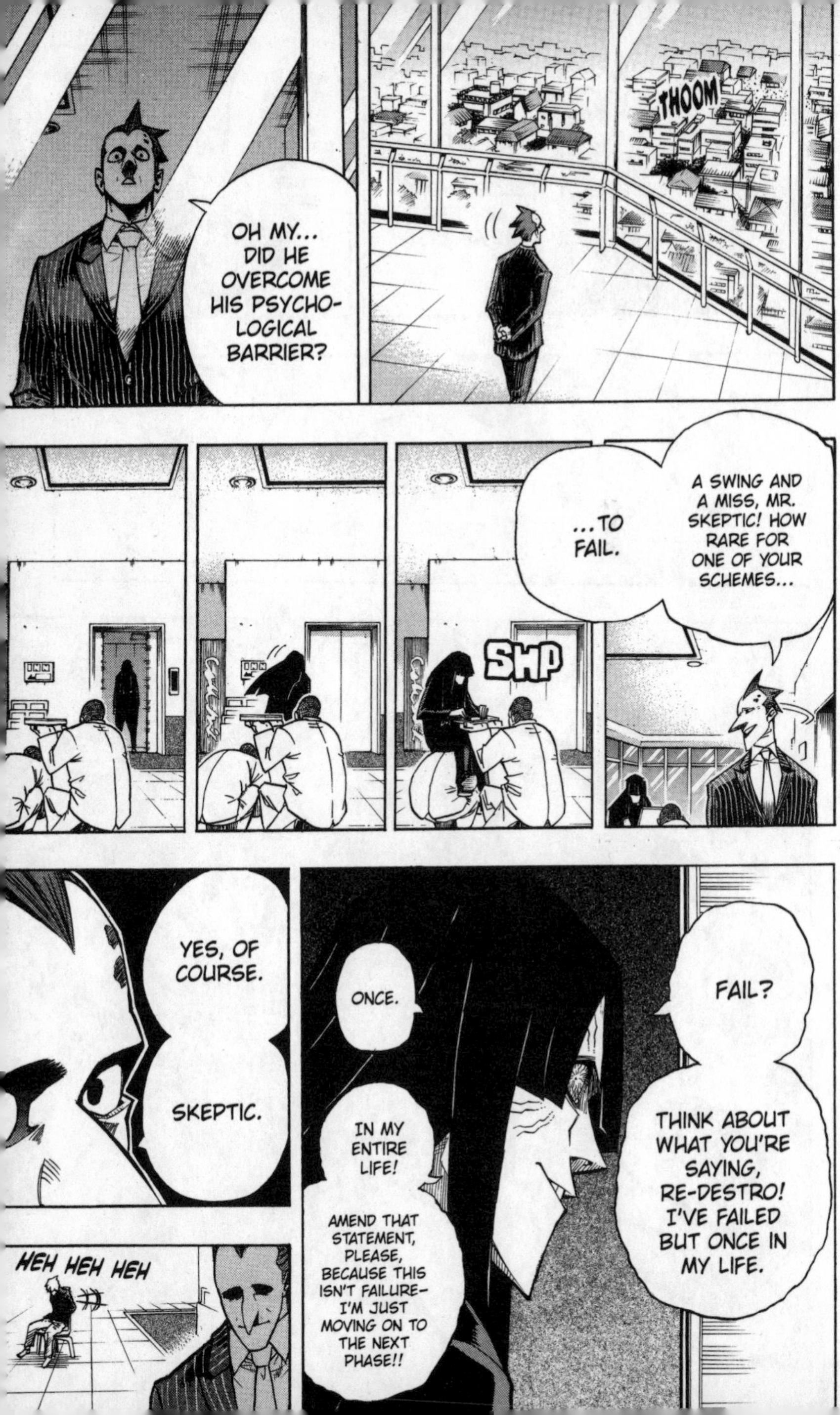
THOOM
OH MY... DID HE OVERCOME HIS PSYCHO-LOGICAL BARRIER?
A SWING AND A MISS, MR. SKEPTIC! HOW RARE FOR ONE OF YOUR SCHEMES...
...TO FAIL.
SHP
FAIL?
THINK ABOUT WHAT YOU'RE SAYING, RE-DESTRO! I'VE FAILED BUT ONCE IN MY LIFE.
ONCE.
IN MY ENTIRE LIFE!
AMEND THAT STATEMENT, PLEASE, BECAUSE THIS ISN'T FAILURE– I'M JUST MOVING ON TO THE NEXT PHASE!!
YES, OF COURSE.
SKEPTIC.
HEH HEH HEH

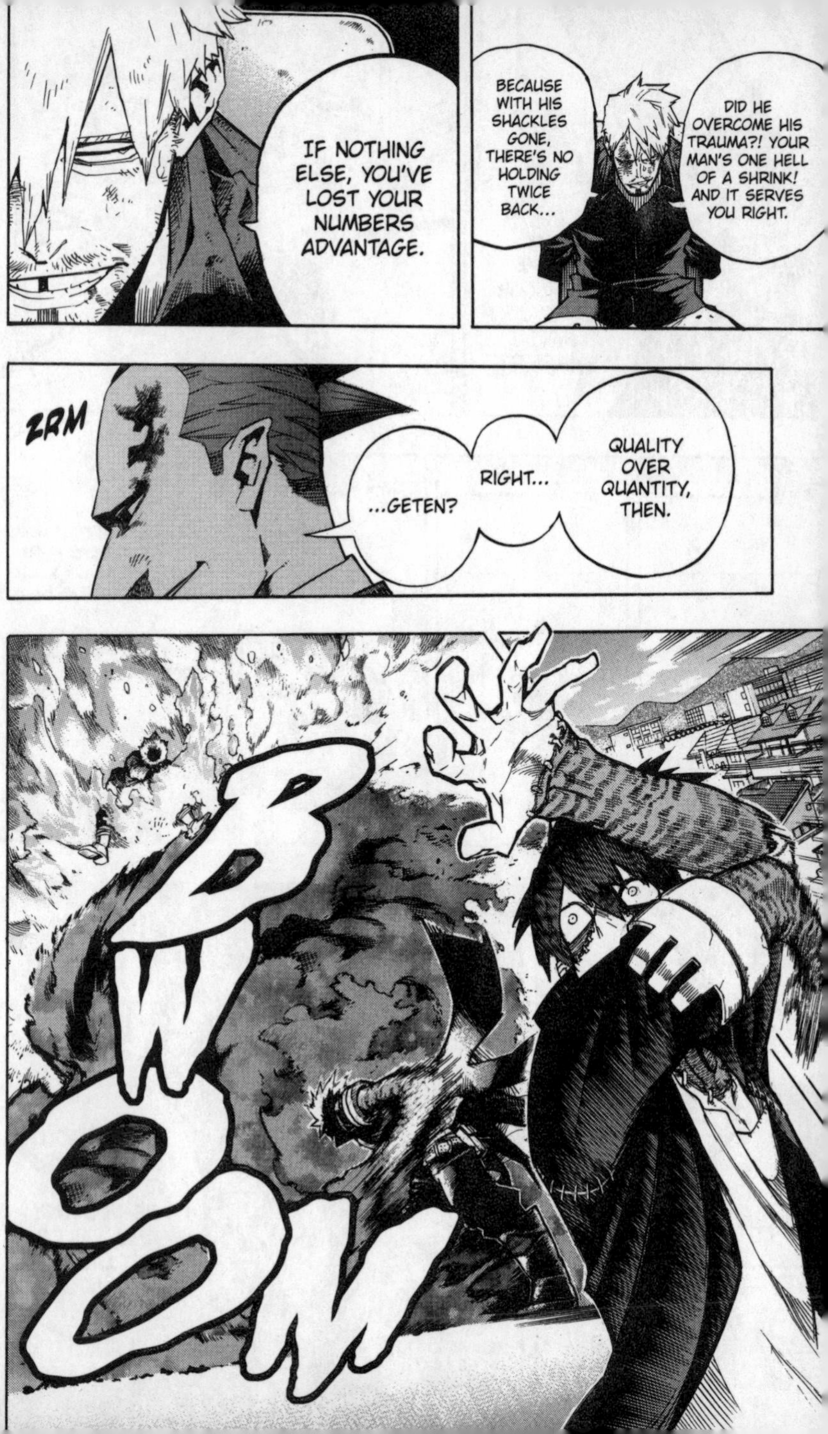

DID HE OVERCOME HIS TRAUMA?! YOUR MAN'S ONE HELL OF A SHRINK! AND IT SERVES YOU RIGHT.
BECAUSE WITH HIS SHACKLES GONE, THERE'S NO HOLDING TWICE BACK...
IF NOTHING ELSE, YOU'VE LOST YOUR NUMBERS ADVANTAGE.
QUALITY OVER QUANTITY, THEN.
RIGHT...
...GETEN?
ZRM
BWOOM

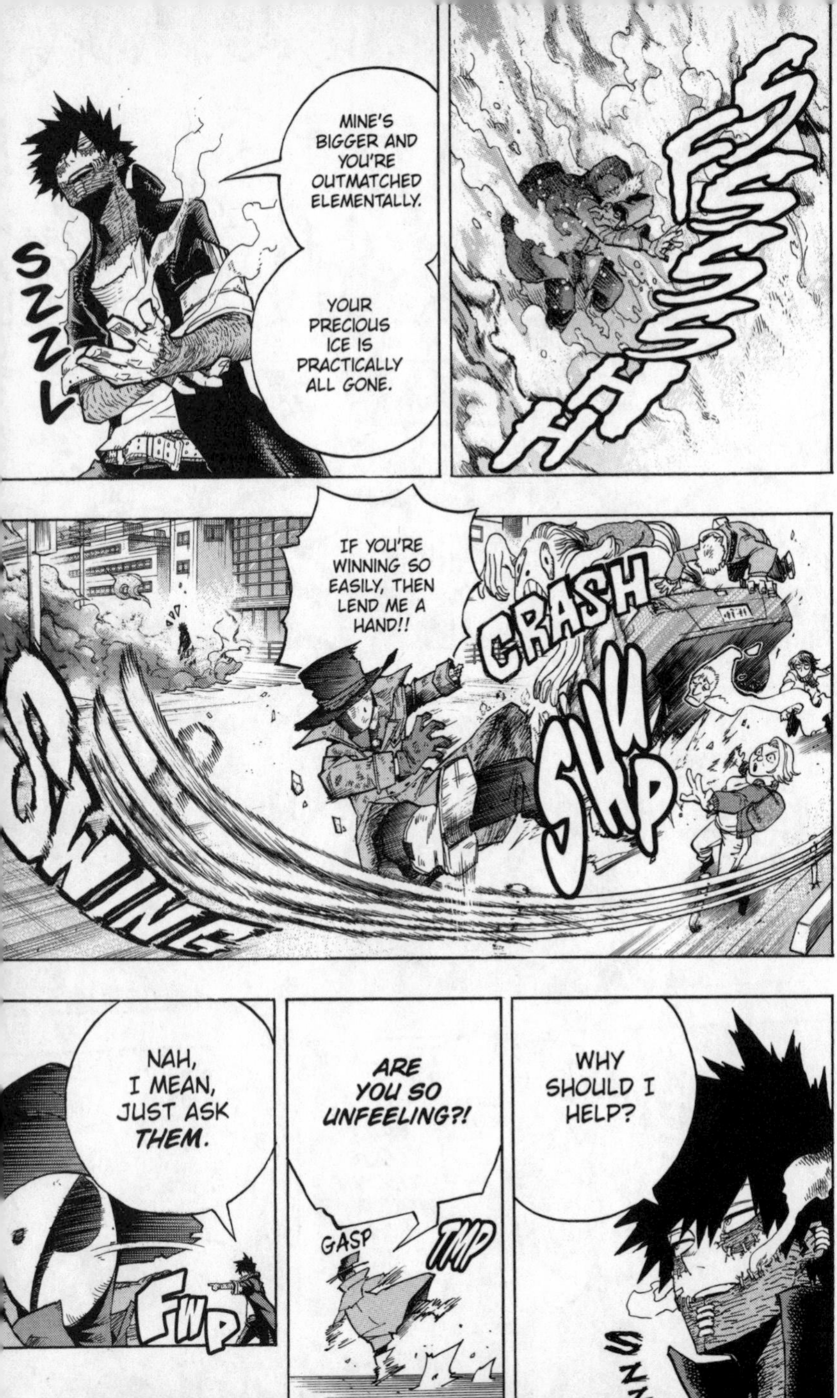
FSSSHH
SZZZL
MINE'S BIGGER AND YOU'RE OUTMATCHED ELEMENTALLY.
YOUR PRECIOUS ICE IS PRACTICALLY ALL GONE.
CRASH
IF YOU'RE WINNING SO EASILY, THEN LEND ME A HAND!!
SHUHP
SWING
WHY SHOULD I HELP?
SZZZL
ARE YOU SO UNFEELING?!
TMP
GASP
NAH, I MEAN, JUST ASK THEM.
FWP

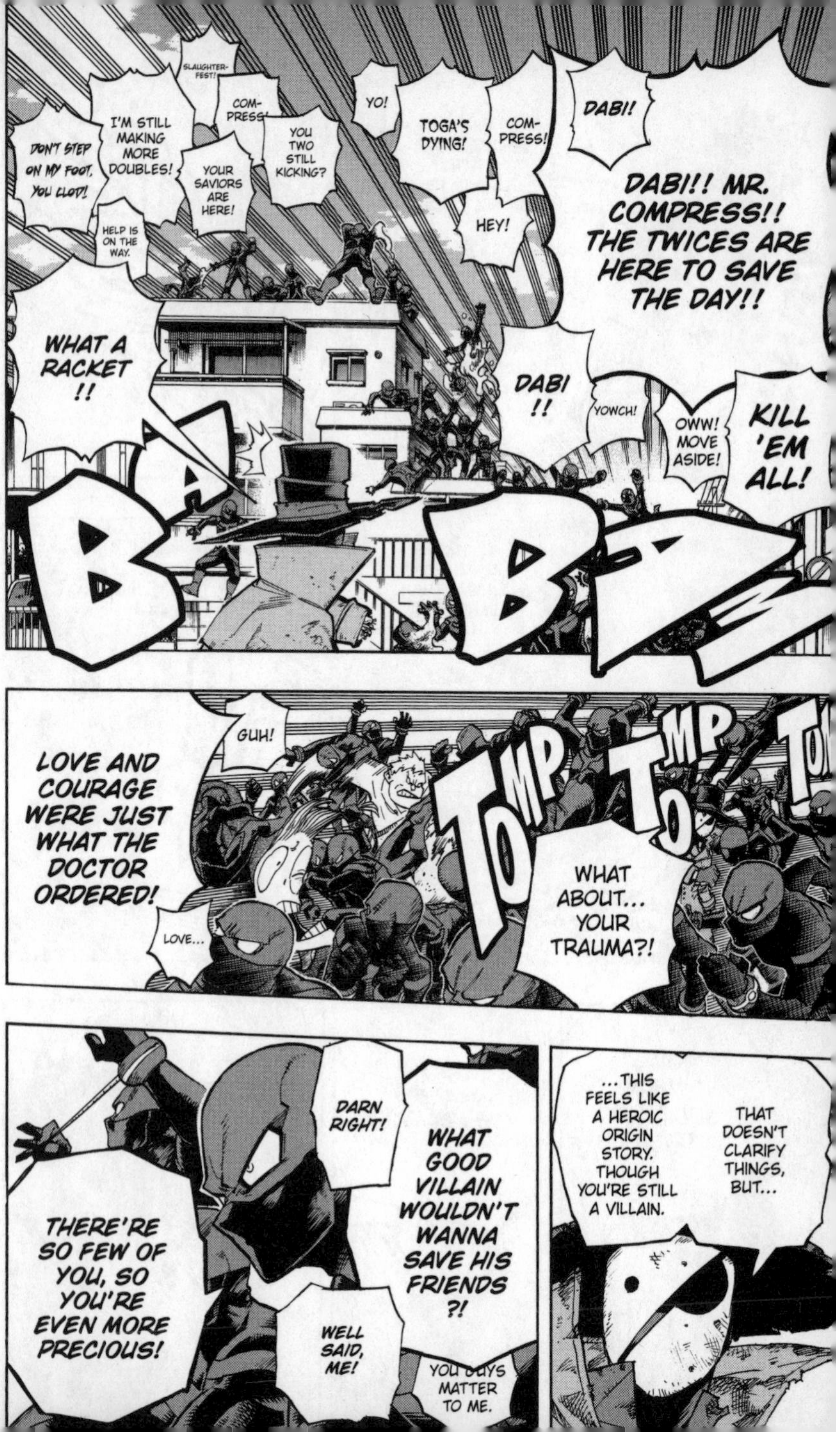
DABI!
DABI!! MR. COMPRESS!! THE TWICES ARE HERE TO SAVE THE DAY!!
COM-PRESS!
TOGA'S DYING!
HEY!
YO!
YOU TWO STILL KICKING?
COM-PRESS!
SLAUGHTER-FEST!
YOUR SAVIORS ARE HERE!
I'M STILL MAKING MORE DOUBLES!
DON'T STEP ON MY FOOT, YOU CLOD!
HELP IS ON THE WAY.
KILL 'EM ALL!
OWW! MOVE ASIDE!
YOWCH!
DABI!!
WHAT A RACKET!!
TOMP TOMP
WHAT ABOUT... YOUR TRAUMA?!
GUH!
LOVE...
LOVE AND COURAGE WERE JUST WHAT THE DOCTOR ORDERED!
THAT DOESN'T CLARIFY THINGS, BUT...
...THIS FEELS LIKE A HEROIC ORIGIN STORY. THOUGH YOU'RE STILL A VILLAIN.
DARN RIGHT!
WHAT GOOD VILLAIN WOULDN'T WANNA SAVE HIS FRIENDS?!
THERE'RE SO FEW OF YOU, SO YOU'RE EVEN MORE PRECIOUS!
WELL SAID, ME!
YOU GUYS MATTER TO ME.

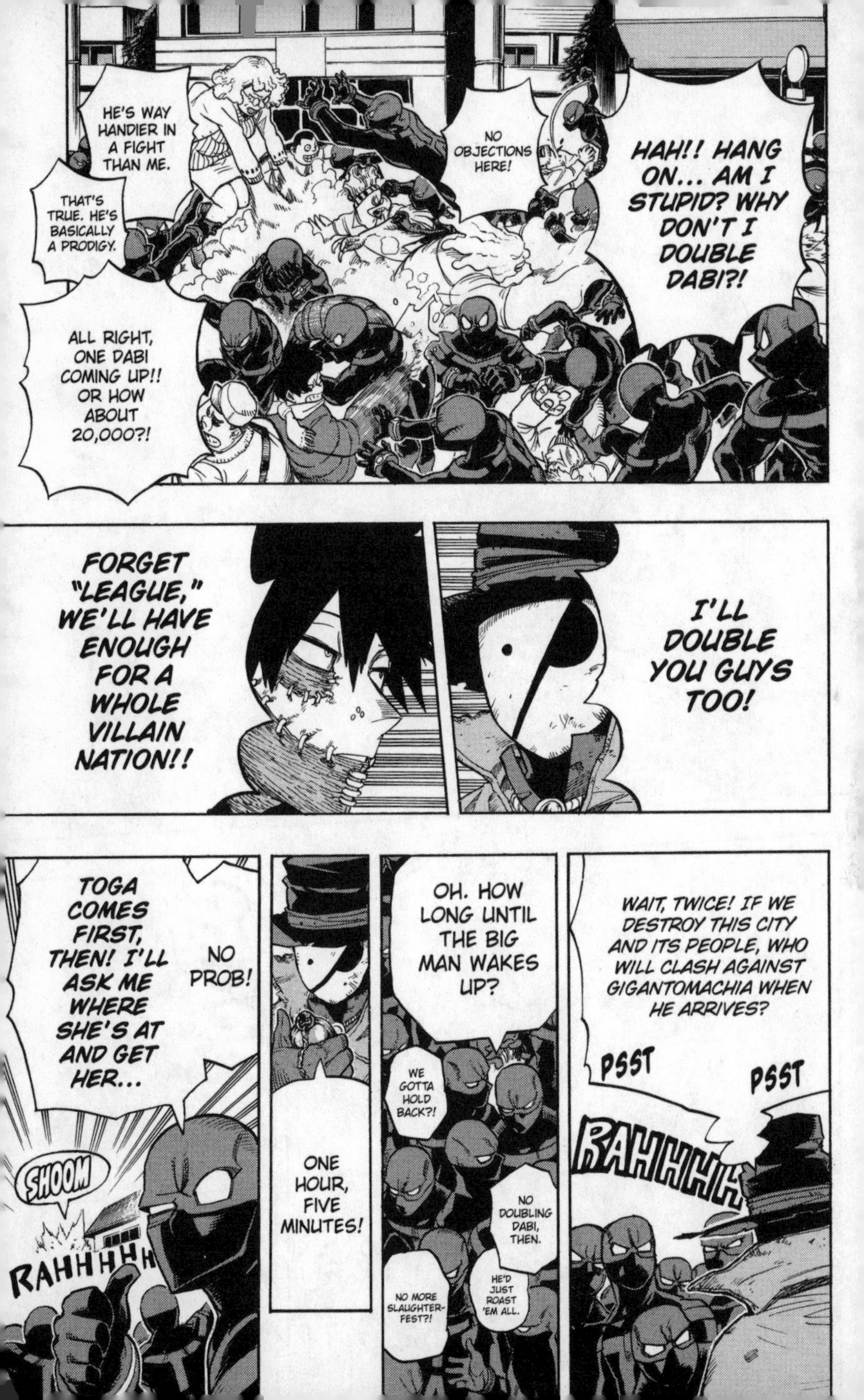
HAH!! HANG ON... AM I STUPID? WHY DON'T I DOUBLE DABI?!
NO OBJECTIONS HERE!
HE'S WAY HANDIER IN A FIGHT THAN ME.
THAT'S TRUE. HE'S BASICALLY A PRODIGY.
ALL RIGHT, ONE DABI COMING UP!! OR HOW ABOUT 20,000?!
I'LL DOUBLE YOU GUYS TOO!
FORGET "LEAGUE," WE'LL HAVE ENOUGH FOR A WHOLE VILLAIN NATION!!
WAIT, TWICE! IF WE DESTROY THIS CITY AND ITS PEOPLE, WHO WILL CLASH AGAINST GIGANTOMACHIA WHEN HE ARRIVES?
PSST
PSST
RAHHHHH
OH. HOW LONG UNTIL THE BIG MAN WAKES UP?
WE GOTTA HOLD BACK?!
NO DOUBLING DABI, THEN.
HE'D JUST ROAST 'EM ALL.
NO MORE SLAUGHTER-FEST?!
ONE HOUR, FIVE MINUTES!
NO PROB!
TOGA COMES FIRST, THEN! I'LL ASK ME WHERE SHE'S AT AND GET HER...
SHOOM
RAHHHHH

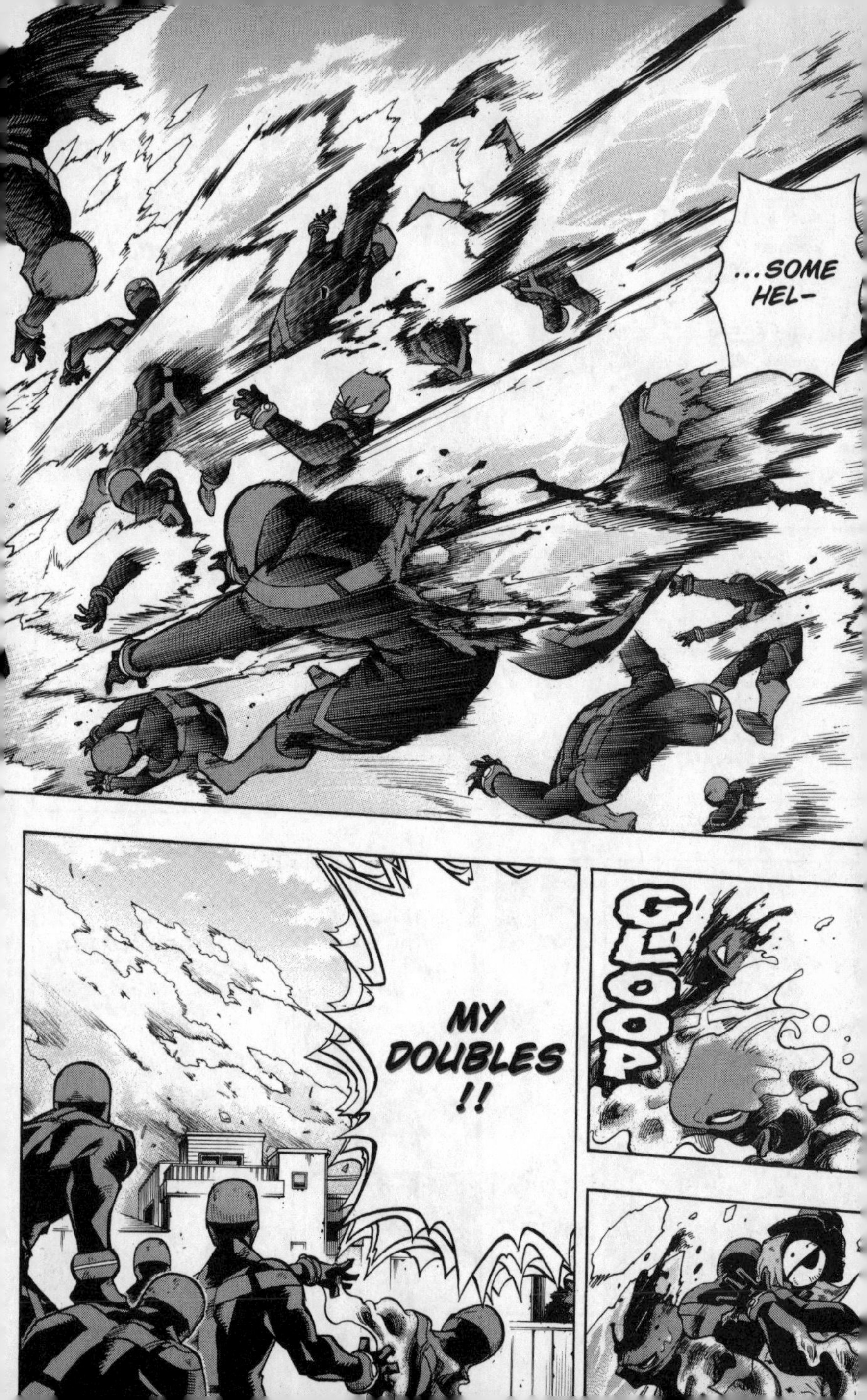
...SOME HEL-
GLOOP
MY DOUBLES !!

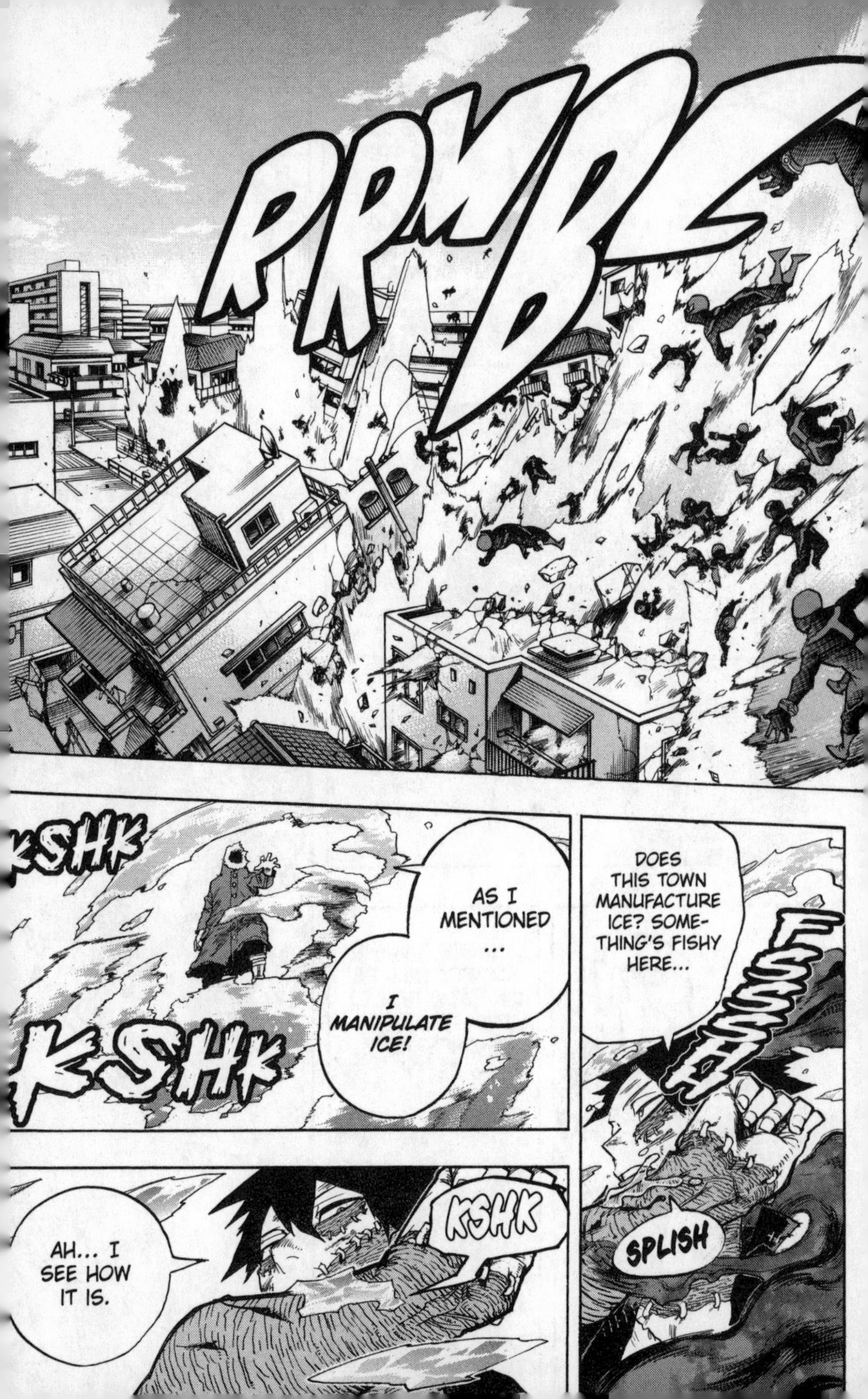
RRMBL
DOES THIS TOWN MANUFACTURE ICE? SOME-THING'S FISHY HERE...
FSSSH
SPLISH
KSHK
AS I MENTIONED ...
I MANIPULATE ICE!
KSHK
KSHK
AH... I SEE HOW IT IS.

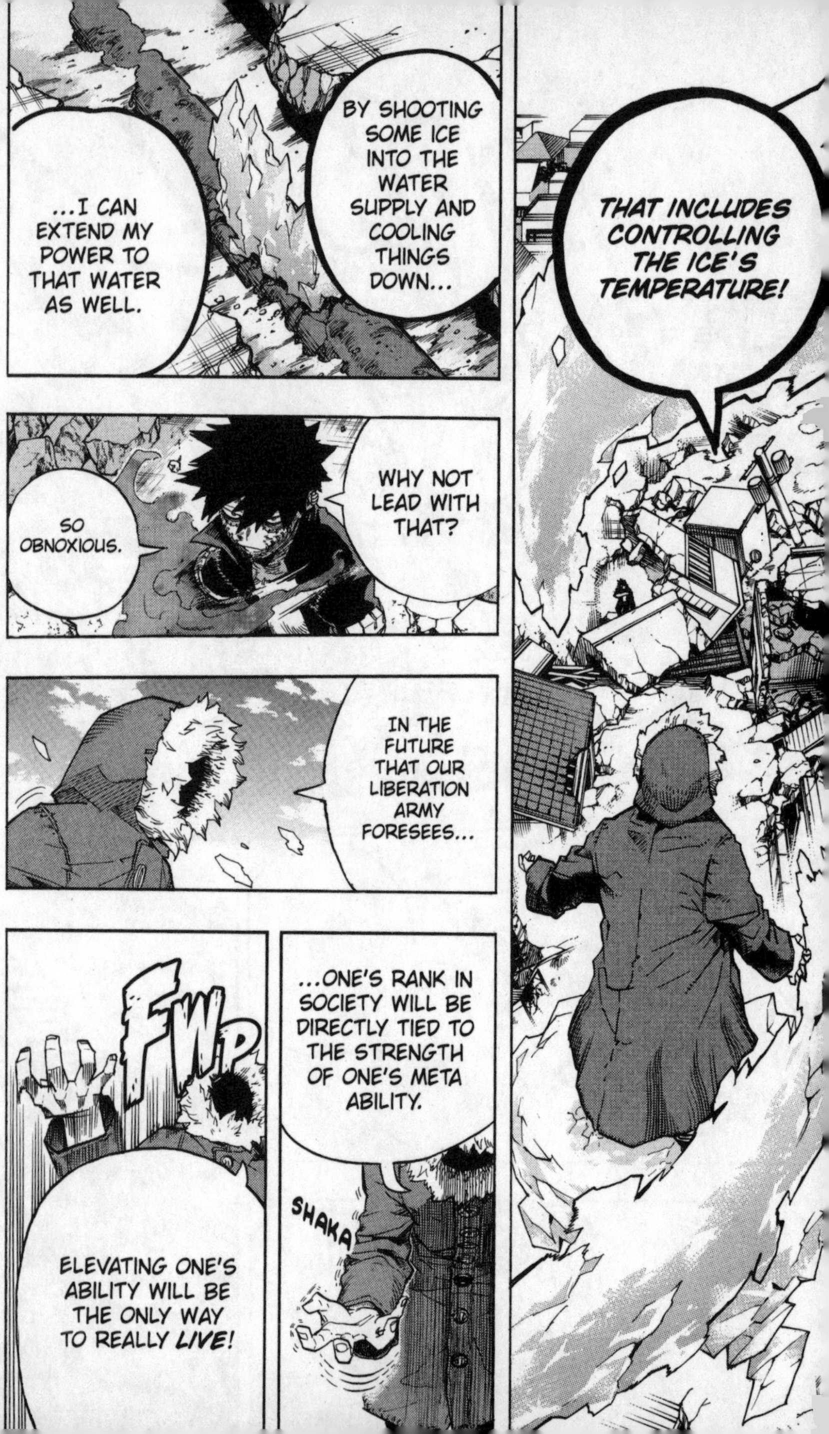
THAT INCLUDES CONTROLLING THE ICE'S TEMPERATURE!
BY SHOOTING SOME ICE INTO THE WATER SUPPLY AND COOLING THINGS DOWN...
...I CAN EXTEND MY POWER TO THAT WATER AS WELL.
WHY NOT LEAD WITH THAT?
SO OBNOXIOUS.
IN THE FUTURE THAT OUR LIBERATION ARMY FORESEES...
...ONE'S RANK IN SOCIETY WILL BE DIRECTLY TIED TO THE STRENGTH OF ONE'S META ABILITY.
SHAKA
FWP
ELEVATING ONE'S ABILITY WILL BE THE ONLY WAY TO REALLY *LIVE*!

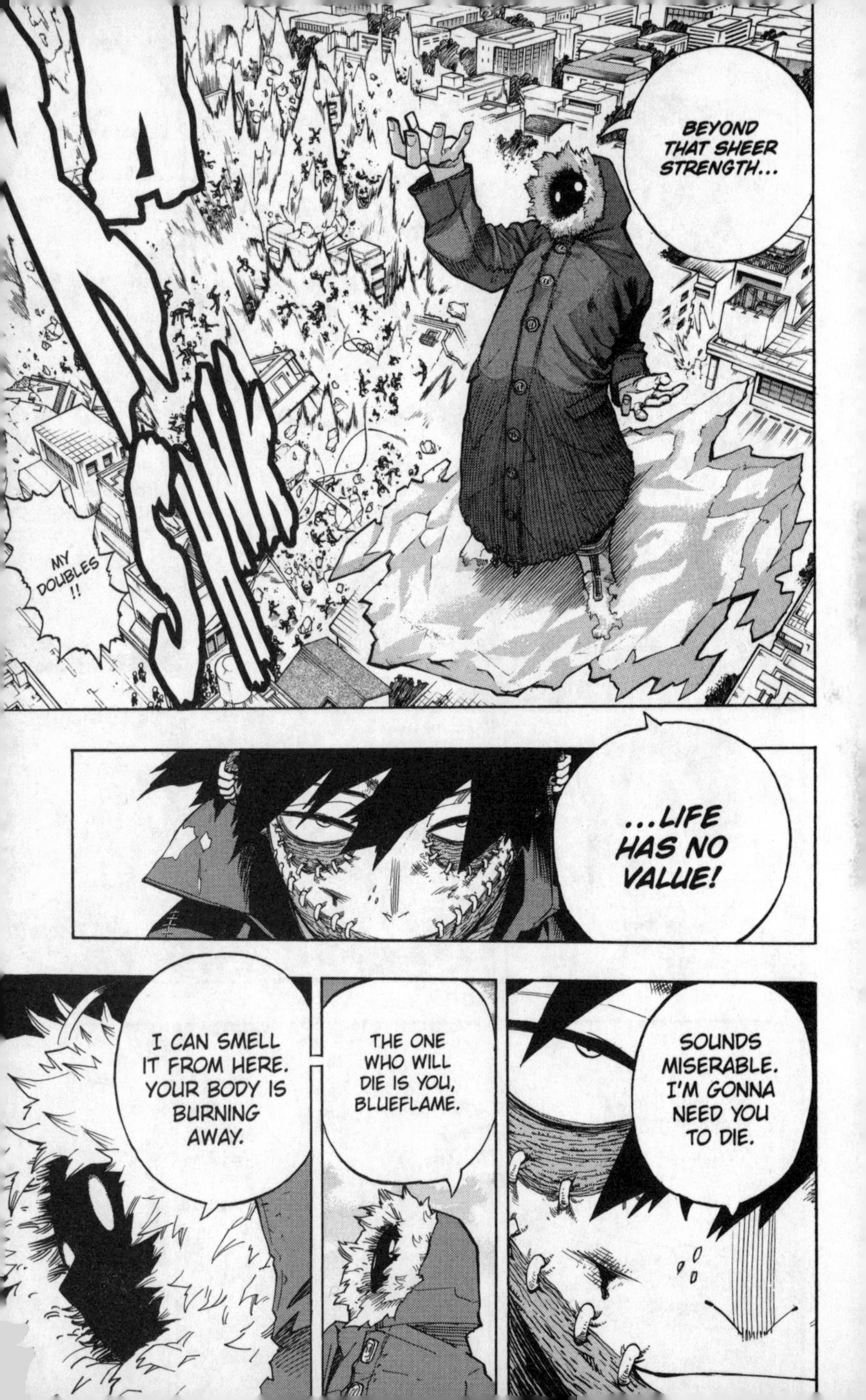
BEYOND THAT SHEER STRENGTH...
MY DOUBLES !!
...LIFE HAS NO VALUE!
SOUNDS MISERABLE. I'M GONNA NEED YOU TO DIE.
THE ONE WHO WILL DIE IS YOU, BLUEFLAME.
I CAN SMELL IT FROM HERE. YOUR BODY IS BURNING AWAY.

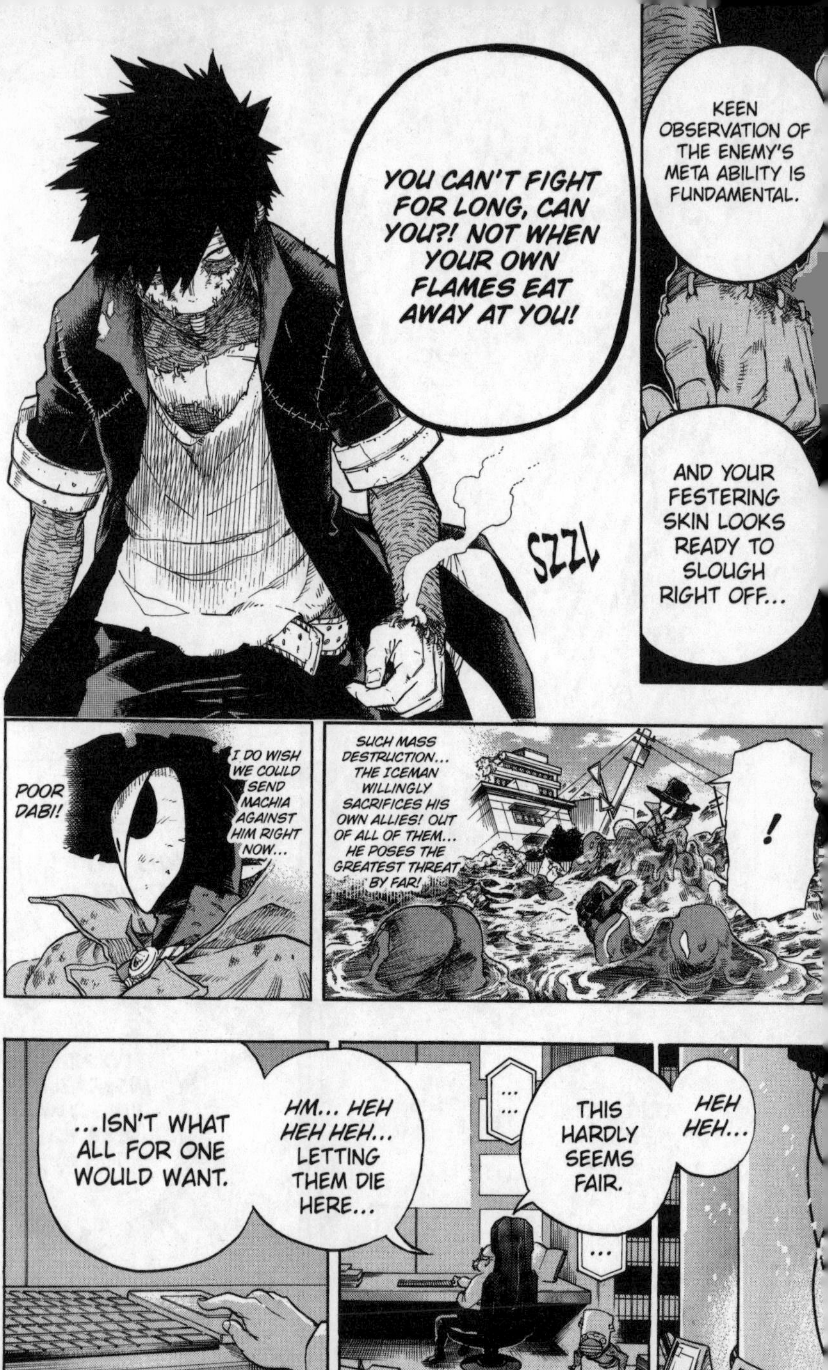
KEEN OBSERVATION OF THE ENEMY'S META ABILITY IS FUNDAMENTAL.
AND YOUR FESTERING SKIN LOOKS READY TO SLOUGH RIGHT OFF...
YOU CAN'T FIGHT FOR LONG, CAN YOU?! NOT WHEN YOUR OWN FLAMES EAT AWAY AT YOU!
SZZL
!
SUCH MASS DESTRUCTION... THE ICEMAN WILLINGLY SACRIFICES HIS OWN ALLIES! OUT OF ALL OF THEM... HE POSES THE GREATEST THREAT BY FAR!
I DO WISH WE COULD SEND MACHIA AGAINST HIM RIGHT NOW...
POOR DABI!
HEH HEH...
THIS HARDLY SEEMS FAIR.
...
... ...
HM... HEH HEH HEH... LETTING THEM DIE HERE...
...ISN'T WHAT ALL FOR ONE WOULD WANT.

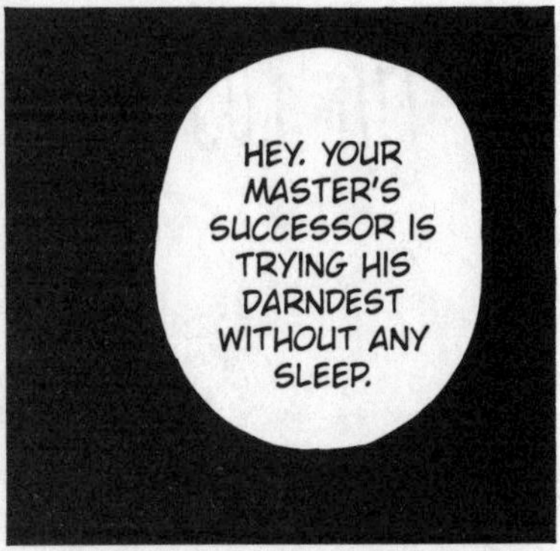
HEY. YOUR MASTER'S SUCCESSOR IS TRYING HIS DARNDEST WITHOUT ANY SLEEP.
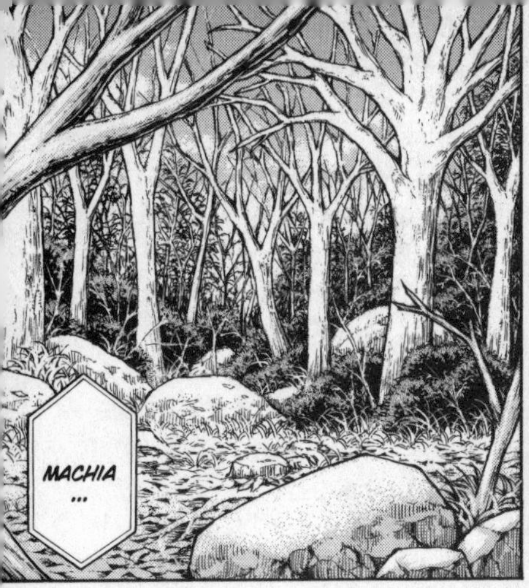
MACHIA ...
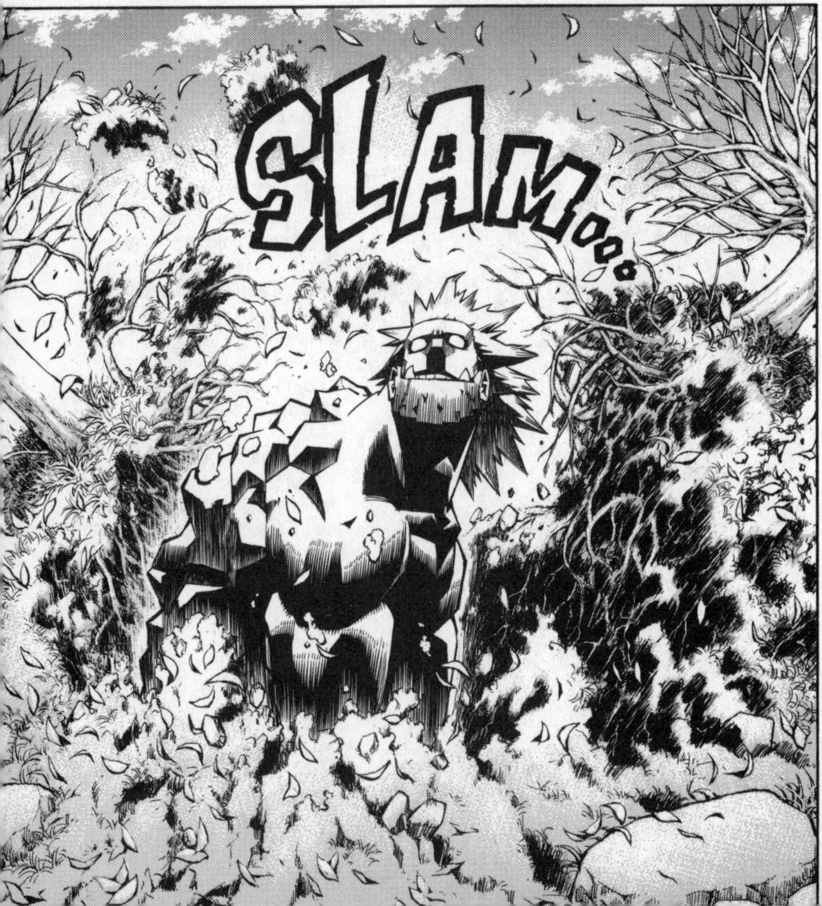
SLAM...

THE COSTUME

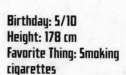
Birthday: 5/10
Height: 178 cm
Favorite Thing: Smoking cigarettes

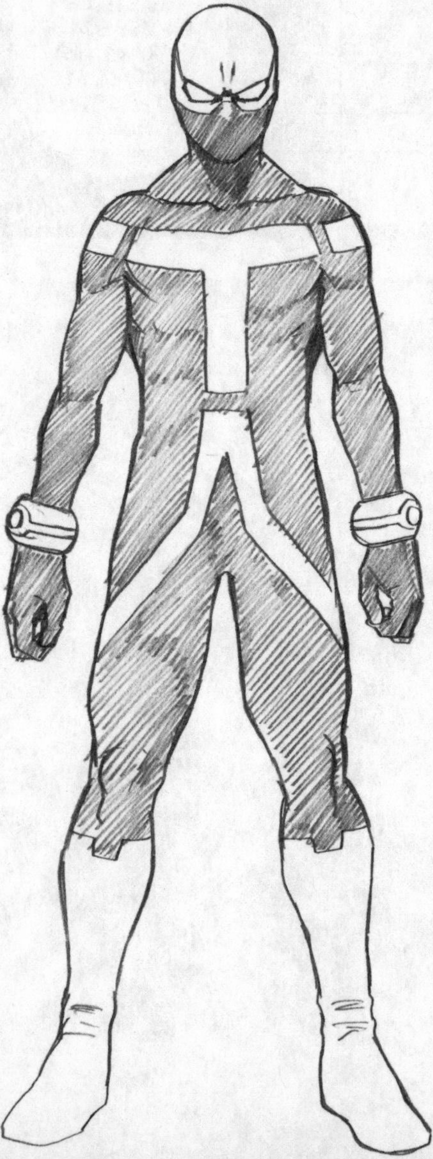

THE SUPPLEMENT

Giran placed a special order for this costume. It's tough, and it's easy on the skin. For Bubaigawara—who couldn't maintain an ordinary life and ended up losing all the money he stole—this was a fancy item he never could've afforded on his own.

At the time, Giran just said, "I'll put it on your tab." He still demanded his intermediary fee as a broker, though.

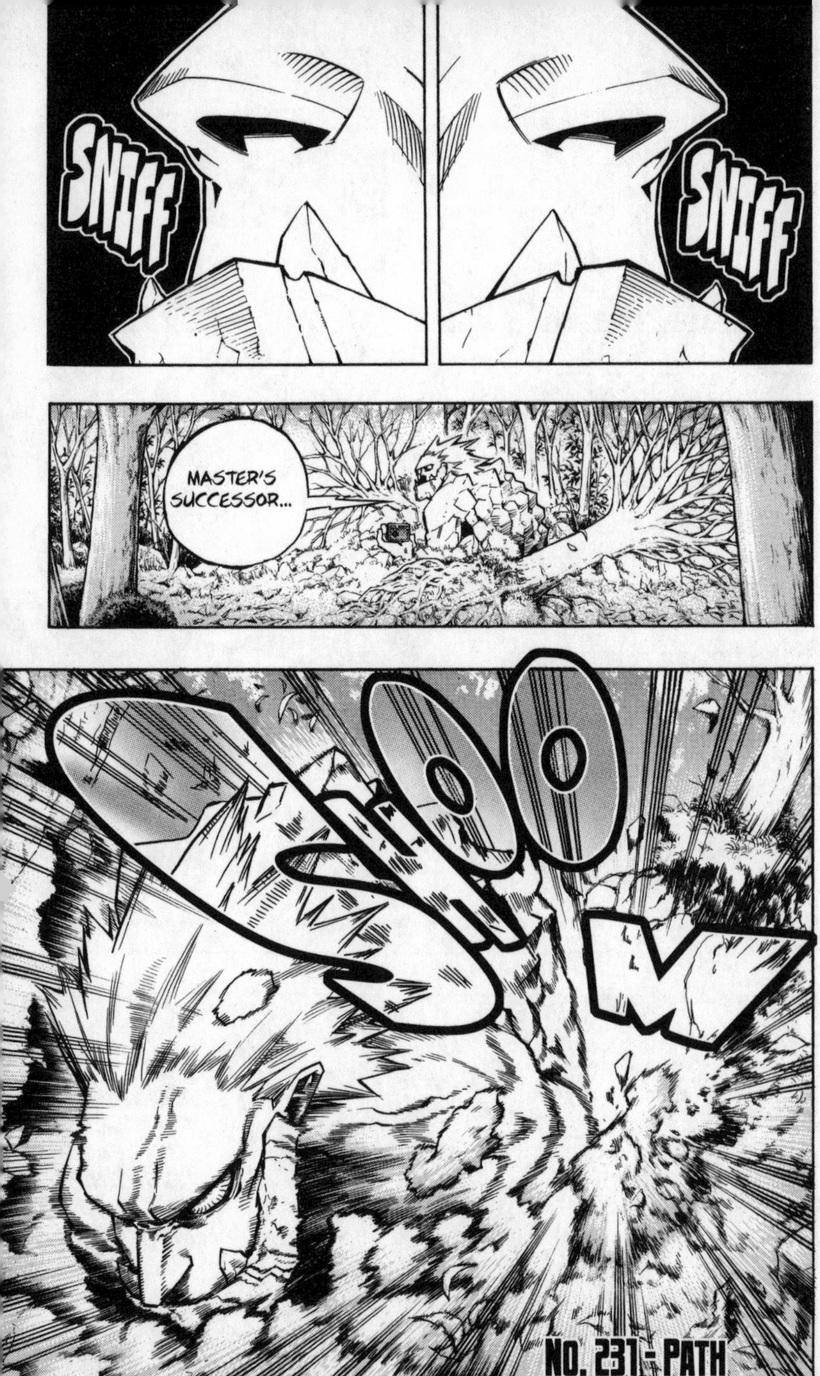
SNIFF
SNIFF
MASTER'S SUCCESSOR...
SHOOM
NO. 231 - PATH

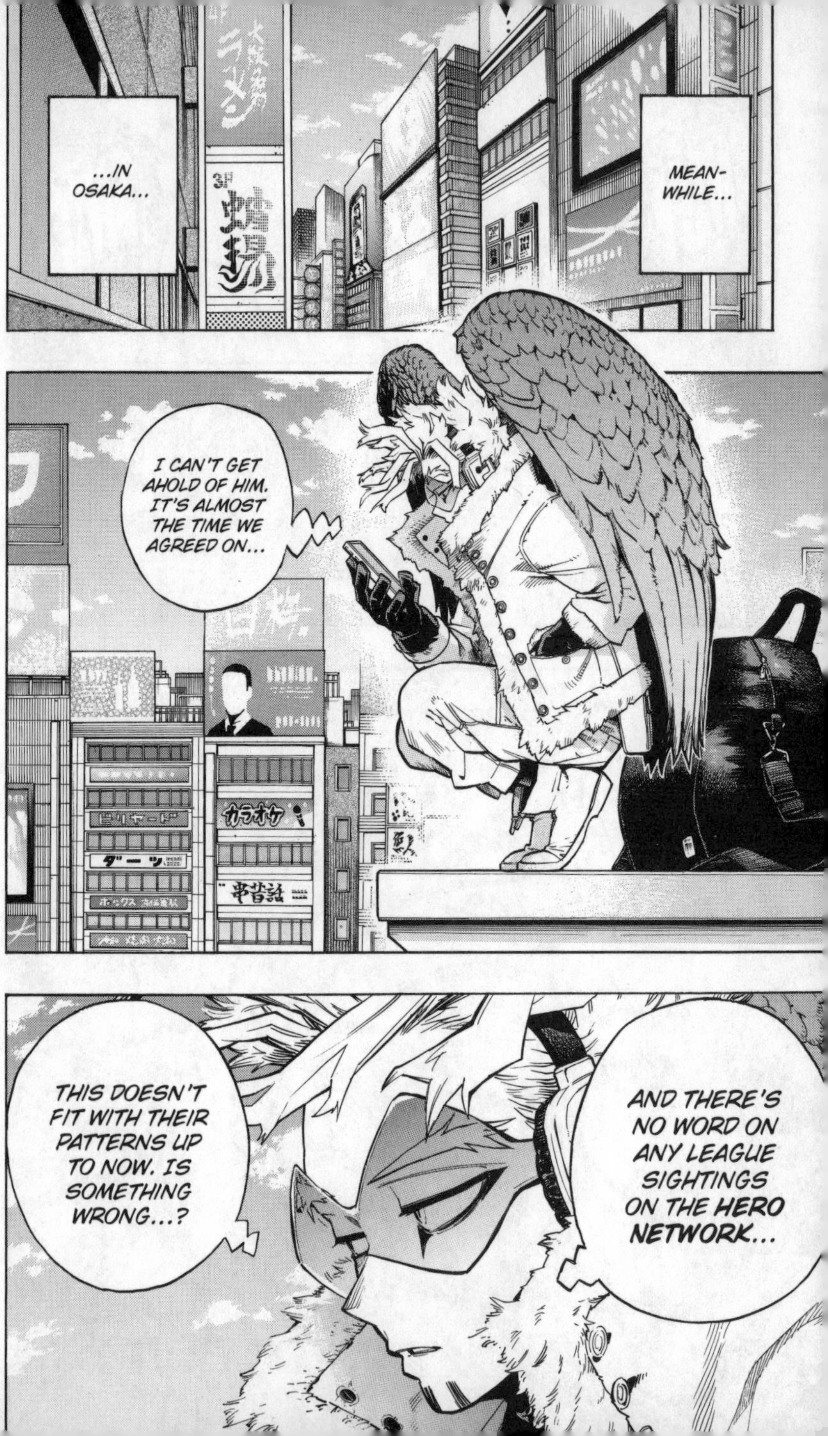
MEAN-WHILE...
...IN OSAKA...
I CAN'T GET AHOLD OF HIM. IT'S ALMOST THE TIME WE AGREED ON...
カラオケ
ダーツ
AND THERE'S NO WORD ON ANY LEAGUE SIGHTINGS ON THE HERO NETWORK...
THIS DOESN'T FIT WITH THEIR PATTERNS UP TO NOW. IS SOMETHING WRONG...?

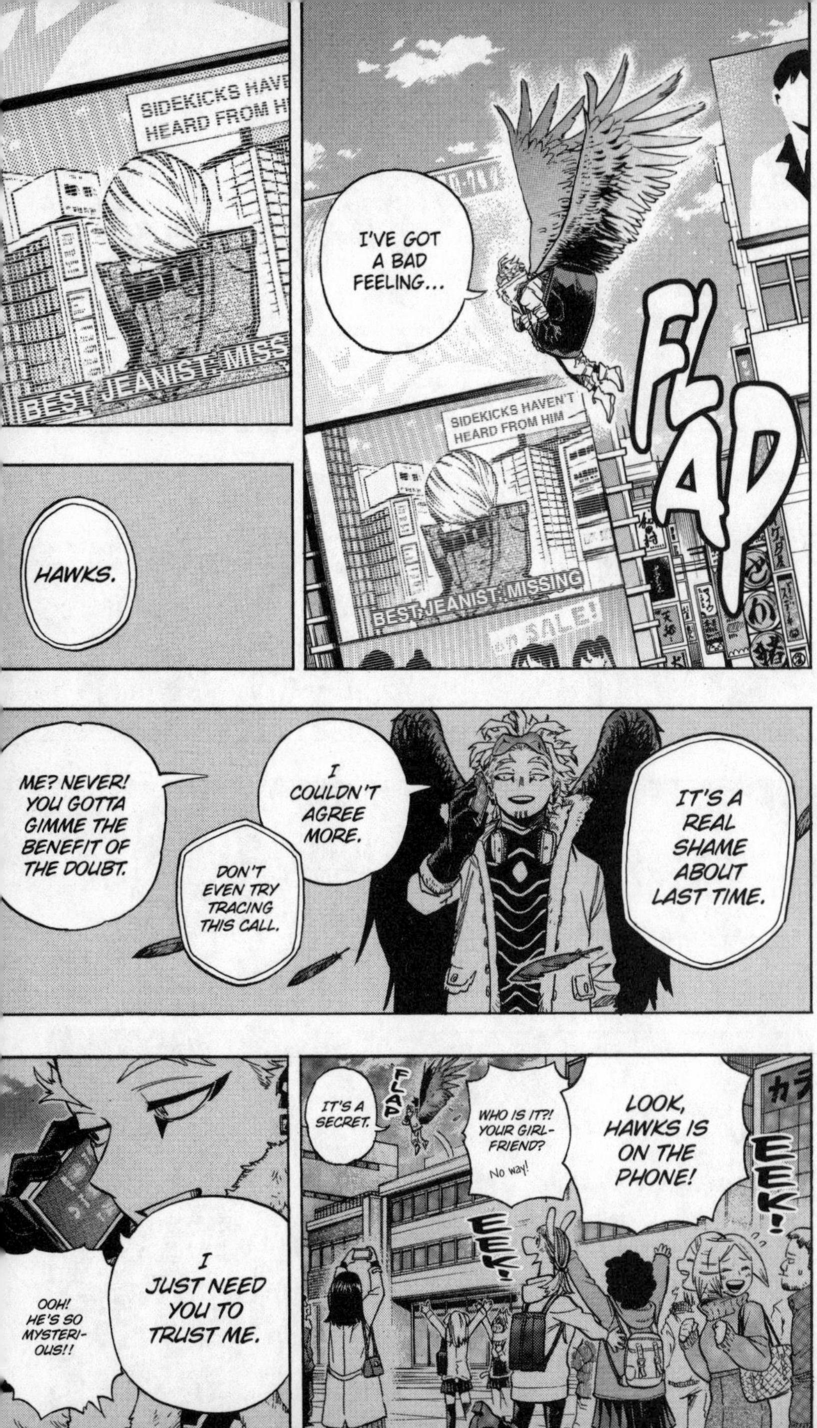
I'VE GOT A BAD FEELING...
FLAP
SIDEKICKS HAVEN'T HEARD FROM HIM
BEST JEANIST: MISSING
SALE!
SIDEKICKS HAVE
HEARD FROM HI
BEST JEANIST: MISS
HAWKS.
IT'S A REAL SHAME ABOUT LAST TIME.
I COULDN'T AGREE MORE.
DON'T EVEN TRY TRACING THIS CALL.
ME? NEVER! YOU GOTTA GIMME THE BENEFIT OF THE DOUBT.
EEK!
LOOK, HAWKS IS ON THE PHONE!
WHO IS IT?! YOUR GIRLFRIEND?
No way!
EEK!
FLAP
IT'S A SECRET.
I JUST NEED YOU TO TRUST ME.
OOH! HE'S SO MYSTERIOUS!!

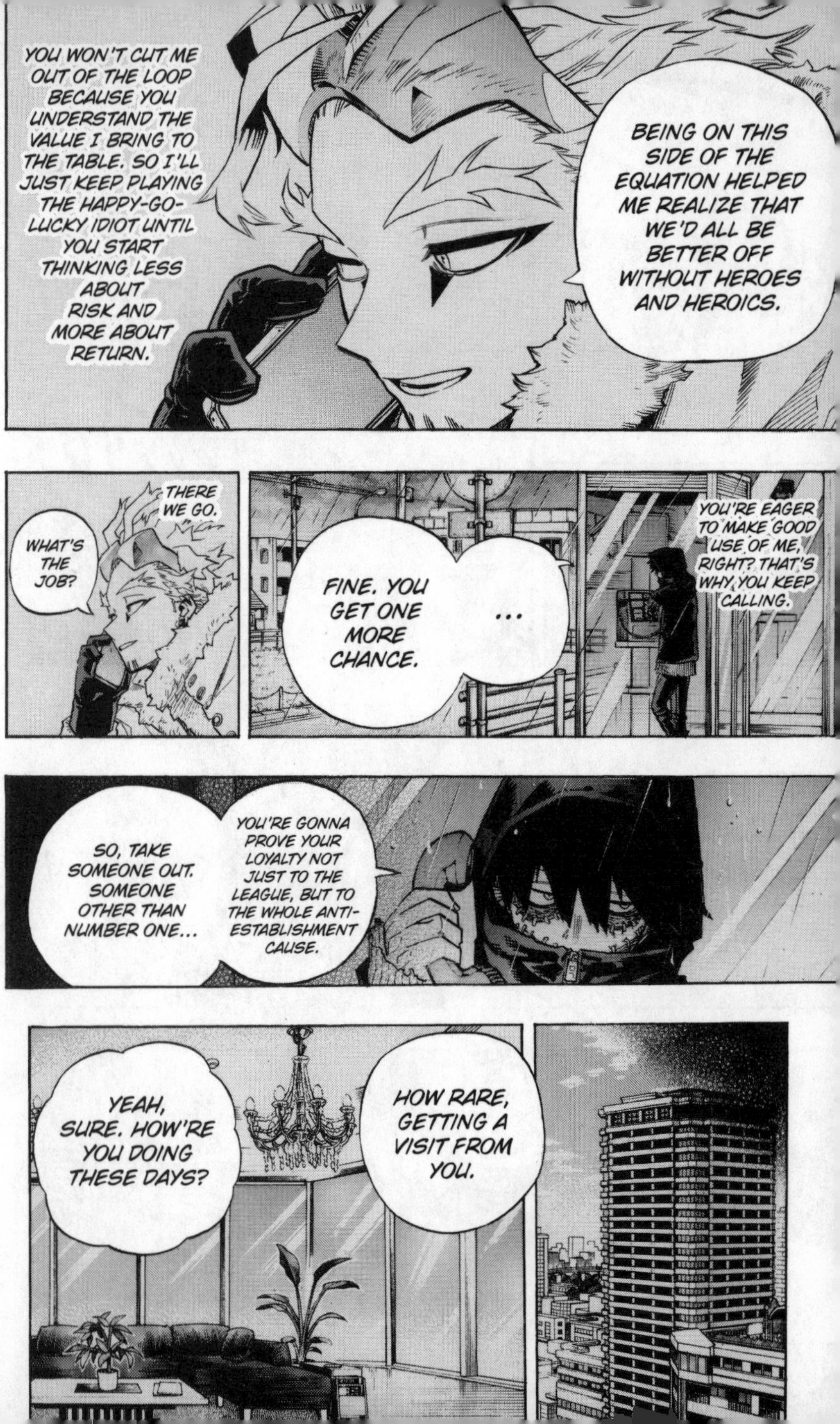
BEING ON THIS SIDE OF THE EQUATION HELPED ME REALIZE THAT WE'D ALL BE BETTER OFF WITHOUT HEROES AND HEROICS.
YOU WON'T CUT ME OUT OF THE LOOP BECAUSE YOU UNDERSTAND THE VALUE I BRING TO THE TABLE. SO I'LL JUST KEEP PLAYING THE HAPPY-GO-LUCKY IDIOT UNTIL YOU START THINKING LESS ABOUT RISK AND MORE ABOUT RETURN.
YOU'RE EAGER TO MAKE GOOD USE OF ME, RIGHT? THAT'S WHY YOU KEEP CALLING.
...
FINE. YOU GET ONE MORE CHANCE.
THERE WE GO.
WHAT'S THE JOB?
YOU'RE GONNA PROVE YOUR LOYALTY NOT JUST TO THE LEAGUE, BUT TO THE WHOLE ANTI-ESTABLISHMENT CAUSE.
SO, TAKE SOMEONE OUT. SOMEONE OTHER THAN NUMBER ONE...
HOW RARE, GETTING A VISIT FROM YOU.
YEAH, SURE. HOW'RE YOU DOING THESE DAYS?

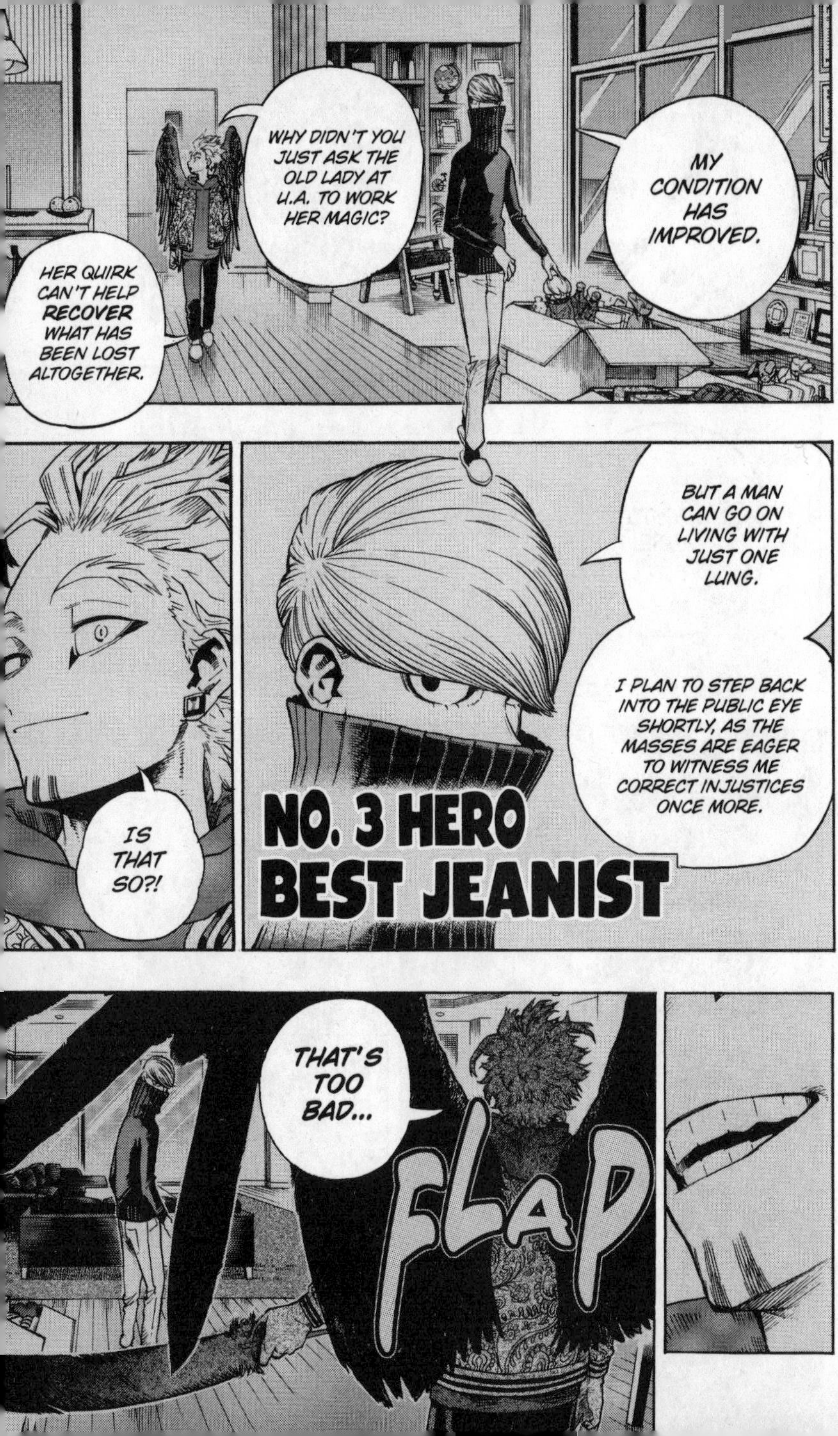
MY CONDITION HAS IMPROVED.
WHY DIDN'T YOU JUST ASK THE OLD LADY AT U.A. TO WORK HER MAGIC?
HER QUIRK CAN'T HELP RECOVER WHAT HAS BEEN LOST ALTOGETHER.
BUT A MAN CAN GO ON LIVING WITH JUST ONE LUNG.
I PLAN TO STEP BACK INTO THE PUBLIC EYE SHORTLY, AS THE MASSES ARE EAGER TO WITNESS ME CORRECT INJUSTICES ONCE MORE.
NO. 3 HERO BEST JEANIST
IS THAT SO?!
THAT'S TOO BAD...
FLAP

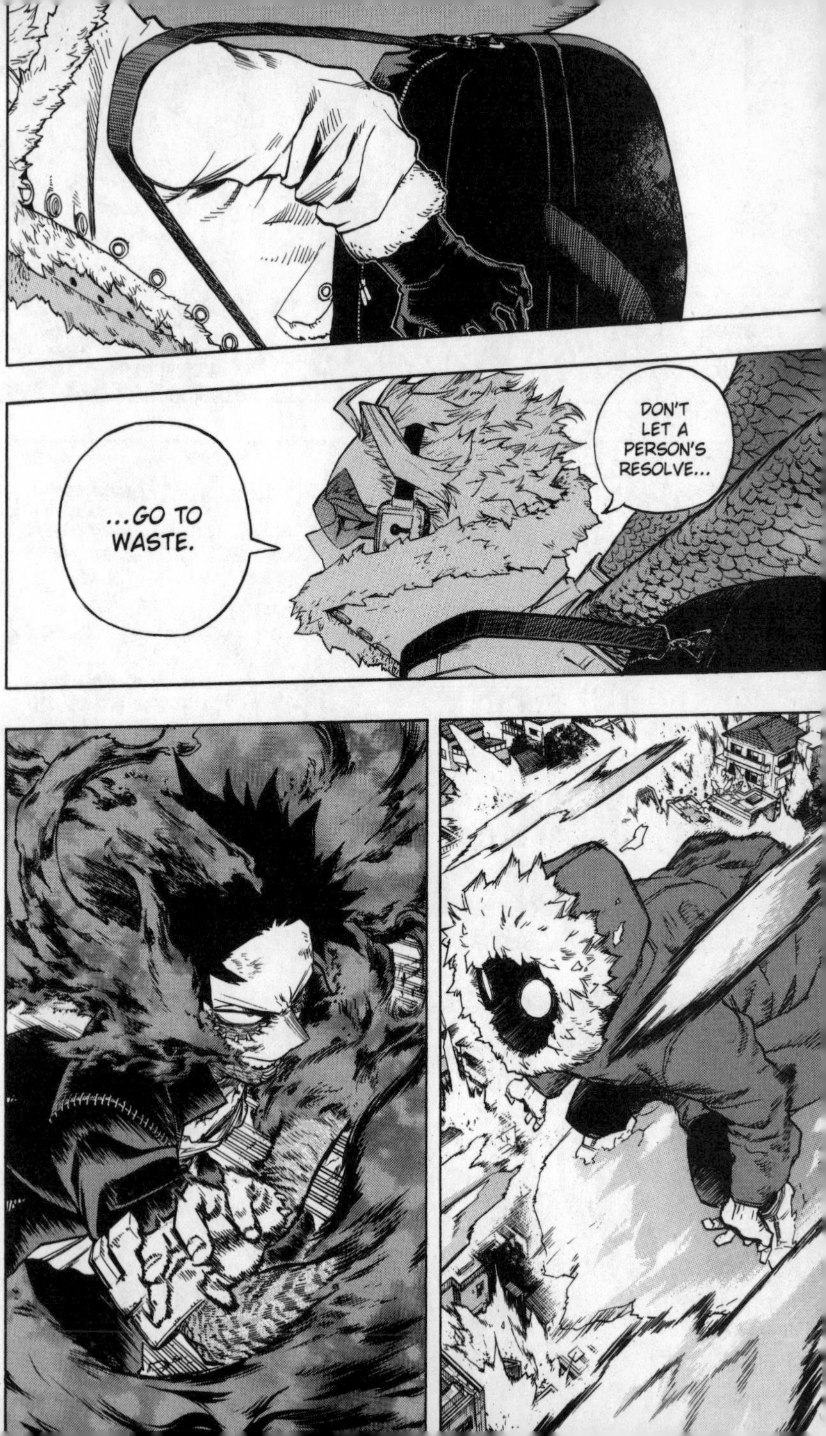
DON'T LET A PERSON'S RESOLVE...
...GO TO WASTE.

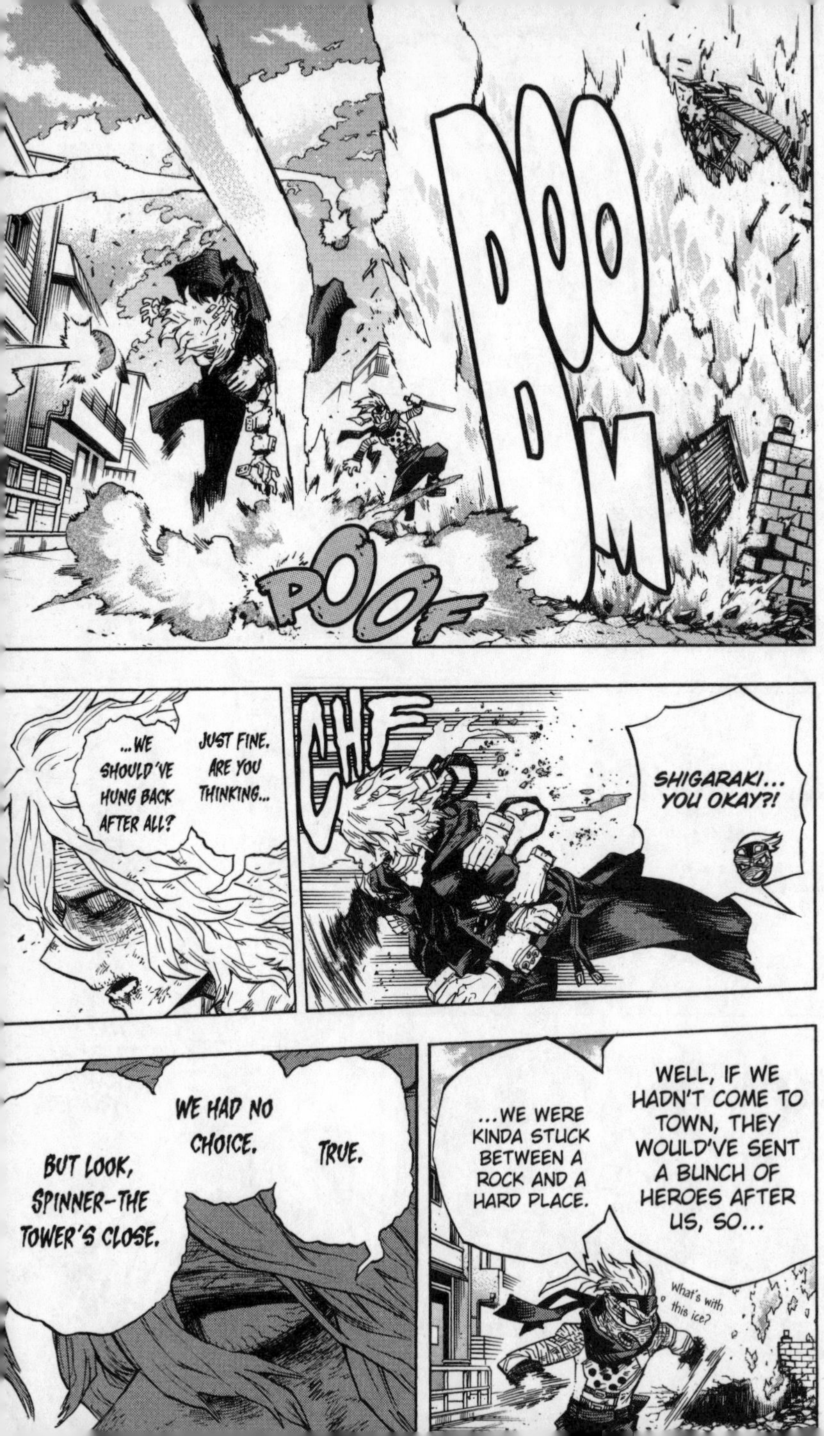
DOOOM
POOF
SHIGARAKI... YOU OKAY?!
CHF
JUST FINE. ARE YOU THINKING...
...WE SHOULD'VE HUNG BACK AFTER ALL?
WELL, IF WE HADN'T COME TO TOWN, THEY WOULD'VE SENT A BUNCH OF HEROES AFTER US, SO...
...WE WERE KINDA STUCK BETWEEN A ROCK AND A HARD PLACE.
What's with this ice?
TRUE.
WE HAD NO CHOICE.
BUT LOOK, SPINNER—THE TOWER'S CLOSE.

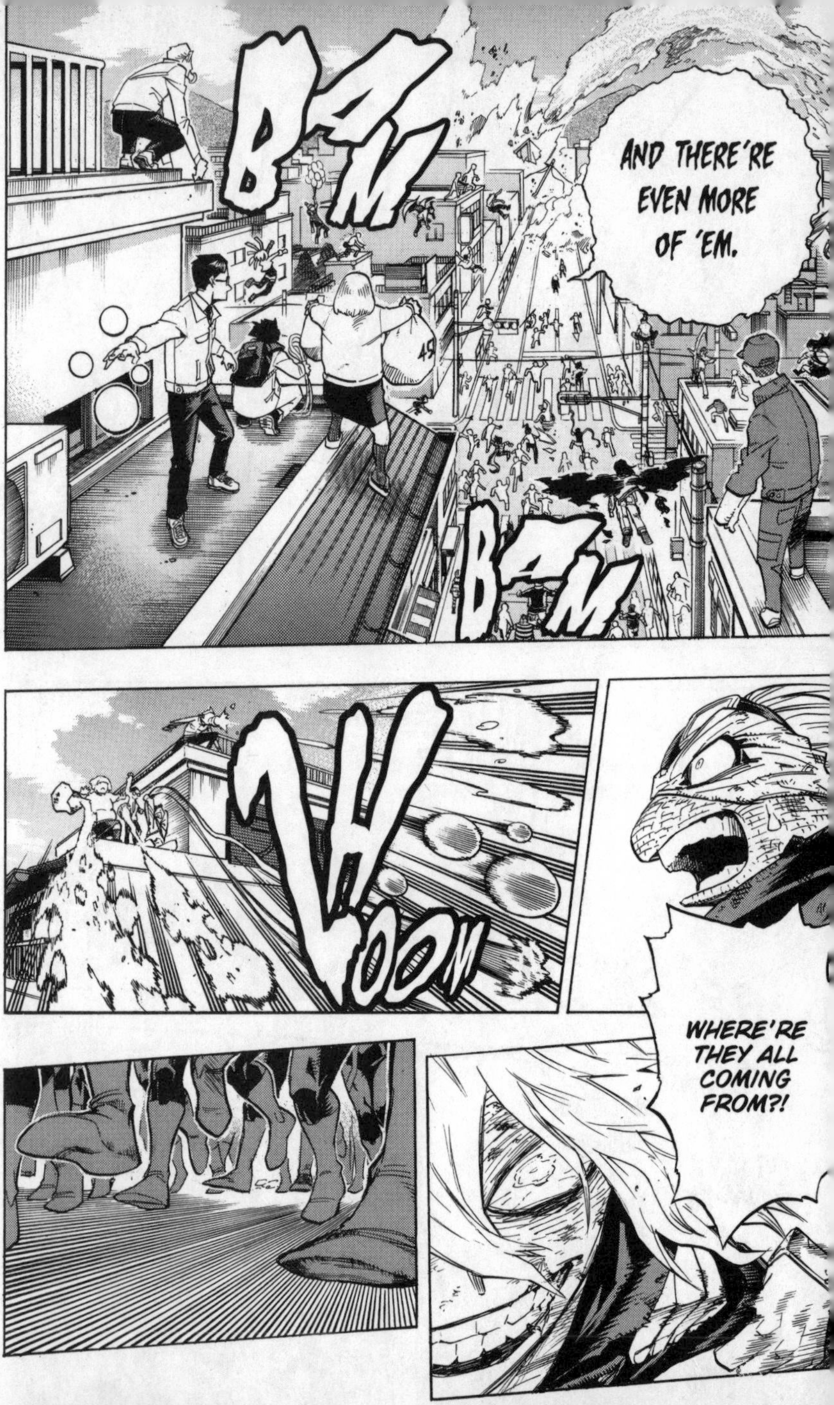
AND THERE'RE EVEN MORE OF 'EM.
BAM
BAM
WHERE'RE THEY ALL COMING FROM?!
ZHVOOM

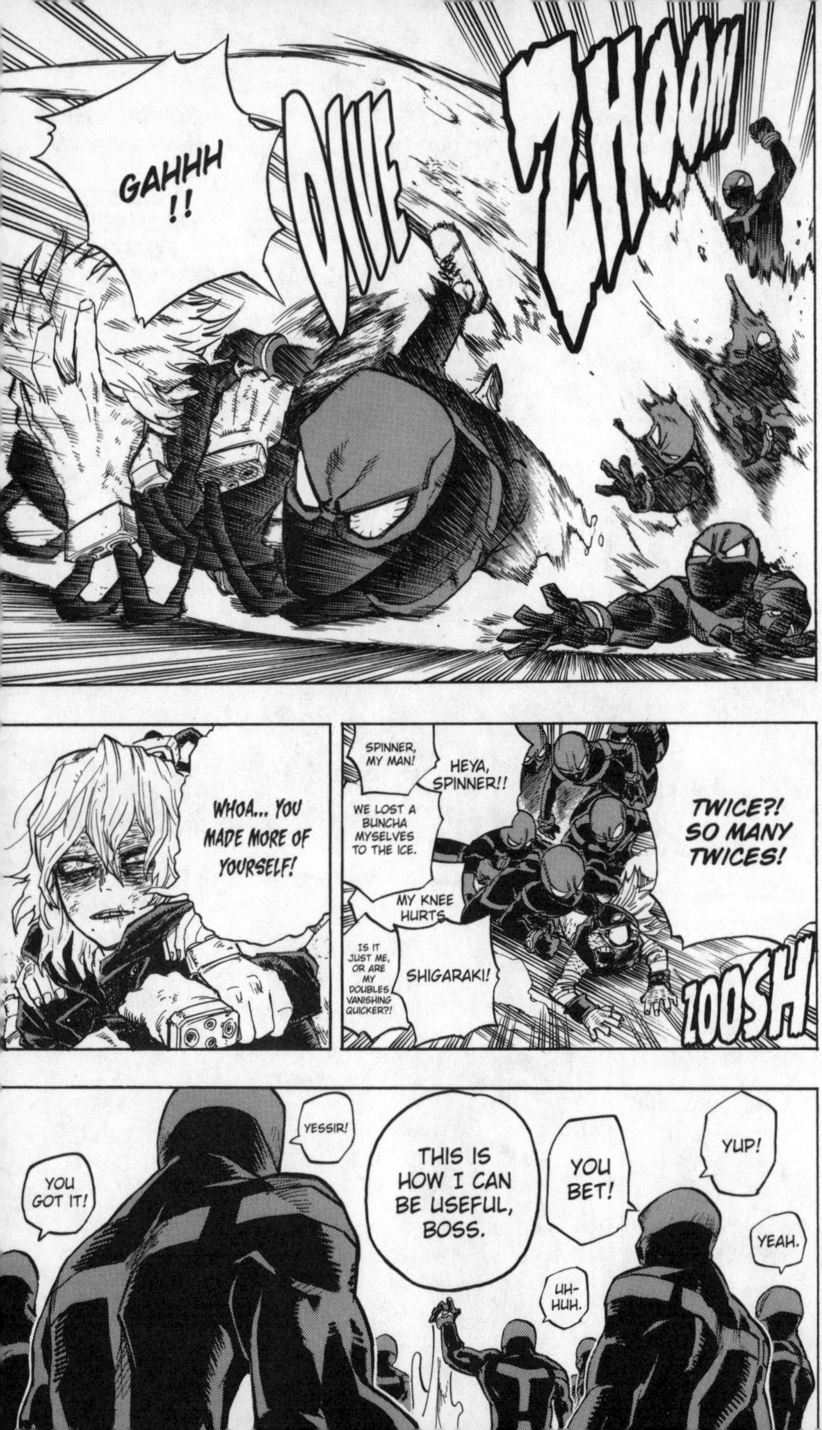
ZHOOM
DIVE
GAHHH !!
TWICE?! SO MANY TWICES!
HEYA, SPINNER!!
SPINNER, MY MAN!
WE LOST A BUNCHA MYSELVES TO THE ICE.
MY KNEE HURTS
SHIGARAKI!
IS IT JUST ME, OR ARE MY DOUBLES VANISHING QUICKER?!
ZOOSH
WHOA... YOU MADE MORE OF YOURSELF!
YUP!
YOU BET!
THIS IS HOW I CAN BE USEFUL, BOSS.
YESSIR!
YOU GOT IT!
YEAH.
UH-HUH.

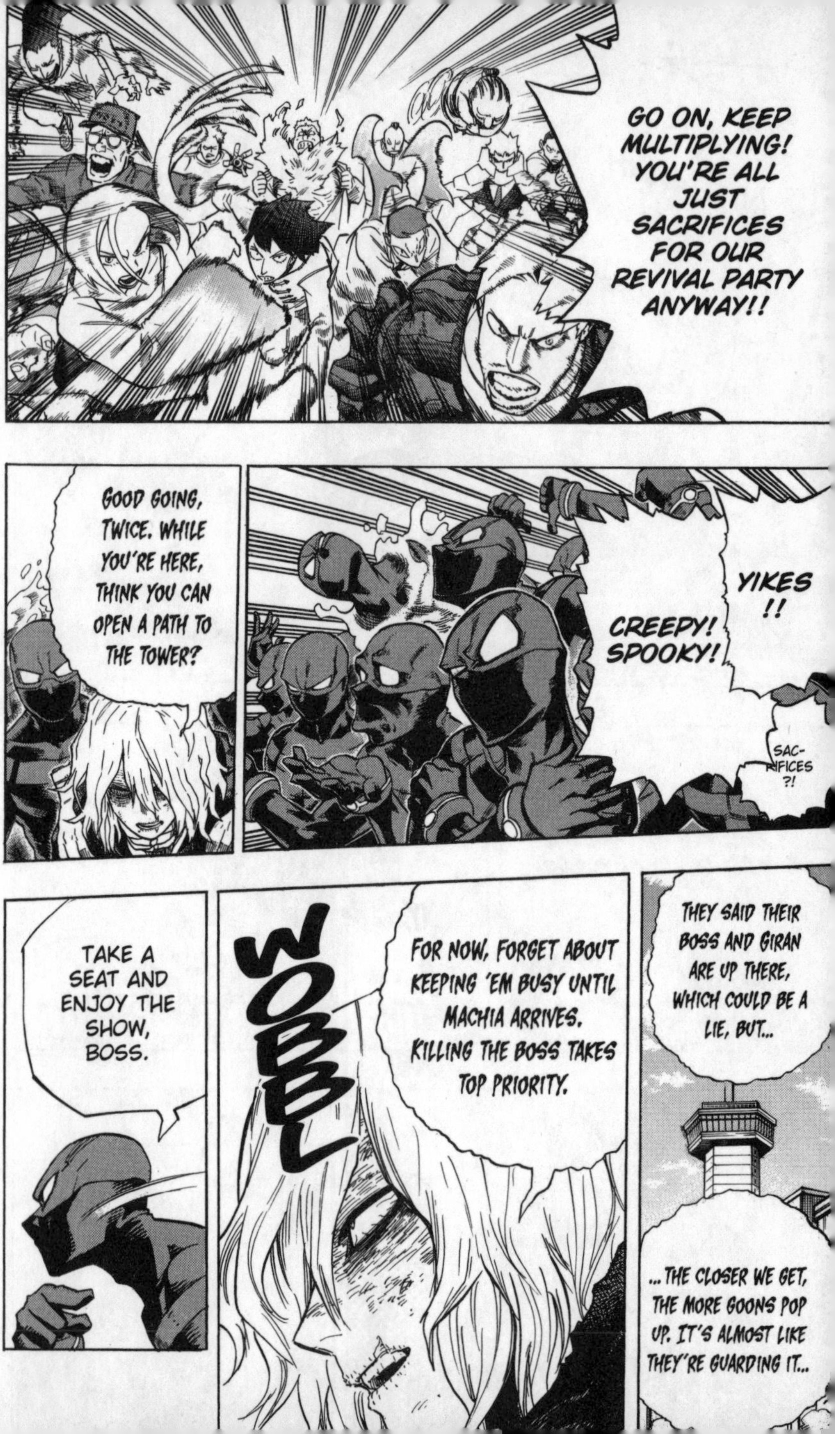
GO ON, KEEP MULTIPLYING! YOU'RE ALL JUST SACRIFICES FOR OUR REVIVAL PARTY ANYWAY!!
YIKES!!
CREEPY! SPOOKY!
SAC-RIFICES?!
GOOD GOING, TWICE. WHILE YOU'RE HERE, THINK YOU CAN OPEN A PATH TO THE TOWER?
THEY SAID THEIR BOSS AND GIRAN ARE UP THERE, WHICH COULD BE A LIE, BUT...
...THE CLOSER WE GET, THE MORE GOONS POP UP. IT'S ALMOST LIKE THEY'RE GUARDING IT...
FOR NOW, FORGET ABOUT KEEPING 'EM BUSY UNTIL MACHIA ARRIVES. KILLING THE BOSS TAKES TOP PRIORITY.
WOBBL
TAKE A SEAT AND ENJOY THE SHOW, BOSS.

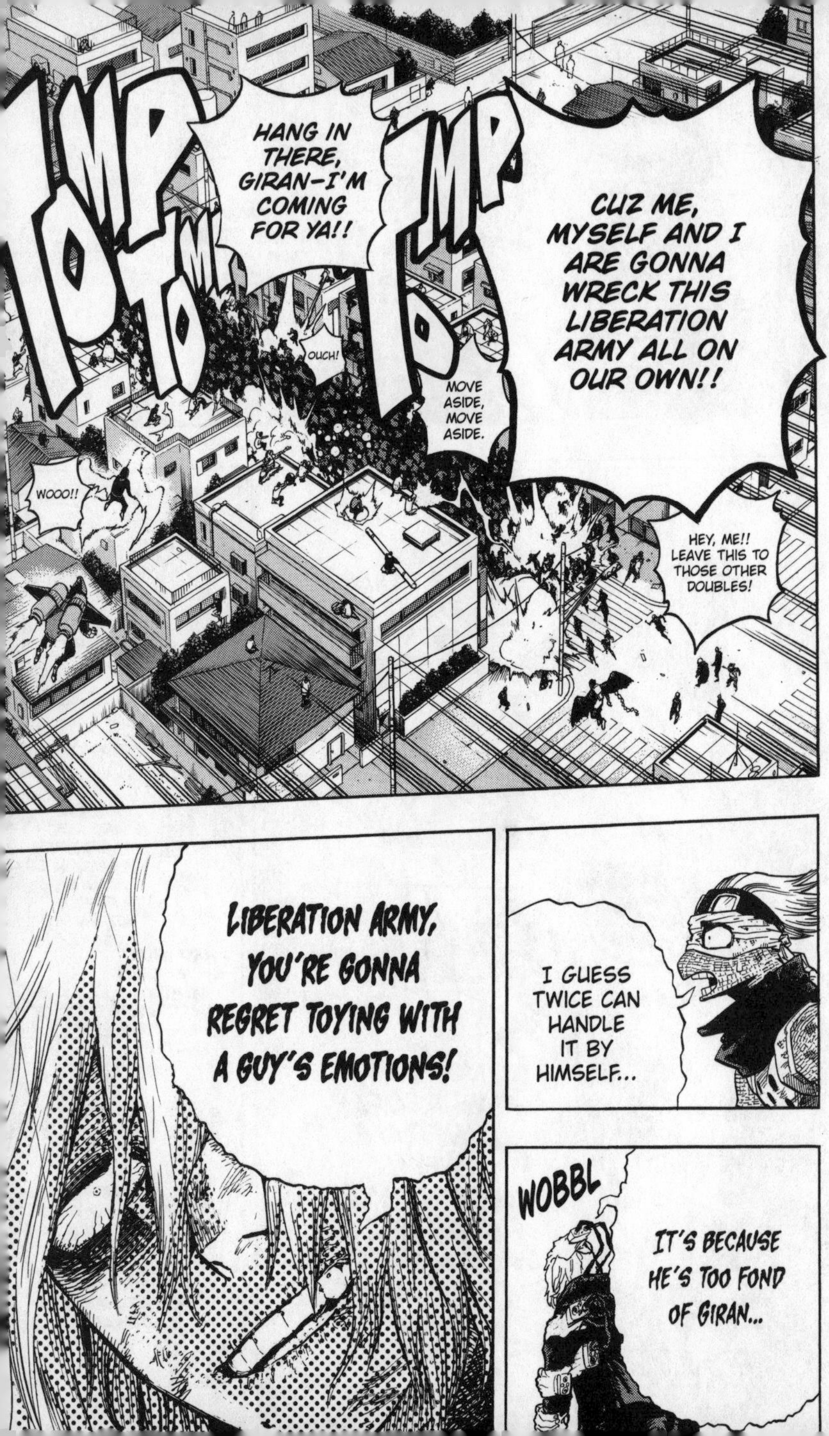
CUZ ME, MYSELF AND I ARE GONNA WRECK THIS LIBERATION ARMY ALL ON OUR OWN!!
TOMP
HANG IN THERE, GIRAN—I'M COMING FOR YA!!
TOMP
TOM
OUCH!
MOVE ASIDE, MOVE ASIDE.
HEY, ME!! LEAVE THIS TO THOSE OTHER DOUBLES!
WOOO!!
I GUESS TWICE CAN HANDLE IT BY HIMSELF...
WOBBL
IT'S BECAUSE HE'S TOO FOND OF GIRAN...
LIBERATION ARMY, YOU'RE GONNA REGRET TOYING WITH A GUY'S EMOTIONS!

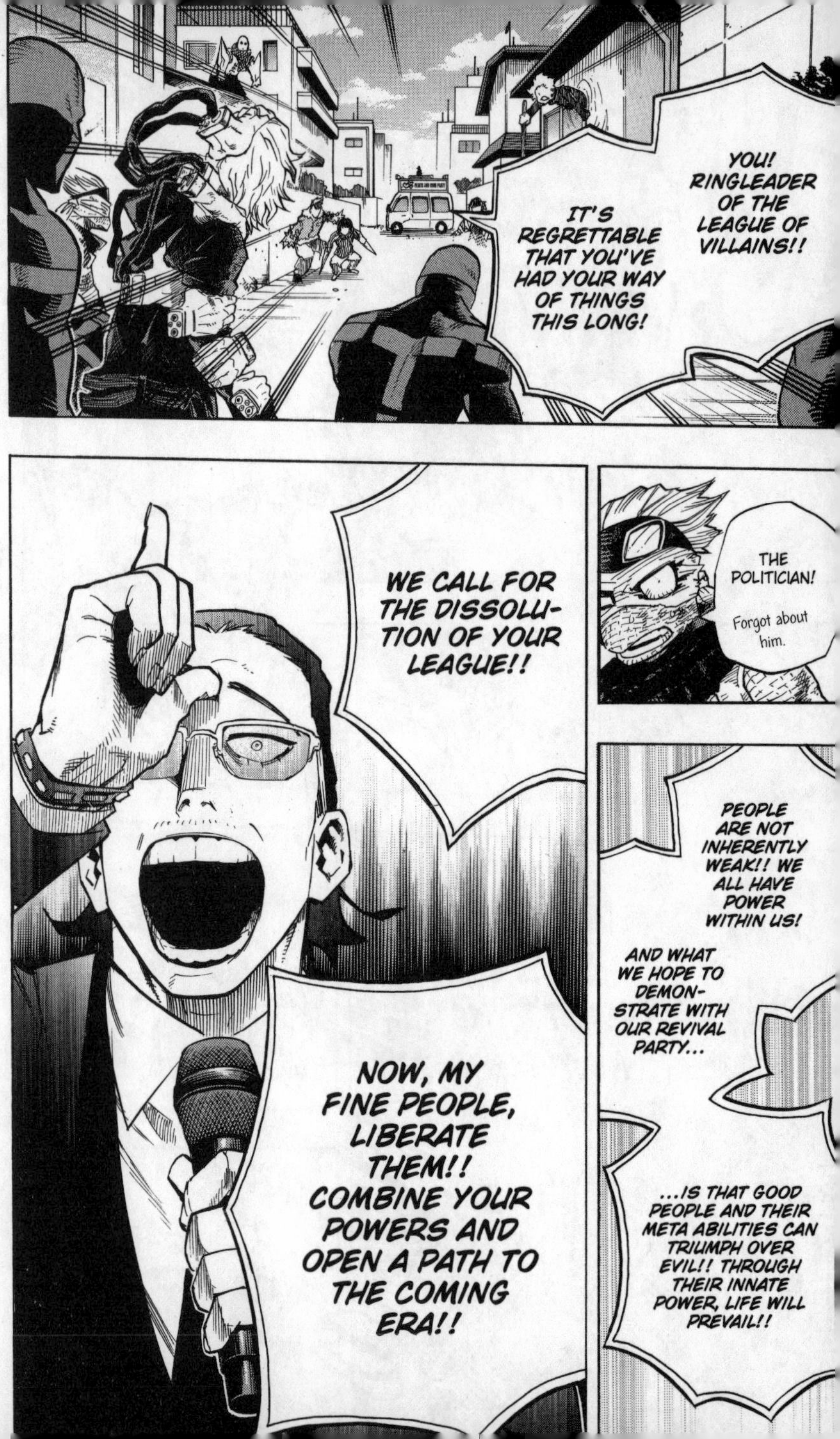
YOU! RINGLEADER OF THE LEAGUE OF VILLAINS!!
IT'S REGRETTABLE THAT YOU'VE HAD YOUR WAY OF THINGS THIS LONG!
THE POLITICIAN!
Forgot about him.
PEOPLE ARE NOT INHERENTLY WEAK!! WE ALL HAVE POWER WITHIN US!
AND WHAT WE HOPE TO DEMON-STRATE WITH OUR REVIVAL PARTY...
...IS THAT GOOD PEOPLE AND THEIR META ABILITIES CAN TRIUMPH OVER EVIL!! THROUGH THEIR INNATE POWER, LIFE WILL PREVAIL!!
WE CALL FOR THE DISSOLU-TION OF YOUR LEAGUE!!
NOW, MY FINE PEOPLE, LIBERATE THEM!! COMBINE YOUR POWERS AND OPEN A PATH TO THE COMING ERA!!

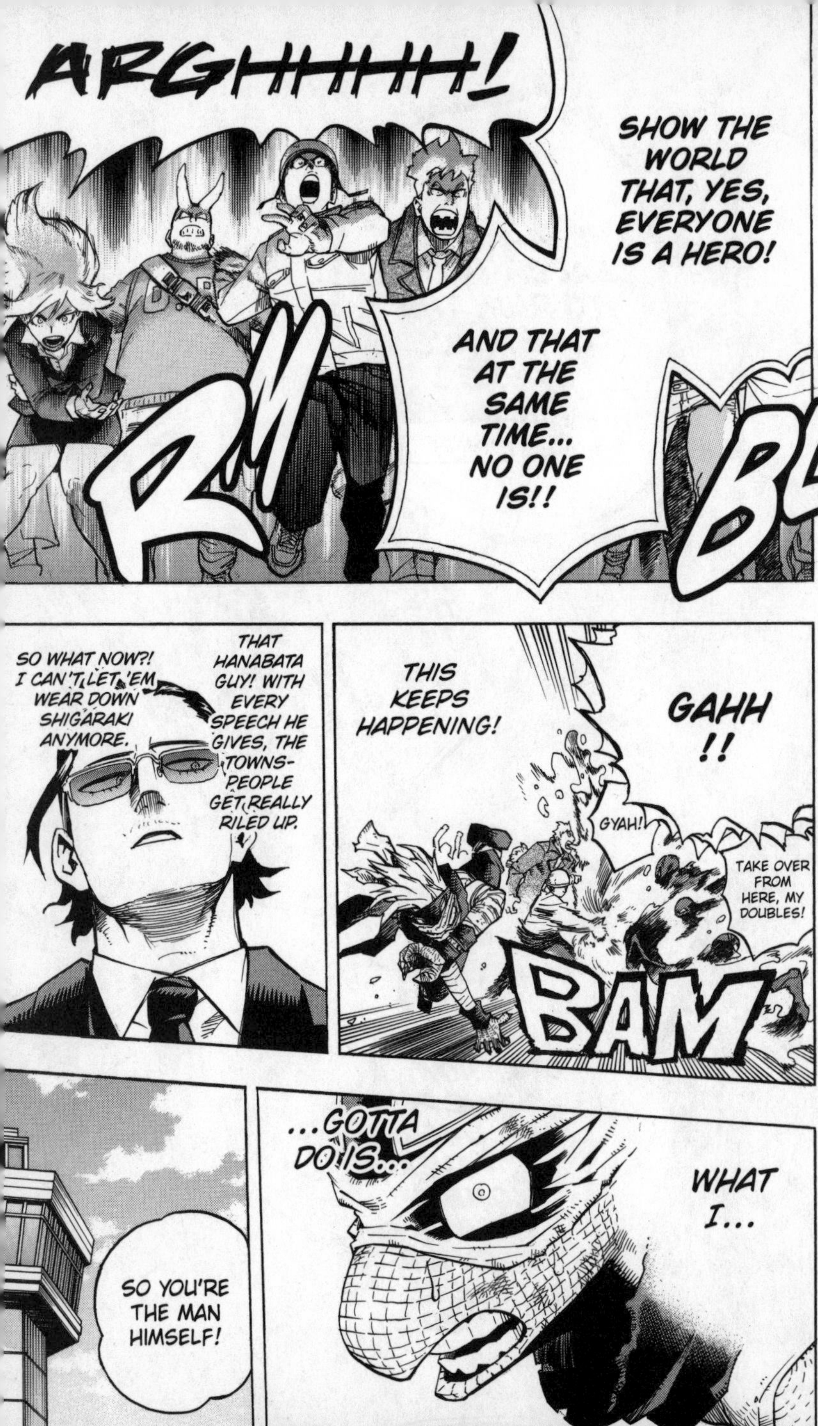
SHOW THE WORLD THAT, YES, EVERYONE IS A HERO!
ARGHHHHH!
AND THAT AT THE SAME TIME... NO ONE IS!!
BL
RM
THIS KEEPS HAPPENING!
GAHH!!
GYAH!
TAKE OVER FROM HERE, MY DOUBLES!
BAM
THAT HANABATA GUY! WITH EVERY SPEECH HE GIVES, THE TOWNSPEOPLE GET REALLY RILED UP.
SO WHAT NOW?! I CAN'T LET 'EM WEAR DOWN SHIGARAKI ANYMORE.
WHAT I...
...GOTTA DO IS...
SO YOU'RE THE MAN HIMSELF!

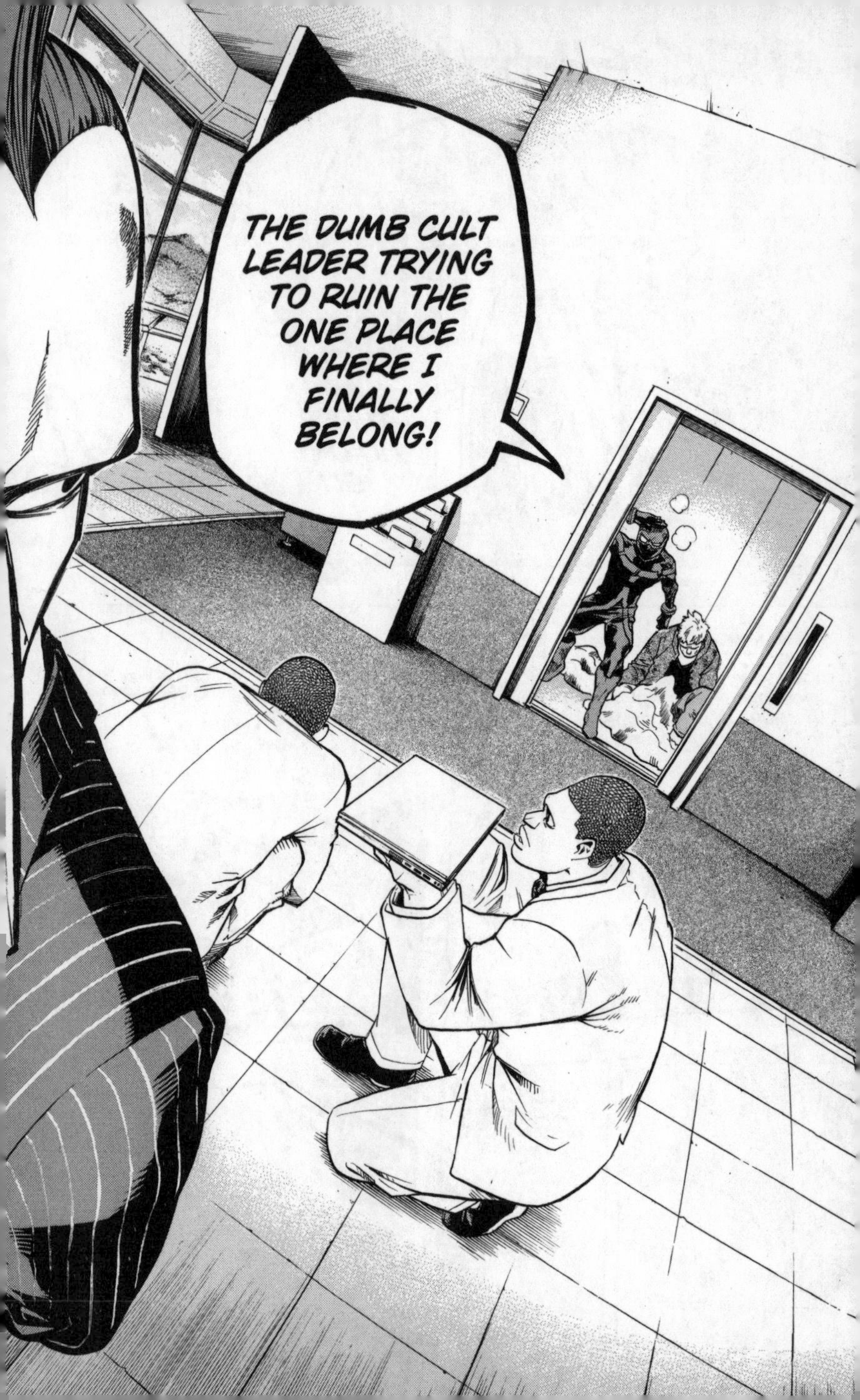
THE DUMB CULT LEADER TRYING TO RUIN THE ONE PLACE WHERE I FINALLY BELONG!

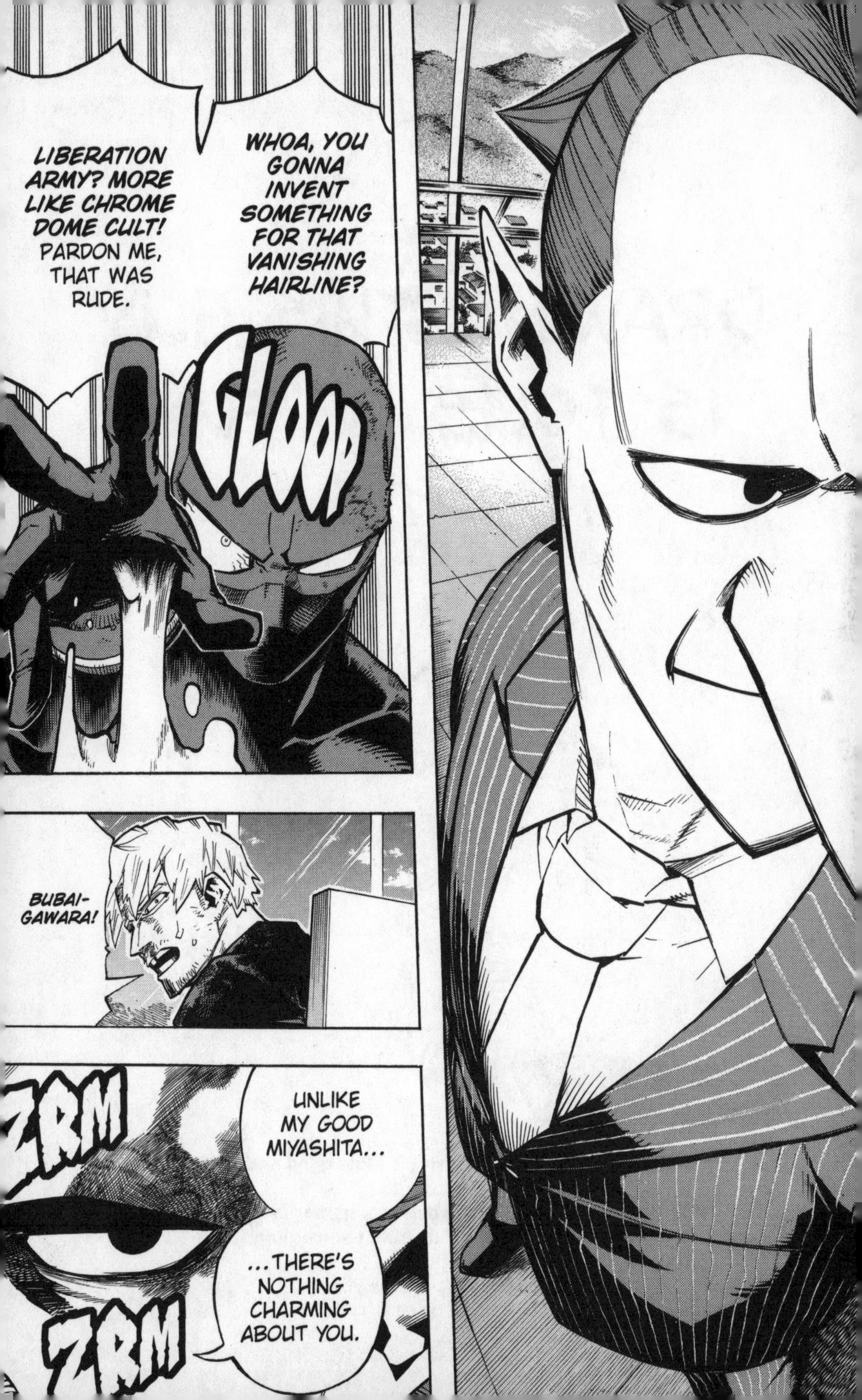
WHOA, YOU GONNA INVENT SOMETHING FOR THAT VANISHING HAIRLINE?
LIBERATION ARMY? MORE LIKE CHROME DOME CULT! PARDON ME, THAT WAS RUDE.
GLOOP
BUBAI-GAWARA!
UNLIKE MY GOOD MIYASHITA...
...THERE'S NOTHING CHARMING ABOUT YOU.
ZRM
ZRM

DRAWING THIS GUY IS TONS OF FUN

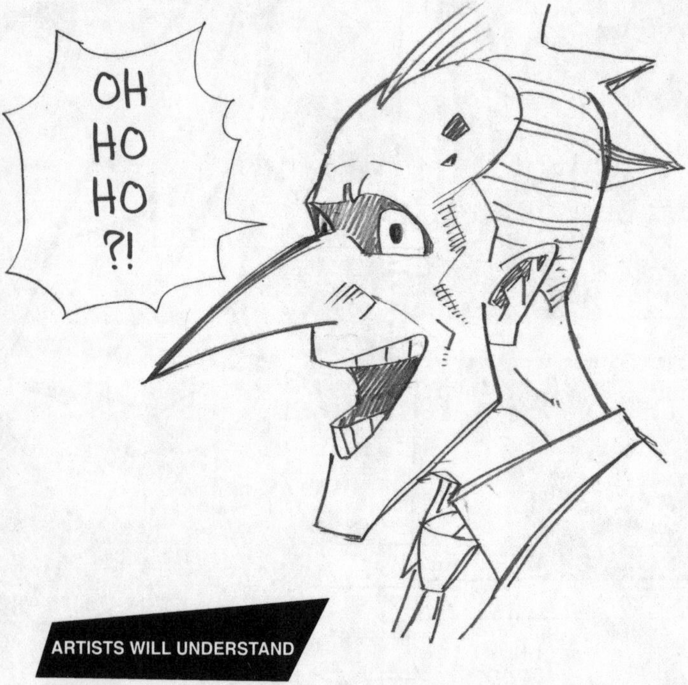
OH HO HO ?!

ARTISTS WILL UNDERSTAND

There's nothing more fun than drawing middle-aged and old men.

With handsome dudes and pretty ladies, it's harder to distort their expressions when they get worked up about something...

Why can't everyone just be a wacky old man?

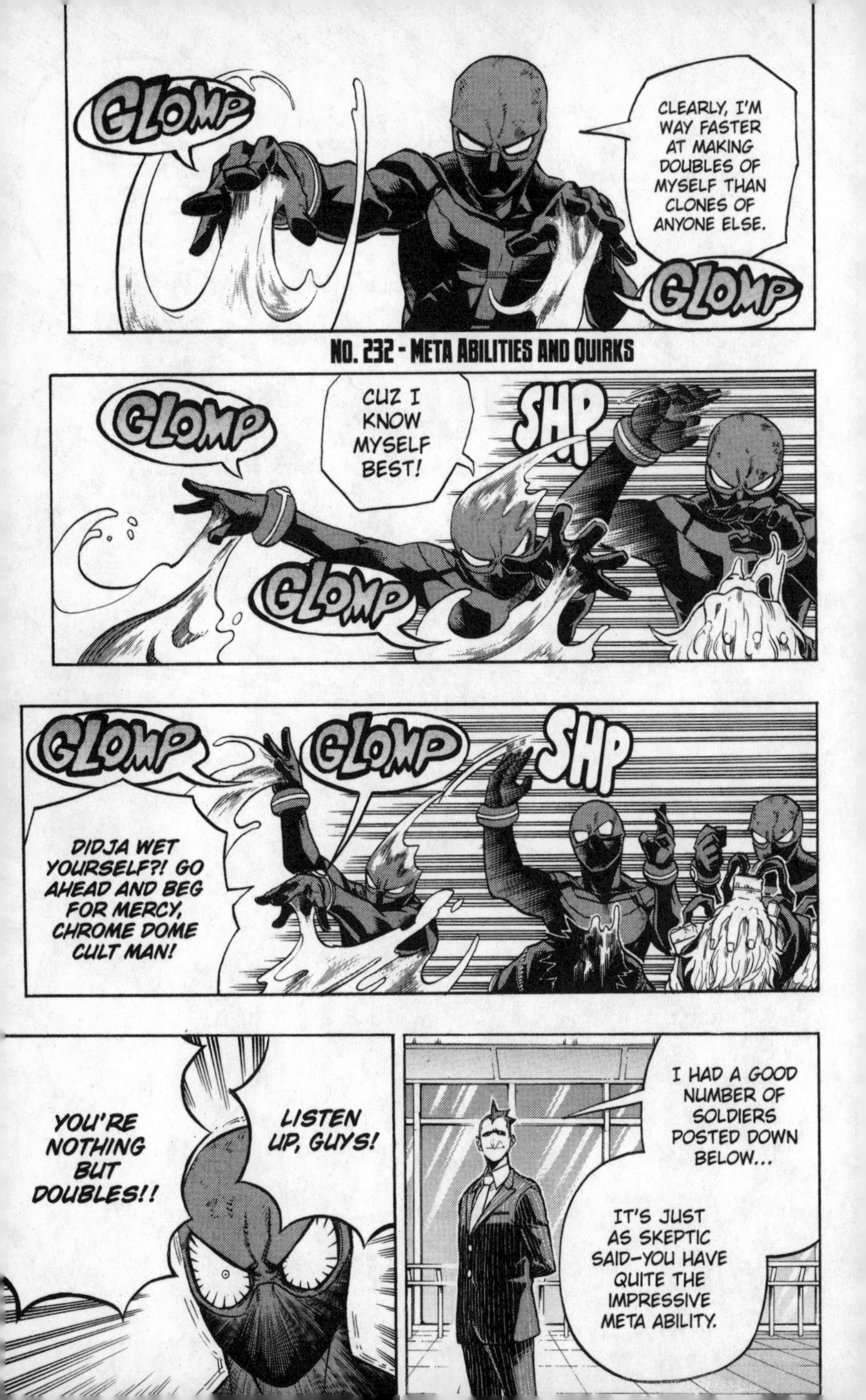
CLEARLY, I'M WAY FASTER AT MAKING DOUBLES OF MYSELF THAN CLONES OF ANYONE ELSE.
GLOMP
GLOMP
NO. 232 - META ABILITIES AND QUIRKS
SHP
CUZ I KNOW MYSELF BEST!
GLOMP
GLOMP
SHP
GLOMP
GLOMP
DIDJA WET YOURSELF?! GO AHEAD AND BEG FOR MERCY, CHROME DOME CULT MAN!
I HAD A GOOD NUMBER OF SOLDIERS POSTED DOWN BELOW...
IT'S JUST AS SKEPTIC SAID—YOU HAVE QUITE THE IMPRESSIVE META ABILITY.
LISTEN UP, GUYS!
YOU'RE NOTHING BUT DOUBLES!!

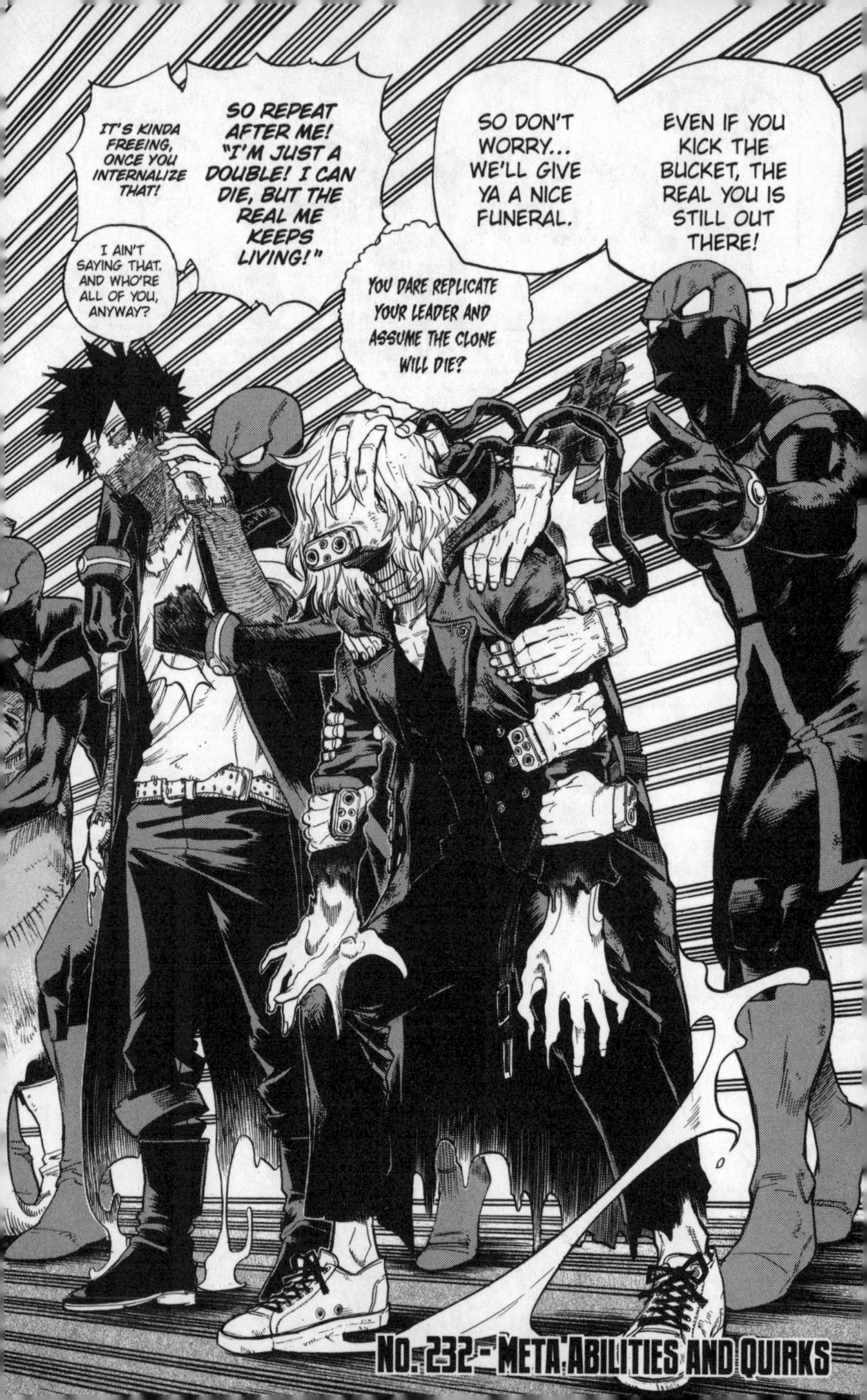
EVEN IF YOU KICK THE BUCKET, THE REAL YOU IS STILL OUT THERE!
SO DON'T WORRY... WE'LL GIVE YA A NICE FUNERAL.
SO REPEAT AFTER ME! "I'M JUST A DOUBLE! I CAN DIE, BUT THE REAL ME KEEPS LIVING!"
IT'S KINDA FREEING, ONCE YOU INTERNALIZE THAT!
YOU DARE REPLICATE YOUR LEADER AND ASSUME THE CLONE WILL DIE?
I AIN'T SAYING THAT. AND WHO'RE ALL OF YOU, ANYWAY?
NO. 232 - META ABILITIES AND QUIRKS

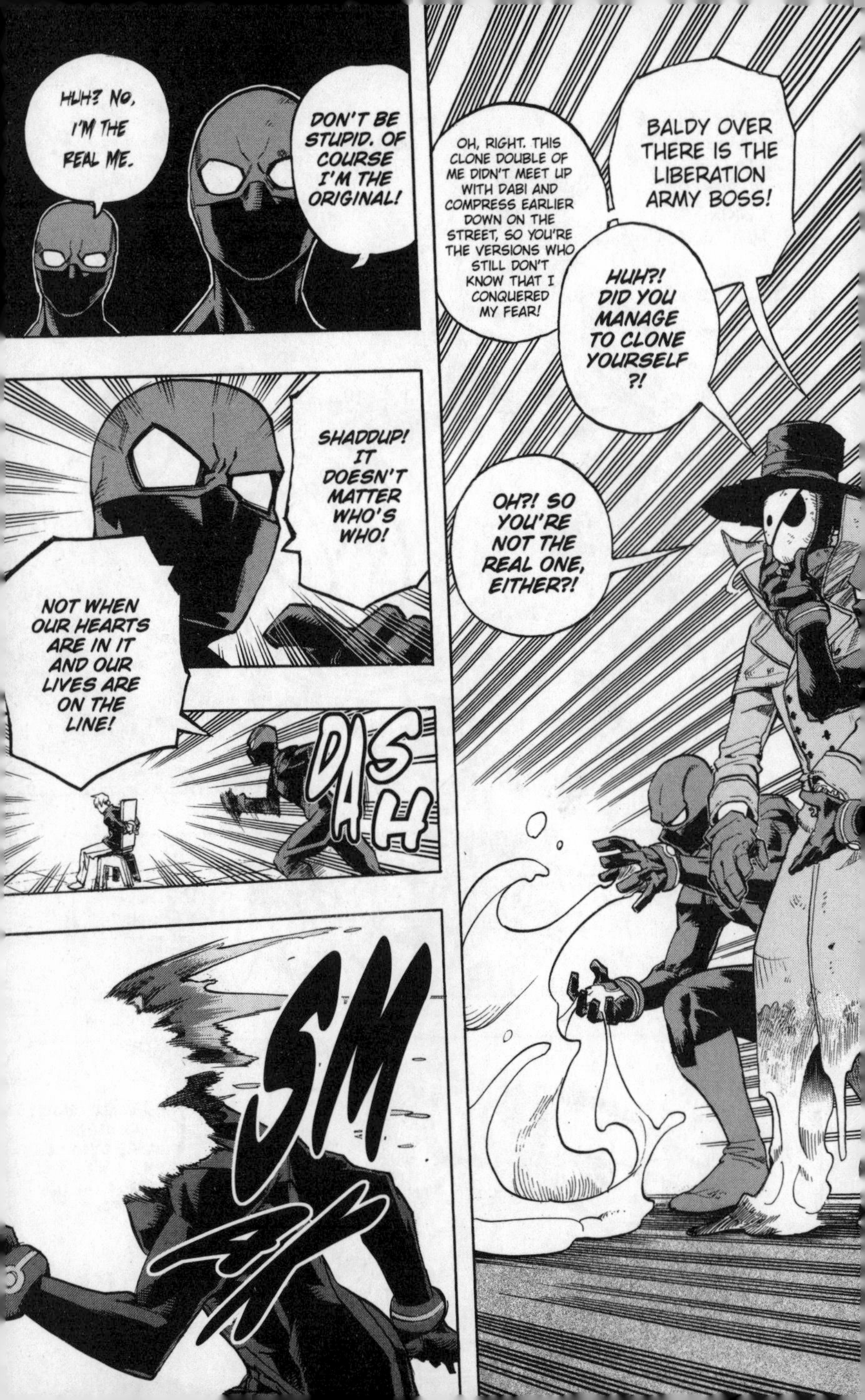
BALDY OVER THERE IS THE LIBERATION ARMY BOSS!
OH, RIGHT. THIS CLONE DOUBLE OF ME DIDN'T MEET UP WITH DABI AND COMPRESS EARLIER DOWN ON THE STREET, SO YOU'RE THE VERSIONS WHO STILL DON'T KNOW THAT I CONQUERED MY FEAR!
HUH?! DID YOU MANAGE TO CLONE YOURSELF?!
OH?! SO YOU'RE NOT THE REAL ONE, EITHER?!
DON'T BE STUPID. OF COURSE I'M THE ORIGINAL!
HUH? NO, I'M THE REAL ME.
SHADDUP! IT DOESN'T MATTER WHO'S WHO!
NOT WHEN OUR HEARTS ARE IN IT AND OUR LIVES ARE ON THE LINE!
DASH
SM

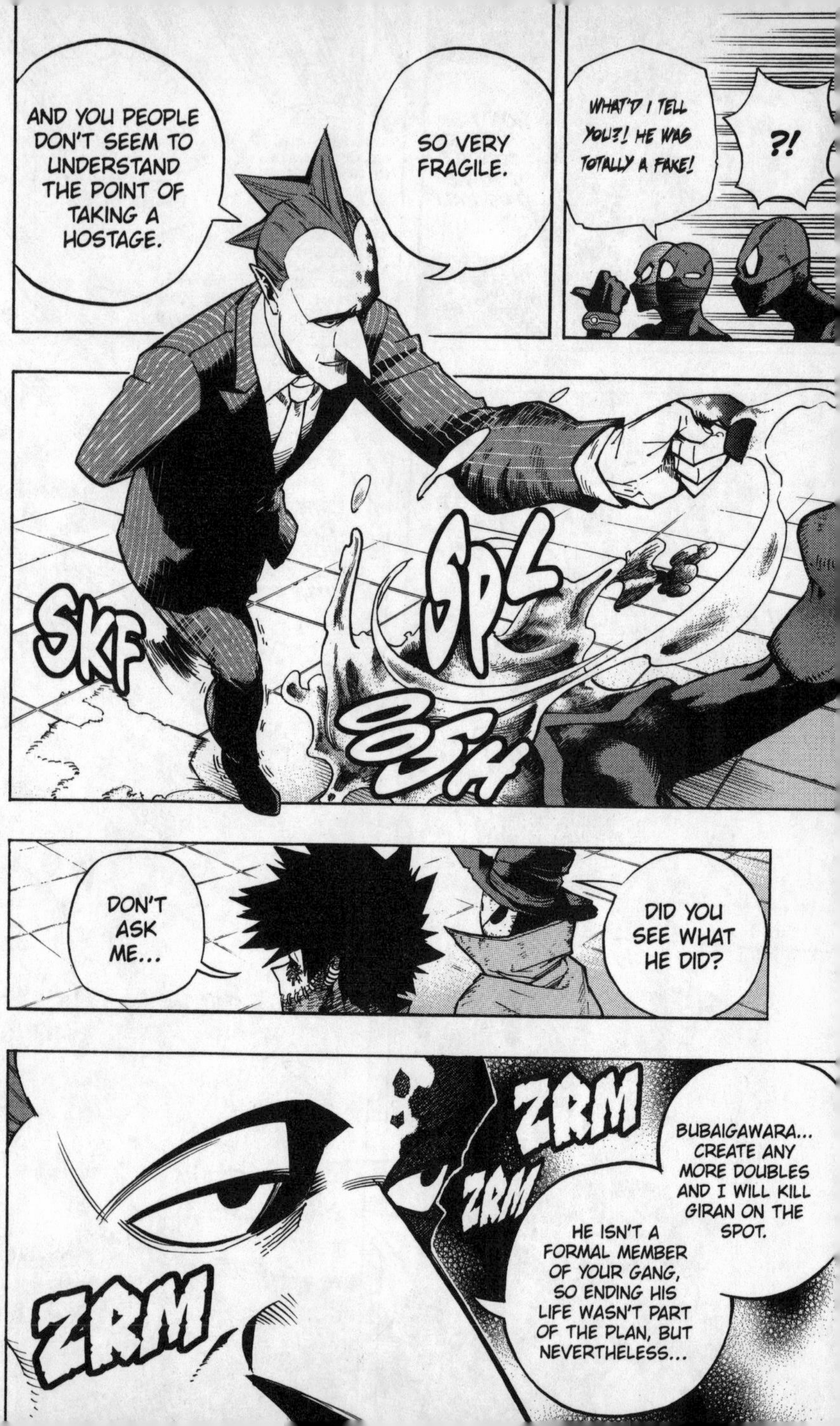
?!
WHAT'D I TELL YOU?! HE WAS TOTALLY A FAKE!
SO VERY FRAGILE.
AND YOU PEOPLE DON'T SEEM TO UNDERSTAND THE POINT OF TAKING A HOSTAGE.
SPL
SKF
OOSH
DID YOU SEE WHAT HE DID?
DON'T ASK ME...
ZRM
BUBAIGAWARA... CREATE ANY MORE DOUBLES AND I WILL KILL GIRAN ON THE SPOT.
ZRM
HE ISN'T A FORMAL MEMBER OF YOUR GANG, SO ENDING HIS LIFE WASN'T PART OF THE PLAN, BUT NEVERTHELESS...
ZRM

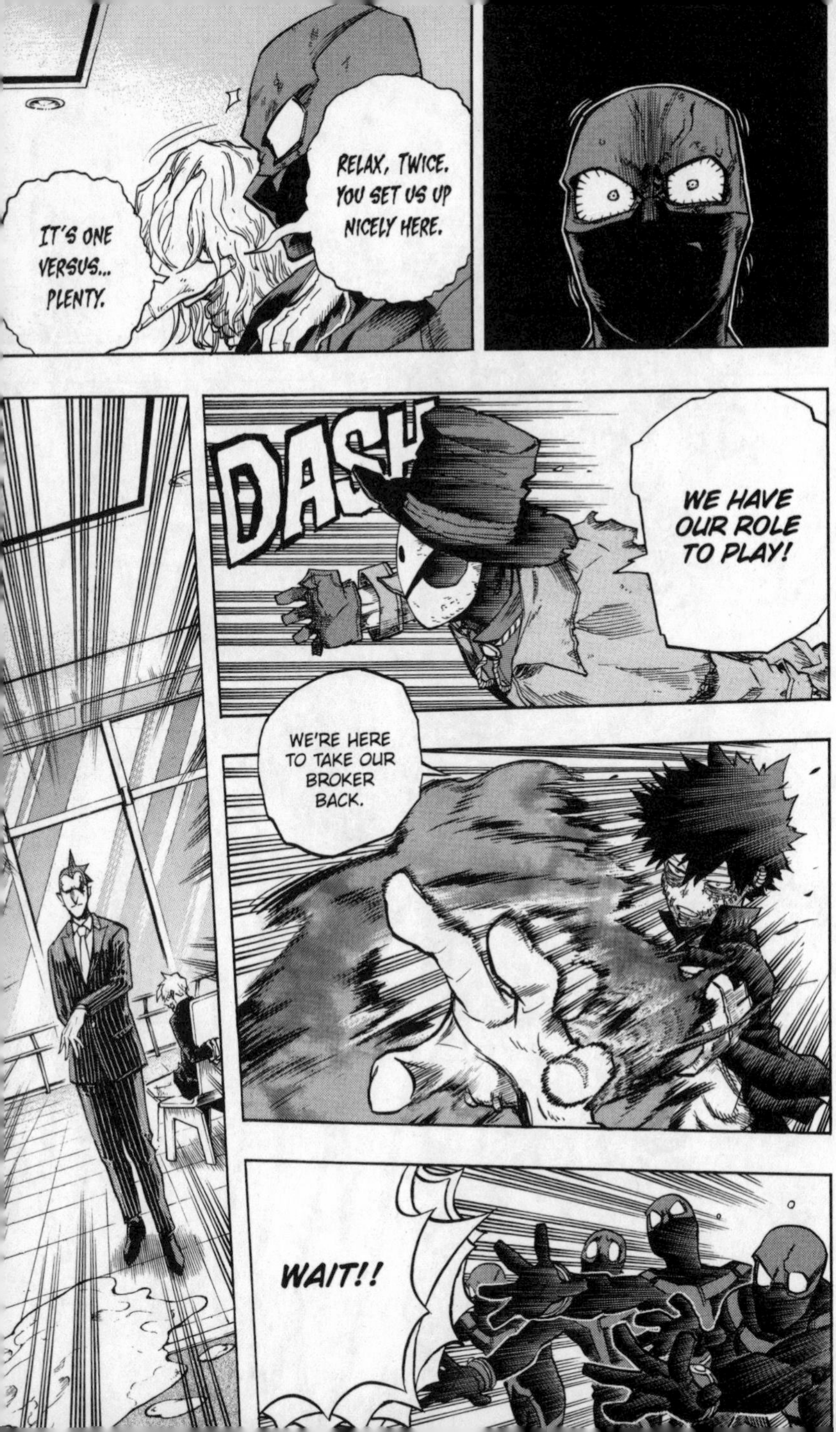
RELAX, TWICE. YOU SET US UP NICELY HERE.
IT'S ONE VERSUS... PLENTY.
WE HAVE OUR ROLE TO PLAY!
DASH
WE'RE HERE TO TAKE OUR BROKER BACK.
WAIT!!

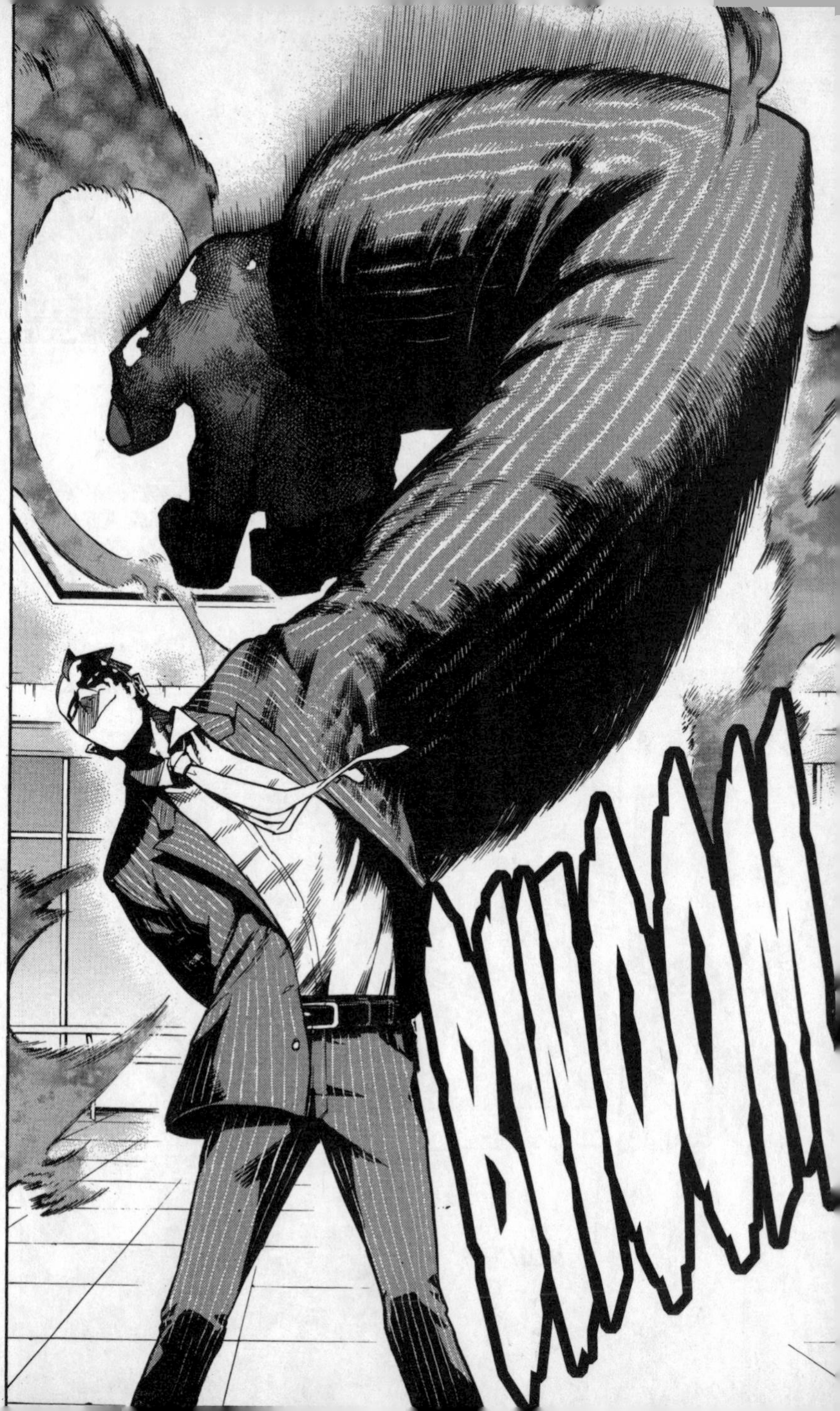
BWOOM

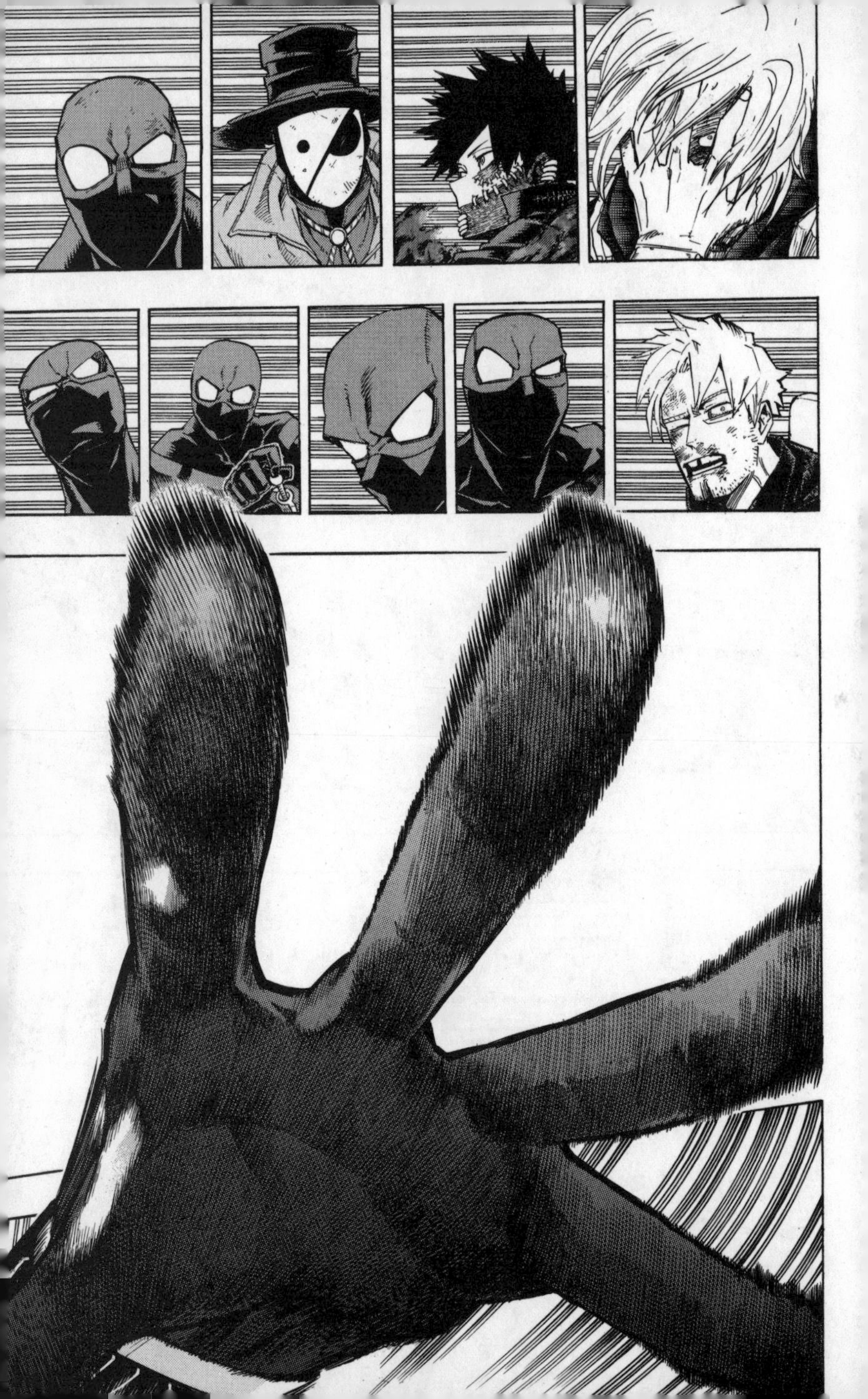

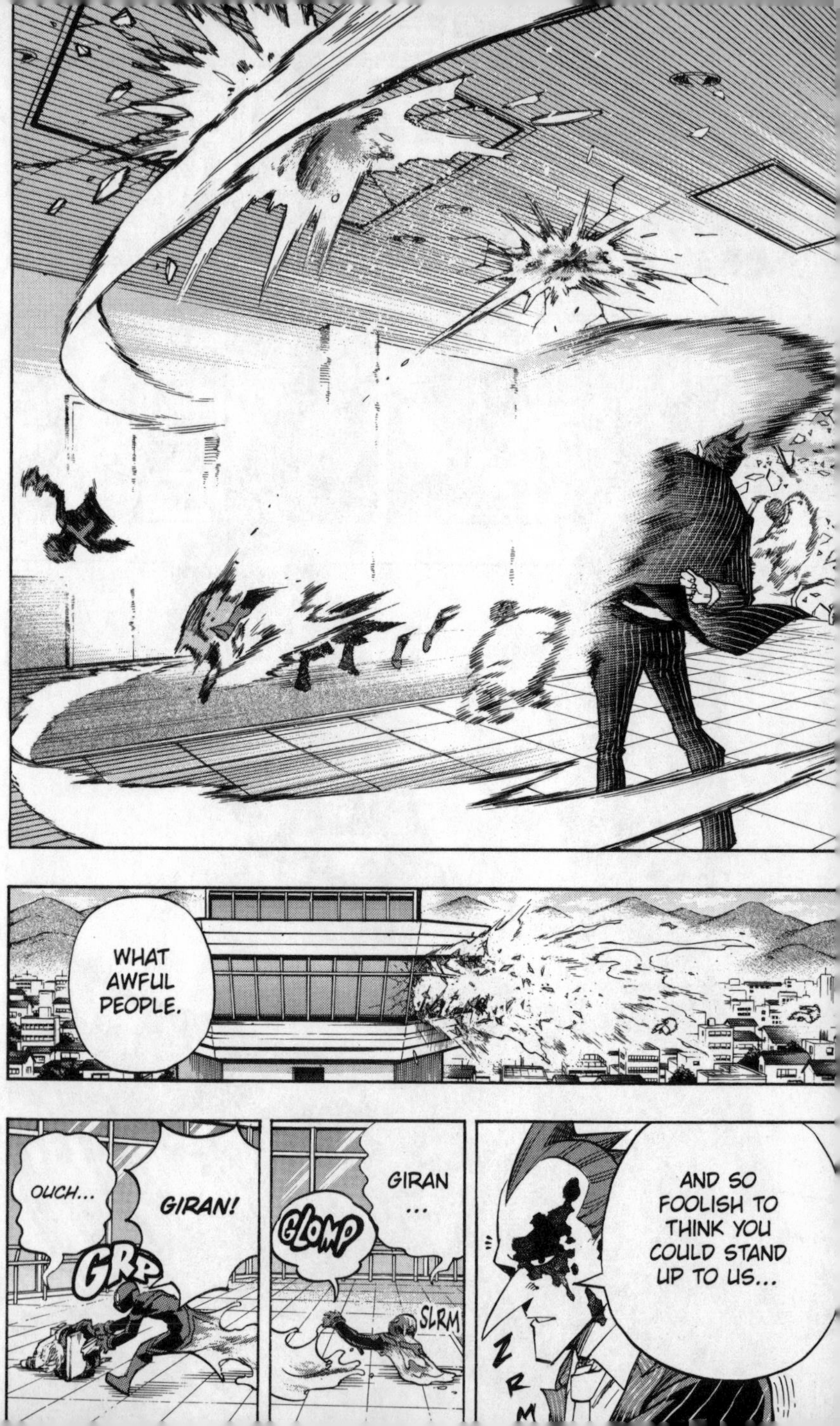
WHAT AWFUL PEOPLE.
AND SO FOOLISH TO THINK YOU COULD STAND UP TO US...
ZRM
GIRAN ...
GLOMP
SLRM
GIRAN!
OUCH...
GRP

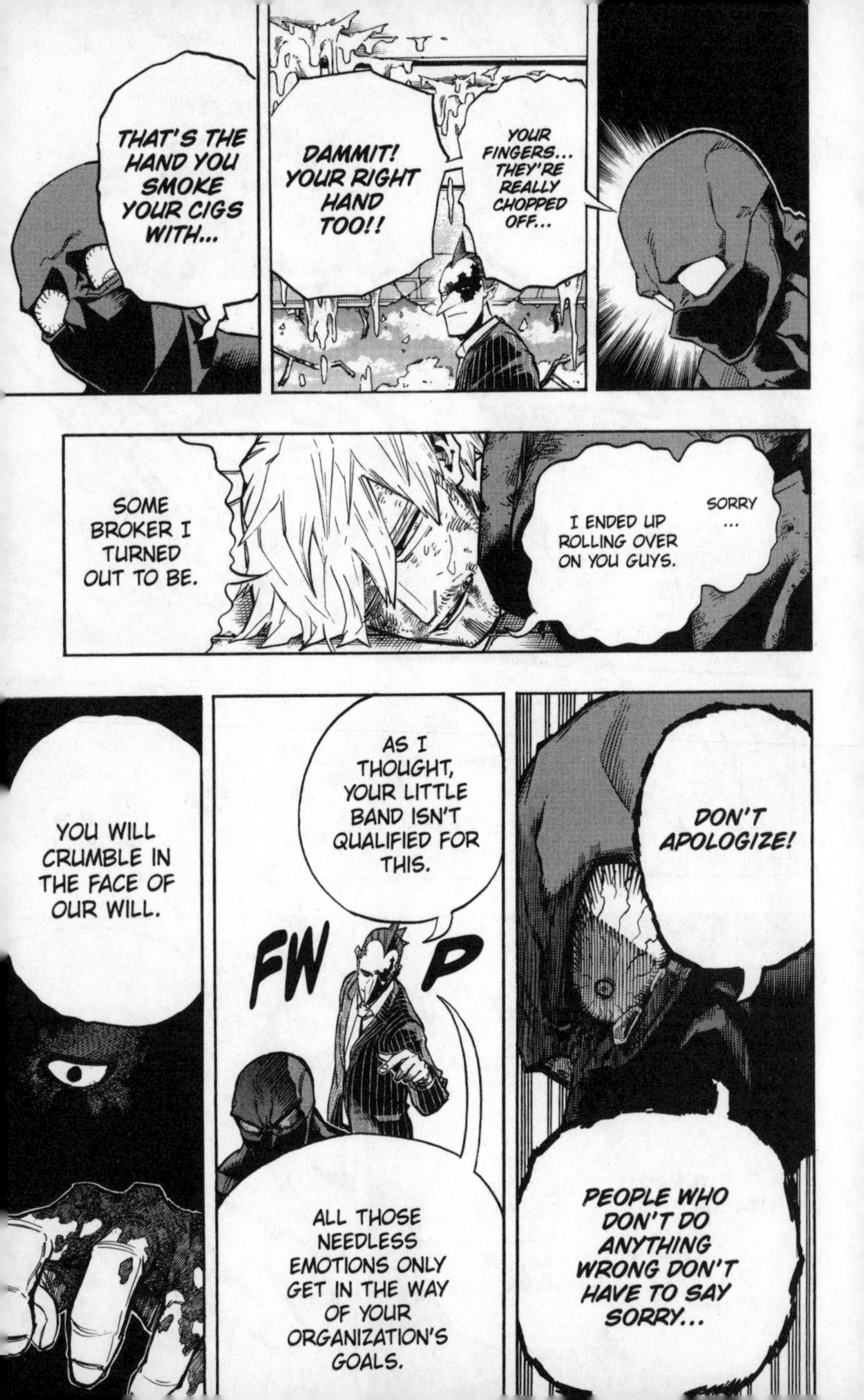
YOUR FINGERS... THEY'RE REALLY CHOPPED OFF...
DAMMIT! YOUR RIGHT HAND TOO!!
THAT'S THE HAND YOU SMOKE YOUR CIGS WITH...
SORRY...
I ENDED UP ROLLING OVER ON YOU GUYS.
SOME BROKER I TURNED OUT TO BE.
DON'T APOLOGIZE!
PEOPLE WHO DON'T DO ANYTHING WRONG DON'T HAVE TO SAY SORRY...
AS I THOUGHT, YOUR LITTLE BAND ISN'T QUALIFIED FOR THIS.
FWP
ALL THOSE NEEDLESS EMOTIONS ONLY GET IN THE WAY OF YOUR ORGANIZATION'S GOALS.
YOU WILL CRUMBLE IN THE FACE OF OUR WILL.

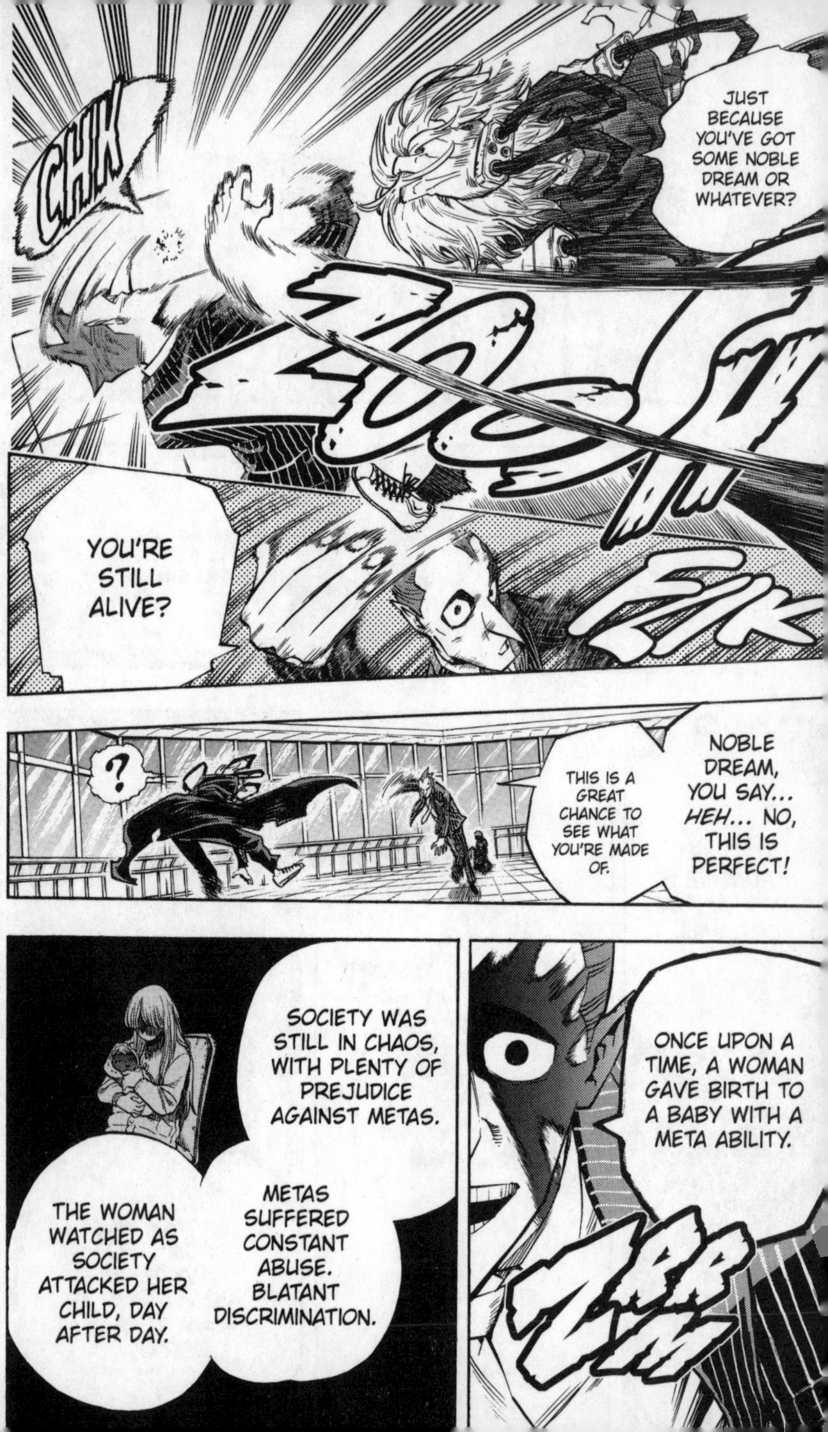
JUST BECAUSE YOU'VE GOT SOME NOBLE DREAM OR WHATEVER?
CHK
YOU'RE STILL ALIVE?
NOBLE DREAM, YOU SAY... *HEH*... NO, THIS IS PERFECT!
THIS IS A GREAT CHANCE TO SEE WHAT YOU'RE MADE OF.
?
ONCE UPON A TIME, A WOMAN GAVE BIRTH TO A BABY WITH A META ABILITY.
SOCIETY WAS STILL IN CHAOS, WITH PLENTY OF PREJUDICE AGAINST METAS.
METAS SUFFERED CONSTANT ABUSE. BLATANT DISCRIMINATION.
THE WOMAN WATCHED AS SOCIETY ATTACKED HER CHILD, DAY AFTER DAY.

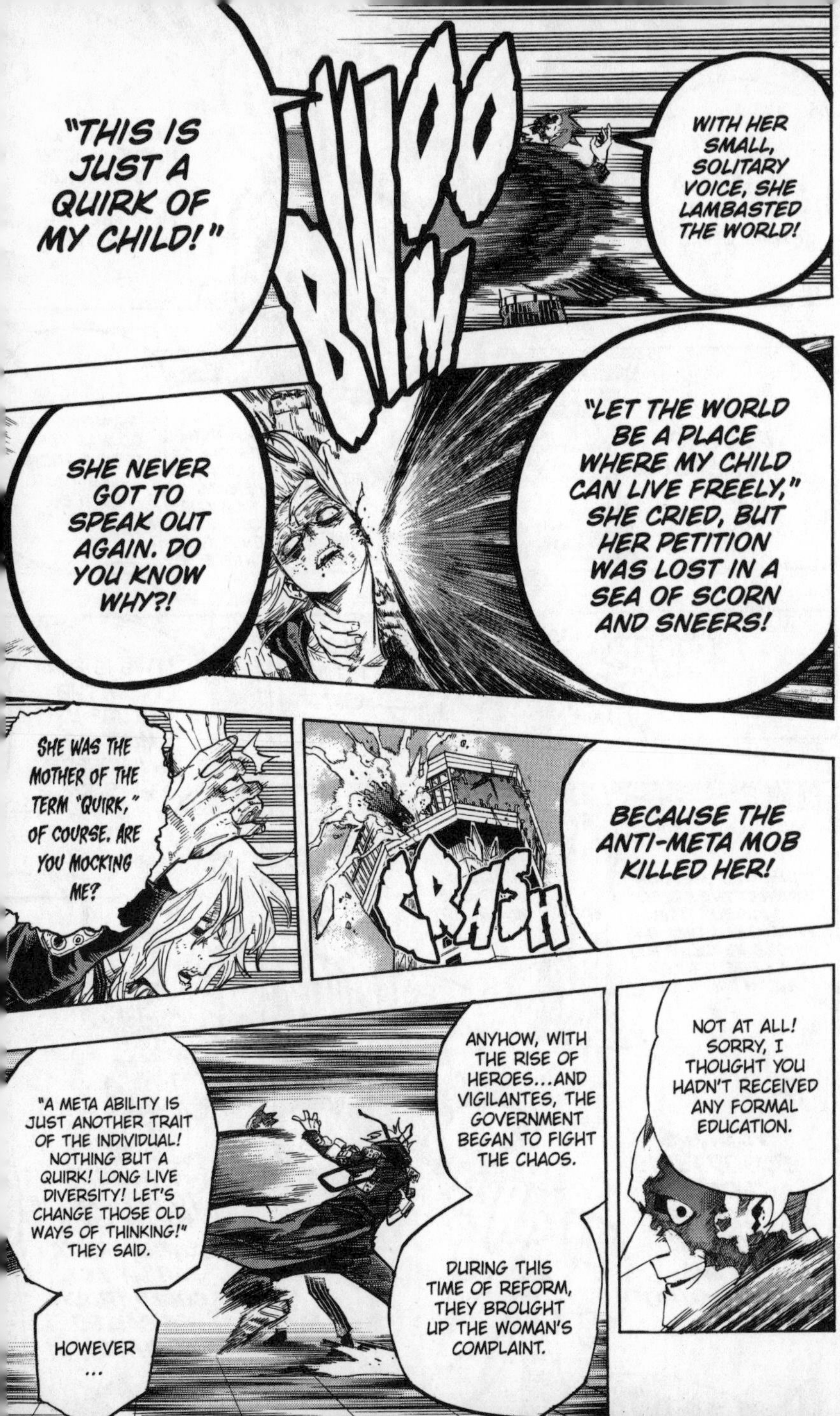

WITH HER SMALL, SOLITARY VOICE, SHE LAMBASTED THE WORLD!
"THIS IS JUST A QUIRK OF MY CHILD!"
"LET THE WORLD BE A PLACE WHERE MY CHILD CAN LIVE FREELY," SHE CRIED, BUT HER PETITION WAS LOST IN A SEA OF SCORN AND SNEERS!
SHE NEVER GOT TO SPEAK OUT AGAIN. DO YOU KNOW WHY?!
BECAUSE THE ANTI-META MOB KILLED HER!
CRASH
SHE WAS THE MOTHER OF THE TERM "QUIRK," OF COURSE. ARE YOU MOCKING ME?
NOT AT ALL! SORRY, I THOUGHT YOU HADN'T RECEIVED ANY FORMAL EDUCATION.
ANYHOW, WITH THE RISE OF HEROES...AND VIGILANTES, THE GOVERNMENT BEGAN TO FIGHT THE CHAOS.
DURING THIS TIME OF REFORM, THEY BROUGHT UP THE WOMAN'S COMPLAINT.
"A META ABILITY IS JUST ANOTHER TRAIT OF THE INDIVIDUAL! NOTHING BUT A QUIRK! LONG LIVE DIVERSITY! LET'S CHANGE THOSE OLD WAYS OF THINKING!" THEY SAID.
HOWEVER ...

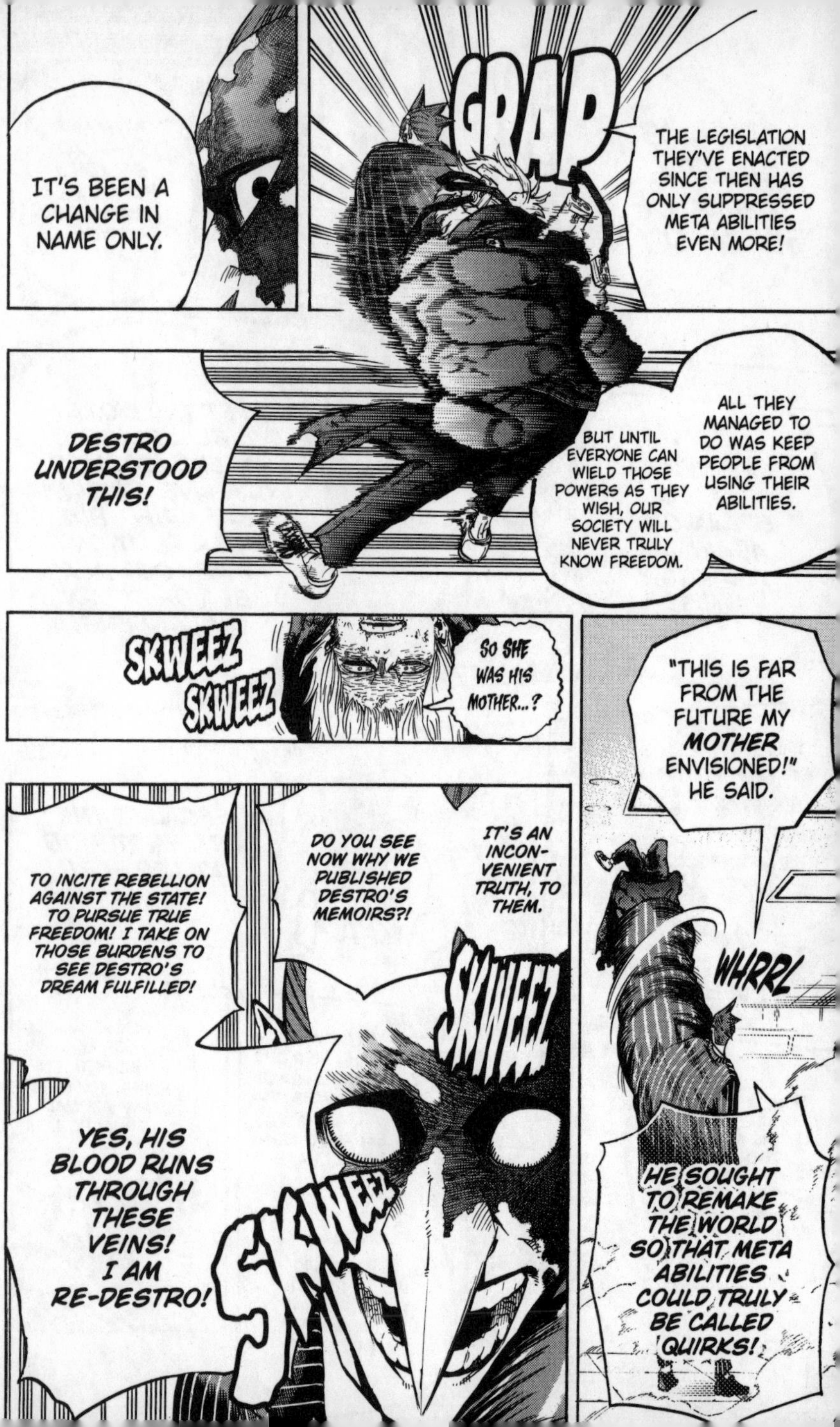
GRAP
THE LEGISLATION THEY'VE ENACTED SINCE THEN HAS ONLY SUPPRESSED META ABILITIES EVEN MORE!
IT'S BEEN A CHANGE IN NAME ONLY.
ALL THEY MANAGED TO DO WAS KEEP PEOPLE FROM USING THEIR ABILITIES.
BUT UNTIL EVERYONE CAN WIELD THOSE POWERS AS THEY WISH, OUR SOCIETY WILL NEVER TRULY KNOW FREEDOM.
DESTRO UNDERSTOOD THIS!
"THIS IS FAR FROM THE FUTURE MY MOTHER ENVISIONED!" HE SAID.
WHRRL
HE SOUGHT TO REMAKE THE WORLD SO THAT META ABILITIES COULD TRULY BE CALLED QUIRKS!
SKWEEZ
SKWEEZ
So SHE WAS HIS MOTHER...?
IT'S AN INCON-VENIENT TRUTH, TO THEM.
DO YOU SEE NOW WHY WE PUBLISHED DESTRO'S MEMOIRS?!
TO INCITE REBELLION AGAINST THE STATE! TO PURSUE TRUE FREEDOM! I TAKE ON THOSE BURDENS TO SEE DESTRO'S DREAM FULFILLED!
SKWEEZ
SKWEEZ
YES, HIS BLOOD RUNS THROUGH THESE VEINS! I AM RE-DESTRO!

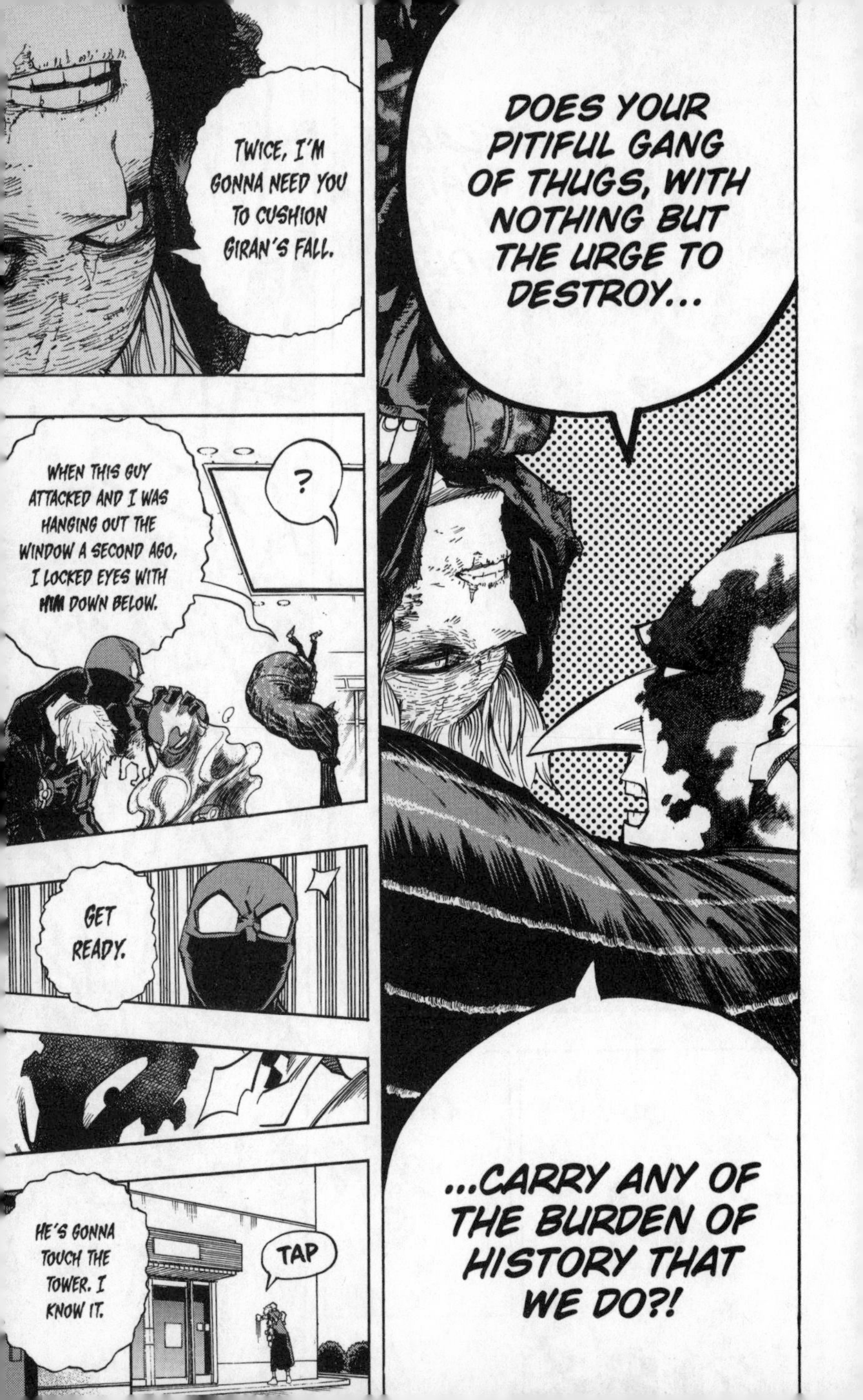
DOES YOUR PITIFUL GANG OF THUGS, WITH NOTHING BUT THE URGE TO DESTROY...
...CARRY ANY OF THE BURDEN OF HISTORY THAT WE DO?!
TWICE, I'M GONNA NEED YOU TO CUSHION GIRAN'S FALL.
?
WHEN THIS GUY ATTACKED AND I WAS HANGING OUT THE WINDOW A SECOND AGO, I LOCKED EYES WITH HIM DOWN BELOW.
GET READY.
TAP
HE'S GONNA TOUCH THE TOWER. I KNOW IT.

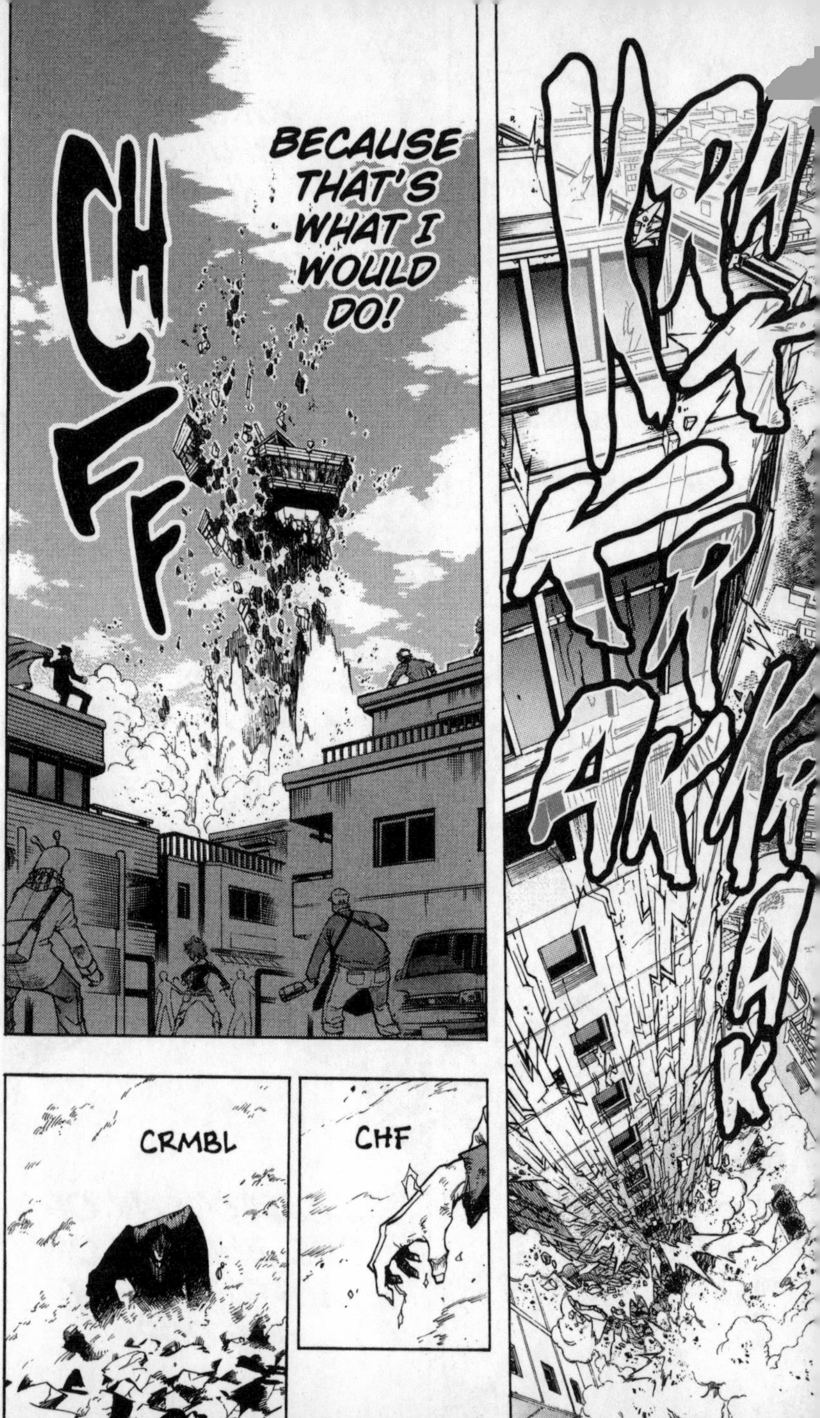
CHFF
BECAUSE THAT'S WHAT I WOULD DO!
CHF
CRMBL

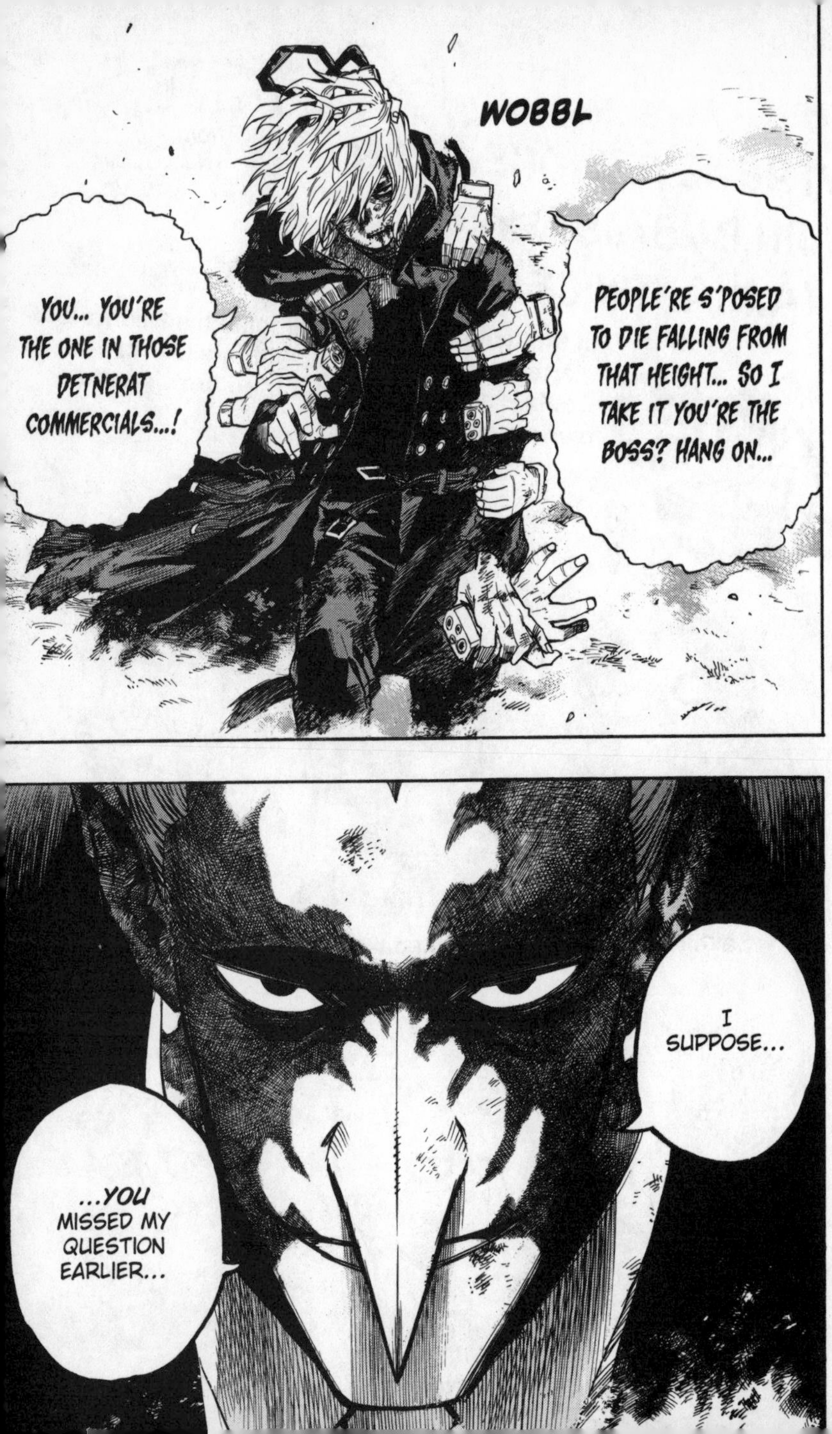
WOBBL
PEOPLE'RE S'POSED TO DIE FALLING FROM THAT HEIGHT... SO I TAKE IT YOU'RE THE BOSS? HANG ON...
YOU... YOU'RE THE ONE IN THOSE DETNERAT COMMERCIALS...!
I SUPPOSE...
...YOU MISSED MY QUESTION EARLIER...

THIS TITLE WRITTEN BY NOGUCHI

THE "EVERYONE DRAW JIN BUBAIGAWARA (A.K.A. TWICE)" CORNER

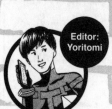

Editor:
Yoritomi

In this volume, Twice overcame his trauma and started doubling himself with his Quirk, so my assistants tried drawing their own versions of Twice.

Sakaino

Ikeda

Imai

Yuzawa

TOGA

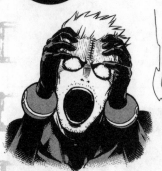

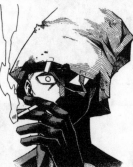

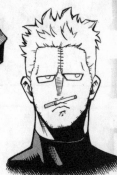

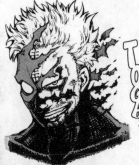

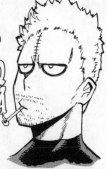

Noguchi

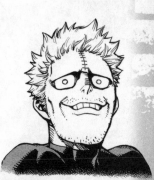

Fushimi

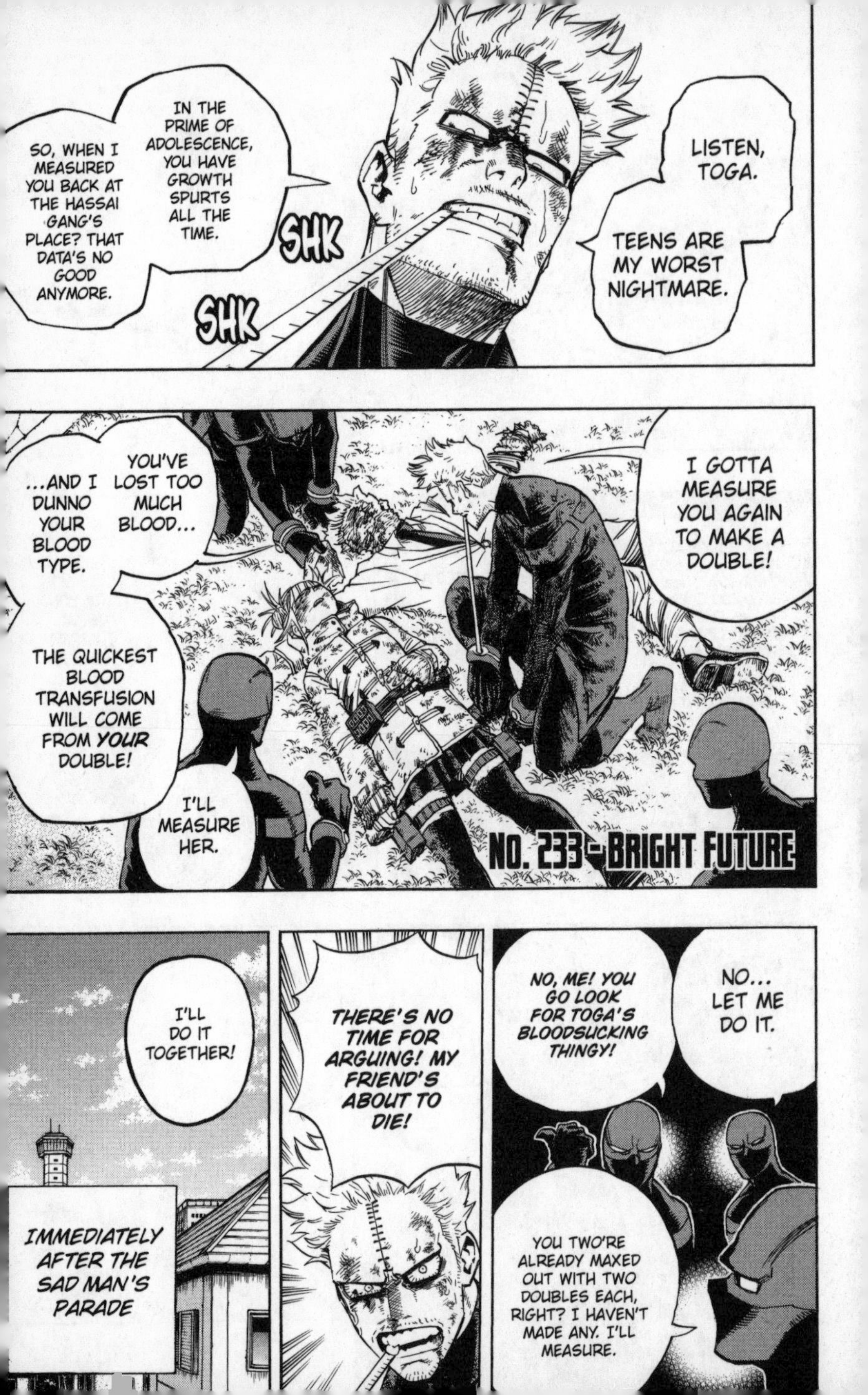
LISTEN, TOGA.
TEENS ARE MY WORST NIGHTMARE.
SHK
IN THE PRIME OF ADOLESCENCE, YOU HAVE GROWTH SPURTS ALL THE TIME.
SO, WHEN I MEASURED YOU BACK AT THE HASSAI GANG'S PLACE? THAT DATA'S NO GOOD ANYMORE.
SHK
I GOTTA MEASURE YOU AGAIN TO MAKE A DOUBLE!
YOU'VE LOST TOO MUCH BLOOD...
...AND I DUNNO YOUR BLOOD TYPE.
THE QUICKEST BLOOD TRANSFUSION WILL COME FROM *YOUR* DOUBLE!
I'LL MEASURE HER.
NO. 233 - BRIGHT FUTURE
NO... LET ME DO IT.
NO, ME! YOU GO LOOK FOR TOGA'S BLOODSUCKING THINGY!
YOU TWO'RE ALREADY MAXED OUT WITH TWO DOUBLES EACH, RIGHT? I HAVEN'T MADE ANY. I'LL MEASURE.
THERE'S NO TIME FOR ARGUING! MY FRIEND'S ABOUT TO DIE!
I'LL DO IT TOGETHER!
IMMEDIATELY AFTER THE SAD MAN'S PARADE

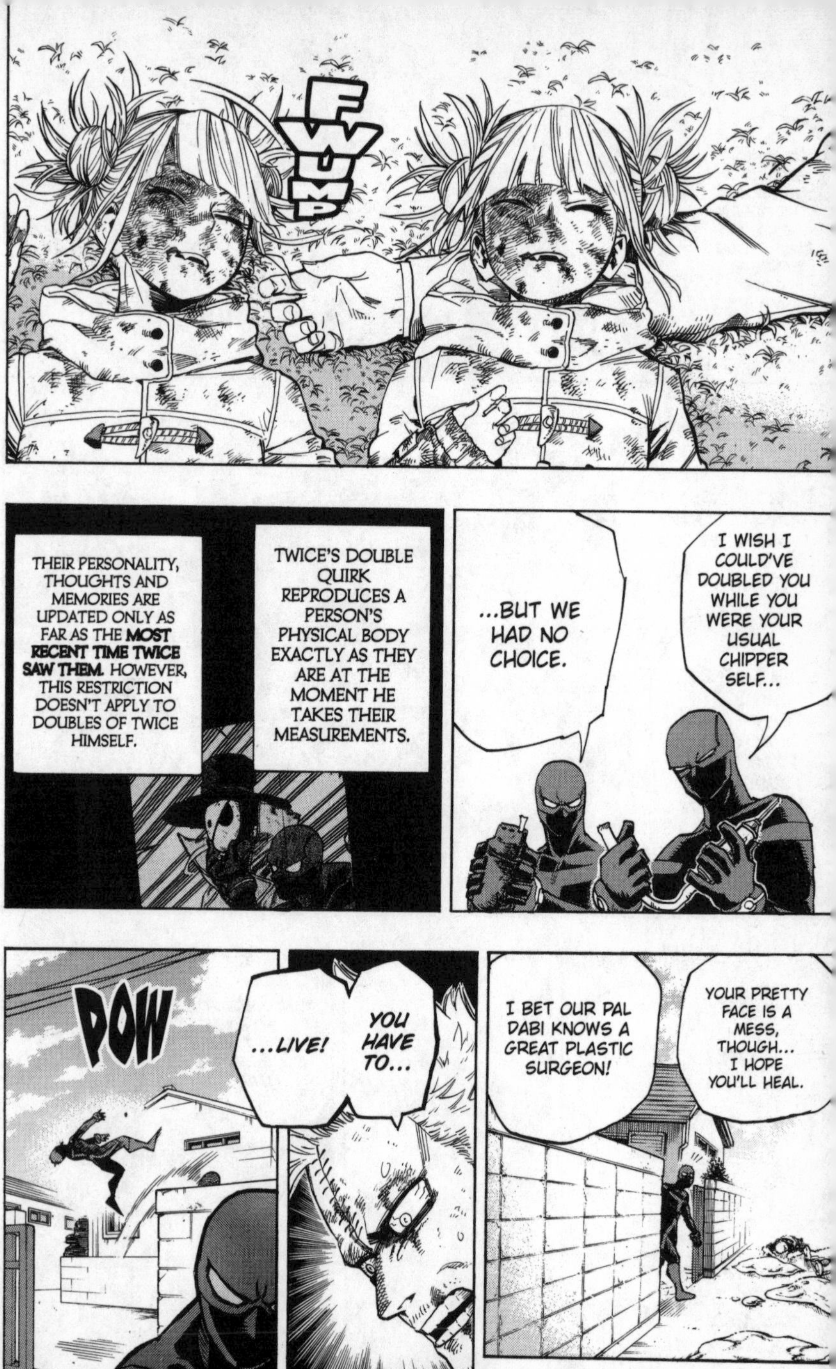
FWUMP
I WISH I COULD'VE DOUBLED YOU WHILE YOU WERE YOUR USUAL CHIPPER SELF...
...BUT WE HAD NO CHOICE.
TWICE'S DOUBLE QUIRK REPRODUCES A PERSON'S PHYSICAL BODY EXACTLY AS THEY ARE AT THE MOMENT HE TAKES THEIR MEASUREMENTS.
THEIR PERSONALITY, THOUGHTS AND MEMORIES ARE UPDATED ONLY AS FAR AS THE **MOST RECENT TIME TWICE SAW THEM.** HOWEVER, THIS RESTRICTION DOESN'T APPLY TO DOUBLES OF TWICE HIMSELF.
YOUR PRETTY FACE IS A MESS, THOUGH... I HOPE YOU'LL HEAL.
I BET OUR PAL DABI KNOWS A GREAT PLASTIC SURGEON!
YOU HAVE TO...
...LIVE!
POW

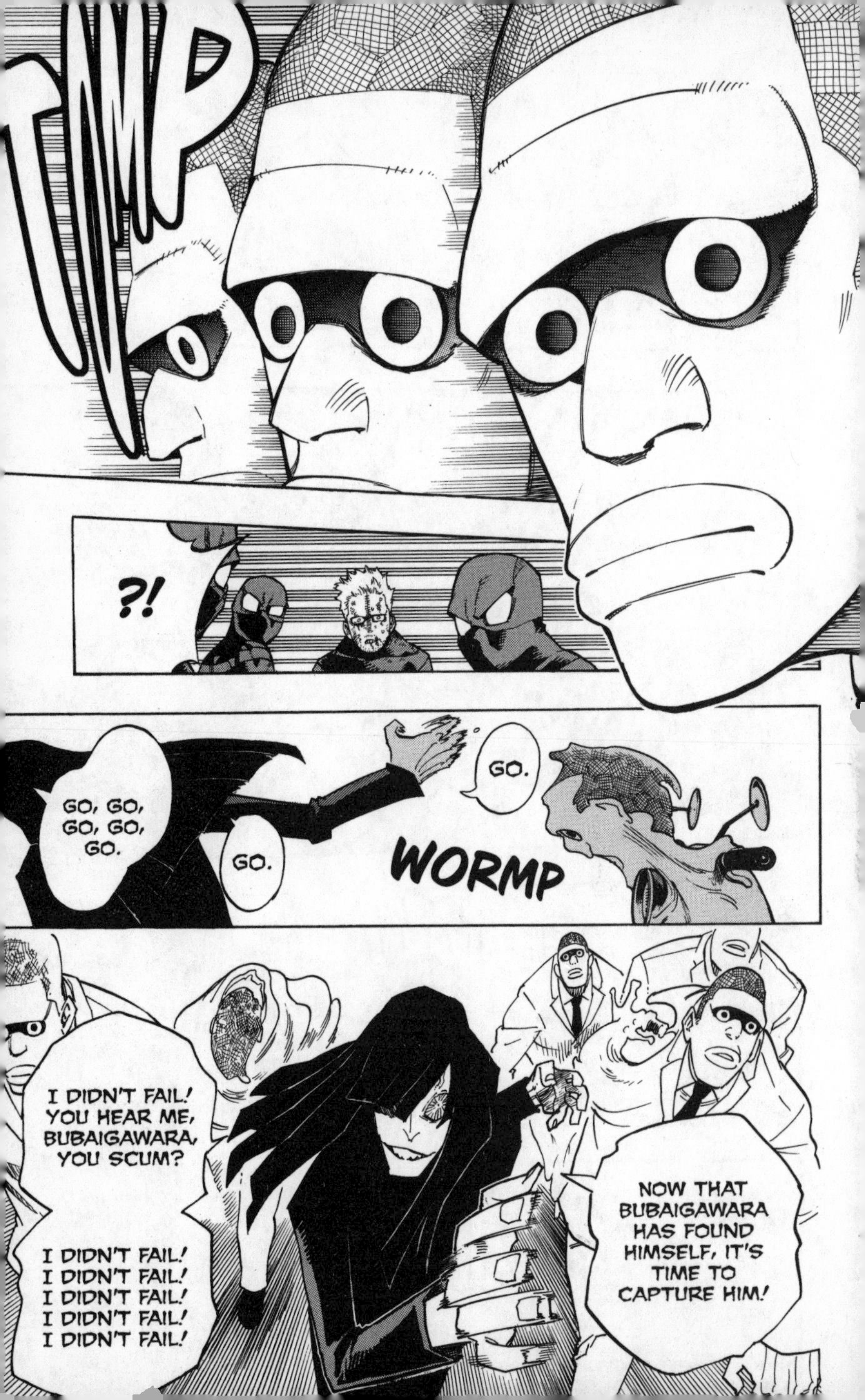
?!
GO.
WORMP
GO.
GO, GO, GO, GO, GO.
NOW THAT BUBAIGAWARA HAS FOUND HIMSELF, IT'S TIME TO CAPTURE HIM!
I DIDN'T FAIL! YOU HEAR ME, BUBAIGAWARA, YOU SCUM?
I DIDN'T FAIL! I DIDN'T FAIL! I DIDN'T FAIL! I DIDN'T FAIL! I DIDN'T FAIL!

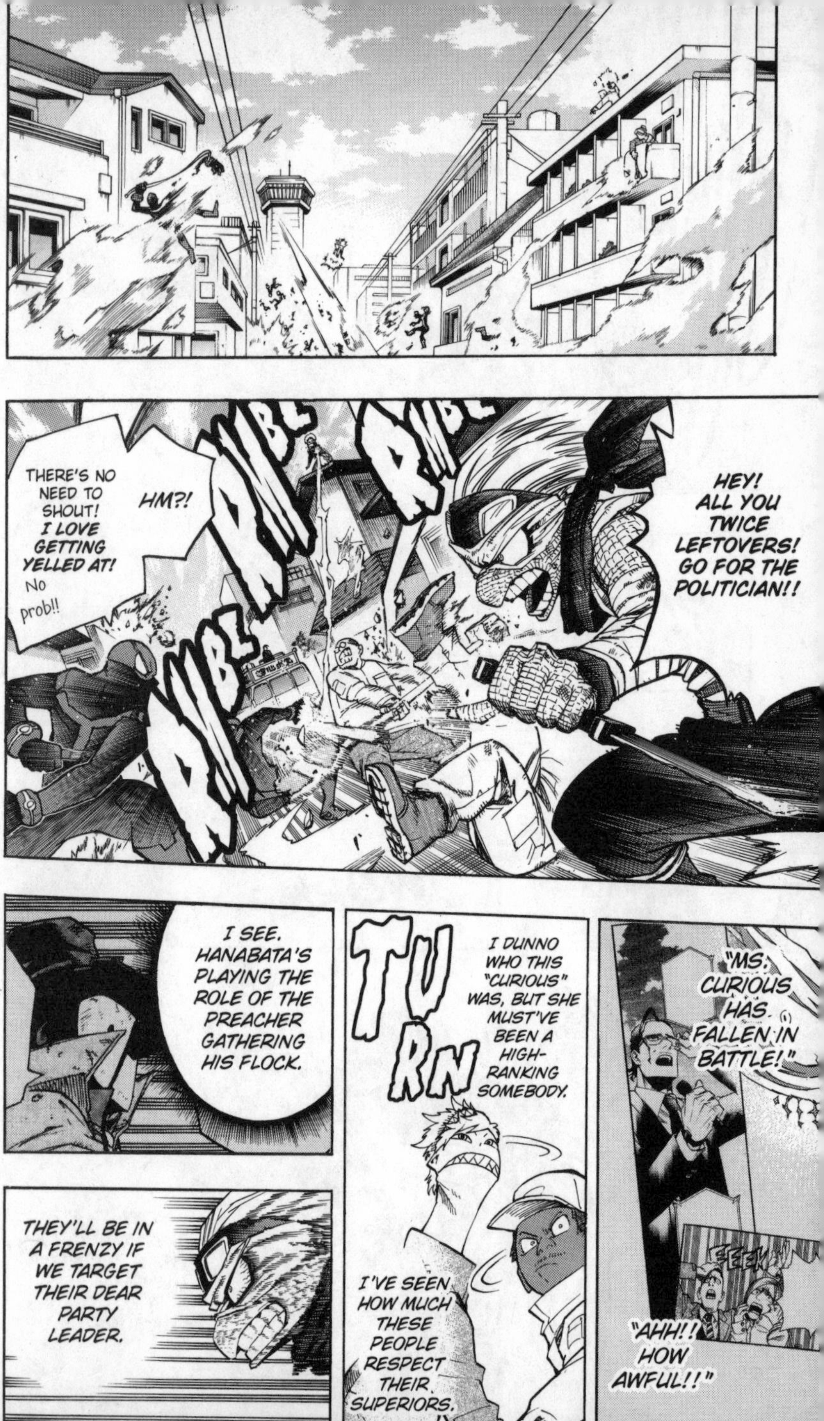
HEY! ALL YOU TWICE LEFTOVERS! GO FOR THE POLITICIAN!!
HM?!
THERE'S NO NEED TO SHOUT! I LOVE GETTING YELLED AT! No prob!!
"MS. CURIOUS HAS FALLEN IN BATTLE!"
"AHH!! HOW AWFUL!!"
TURN
I DUNNO WHO THIS "CURIOUS" WAS, BUT SHE MUST'VE BEEN A HIGH-RANKING SOMEBODY.
I'VE SEEN HOW MUCH THESE PEOPLE RESPECT THEIR SUPERIORS.
I SEE. HANABATA'S PLAYING THE ROLE OF THE PREACHER GATHERING HIS FLOCK.
THEY'LL BE IN A FRENZY IF WE TARGET THEIR DEAR PARTY LEADER.

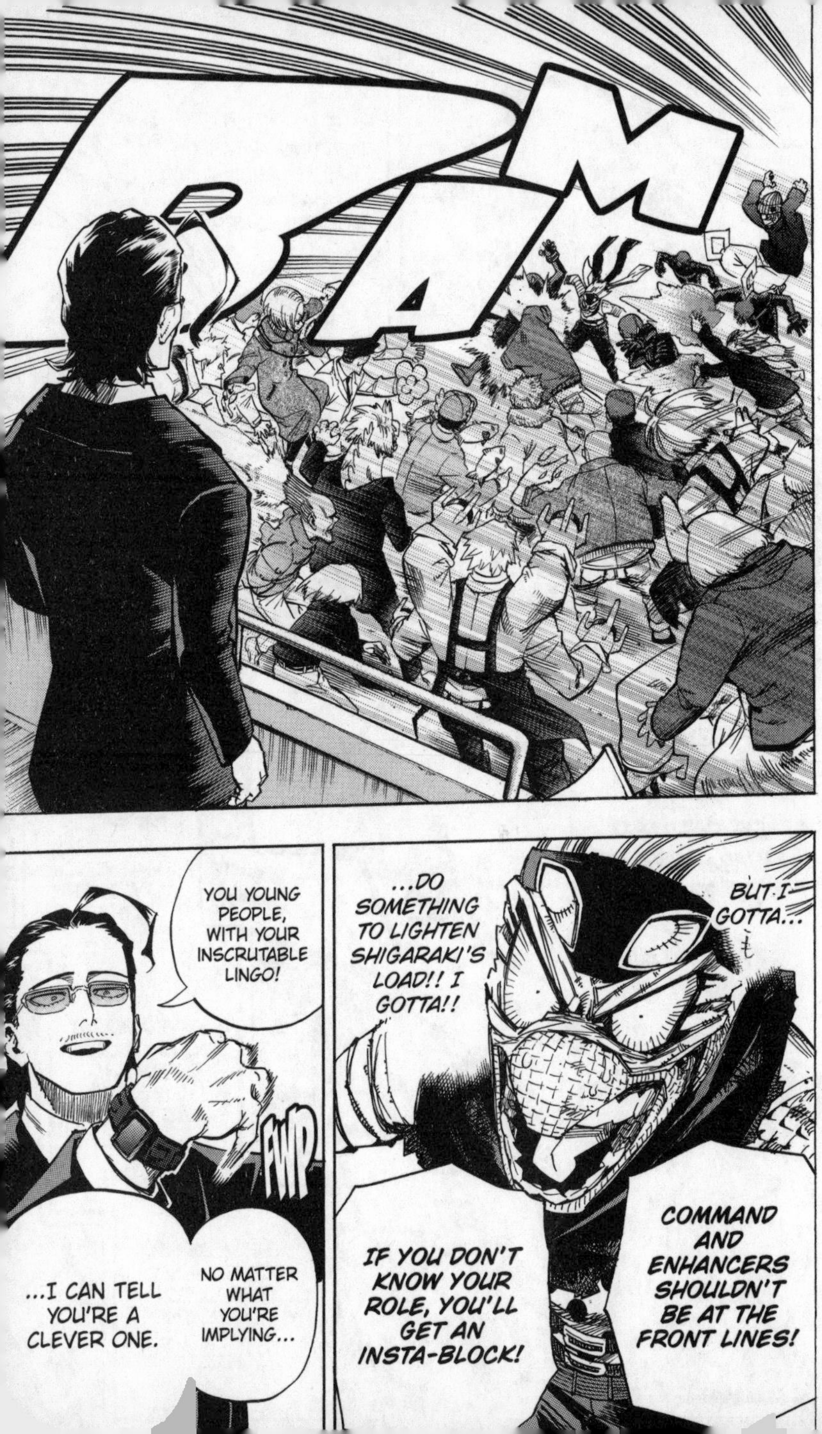
BUT I- GOTTA...
...DO SOMETHING TO LIGHTEN SHIGARAKI'S LOAD!! I GOTTA!!
COMMAND AND ENHANCERS SHOULDN'T BE AT THE FRONT LINES!
IF YOU DON'T KNOW YOUR ROLE, YOU'LL GET AN INSTA-BLOCK!
YOU YOUNG PEOPLE, WITH YOUR INSCRUTABLE LINGO!
FWP
NO MATTER WHAT YOU'RE IMPLYING...
...I CAN TELL YOU'RE A CLEVER ONE.

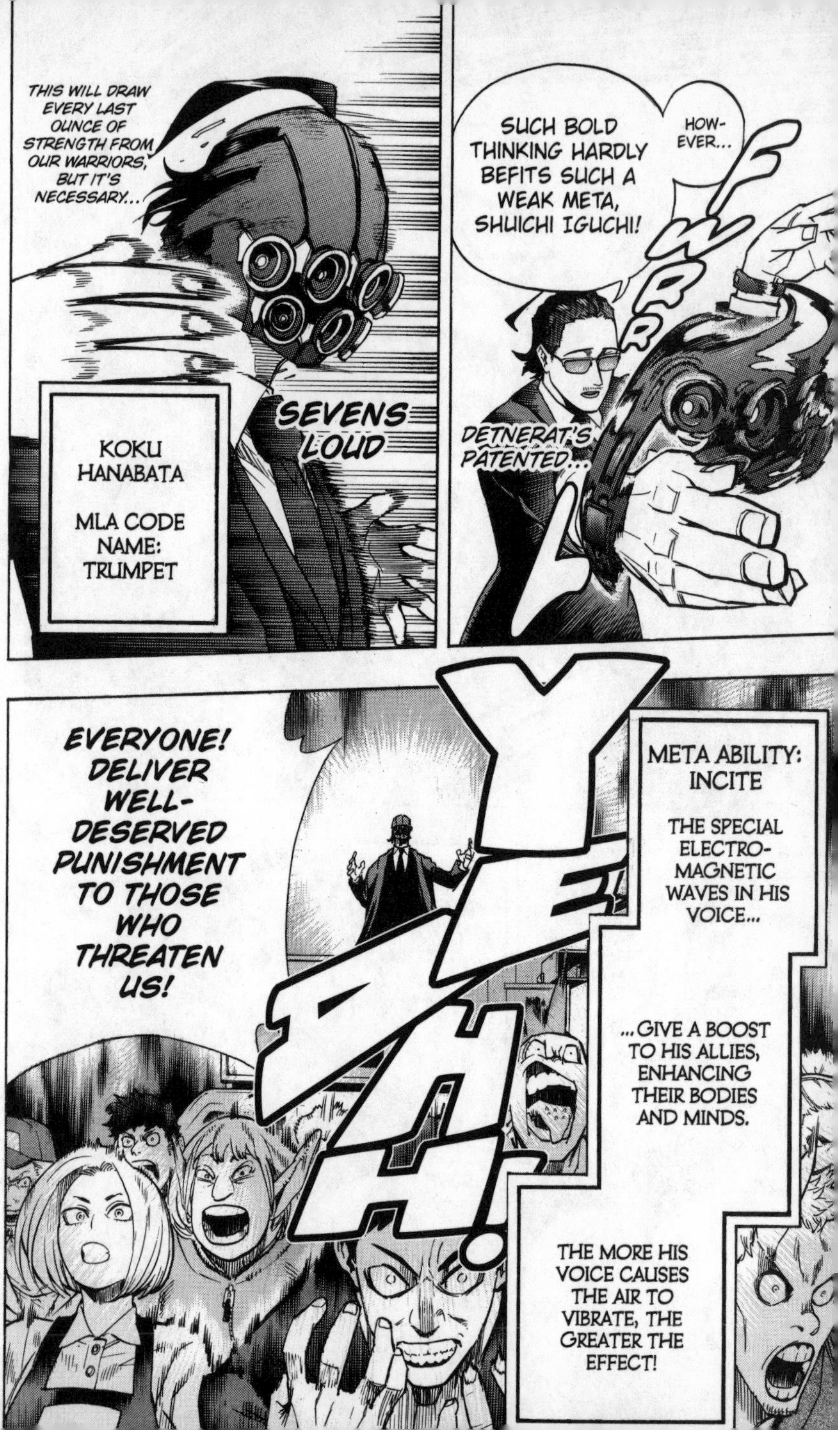
SUCH BOLD THINKING HARDLY BEFITS SUCH A WEAK META, SHUICHI IGUCHI!
HOW-EVER...
FWRR
DETNERAT'S PATENTED...
THIS WILL DRAW EVERY LAST OUNCE OF STRENGTH FROM OUR WARRIORS, BUT IT'S NECESSARY...
SEVENS LOUD
KOKU HANABATA
MLA CODE NAME: TRUMPET
META ABILITY: INCITE
THE SPECIAL ELECTRO-MAGNETIC WAVES IN HIS VOICE...
YEAH!
EVERYONE! DELIVER WELL-DESERVED PUNISHMENT TO THOSE WHO THREATEN US!
...GIVE A BOOST TO HIS ALLIES, ENHANCING THEIR BODIES AND MINDS.
THE MORE HIS VOICE CAUSES THE AIR TO VIBRATE, THE GREATER THE EFFECT!

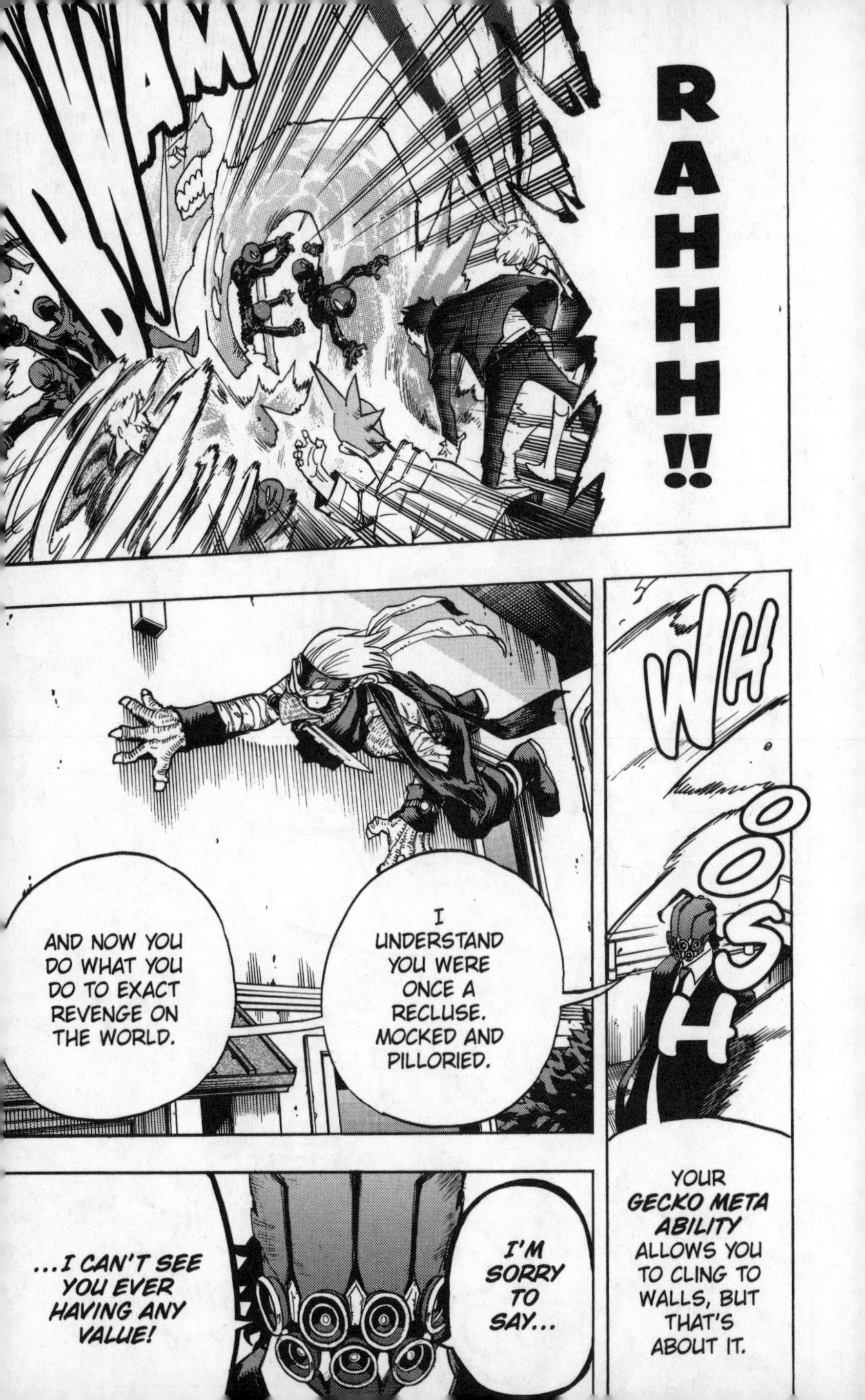
RAHHHH!!
WHAM
WHOOOSH
I UNDERSTAND YOU WERE ONCE A RECLUSE. MOCKED AND PILLORIED.
AND NOW YOU DO WHAT YOU DO TO EXACT REVENGE ON THE WORLD.
YOUR *GECKO META ABILITY* ALLOWS YOU TO CLING TO WALLS, BUT THAT'S ABOUT IT.
I'M SORRY TO SAY...
...I CAN'T SEE YOU EVER HAVING ANY VALUE!

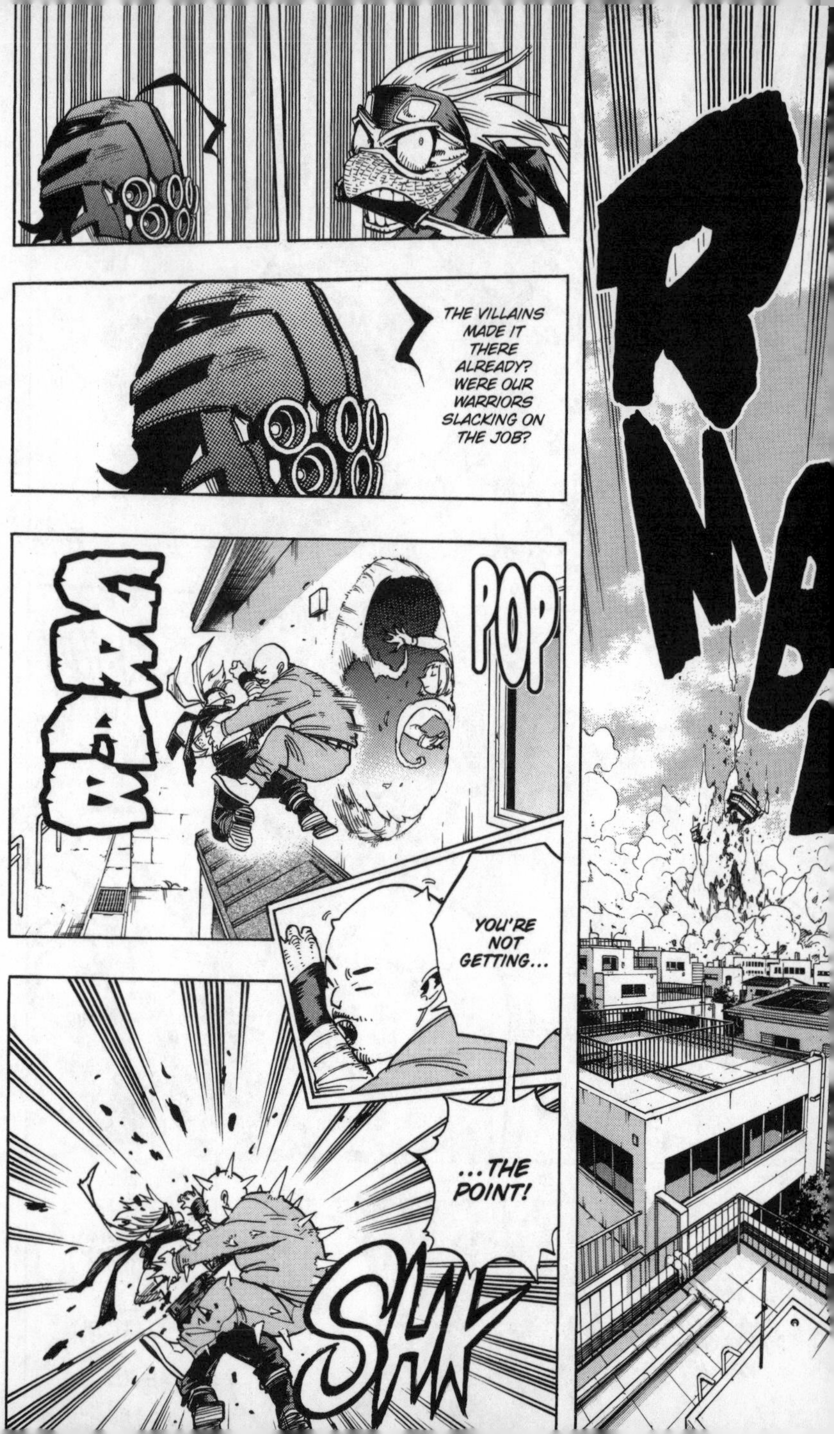
RMB
THE VILLAINS MADE IT THERE ALREADY? WERE OUR WARRIORS SLACKING ON THE JOB?
POP
GRAB
YOU'RE NOT GETTING...
...THE POINT!
SHK

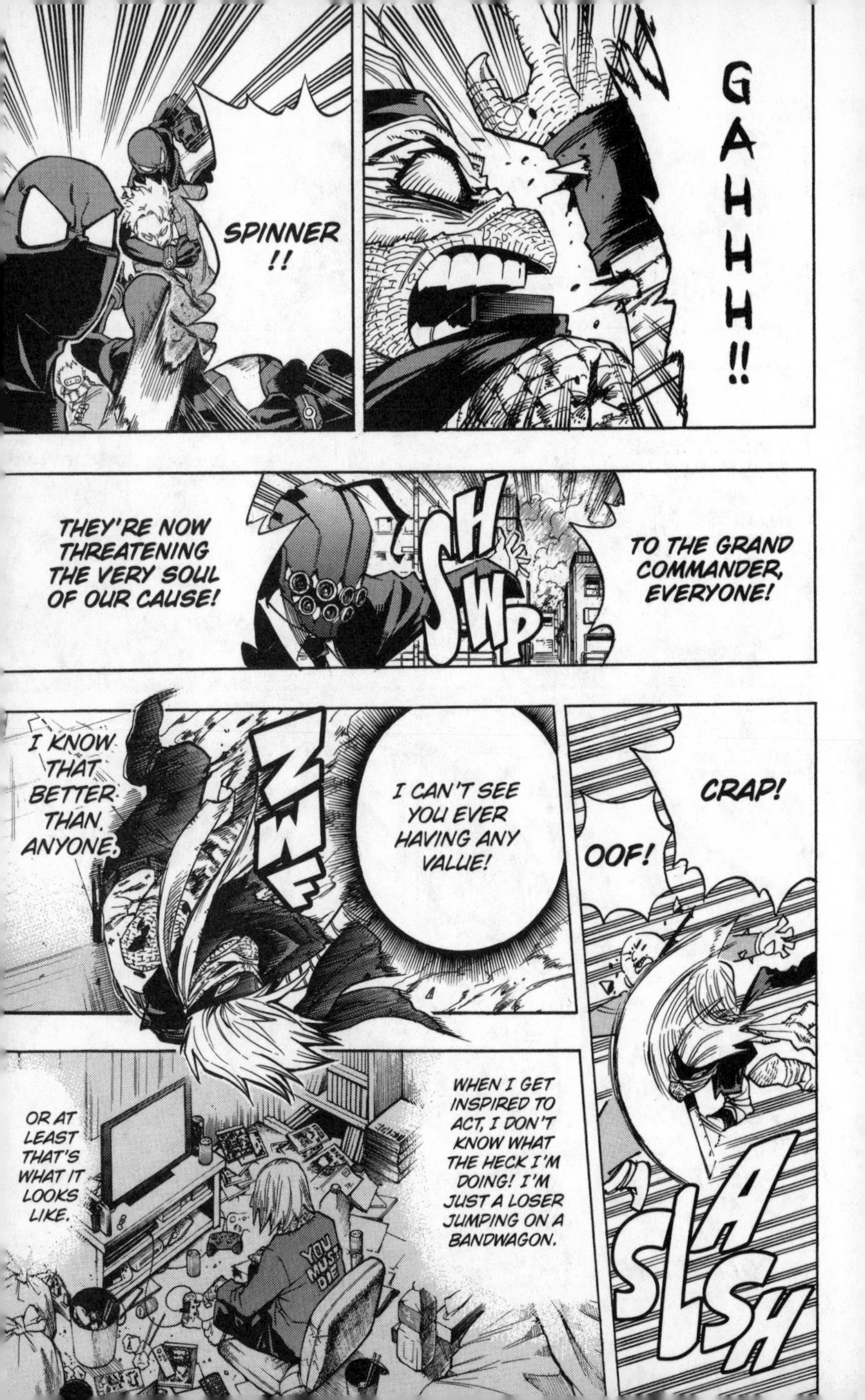
GAHHH!!
SPINNER!!
TO THE GRAND COMMANDER, EVERYONE!
THEY'RE NOW THREATENING THE VERY SOUL OF OUR CAUSE!
CRAP!
OOF!
I CAN'T SEE YOU EVER HAVING ANY VALUE!
I KNOW THAT BETTER THAN ANYONE.
WHEN I GET INSPIRED TO ACT, I DON'T KNOW WHAT THE HECK I'M DOING! I'M JUST A LOSER JUMPING ON A BANDWAGON.
YOU MUST DIE
OR AT LEAST THAT'S WHAT IT LOOKS LIKE.

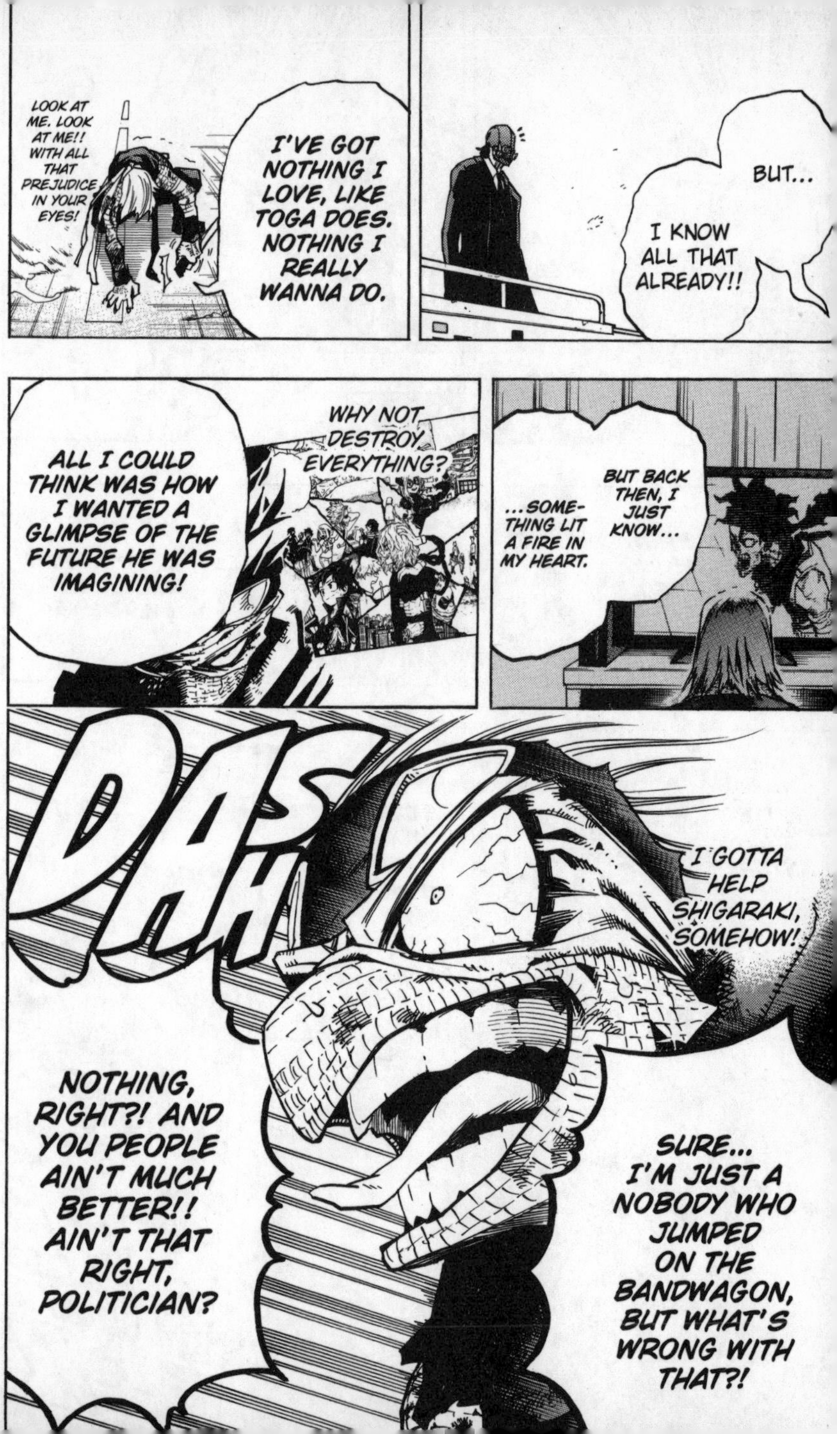
BUT...
I KNOW ALL THAT ALREADY!!
I'VE GOT NOTHING I LOVE, LIKE TOGA DOES. NOTHING I REALLY WANNA DO.
LOOK AT ME. LOOK AT ME!! WITH ALL THAT PREJUDICE IN YOUR EYES!
BUT BACK THEN, I JUST KNOW...
...SOMETHING LIT A FIRE IN MY HEART.
WHY NOT DESTROY EVERYTHING?
ALL I COULD THINK WAS HOW I WANTED A GLIMPSE OF THE FUTURE HE WAS IMAGINING!
I GOTTA HELP SHIGARAKI, SOMEHOW!
DASH
SURE... I'M JUST A NOBODY WHO JUMPED ON THE BANDWAGON, BUT WHAT'S WRONG WITH THAT?!
NOTHING, RIGHT?! AND YOU PEOPLE AIN'T MUCH BETTER!! AIN'T THAT RIGHT, POLITICIAN?

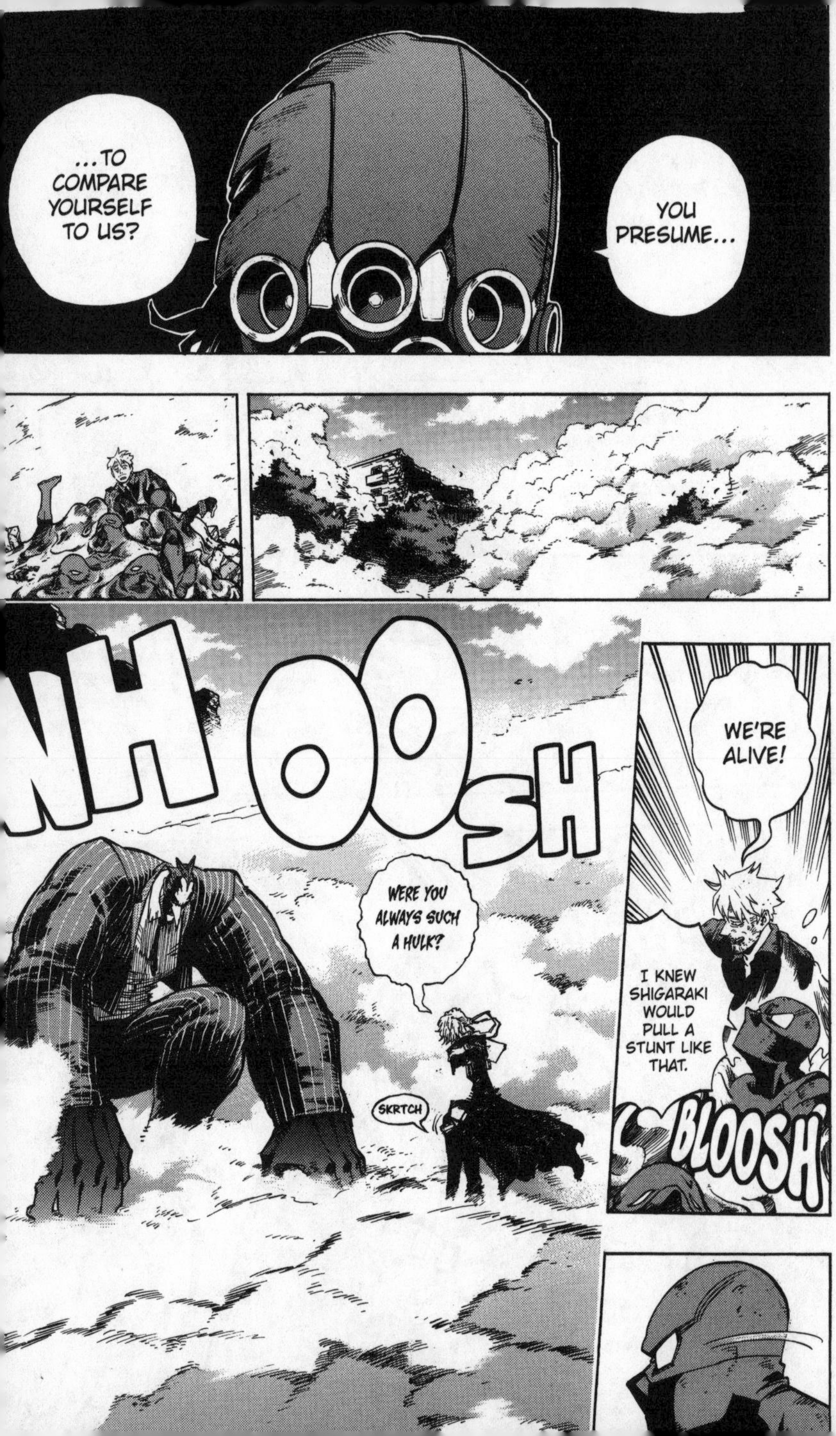
YOU PRESUME...
...TO COMPARE YOURSELF TO US?
WE'RE ALIVE!
I KNEW SHIGARAKI WOULD PULL A STUNT LIKE THAT.
BLOOSH
WHOOSH
WERE YOU ALWAYS SUCH A HULK?
SKRTCH

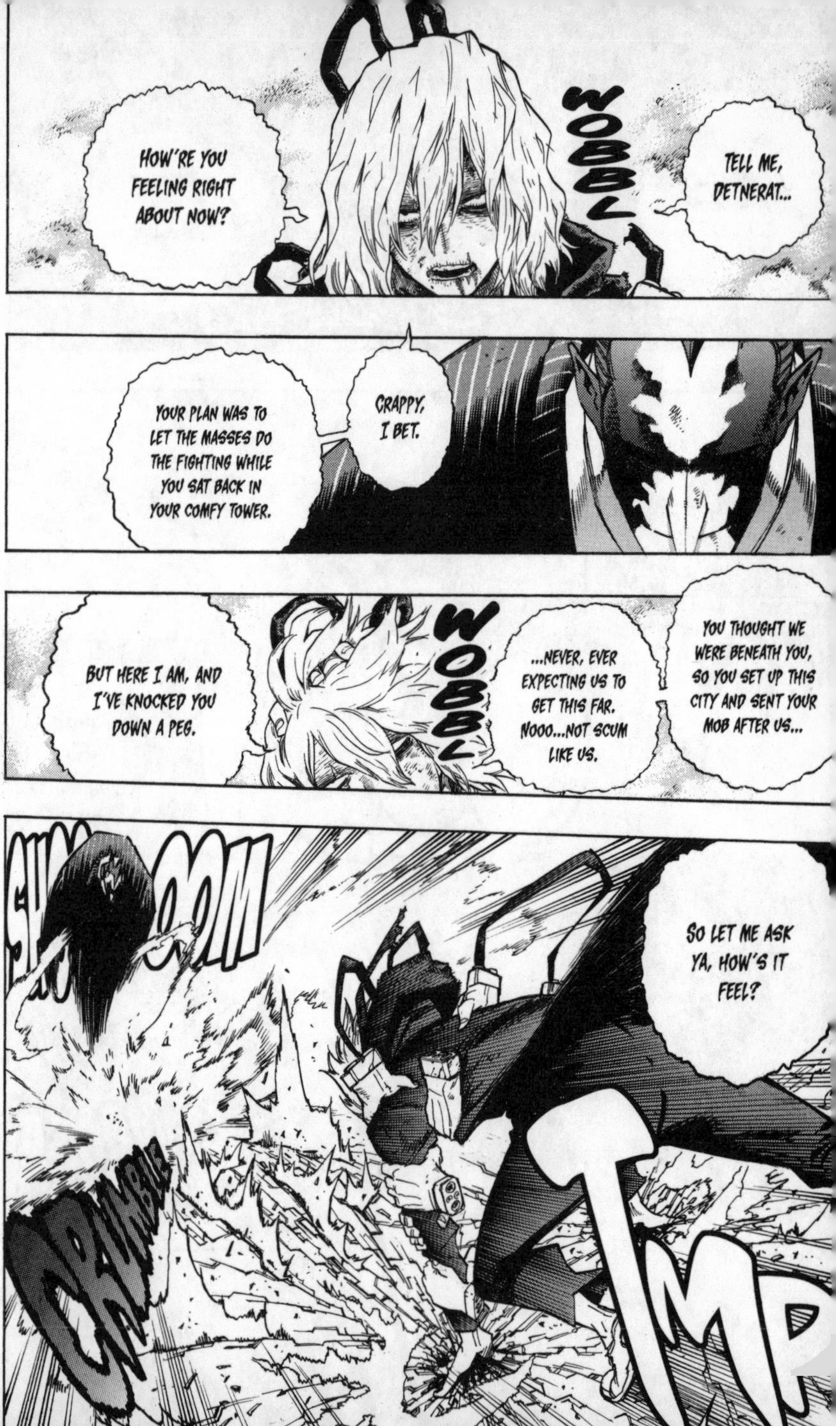
TELL ME, DETNERAT...
WOBBL
HOW'RE YOU FEELING RIGHT ABOUT NOW?
CRAPPY, I BET.
YOUR PLAN WAS TO LET THE MASSES DO THE FIGHTING WHILE YOU SAT BACK IN YOUR COMFY TOWER.
YOU THOUGHT WE WERE BENEATH YOU, SO YOU SET UP THIS CITY AND SENT YOUR MOB AFTER US...
...NEVER, EVER EXPECTING US TO GET THIS FAR. NOOO...NOT SCUM LIKE US.
WOBBL
BUT HERE I AM, AND I'VE KNOCKED YOU DOWN A PEG.
SO LET ME ASK YA, HOW'S IT FEEL?

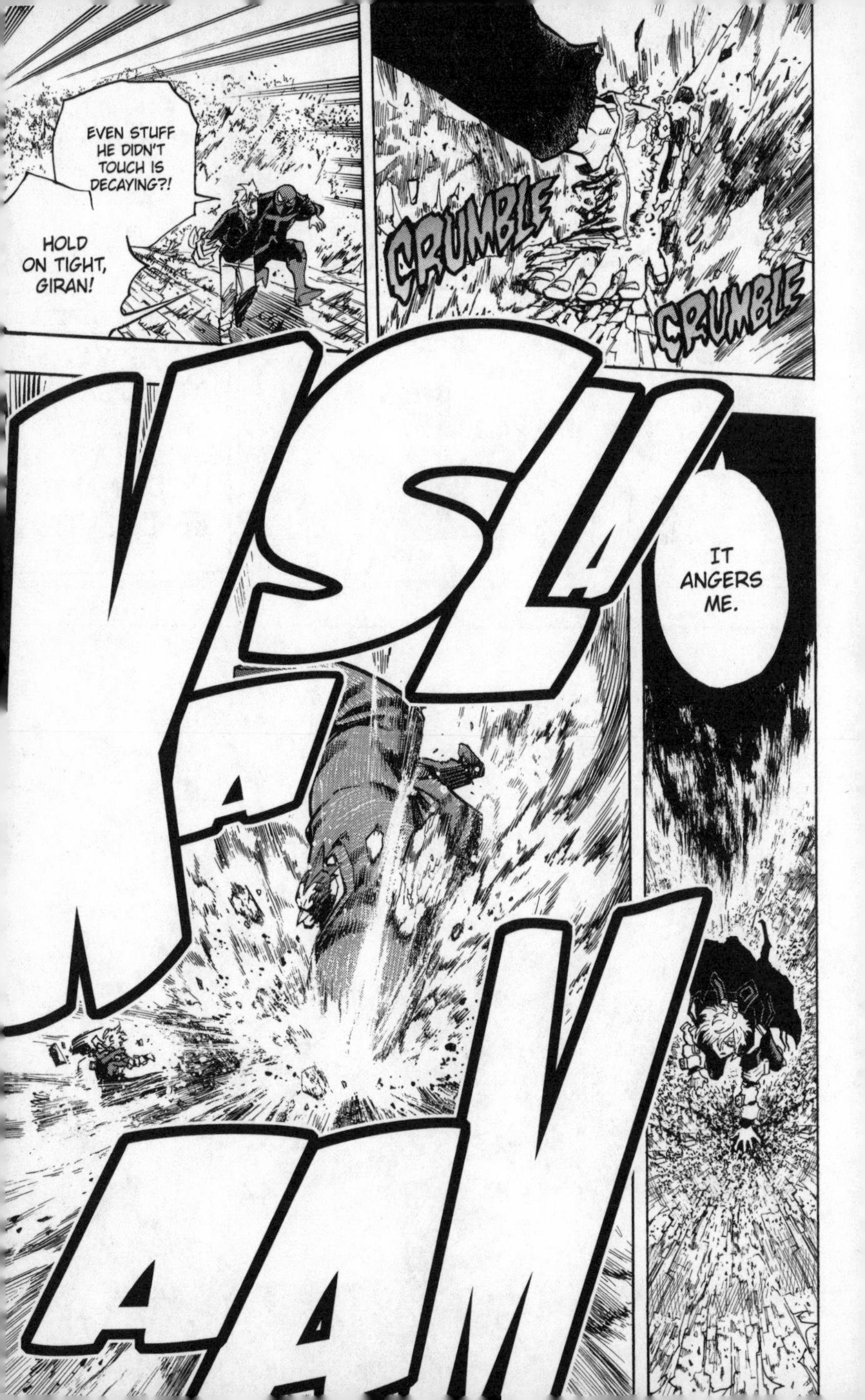
CRUMBLE
CRUMBLE
EVEN STUFF HE DIDN'T TOUCH IS DECAYING?!
HOLD ON TIGHT, GIRAN!
IT ANGERS ME.
SLAAAM

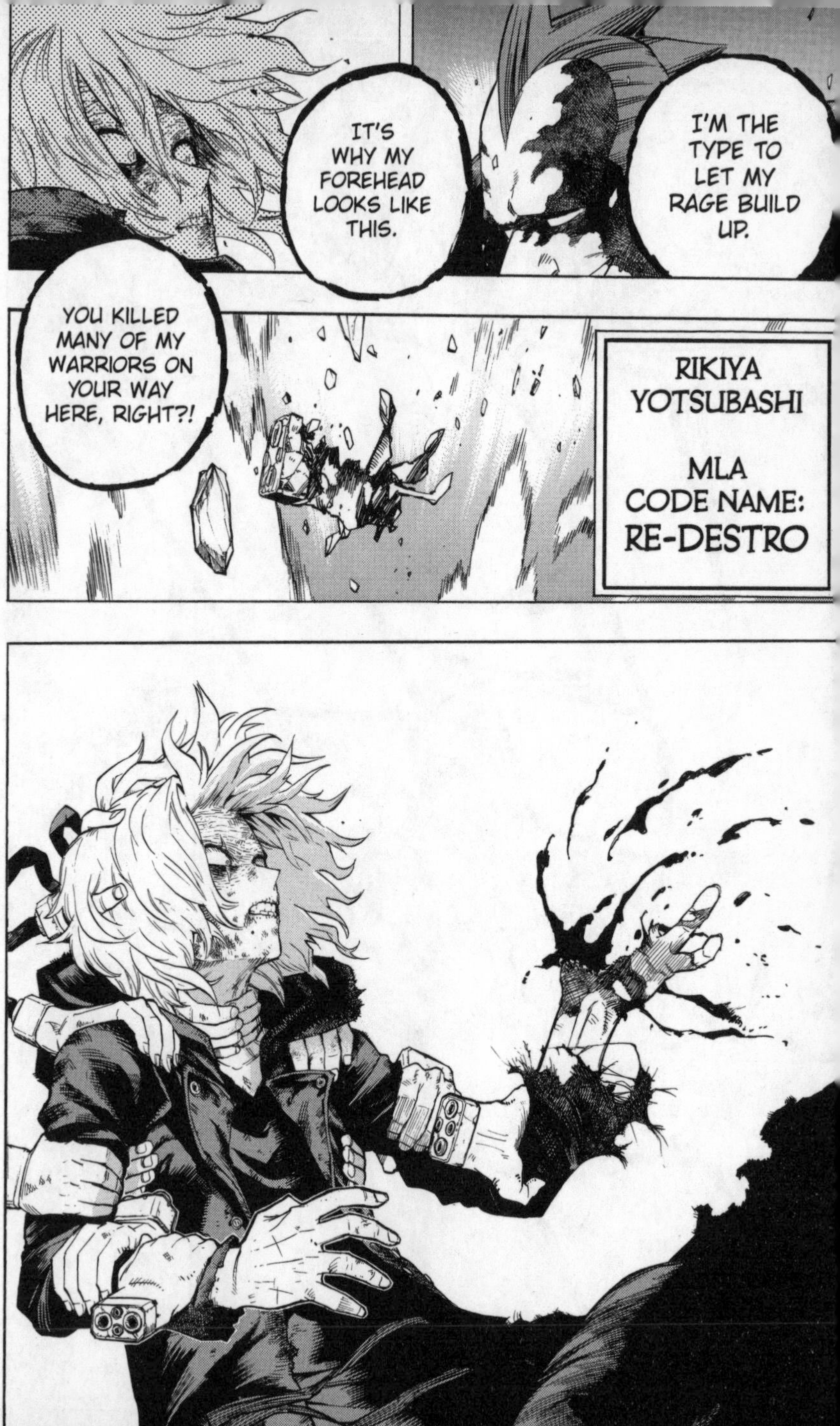
I'M THE TYPE TO LET MY RAGE BUILD UP.
IT'S WHY MY FOREHEAD LOOKS LIKE THIS.
YOU KILLED MANY OF MY WARRIORS ON YOUR WAY HERE, RIGHT?!
RIKIYA YOTSUBASHI
MLA CODE NAME: RE-DESTRO

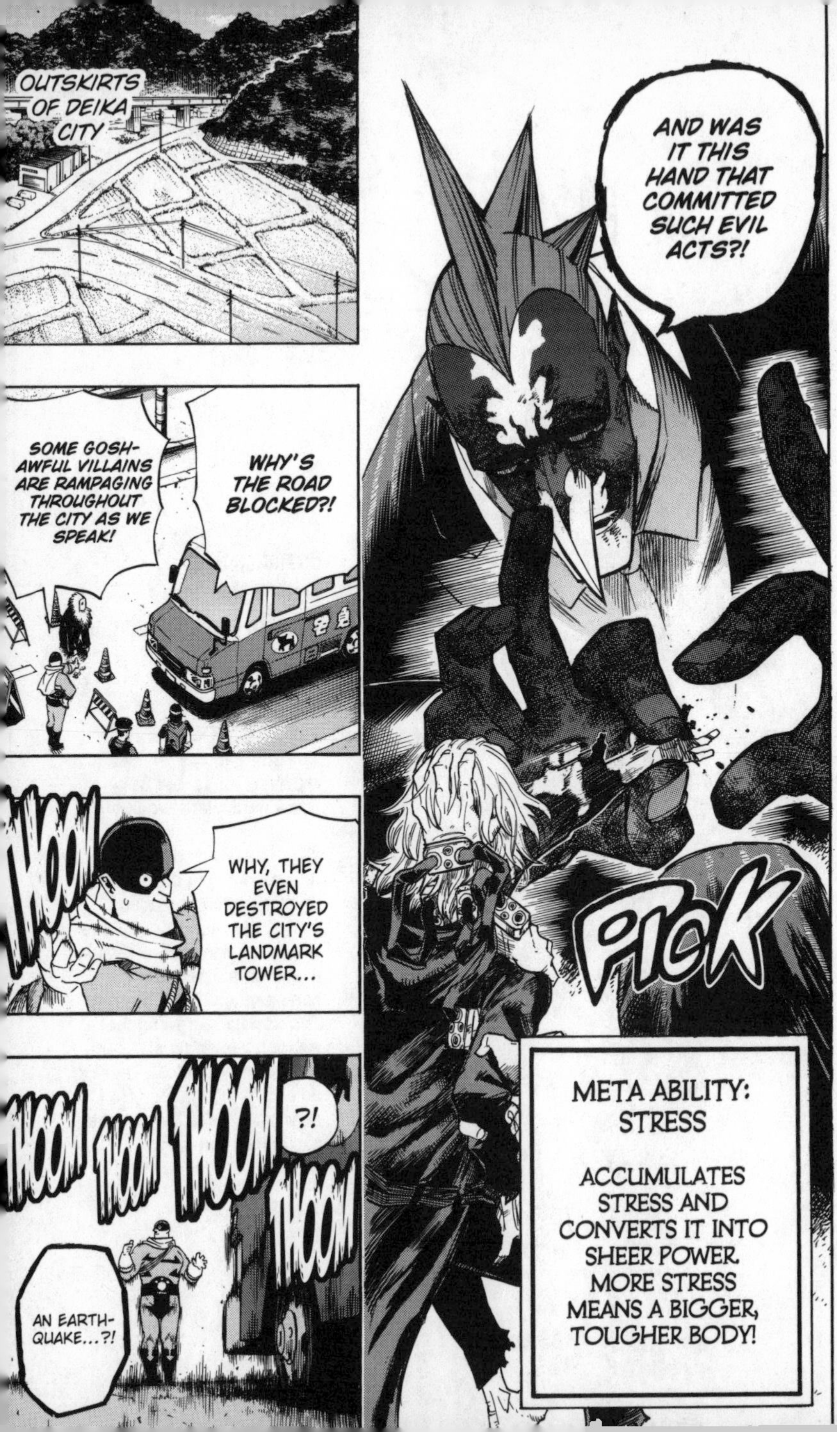
AND WAS IT THIS HAND THAT COMMITTED SUCH EVIL ACTS?!
PICK
META ABILITY: STRESS
ACCUMULATES STRESS AND CONVERTS IT INTO SHEER POWER. MORE STRESS MEANS A BIGGER, TOUGHER BODY!
OUTSKIRTS OF DEIKA CITY
WHY'S THE ROAD BLOCKED?!
SOME GOSH-AWFUL VILLAINS ARE RAMPAGING THROUGHOUT THE CITY AS WE SPEAK!
WHY, THEY EVEN DESTROYED THE CITY'S LANDMARK TOWER...
THOOM
THOOM THOOM THOOM THOOM
?!
AN EARTH-QUAKE...?!

SPINNER (21) (SHUICHI IGUCHI)

THE COSPLAY

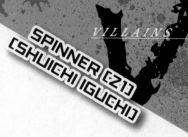

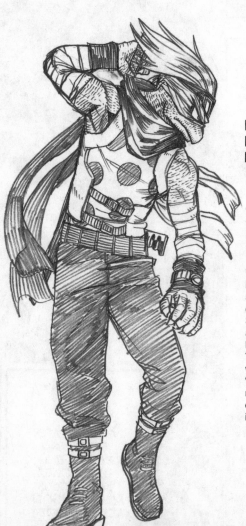

Birthday: 8/8
Height: 174 cm
Favorite Thing: Video games

THE SUPPLEMENT

The entire Iguchi family has reptilian Quirks, but Spinner has a particularly weak one.

When he first appeared, he was wielding an amalgamation of blades I called "the Super Knife Knife Sword," which was really just a bluff on his part to make him seem more threatening. The assistant drawing that weapon went pale and said, "This is impossible… There's no end to the blades!" So I decided to have Deku smash it to pieces with a kick.

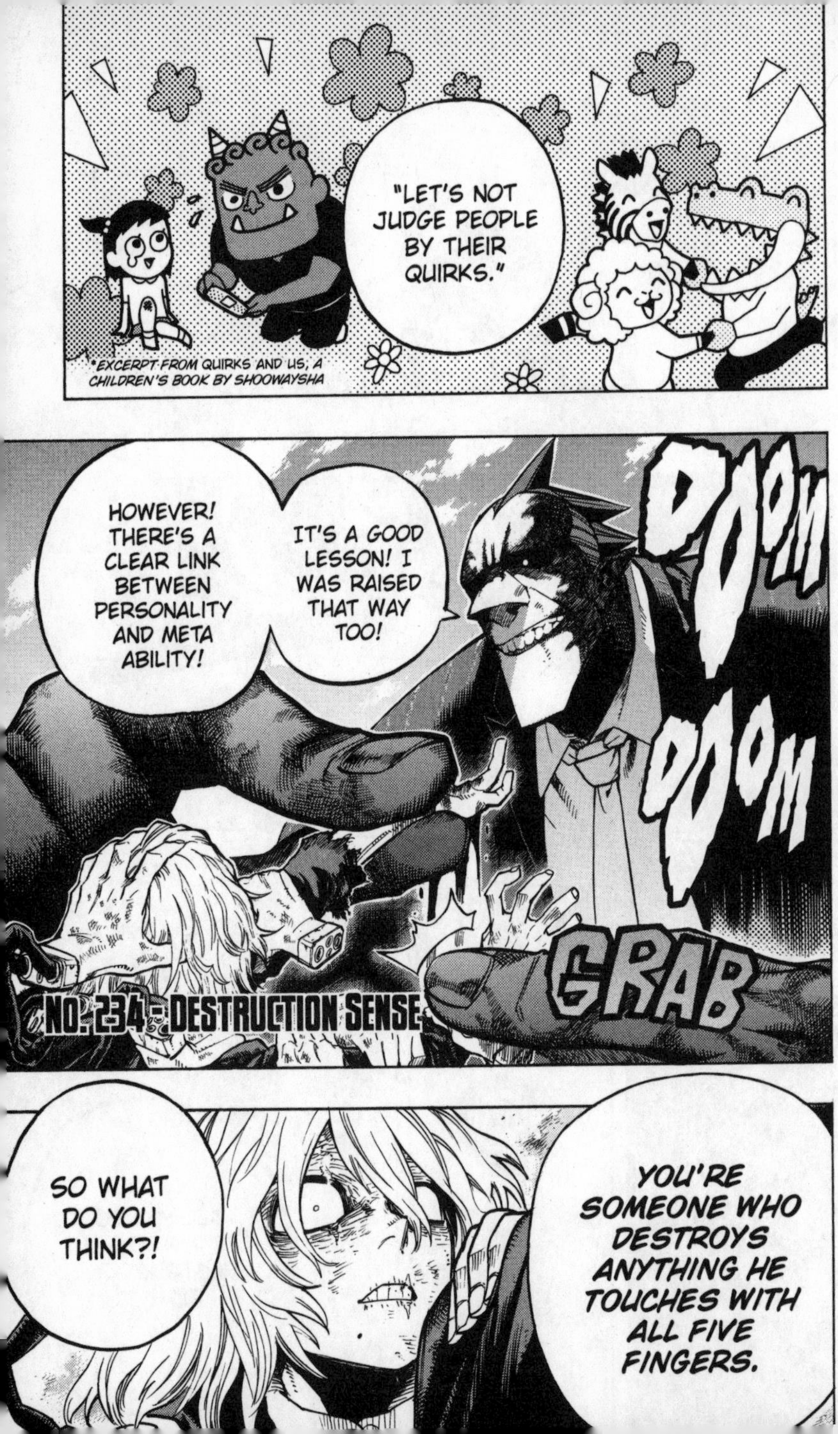
"LET'S NOT JUDGE PEOPLE BY THEIR QUIRKS."
*EXCERPT FROM QUIRKS AND US, A CHILDREN'S BOOK BY SHOOWAYSHA
DOOM DOOM
IT'S A GOOD LESSON! I WAS RAISED THAT WAY TOO!
HOWEVER! THERE'S A CLEAR LINK BETWEEN PERSONALITY AND META ABILITY!
GRAB
NO. 234 - DESTRUCTION SENSE
YOU'RE SOMEONE WHO DESTROYS ANYTHING HE TOUCHES WITH ALL FIVE FINGERS.
SO WHAT DO YOU THINK?!

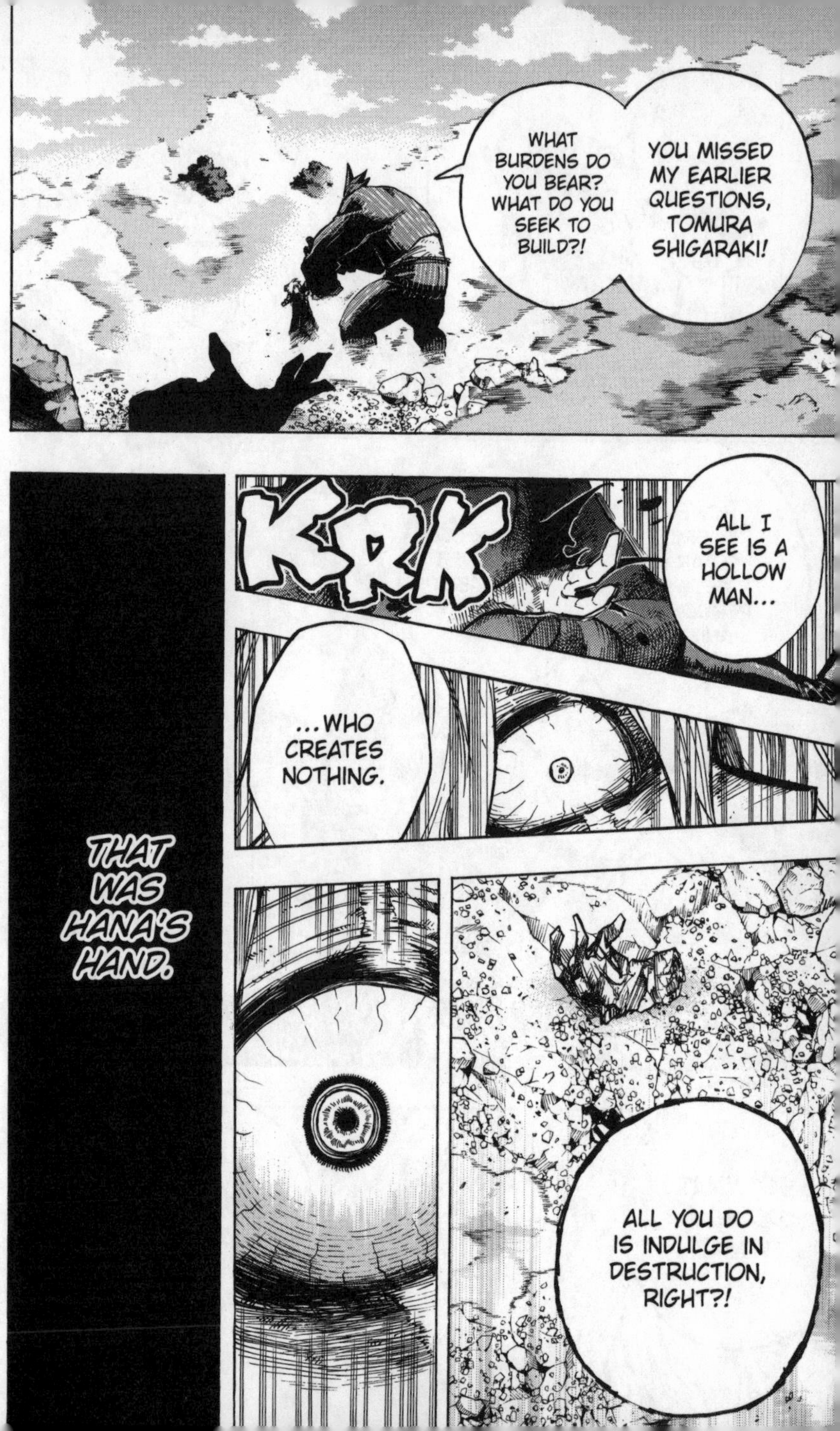
YOU MISSED MY EARLIER QUESTIONS, TOMURA SHIGARAKI!
WHAT BURDENS DO YOU BEAR? WHAT DO YOU SEEK TO BUILD?!
KRK
ALL I SEE IS A HOLLOW MAN...
...WHO CREATES NOTHING.
ALL YOU DO IS INDULGE IN DESTRUCTION, RIGHT?!
THAT WAS HANA'S HAND.

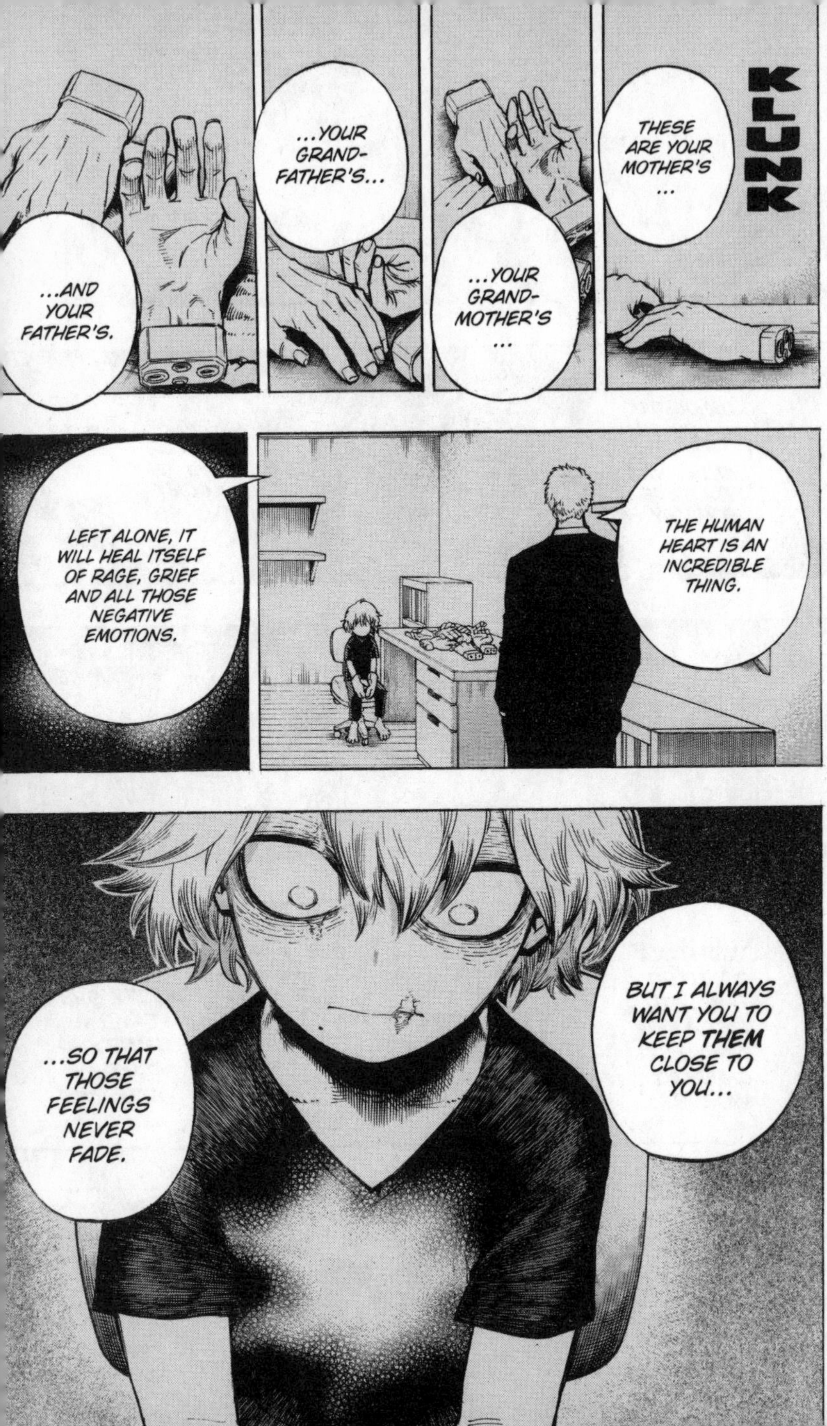
KLUNK
THESE ARE YOUR MOTHER'S ...
...YOUR GRAND-MOTHER'S ...
...YOUR GRAND-FATHER'S...
...AND YOUR FATHER'S.
THE HUMAN HEART IS AN INCREDIBLE THING.
LEFT ALONE, IT WILL HEAL ITSELF OF RAGE, GRIEF AND ALL THOSE NEGATIVE EMOTIONS.
BUT I ALWAYS WANT YOU TO KEEP **THEM** CLOSE TO YOU...
...SO THAT THOSE FEELINGS NEVER FADE.

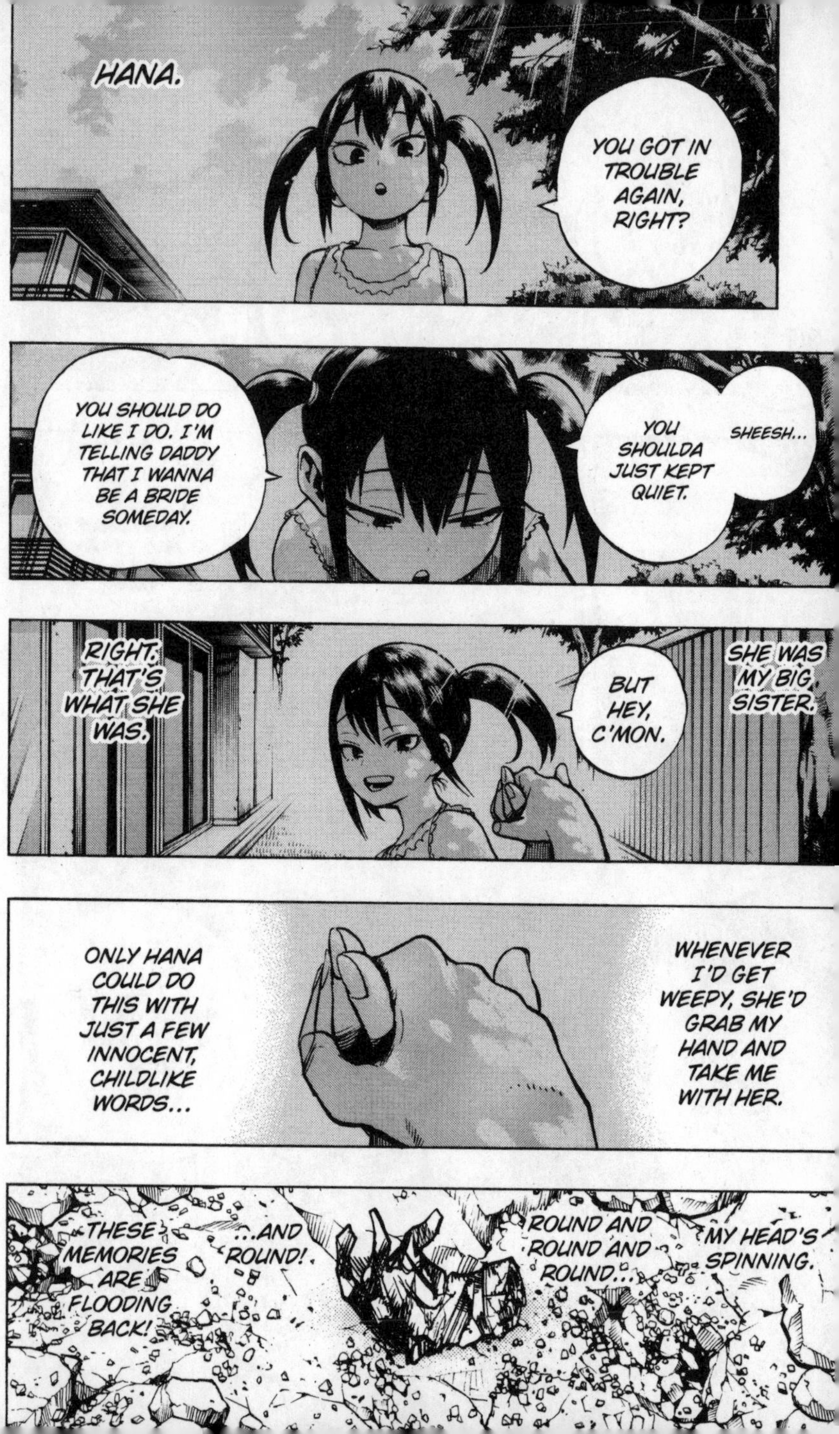
HANA.
YOU GOT IN TROUBLE AGAIN, RIGHT?
SHEESH...
YOU SHOULDA JUST KEPT QUIET.
YOU SHOULD DO LIKE I DO. I'M TELLING DADDY THAT I WANNA BE A BRIDE SOMEDAY.
SHE WAS MY BIG SISTER.
BUT HEY, C'MON.
RIGHT. THAT'S WHAT SHE WAS.
WHENEVER I'D GET WEEPY, SHE'D GRAB MY HAND AND TAKE ME WITH HER.
ONLY HANA COULD DO THIS WITH JUST A FEW INNOCENT, CHILDLIKE WORDS...
MY HEAD'S SPINNING.
ROUND AND ROUND AND ROUND...
...AND ROUND!
THESE MEMORIES ARE FLOODING BACK!

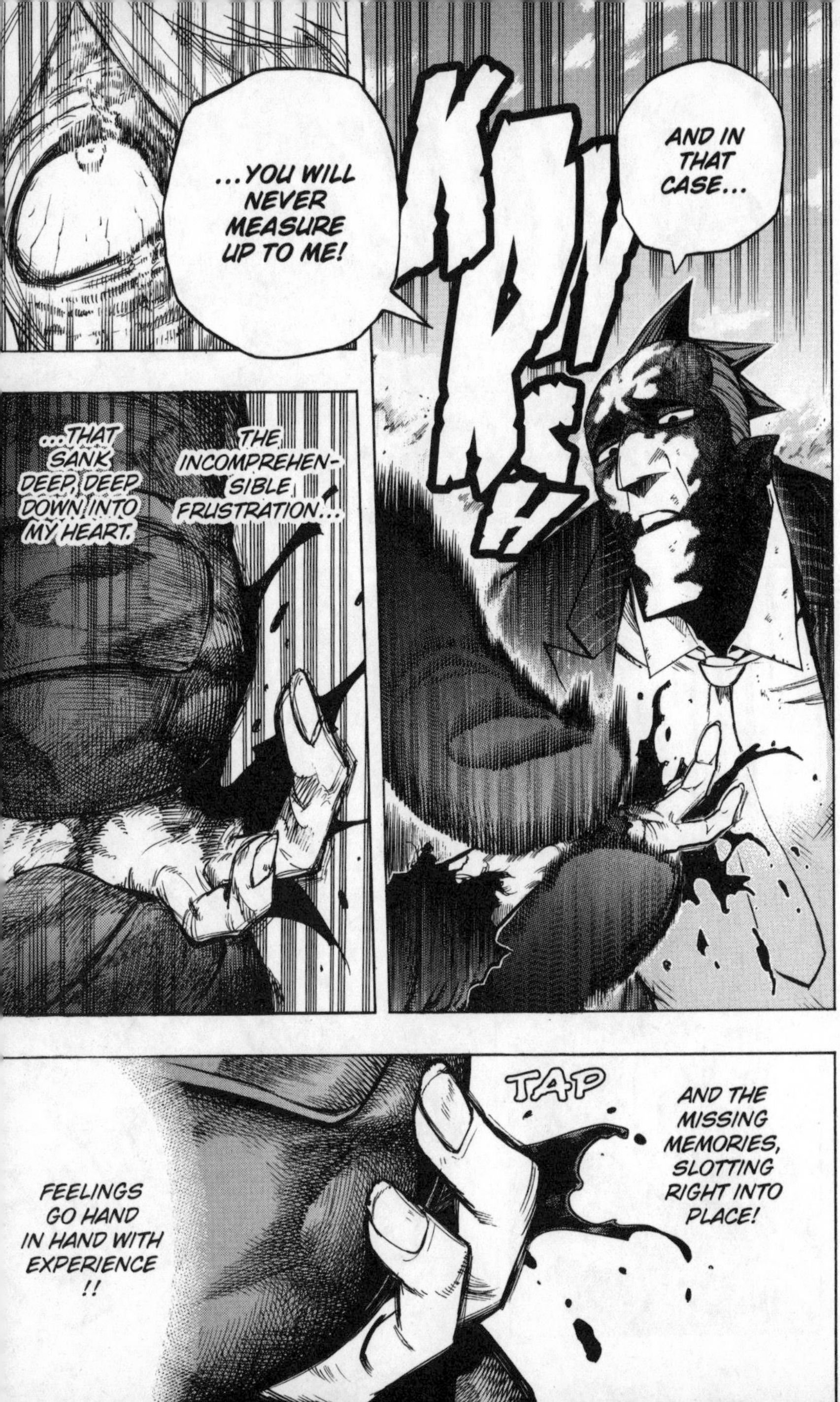
KRASH
AND IN THAT CASE...
...YOU WILL NEVER MEASURE UP TO ME!
THE INCOMPREHENSIBLE FRUSTRATION...
...THAT SANK DEEP, DEEP DOWN INTO MY HEART.
TAP
AND THE MISSING MEMORIES, SLOTTING RIGHT INTO PLACE!
FEELINGS GO HAND IN HAND WITH EXPERIENCE !!

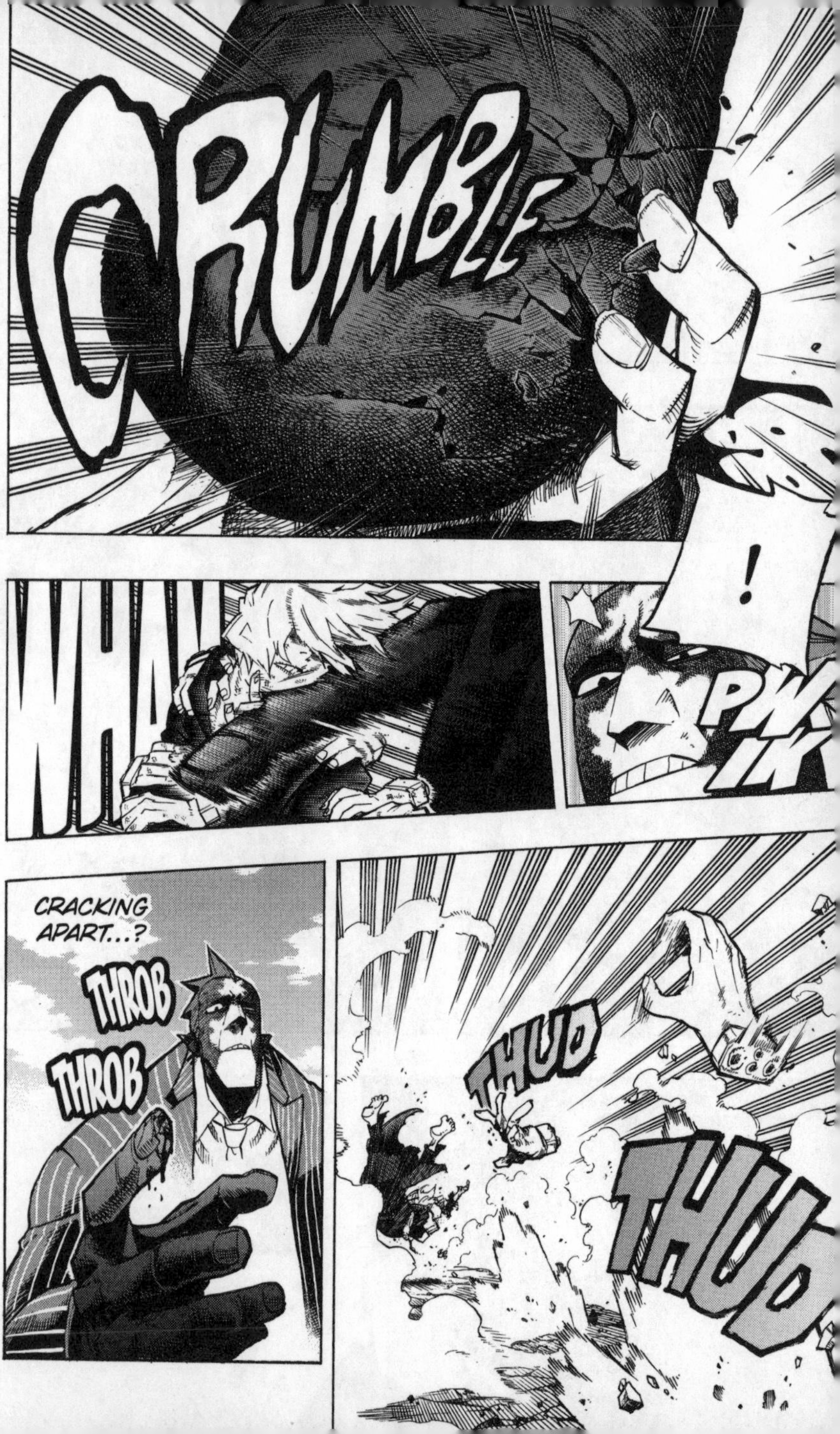
CRUMBLE
!
PWIK
WHAM
THUD
THUD
CRACKING APART...?
THROB
THROB

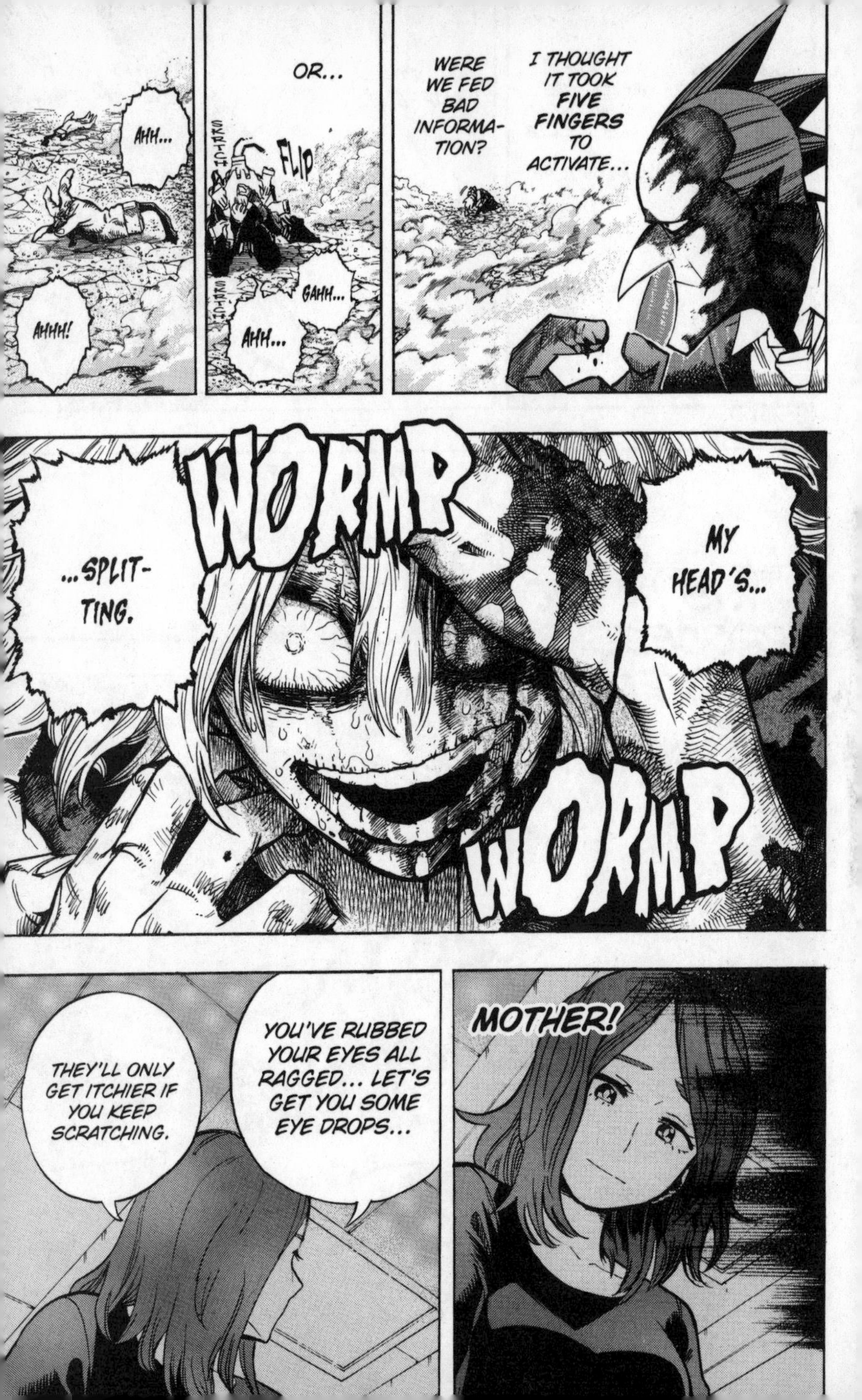

I THOUGHT IT TOOK FIVE FINGERS TO ACTIVATE...
WERE WE FED BAD INFORMATION?
OR...
SKRTCH
FLIP
GAHH...
SKRTCH
AHH...
AHH...
AHHH!
WORMP
MY HEAD'S...
...SPLIT-TING.
WORMP
MOTHER!
YOU'VE RUBBED YOUR EYES ALL RAGGED... LET'S GET YOU SOME EYE DROPS...
THEY'LL ONLY GET ITCHIER IF YOU KEEP SCRATCHING.

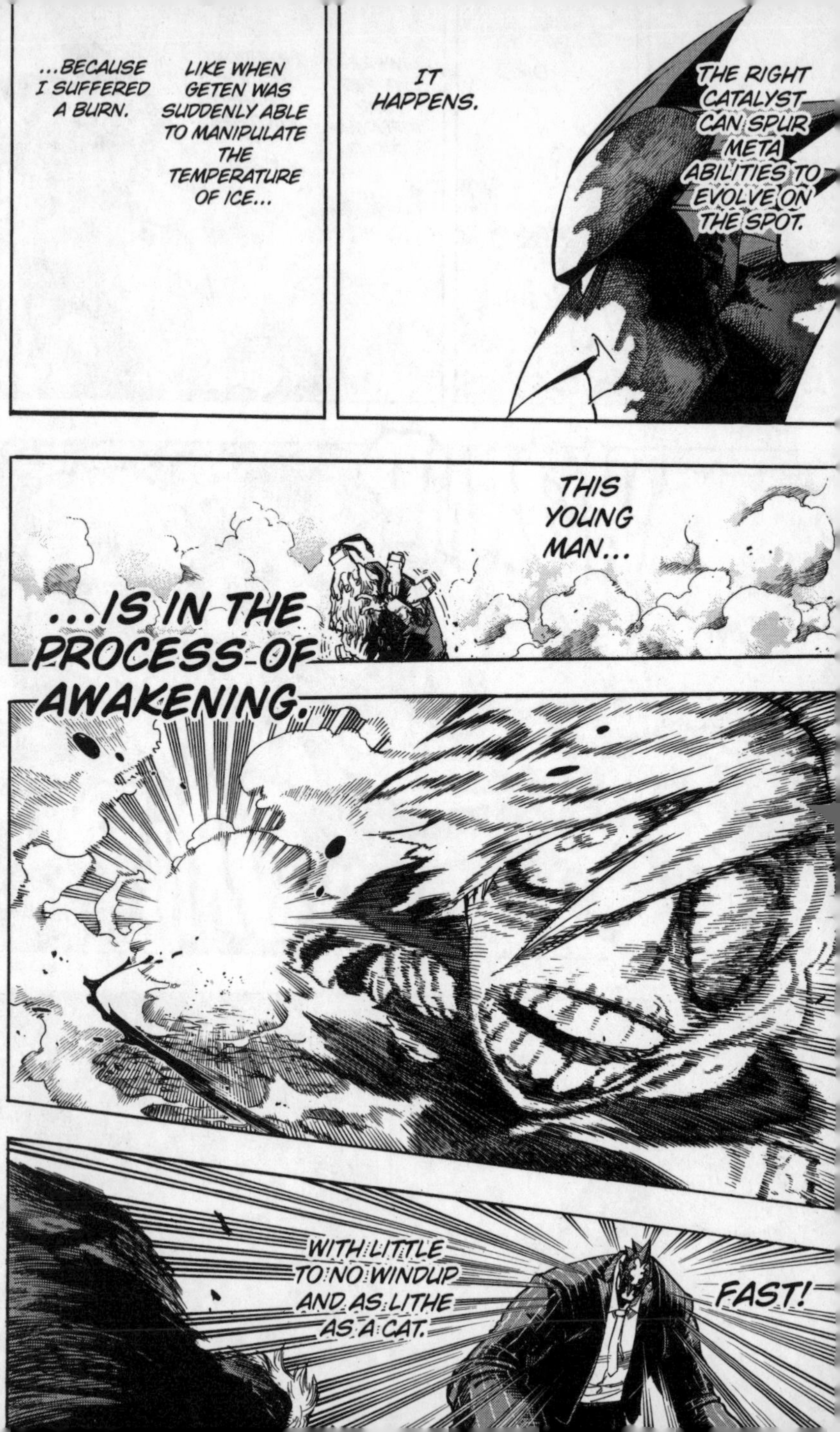
THE RIGHT CATALYST CAN SPUR META ABILITIES TO EVOLVE ON THE SPOT.
IT HAPPENS.
LIKE WHEN GETEN WAS SUDDENLY ABLE TO MANIPULATE THE TEMPERATURE OF ICE...
...BECAUSE I SUFFERED A BURN.
THIS YOUNG MAN...
...IS IN THE PROCESS OF AWAKENING.
FAST!
WITH LITTLE TO NO WINDUP AND AS LITHE AS A CAT.

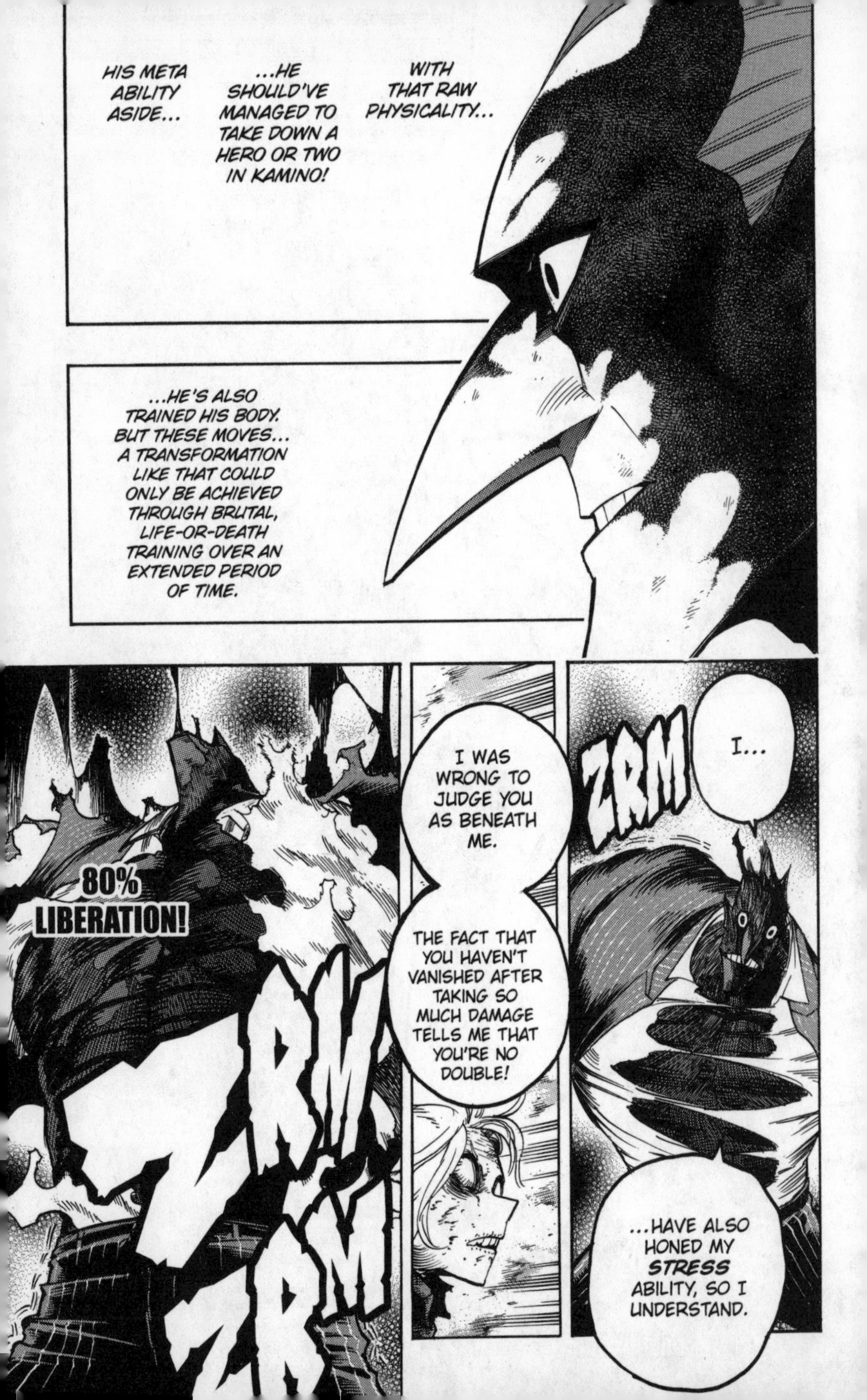
WITH THAT RAW PHYSICALITY...
...HE SHOULD'VE MANAGED TO TAKE DOWN A HERO OR TWO IN KAMINO!
HIS META ABILITY ASIDE...
...HE'S ALSO TRAINED HIS BODY. BUT THESE MOVES... A TRANSFORMATION LIKE THAT COULD ONLY BE ACHIEVED THROUGH BRUTAL, LIFE-OR-DEATH TRAINING OVER AN EXTENDED PERIOD OF TIME.
ZRM
I...
...HAVE ALSO HONED MY ***STRESS*** ABILITY, SO I UNDERSTAND.
I WAS WRONG TO JUDGE YOU AS BENEATH ME.
THE FACT THAT YOU HAVEN'T VANISHED AFTER TAKING SO MUCH DAMAGE TELLS ME THAT YOU'RE NO DOUBLE!
80% LIBERATION!
ZRM
ZRM

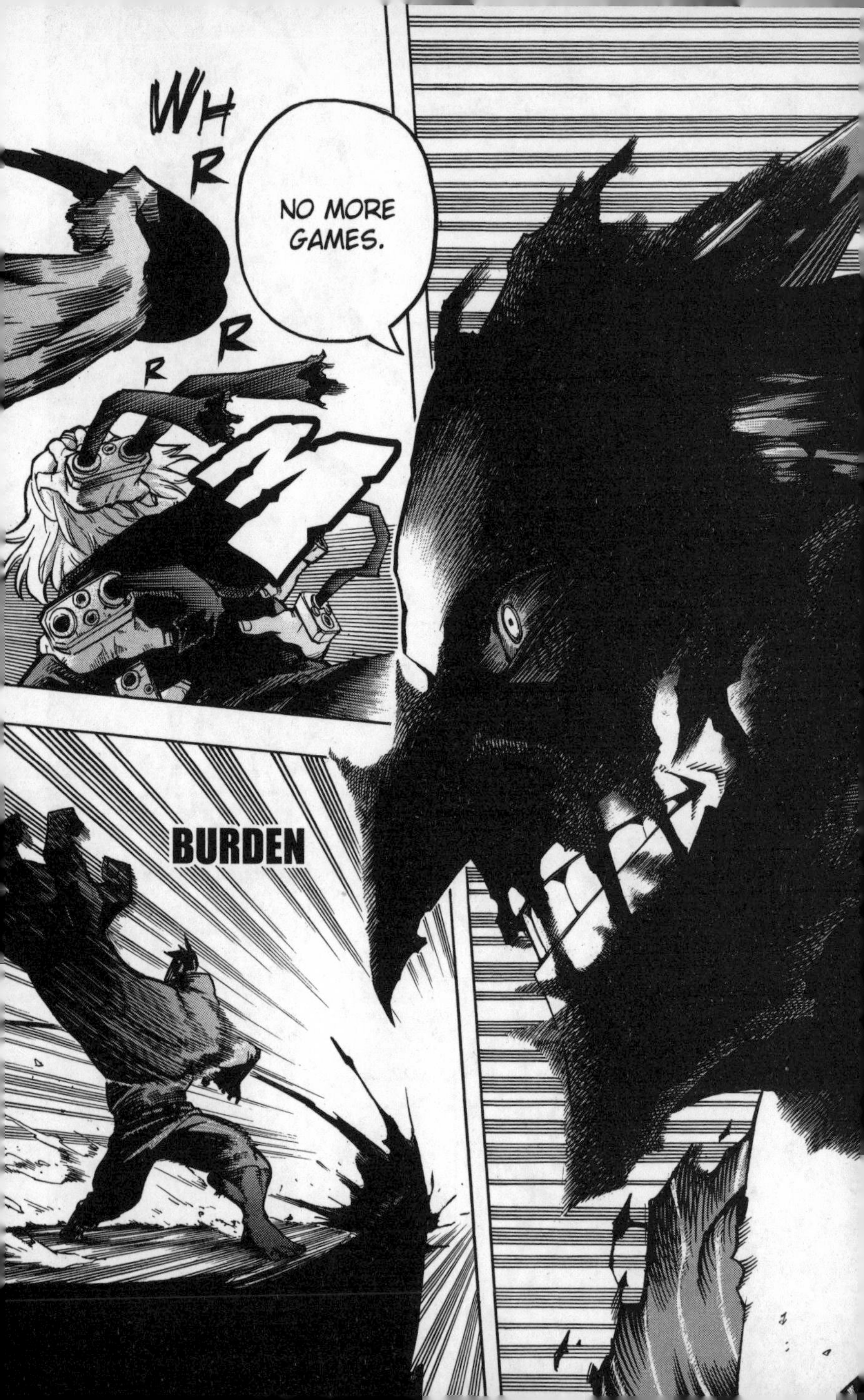
NO MORE GAMES.
WHRRRR
BURDEN

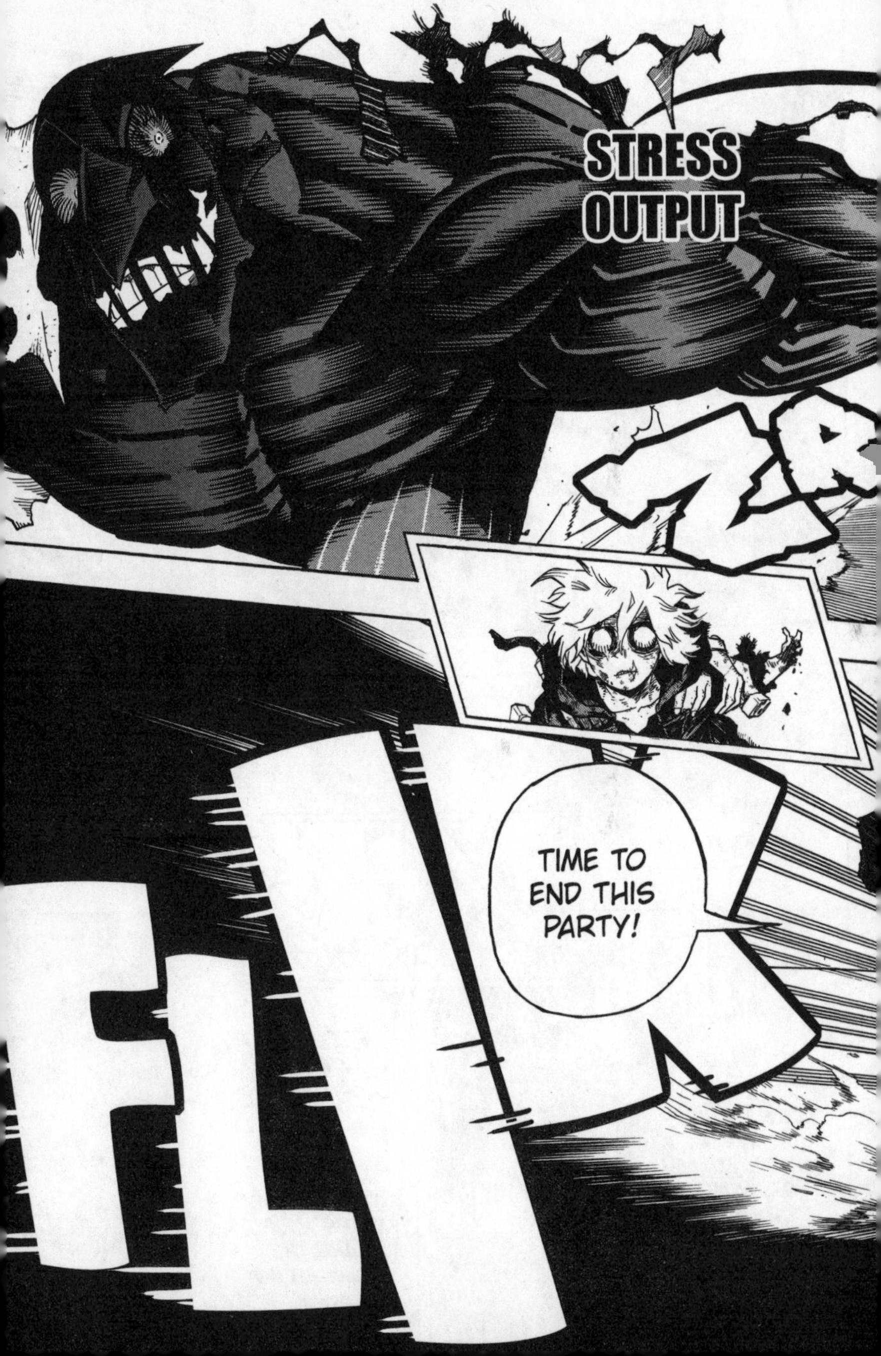
STRESS
OUTPUT
TIME TO END THIS PARTY!

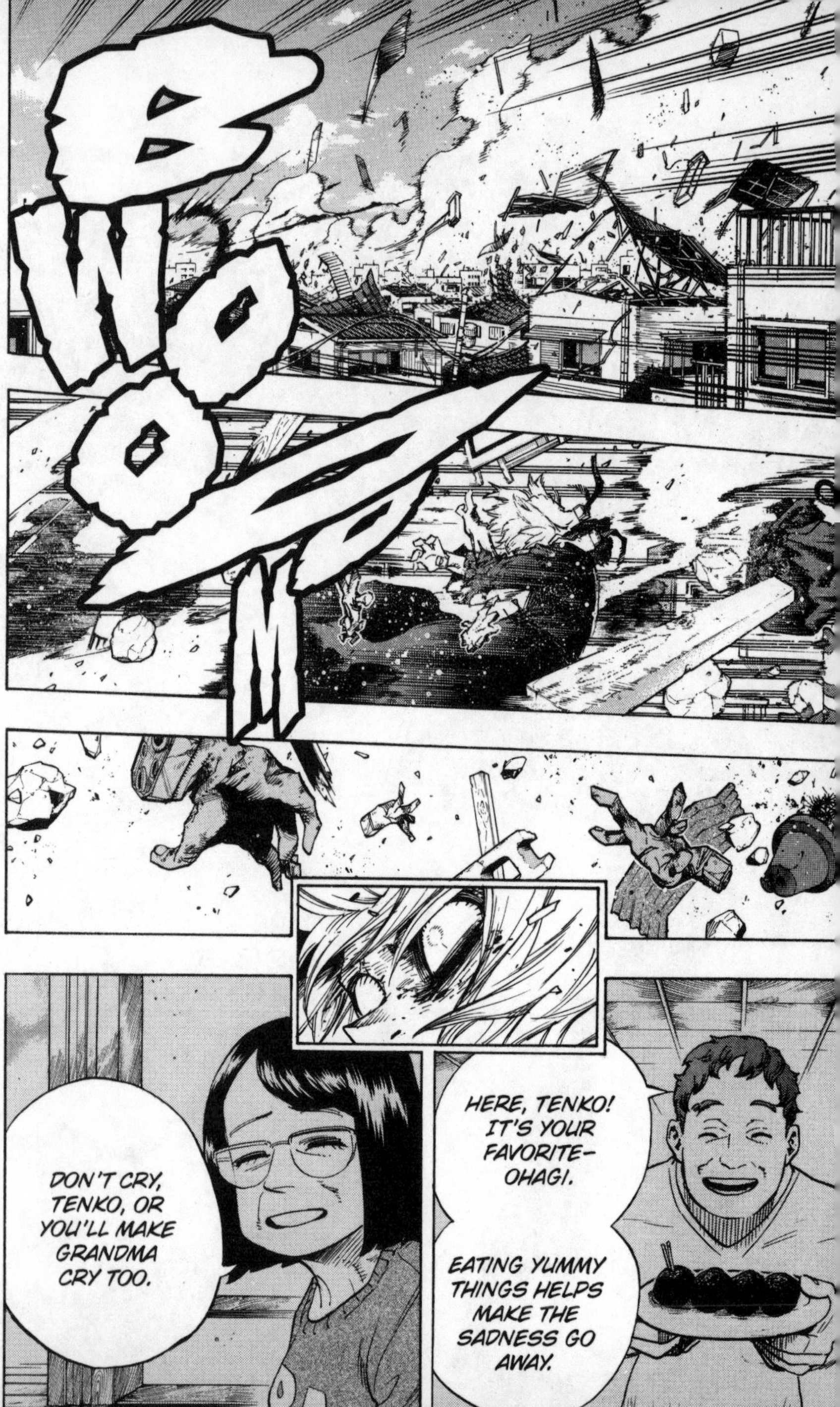
BWOOM
HERE, TENKO! IT'S YOUR FAVORITE— OHAGI.
EATING YUMMY THINGS HELPS MAKE THE SADNESS GO AWAY.
DON'T CRY, TENKO, OR YOU'LL MAKE GRANDMA CRY TOO.

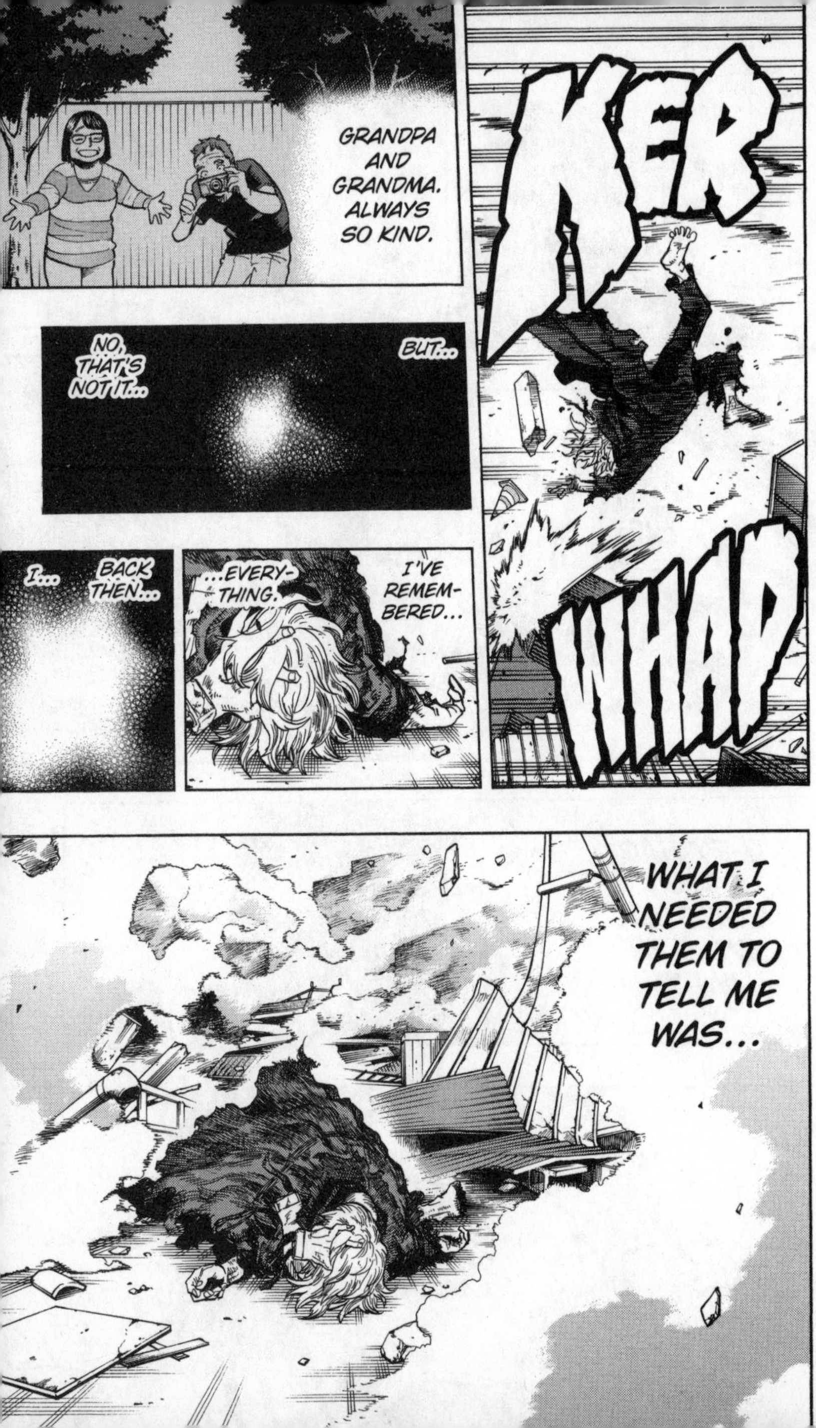
KER
WHAP
GRANDPA AND GRANDMA. ALWAYS SO KIND.
BUT...
NO, THAT'S NOT IT...
I'VE REMEMBERED...
...EVERYTHING.
BACK THEN...
I...
WHAT I NEEDED THEM TO TELL ME WAS...

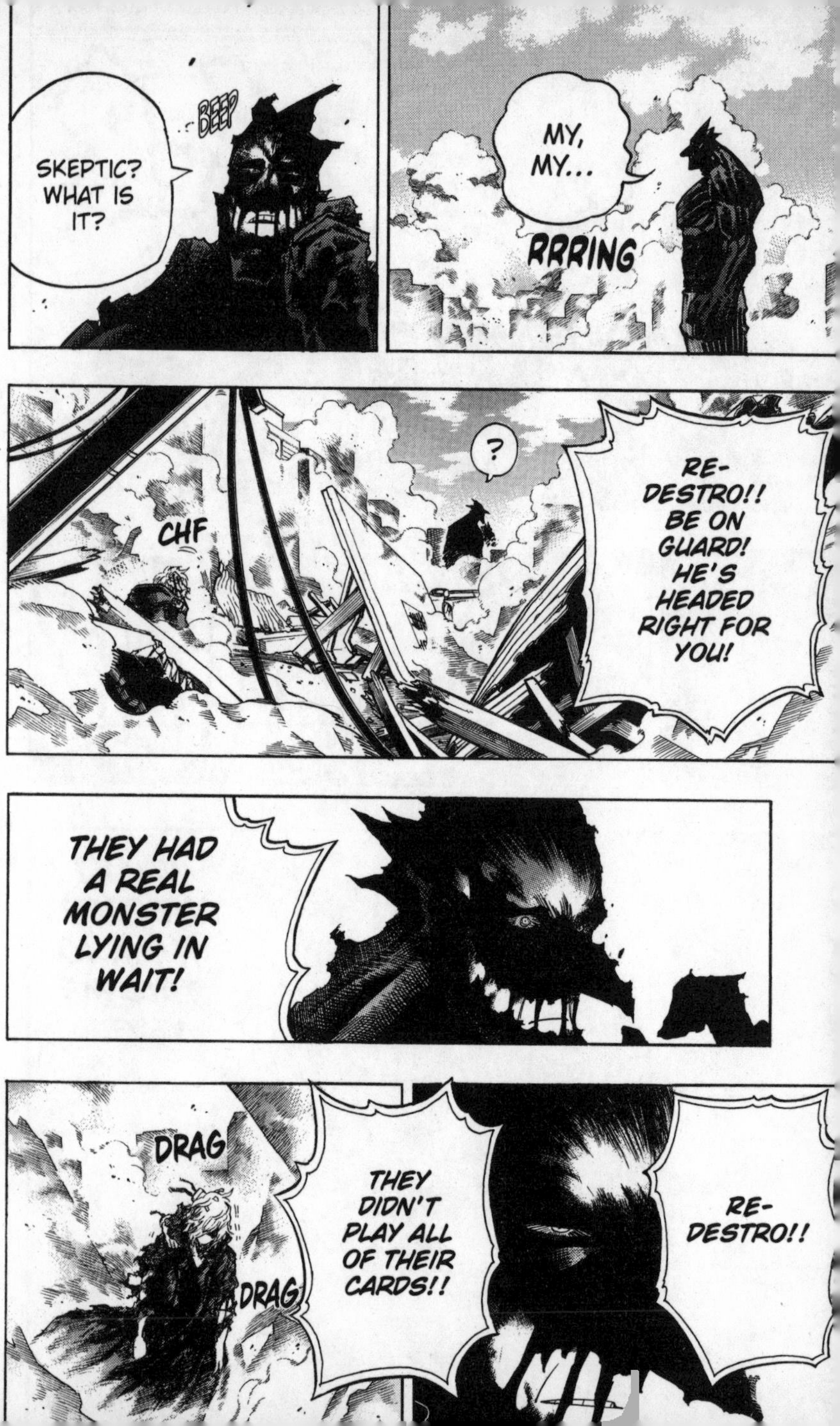
MY, MY...
RRRING
BEEP
SKEPTIC? WHAT IS IT?
RE-DESTRO!! BE ON GUARD! HE'S HEADED RIGHT FOR YOU!
?
CHF
THEY HAD A REAL MONSTER LYING IN WAIT!
RE-DESTRO!!
THEY DIDN'T PLAY ALL OF THEIR CARDS!!
DRAG
DRAG

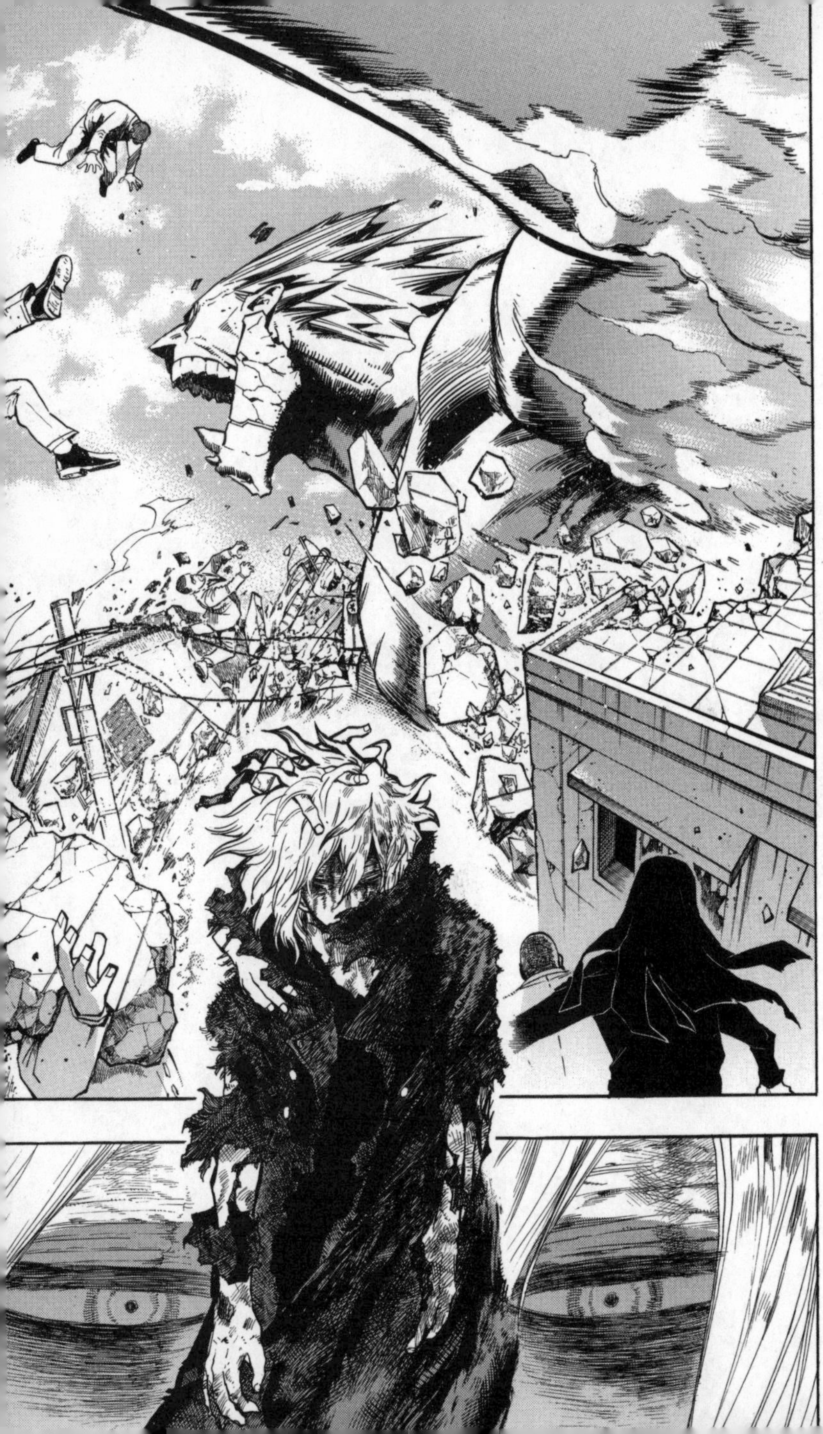

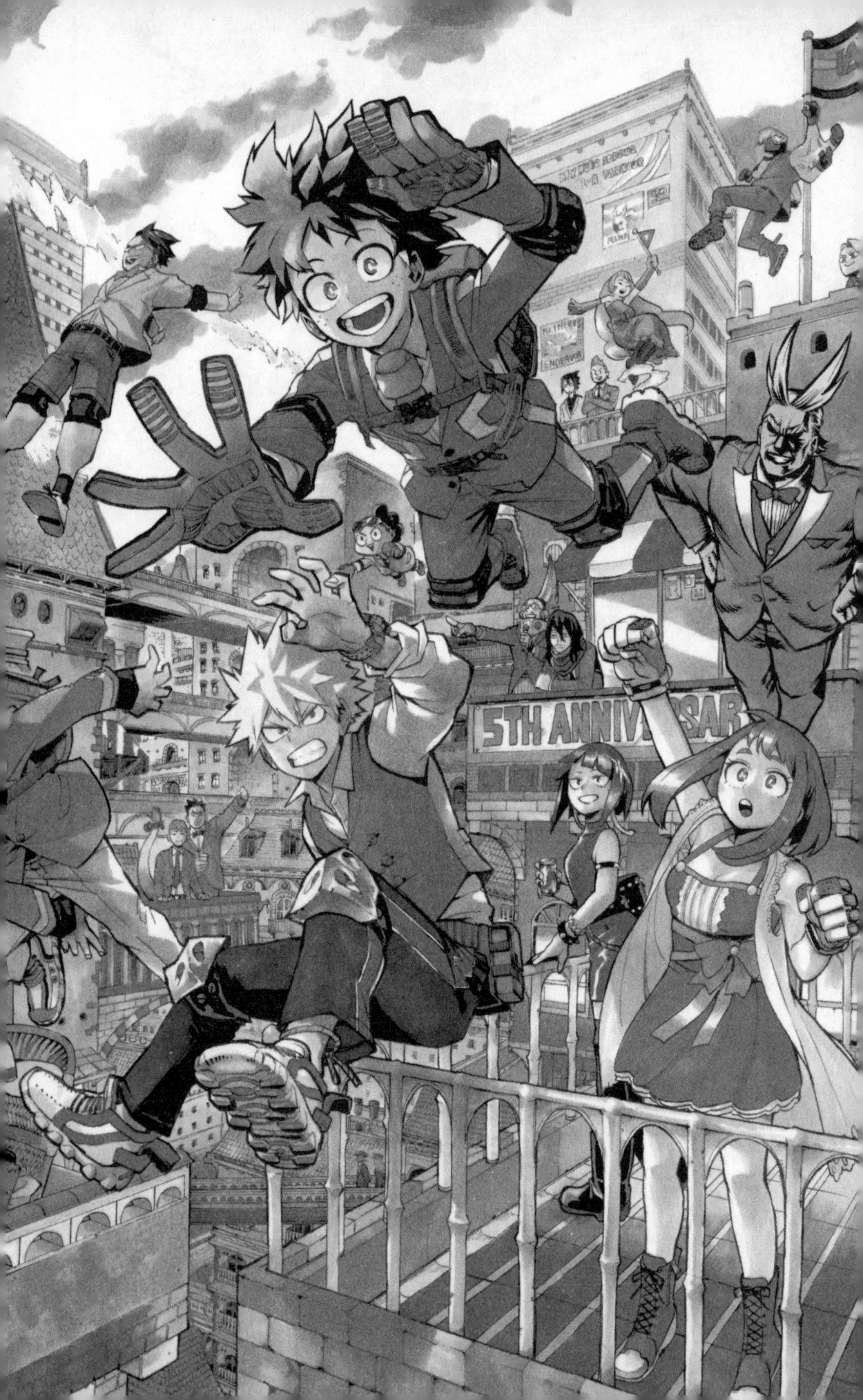
ENDEAVOR
5TH ANNIV
SAR

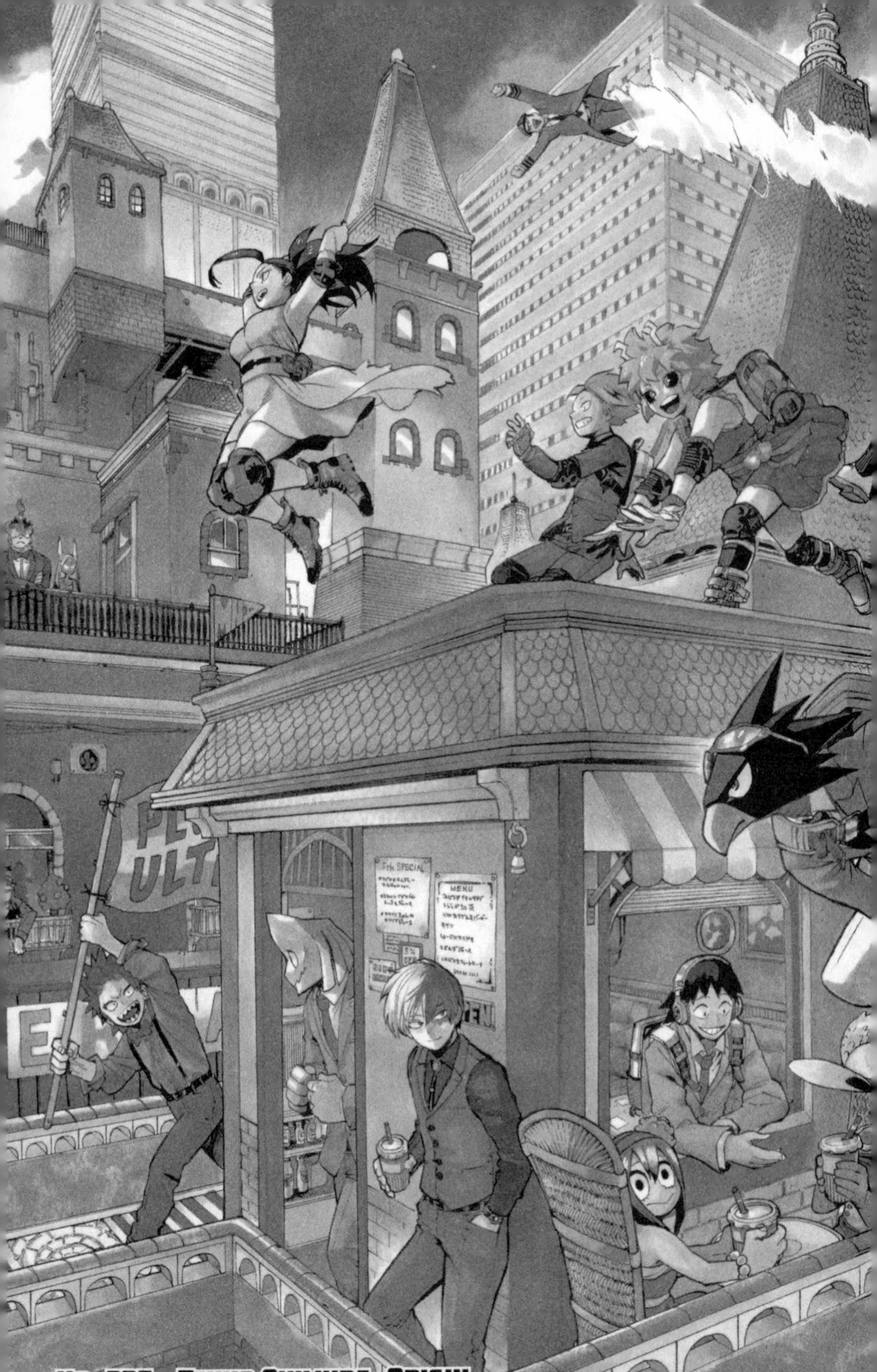
5th SPECIAL
MENU

NO. 235 - TENKO SHIMURA: ORIGIN

MY HERO ACADEMIA

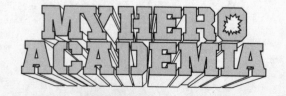

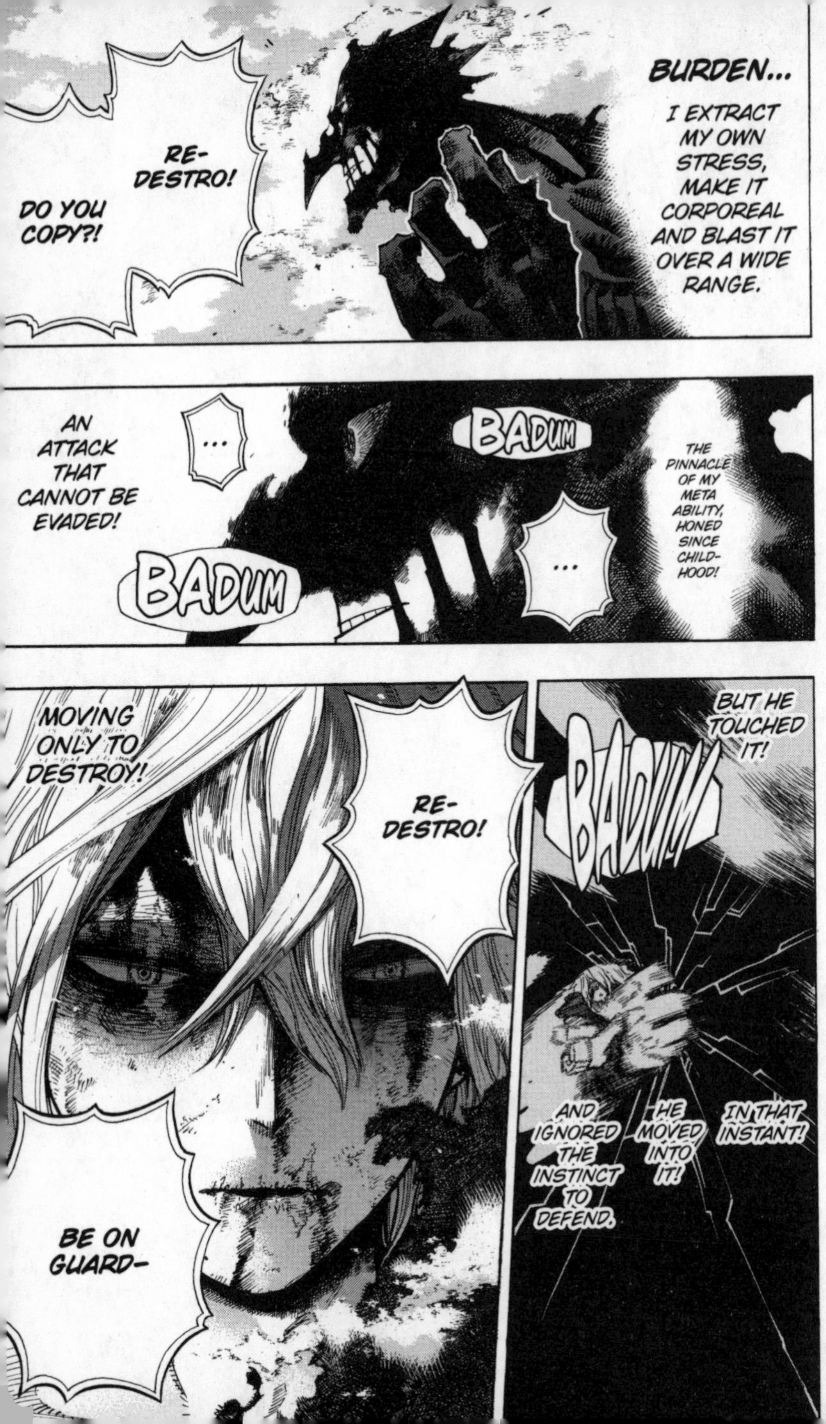
BURDEN...
I EXTRACT MY OWN STRESS, MAKE IT CORPOREAL AND BLAST IT OVER A WIDE RANGE.
RE-DESTRO! DO YOU COPY?!
THE PINNACLE OF MY META ABILITY, HONED SINCE CHILDHOOD!
BADUM
...
...
AN ATTACK THAT CANNOT BE EVADED!
BADUM
BUT HE TOUCHED IT!
BADUMM
IN THAT INSTANT!
HE MOVED INTO IT!
AND IGNORED THE INSTINCT TO DEFEND.
RE-DESTRO!
MOVING ONLY TO DESTROY!
BE ON GUARD-

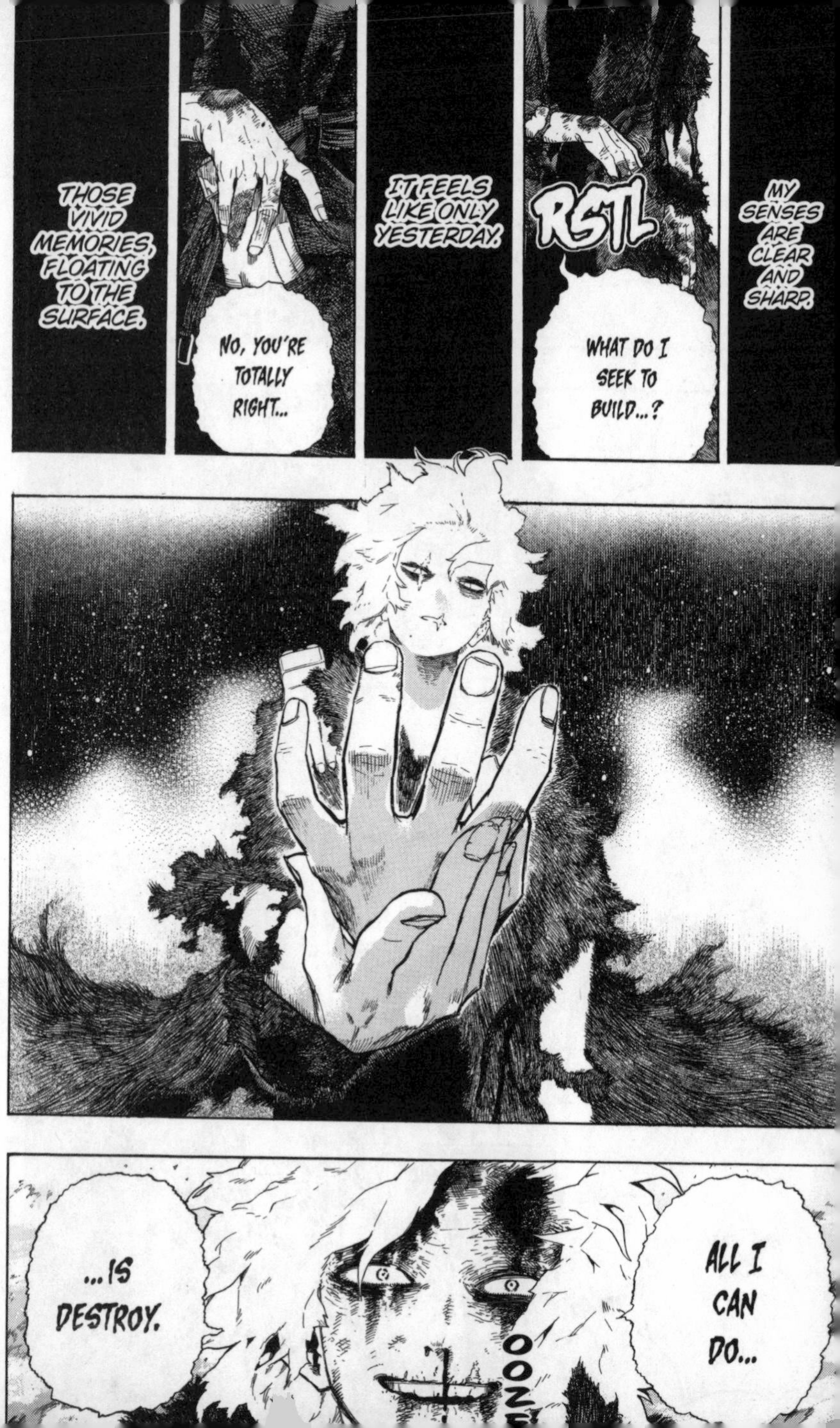
MY SENSES ARE CLEAR AND SHARP.
RSTL
WHAT DO I SEEK TO BUILD...?
IT FEELS LIKE ONLY YESTERDAY.
NO, YOU'RE TOTALLY RIGHT...
THOSE VIVID MEMORIES, FLOATING TO THE SURFACE.
ALL I CAN DO...
OOZ
...IS DESTROY.

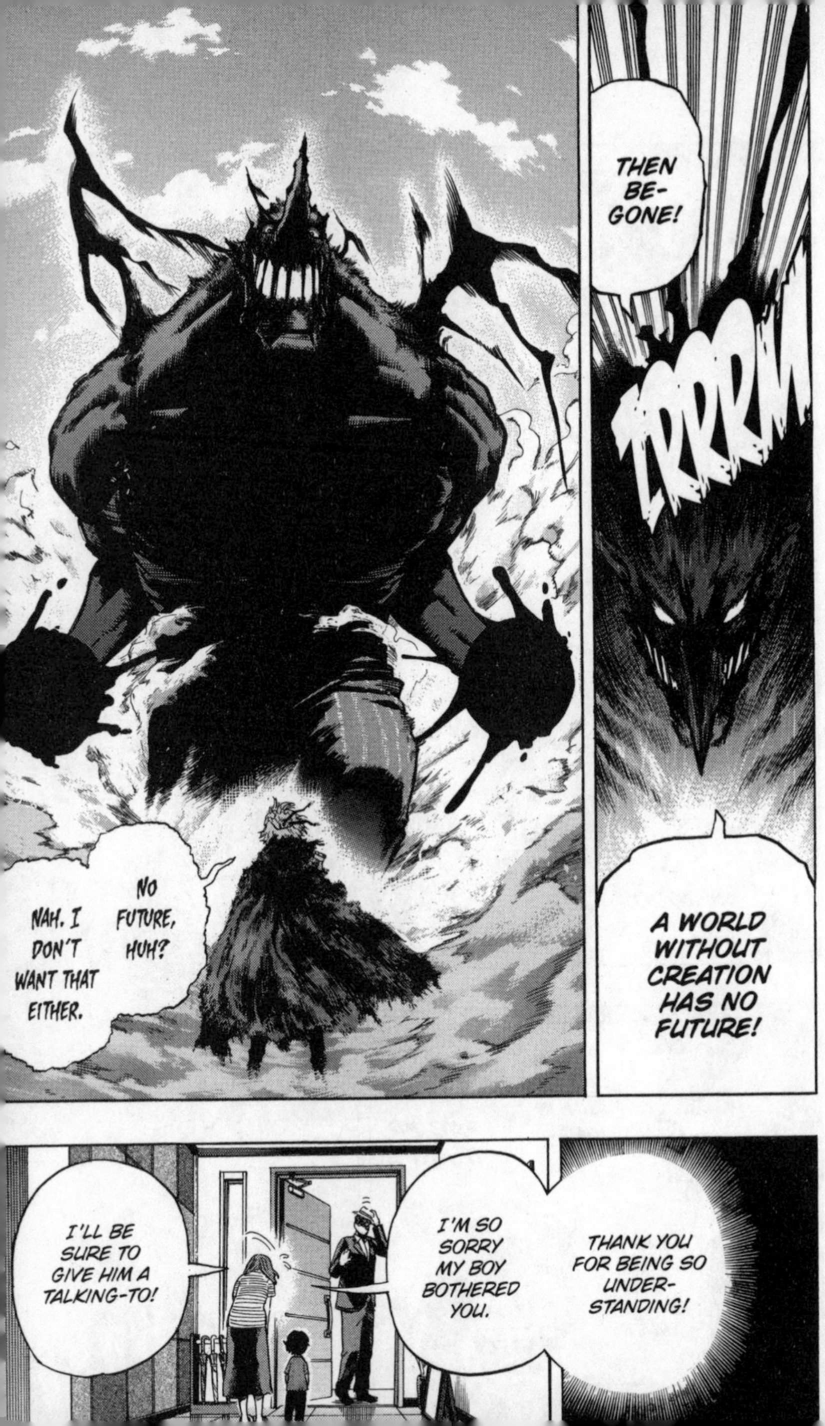
THEN BE-GONE!
ZRRRM
A WORLD WITHOUT CREATION HAS NO FUTURE!
NO FUTURE, HUH?
NAH. I DON'T WANT THAT EITHER.
THANK YOU FOR BEING SO UNDER-STANDING!
I'M SO SORRY MY BOY BOTHERED YOU.
I'LL BE SURE TO GIVE HIM A TALKING-TO!

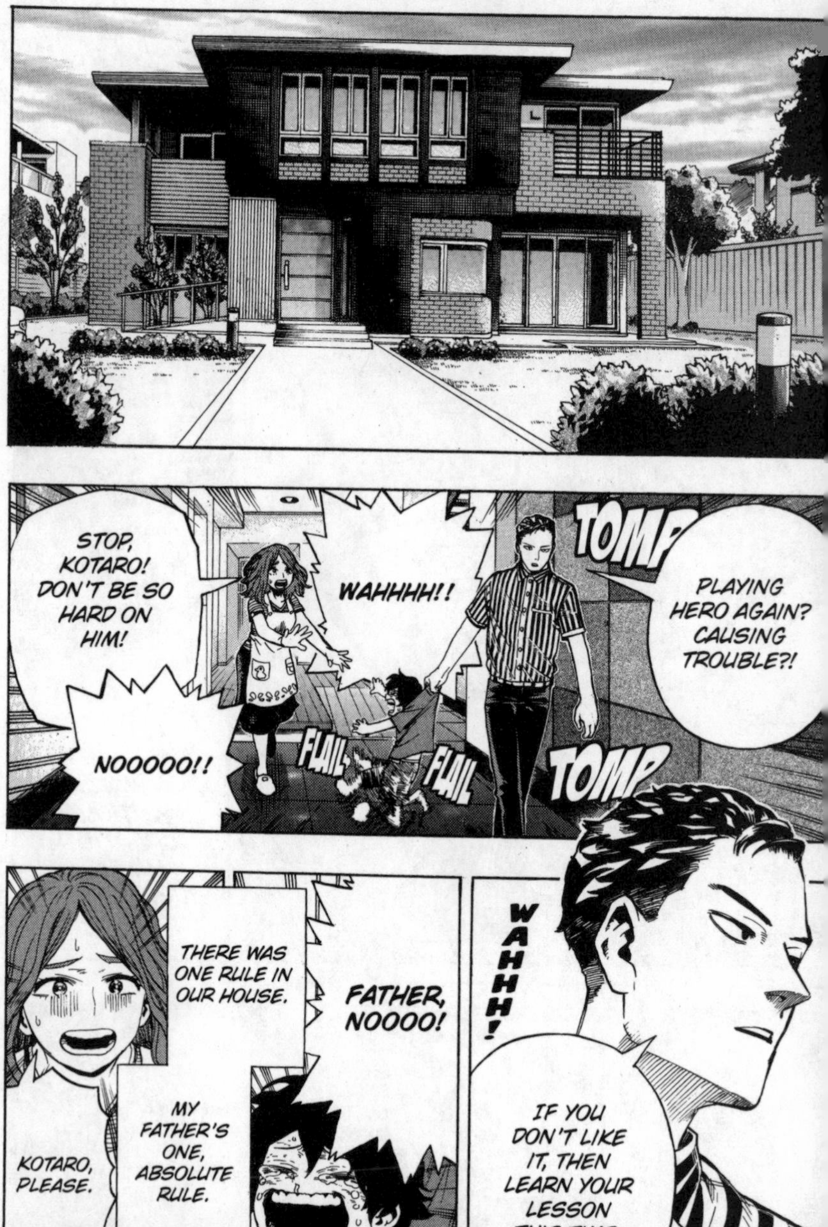
TOMP
PLAYING HERO AGAIN? CAUSING TROUBLE?!
TOMP
WAHHHH!!
FLAIL
FLAIL
STOP, KOTARO! DON'T BE SO HARD ON HIM!
NOOOOO!!
WAHHHH!
IF YOU DON'T LIKE IT, THEN LEARN YOUR LESSON THIS TIME.
THERE WAS ONE RULE IN OUR HOUSE.
FATHER, NOOOO!
MY FATHER'S ONE, ABSOLUTE RULE.
KOTARO, PLEASE.

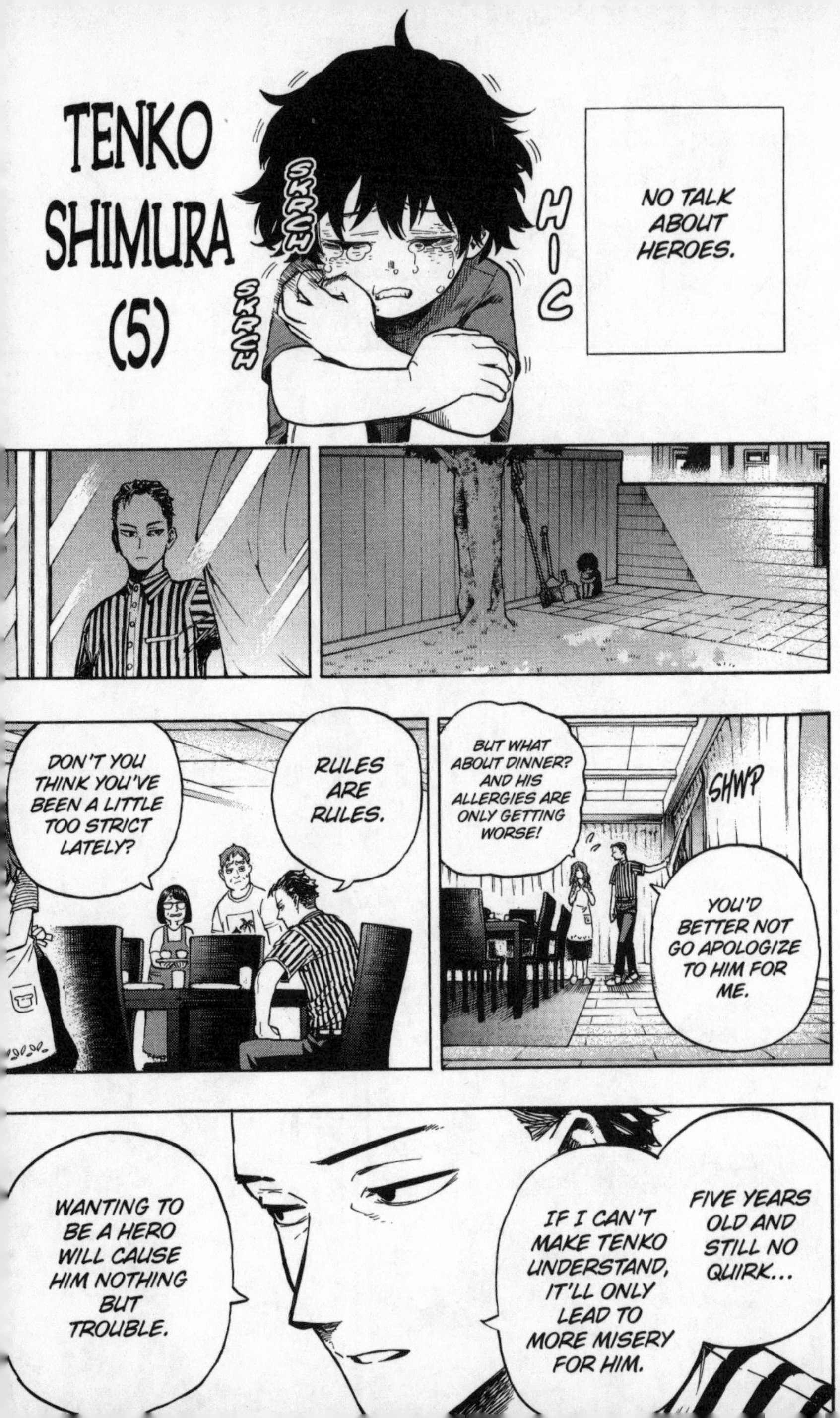
NO TALK ABOUT HEROES.
HIC
SKRCH
SKRCH
TENKO SHIMURA (5)
BUT WHAT ABOUT DINNER? AND HIS ALLERGIES ARE ONLY GETTING WORSE!
SHWP
YOU'D BETTER NOT GO APOLOGIZE TO HIM FOR ME.
RULES ARE RULES.
DON'T YOU THINK YOU'VE BEEN A LITTLE TOO STRICT LATELY?
FIVE YEARS OLD AND STILL NO QUIRK...
IF I CAN'T MAKE TENKO UNDERSTAND, IT'LL ONLY LEAD TO MORE MISERY FOR HIM.
WANTING TO BE A HERO WILL CAUSE HIM NOTHING BUT TROUBLE.

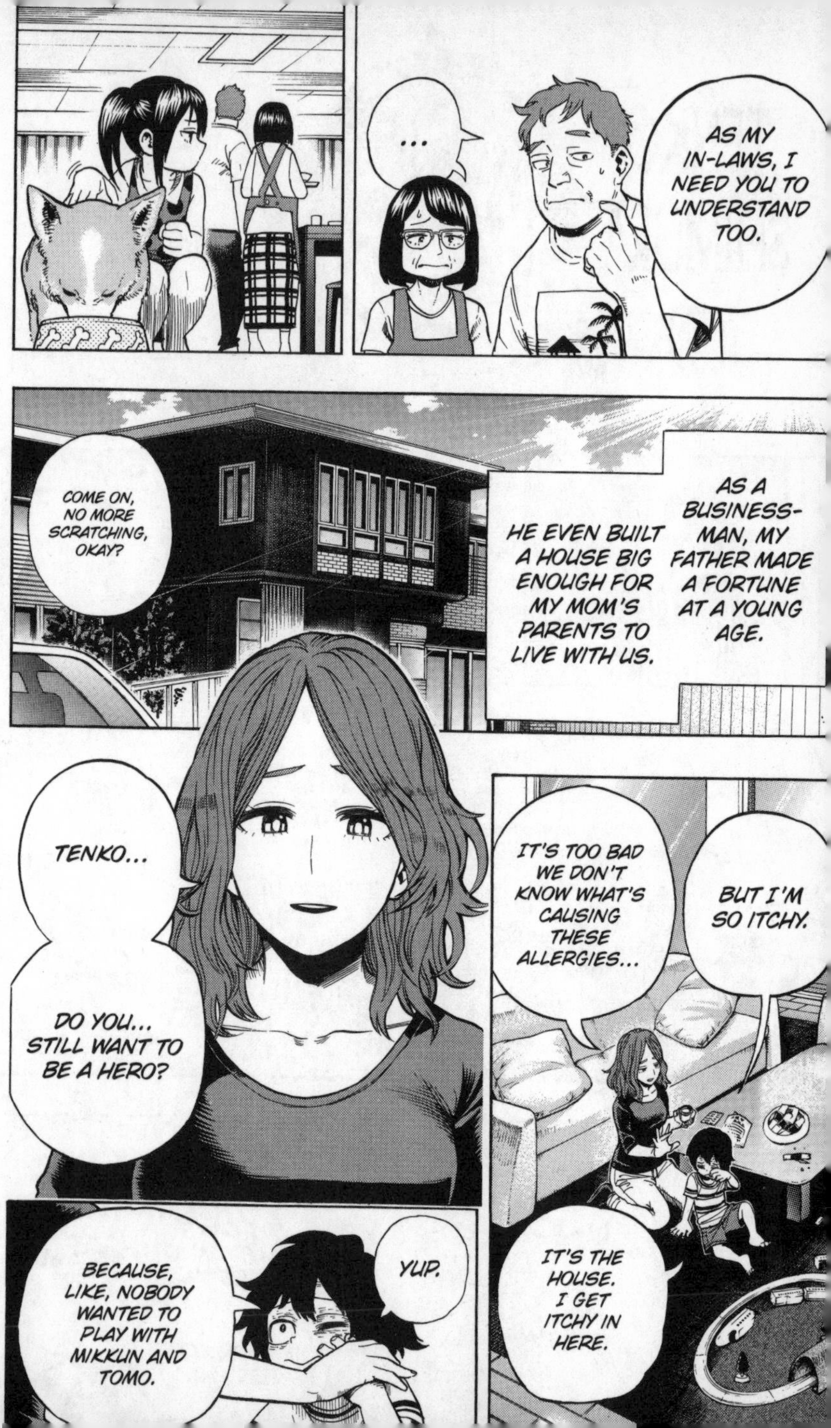
AS MY IN-LAWS, I NEED YOU TO UNDERSTAND TOO.
...
AS A BUSINESS-MAN, MY FATHER MADE A FORTUNE AT A YOUNG AGE.
HE EVEN BUILT A HOUSE BIG ENOUGH FOR MY MOM'S PARENTS TO LIVE WITH US.
COME ON, NO MORE SCRATCHING, OKAY?
BUT I'M SO ITCHY.
IT'S TOO BAD WE DON'T KNOW WHAT'S CAUSING THESE ALLERGIES...
IT'S THE HOUSE. I GET ITCHY IN HERE.
TENKO...
DO YOU... STILL WANT TO BE A HERO?
YUP.
BECAUSE, LIKE, NOBODY WANTED TO PLAY WITH MIKKUN AND TOMO.

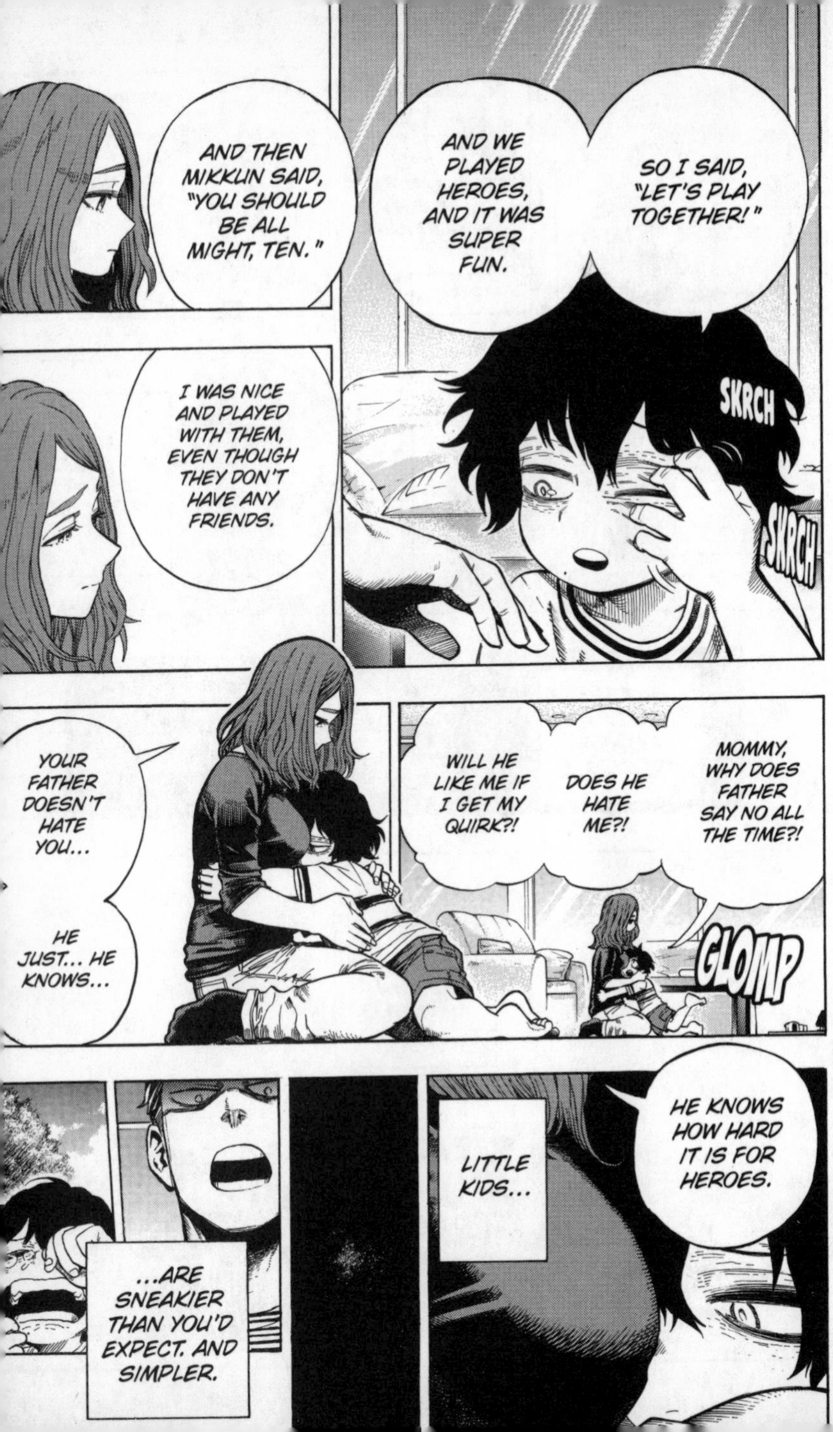
SO I SAID, "LET'S PLAY TOGETHER!"
AND WE PLAYED HEROES, AND IT WAS SUPER FUN.
SKRCH
SKRCH
AND THEN MIKKUN SAID, "YOU SHOULD BE ALL MIGHT, TEN."
I WAS NICE AND PLAYED WITH THEM, EVEN THOUGH THEY DON'T HAVE ANY FRIENDS.
MOMMY, WHY DOES FATHER SAY NO ALL THE TIME?!
DOES HE HATE ME?!
WILL HE LIKE ME IF I GET MY QUIRK?!
GLOMP
YOUR FATHER DOESN'T HATE YOU...
HE JUST... HE KNOWS...
HE KNOWS HOW HARD IT IS FOR HEROES.
LITTLE KIDS...
...ARE SNEAKIER THAN YOU'D EXPECT. AND SIMPLER.

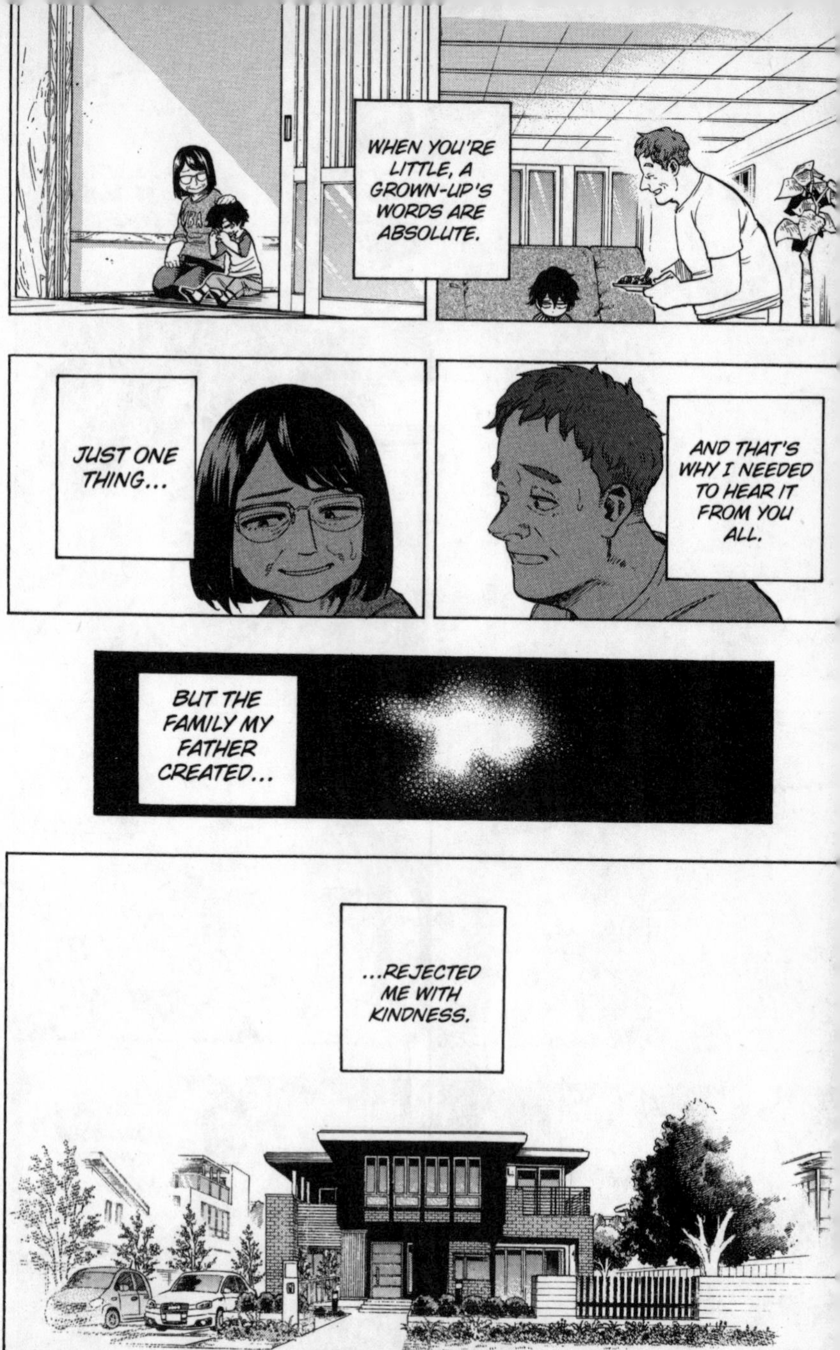
WHEN YOU'RE LITTLE, A GROWN-UP'S WORDS ARE ABSOLUTE.
AND THAT'S WHY I NEEDED TO HEAR IT FROM YOU ALL.
JUST ONE THING...
BUT THE FAMILY MY FATHER CREATED...
...REJECTED ME WITH KINDNESS.

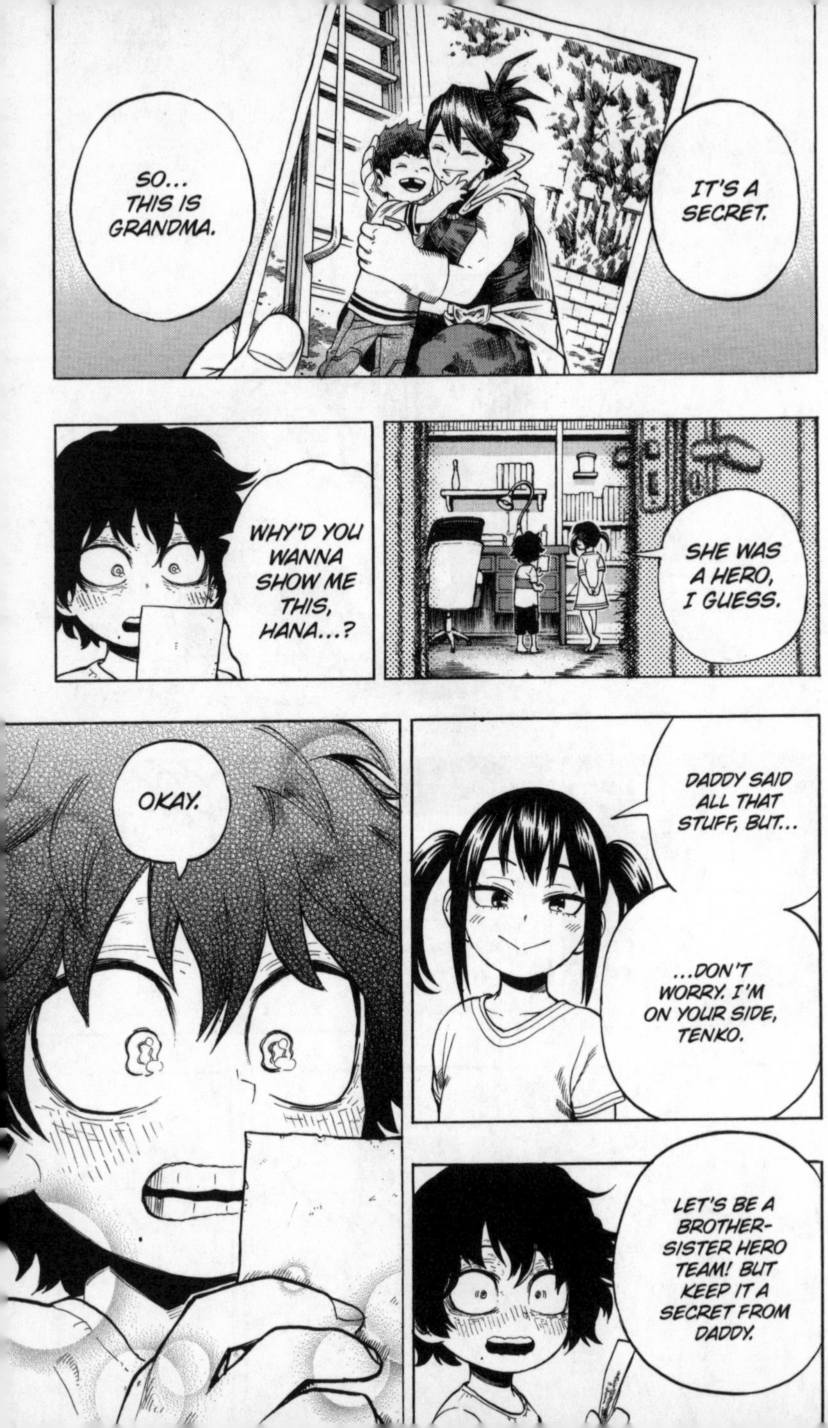
IT'S A SECRET.
SO... THIS IS GRANDMA.
SHE WAS A HERO, I GUESS.
WHY'D YOU WANNA SHOW ME THIS, HANA...?
DADDY SAID ALL THAT STUFF, BUT...
...DON'T WORRY. I'M ON YOUR SIDE, TENKO.
LET'S BE A BROTHER-SISTER HERO TEAM! BUT KEEP IT A SECRET FROM DADDY.
OKAY.

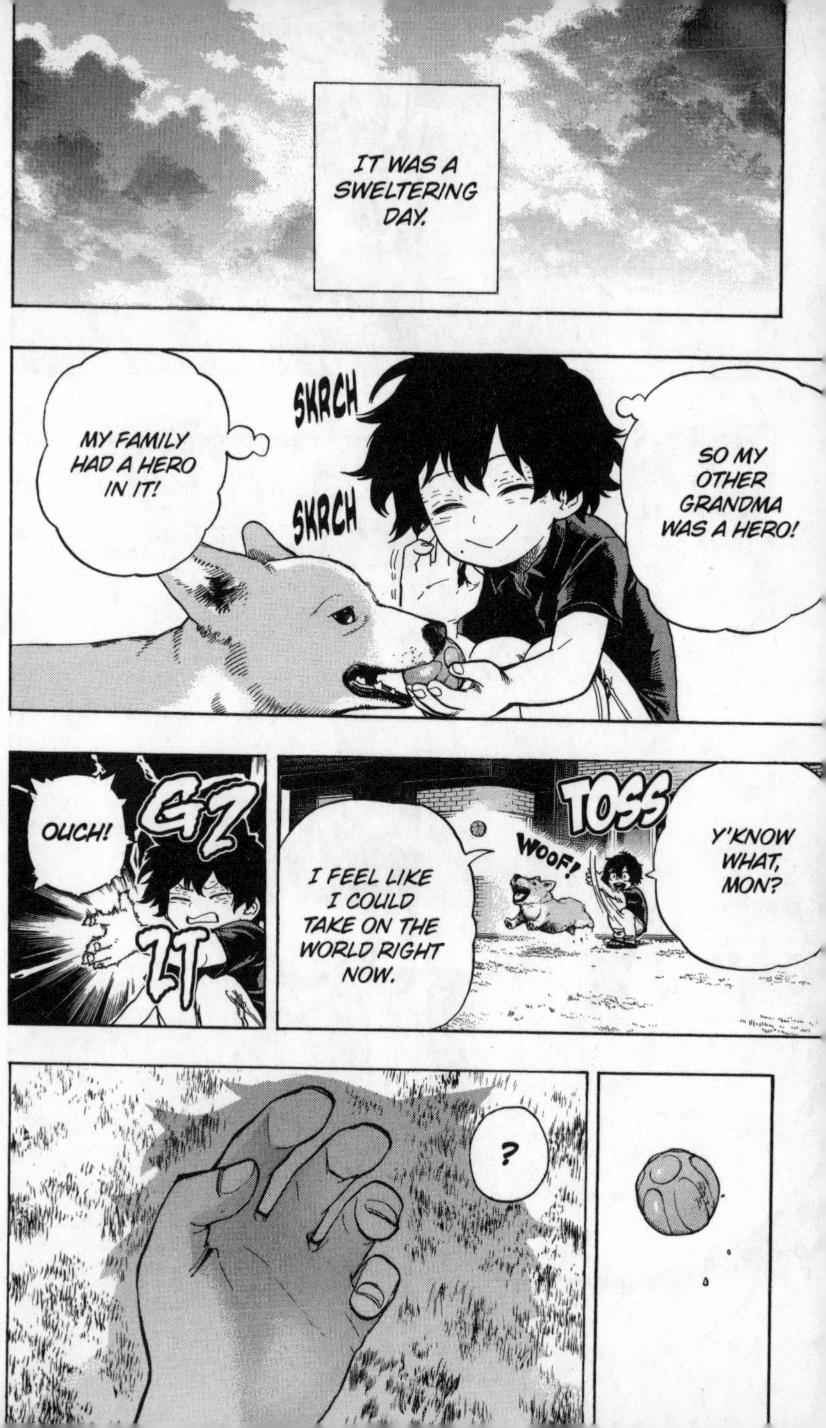
IT WAS A SWELTERING DAY.
SO MY OTHER GRANDMA WAS A HERO!
SKRCH
SKRCH
MY FAMILY HAD A HERO IN IT!
Y'KNOW WHAT, MON?
TOSS
WOOF!
I FEEL LIKE I COULD TAKE ON THE WORLD RIGHT NOW.
GZ
ZT
OUCH!
?

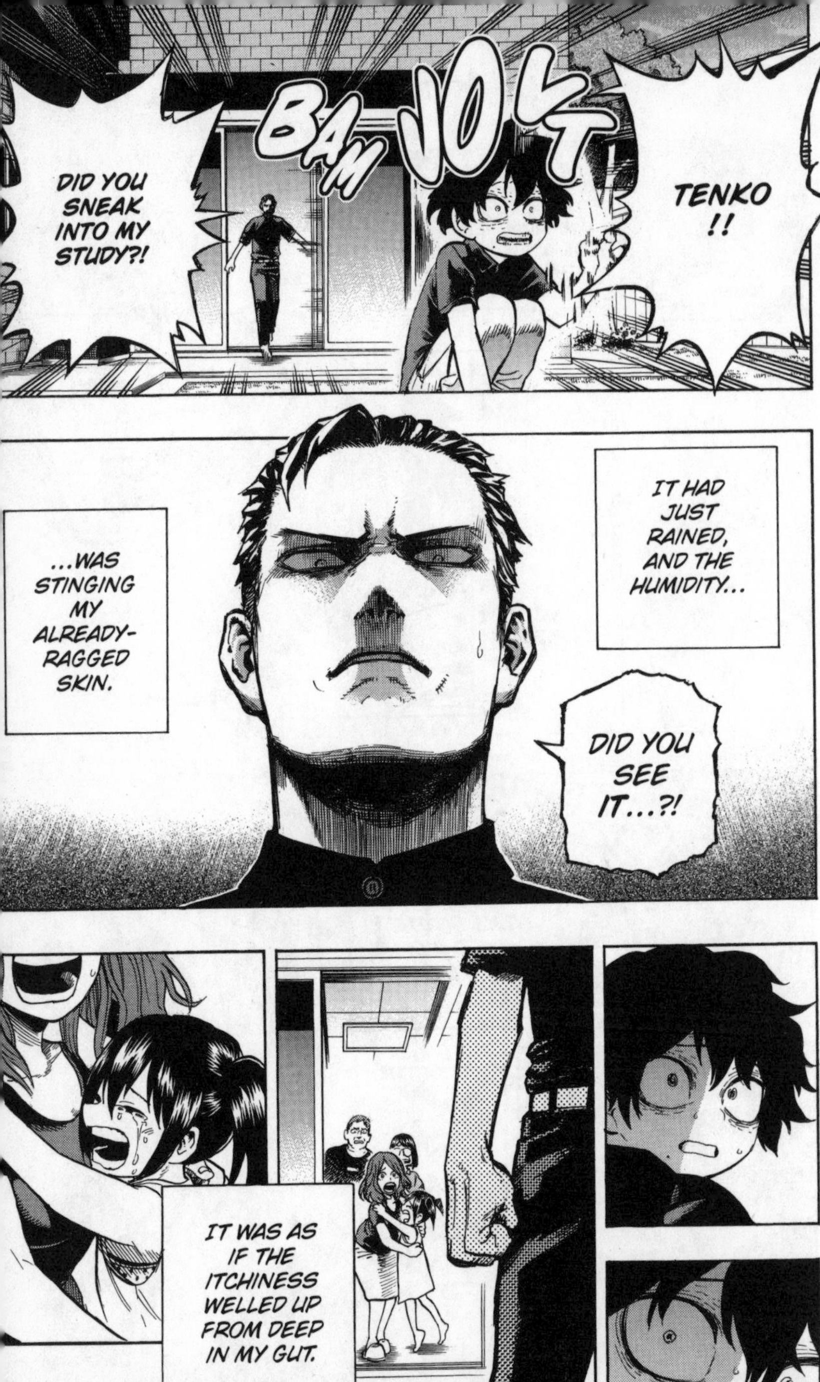
TENKO !!
JOLT
BAM
DID YOU SNEAK INTO MY STUDY?!
IT HAD JUST RAINED, AND THE HUMIDITY...
...WAS STINGING MY ALREADY-RAGGED SKIN.
DID YOU SEE IT...?!
IT WAS AS IF THE ITCHINESS WELLED UP FROM DEEP IN MY GUT.

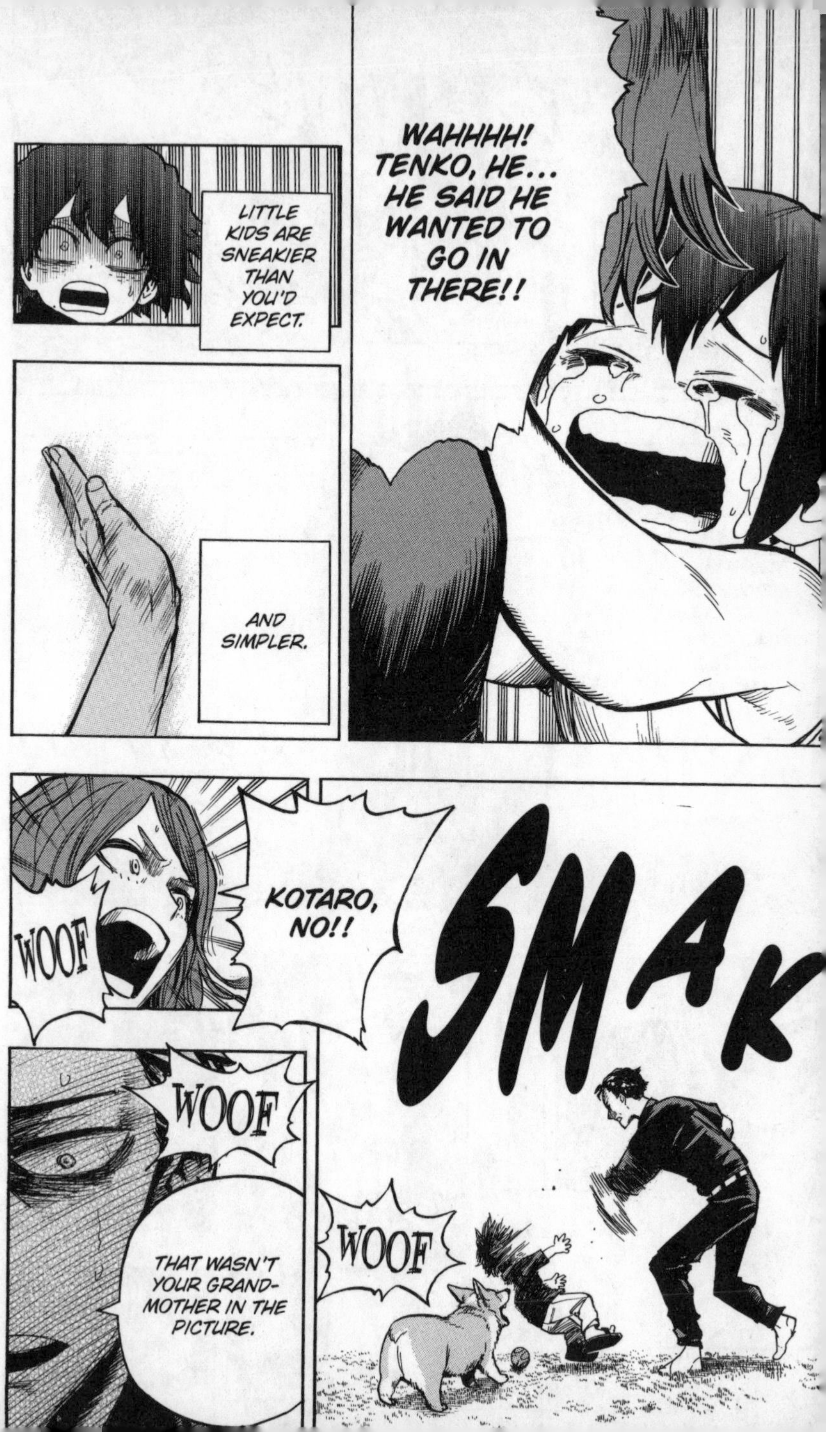
WAHHHH! TENKO, HE... HE SAID HE WANTED TO GO IN THERE!!
LITTLE KIDS ARE SNEAKIER THAN YOU'D EXPECT.
AND SIMPLER.
SMAK
WOOF
KOTARO, NO!!
WOOF
WOOF
THAT WASN'T YOUR GRAND-MOTHER IN THE PICTURE.

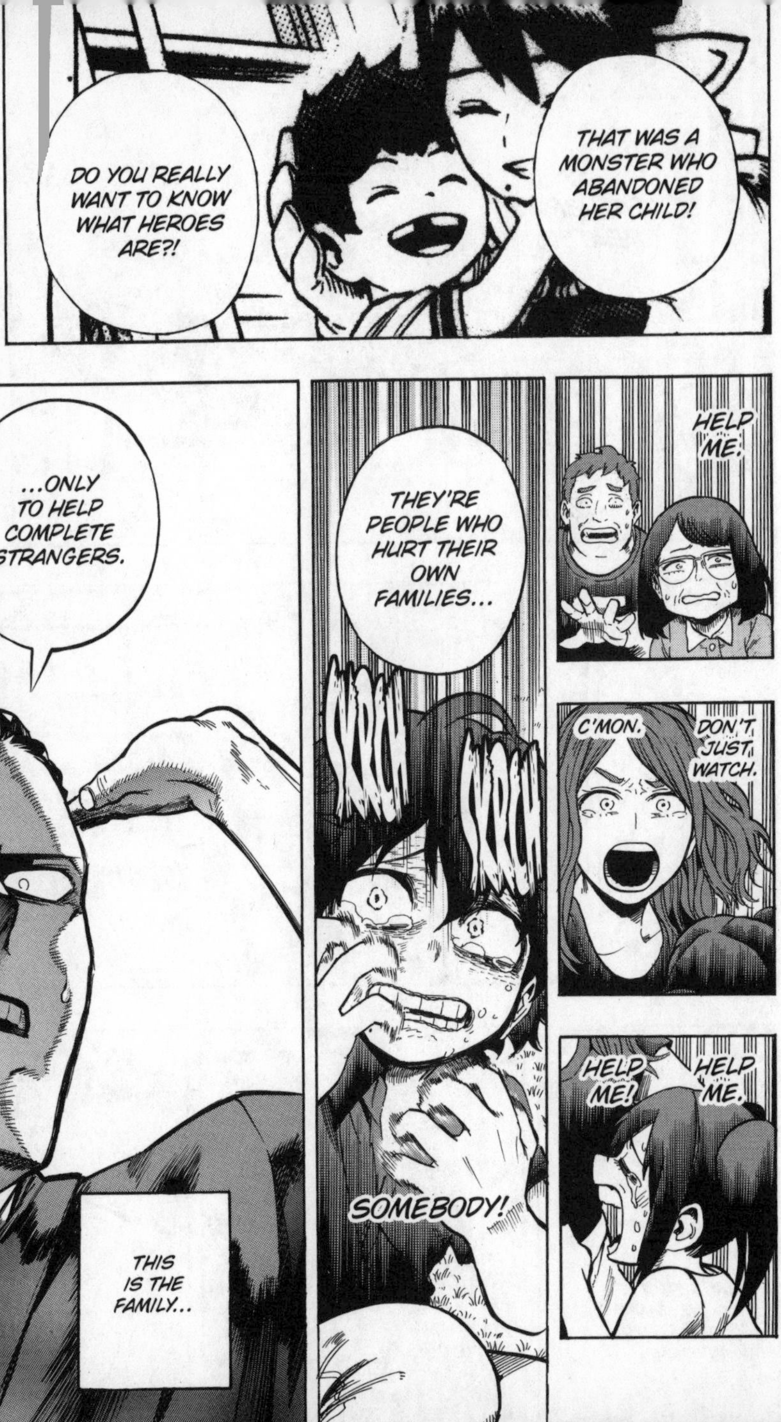
THAT WAS A MONSTER WHO ABANDONED HER CHILD!
DO YOU REALLY WANT TO KNOW WHAT HEROES ARE?!
HELP ME.
DON'T JUST WATCH.
C'MON.
HELP ME.
HELP ME!
THEY'RE PEOPLE WHO HURT THEIR OWN FAMILIES...
SCRCH
SCRCH
SOMEBODY!
...ONLY TO HELP COMPLETE STRANGERS.
THIS IS THE FAMILY...

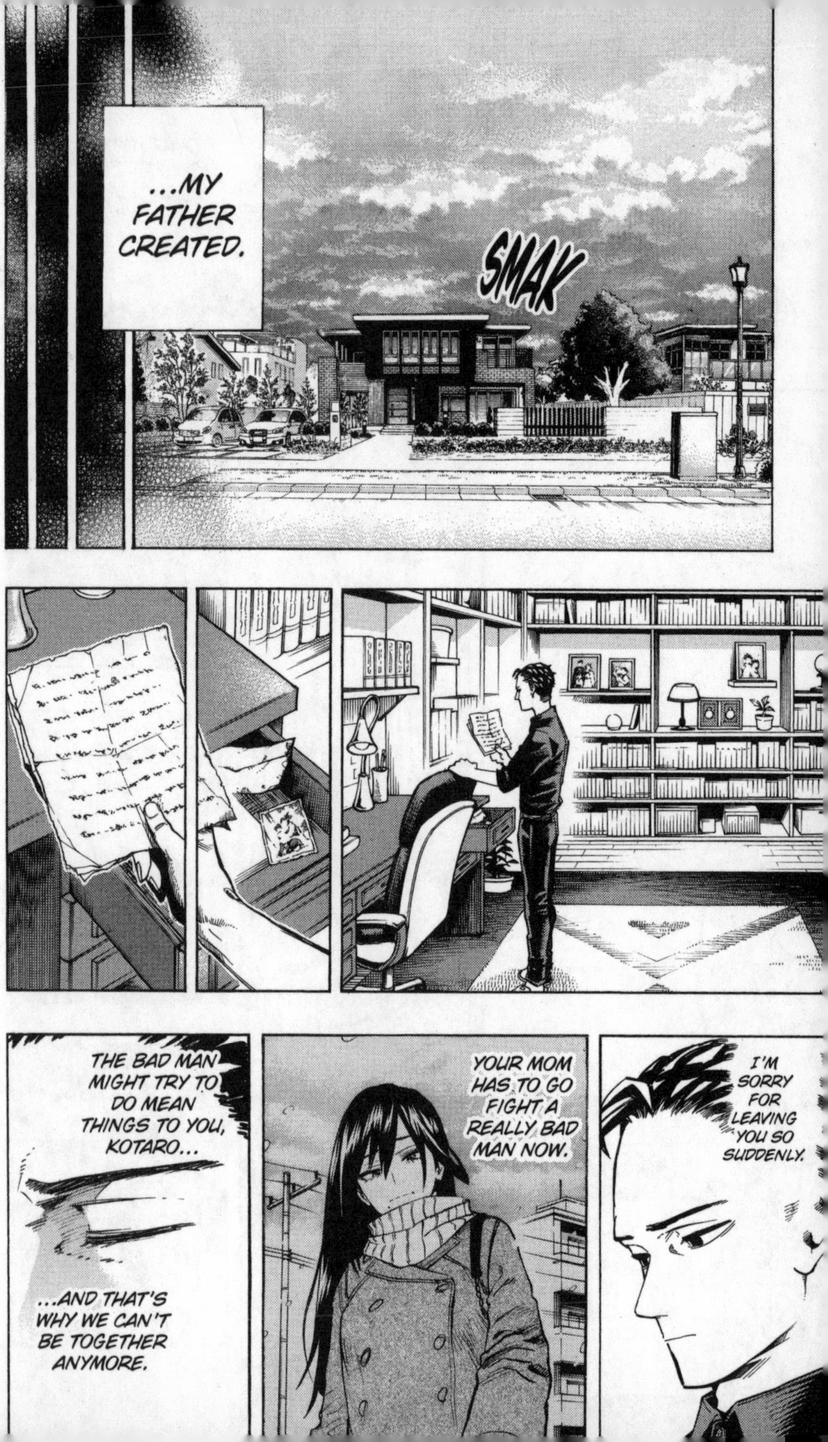
...MY FATHER CREATED.
SMAK
I'M SORRY FOR LEAVING YOU SO SUDDENLY.
YOUR MOM HAS TO GO FIGHT A REALLY BAD MAN NOW.
THE BAD MAN MIGHT TRY TO DO MEAN THINGS TO YOU, KOTARO...
...AND THAT'S WHY WE CAN'T BE TOGETHER ANYMORE.

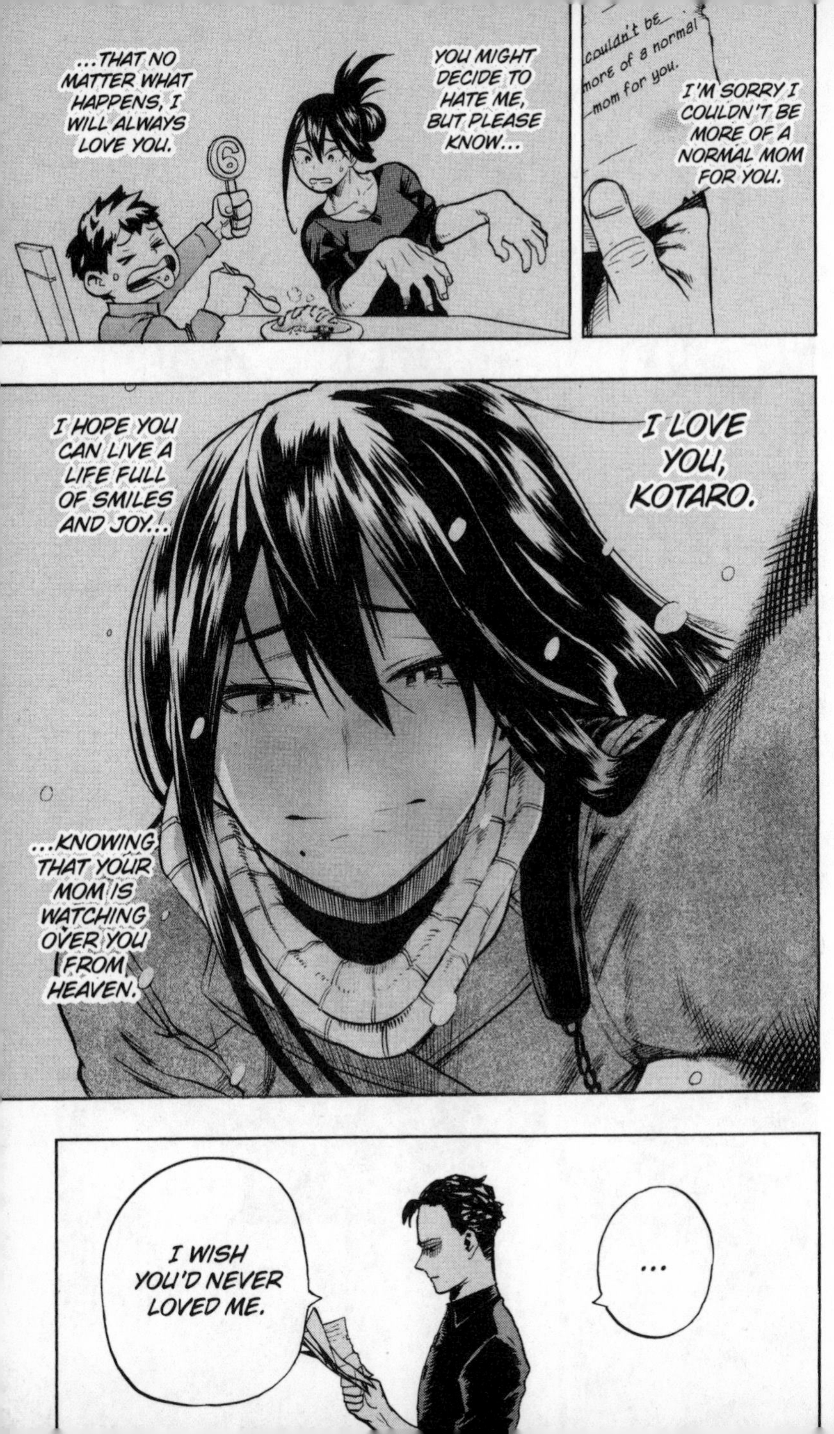
couldn't be more of a normal mom for you.
I'M SORRY I COULDN'T BE MORE OF A NORMAL MOM FOR YOU.
YOU MIGHT DECIDE TO HATE ME, BUT PLEASE KNOW...
...THAT NO MATTER WHAT HAPPENS, I WILL ALWAYS LOVE YOU.
I LOVE YOU, KOTARO.
I HOPE YOU CAN LIVE A LIFE FULL OF SMILES AND JOY...
...KNOWING THAT YOUR MOM IS WATCHING OVER YOU FROM HEAVEN.
...
I WISH YOU'D NEVER LOVED ME.

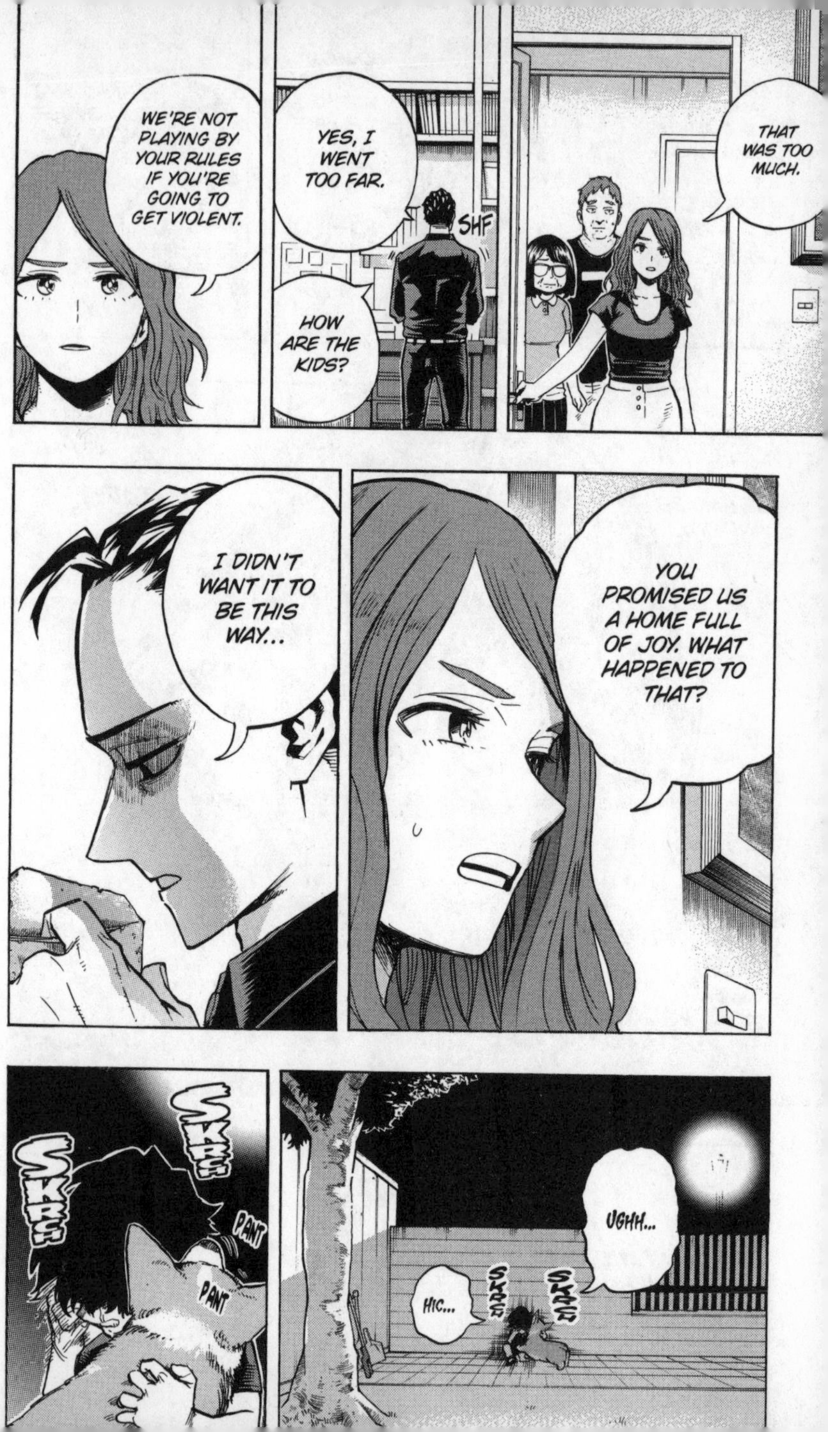
THAT WAS TOO MUCH.
YES, I WENT TOO FAR.
SHF
HOW ARE THE KIDS?
WE'RE NOT PLAYING BY YOUR RULES IF YOU'RE GOING TO GET VIOLENT.
YOU PROMISED US A HOME FULL OF JOY. WHAT HAPPENED TO THAT?
I DIDN'T WANT IT TO BE THIS WAY...
UGHH...
SKRCH
SKRCH
HIC...
SKRCH
SKRCH
PANT
PANT

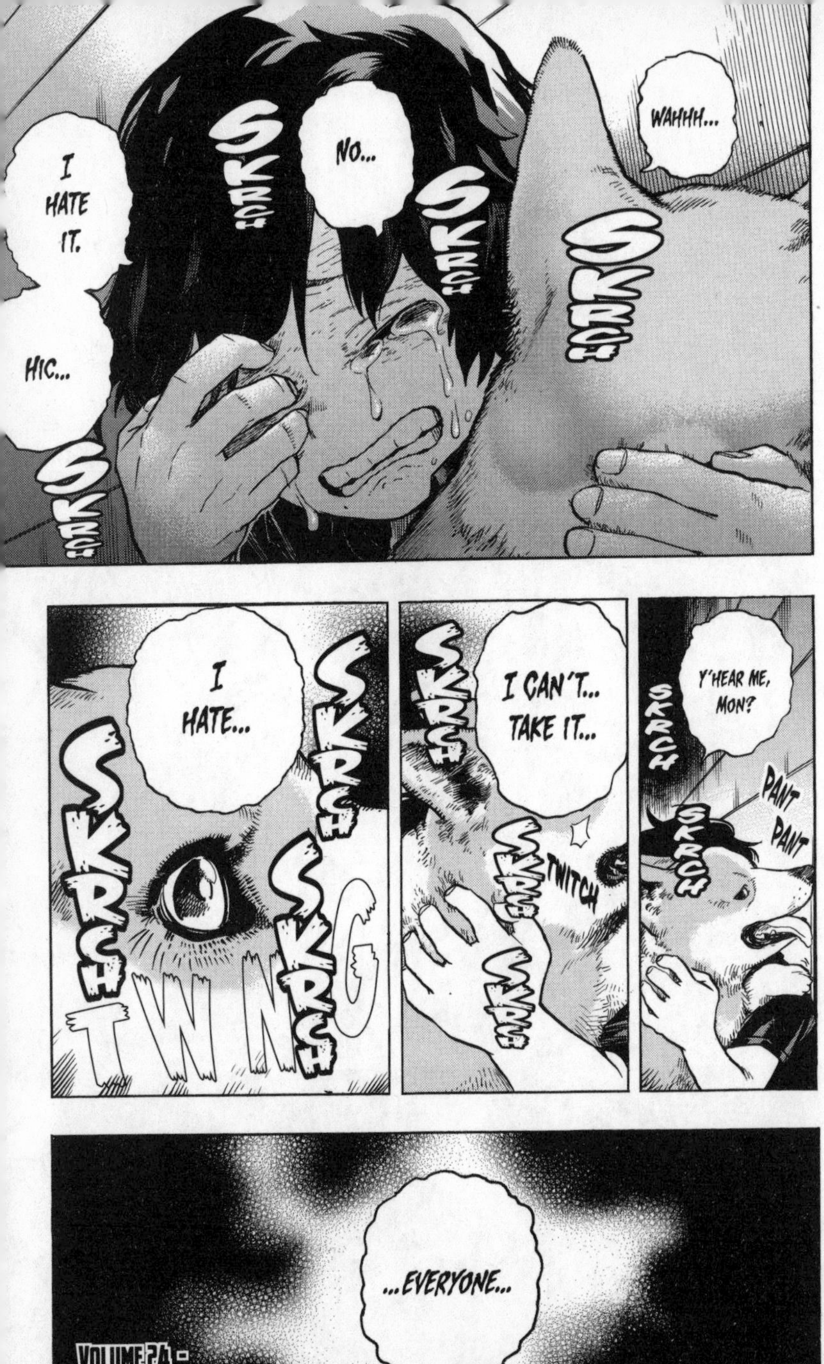
WAHHH...
SKRCH
SKRCH
NO...
SKRCH
I HATE IT.
HIC...
SKRCH
Y'HEAR ME, MON?
SKRCH
PANT PANT
SKRCH
I CAN'T... TAKE IT...
SKRCH
!
TWITCH
SKRCH
SKRCH
I HATE...
SKRCH
SKRCH
TWNG
SKRCH
...EVERYONE...
VOLUME 24 -
ALL IT TAKES IS ONE BAD DAY (END)

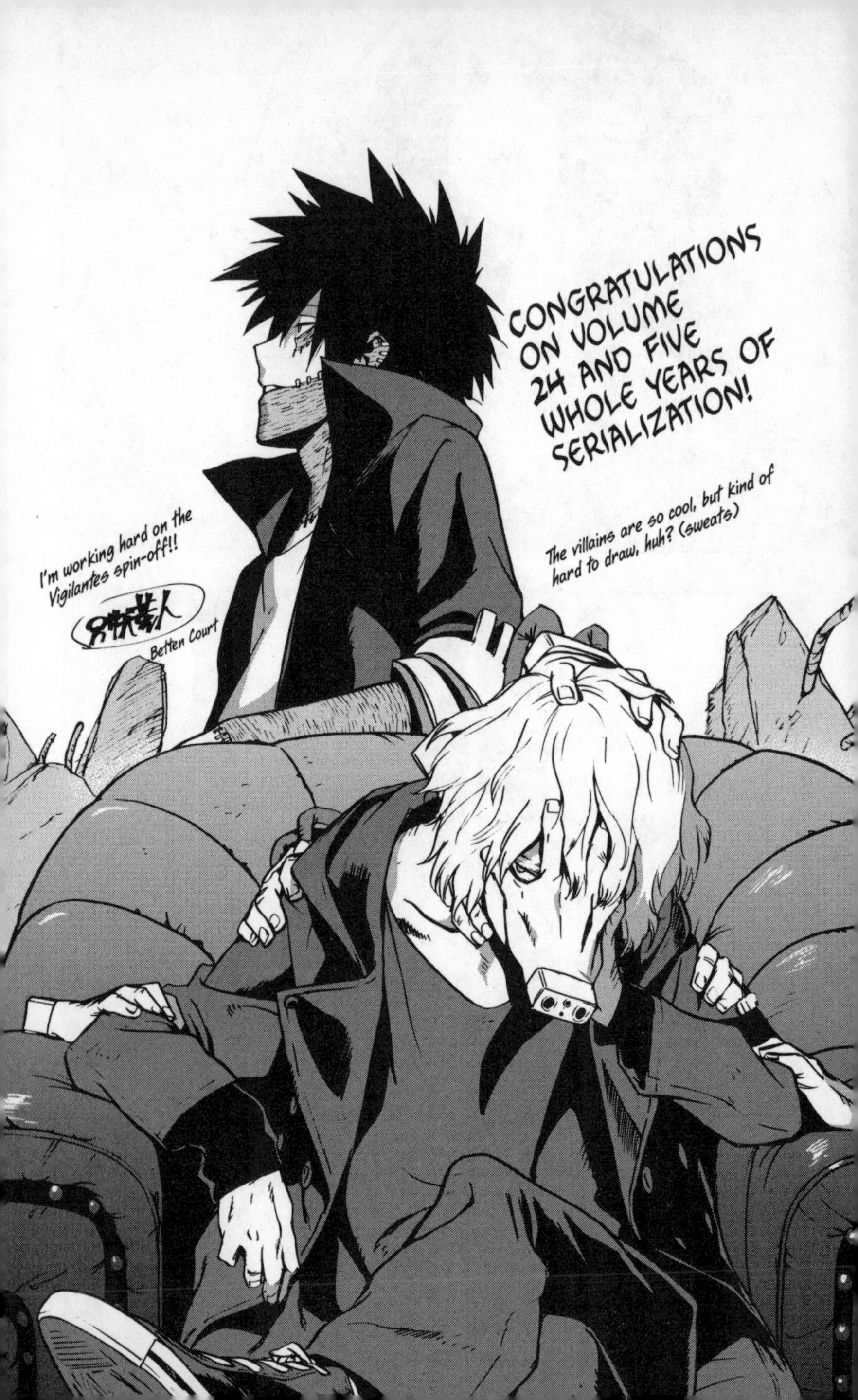
CONGRATULATIONS ON VOLUME 24 AND FIVE WHOLE YEARS OF SERIALIZATION!
The villains are so cool, but kind of hard to draw, huh? (sweats)
I'm working hard on the Vigilantes spin-off!!
Betten Court

I got another special illustration from *MHA: Vigilantes* artist Betten Sensei! Thank you!!

Vigilantes volume 7 is out now, so be sure to pick that up as well!

The two stories mesh together in a few ways, so it's fun to read both at once.

Anyhow, Deku and friends haven't shown up in a while, huh…

This is supposed to be the story of how Deku becomes a great hero, so I'm thinking we'll mosey on back to U.A. High in the next volume! Just hang in there a little while longer!

See you again in volume 25!

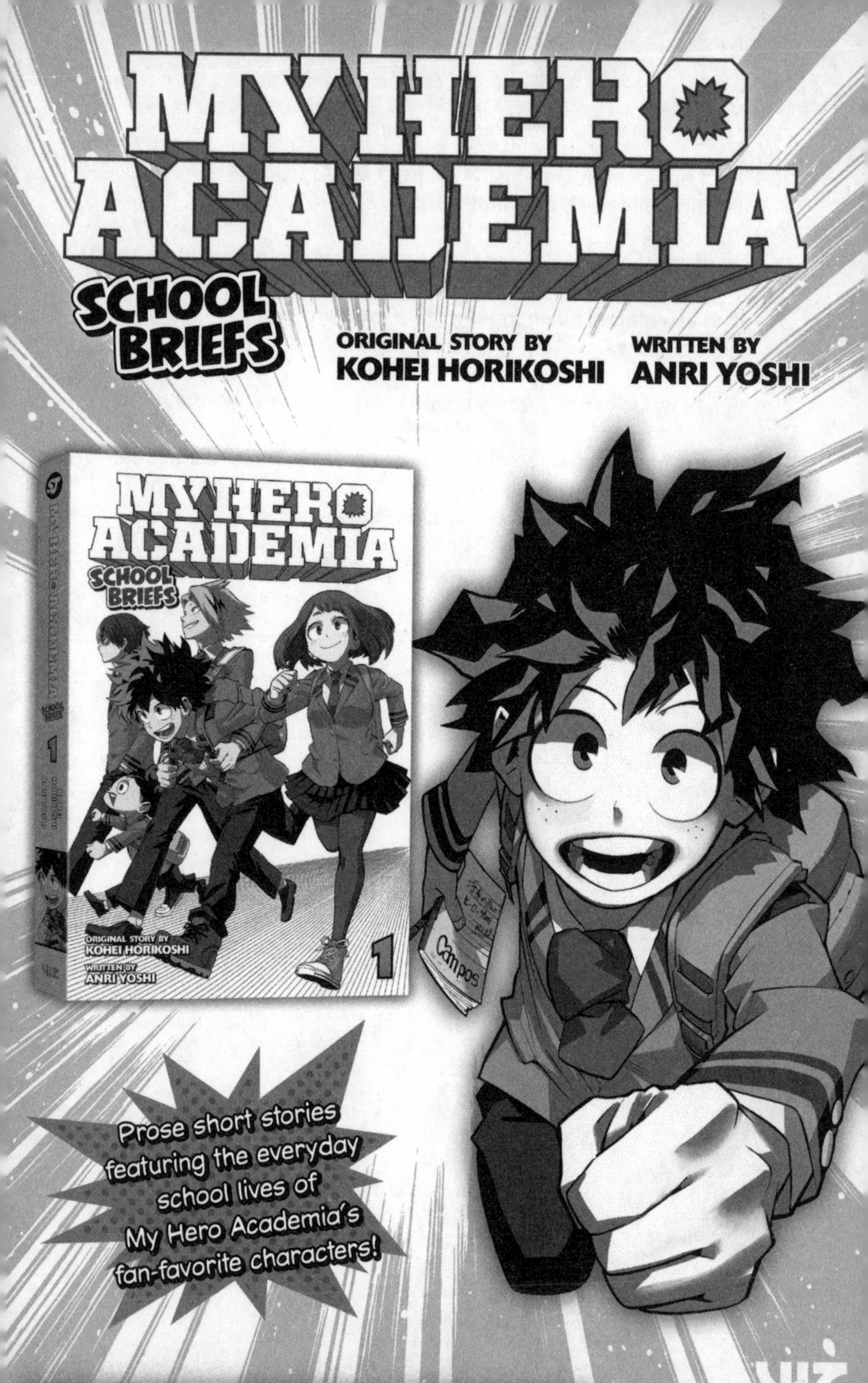
MY HERO ACADEMIA
SCHOOL BRIEFS
ORIGINAL STORY BY
KOHEI HORIKOSHI
WRITTEN BY
ANRI YOSHI
MY HERO ACADEMIA
SCHOOL BRIEFS
1
ORIGINAL STORY BY
KOHEI HORIKOSHI
WRITTEN BY
ANRI YOSHI
Prose short stories featuring the everyday school lives of My Hero Academia's fan-favorite characters!

MY HERO ACADEMIA

SMASH!!

Story and Art by Hirofumi Neda
Original Concept by Kohei Horikoshi

1

MY HERO ACADEMIA SMASH!!

STORY AND ART BY
HIROFUMI NEDA
ORIGINAL CONCEPT BY KOHEI HORIKOSHI

The superpowered society of *My Hero Academia* takes a
hilarious turn in this reimagining of the best-selling series! Join
Midoriya, All Might and all the aspiring heroes of U.A. High, plus
memorable villains, in an irreverent take on the main events
of the series, complete with funny gags, ridiculous jokes and

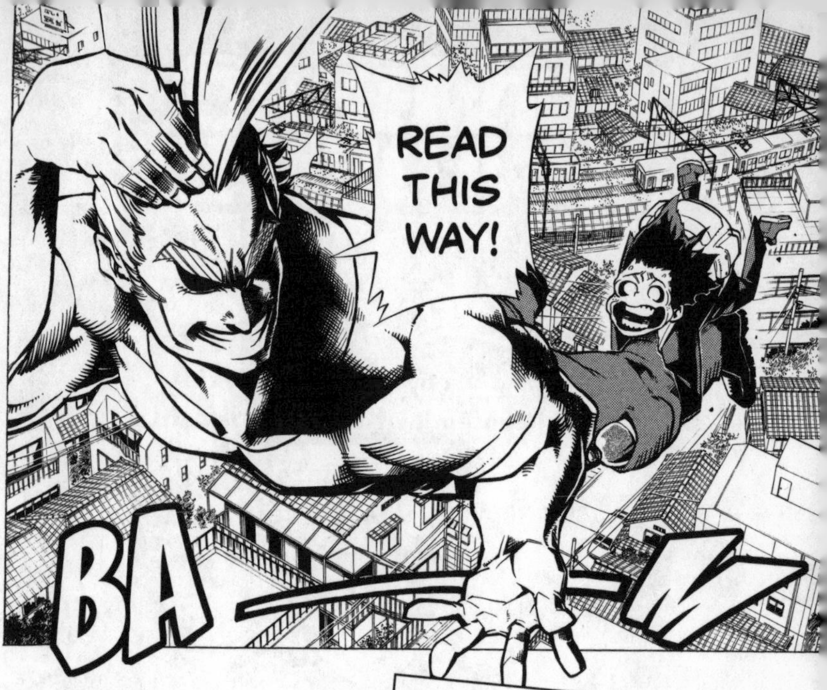
READ THIS WAY!
BA—M

MY HERO ACADEMIA

reads from right to left, starting in the upper-right corner. Japanese is read from right to left, meaning that action, sound effects and word-balloon order are completely reversed from English order.

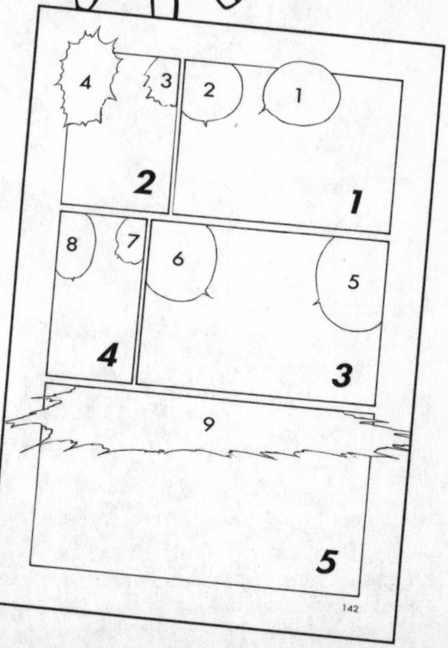